THE LAST THURSDAY
IN JULY

THE LAST THURSDAY
IN JULY

ANDRÉ HANSCOMBE

C
Century · London

Published by Century Books in 1996

1 3 5 7 9 10 8 6 4 2

Copyright © André Hanscombe 1996

"Old Man" © 1995 Broken Fiddle Music
Warner/Chappell Music Ltd. London W1Y 3FA
Reproduced by kind permission of International Publications Ltd.

Published in the United Kingdom by
Century Books, Random House UK Limited
20 Vauxhall Bridge Road, London, SW1V 2SA

Random House Australia (Pty) Limited
16 Dalmore Drive, Scoresby, Victoria 3179, Australia

Random House New Zealand Limited
18 Poland Road, Glenfield, Auckland 10, New Zealand

Random House South Africa (Pty) Limited
PO Box 2263, Rosebank 2121, South Africa

Random House UK Limited Reg. No. 954009

A CIP catalogue record for this book is available from the British Library

Papers used by Random House UK Limited are natural, recyclable products made from
wood grown in sustainable forests. The manufacturing processes conform to the envi-
ronmental regulations of the country of origin

ISBN 0 71 2677321

Typeset by SX Composing DTP, Rayleigh, Essex
Printed and bound in Great Britain by Mackay's of Chatham, PLC, Chatham, Kent

For those who have lost someone

Acknowledgements

To my editor, Oliver Johnson, for his patience with a novice writer, but more importantly for his sensitivity. Some things are hard to help someone express. To Beth Humphries for her copy-editing of this text. To those whose love and support and encouragement have helped to buoy me up, in those moments when I would have preferred to have sunk. I will never be able to return even a part of all that we have received.

Foreword

ON A BEAUTIFUL July morning in 1992, Rachel Nickell left her flat in Balham in South London with her son, Alex, who was almost three years old. She was never to return.

Shortly after ten o'clock that same day her body was found by a man walking his dog on Wimbledon Common. The place where she was discovered was only a hundred yards from the Common's main beauty spot and carpark. Alex, battered and covered with his mother's blood, was clinging to her. Rachel had been stabbed forty-nine times and sexually assaulted.

Since that day, the Rachel Nickell case has seldom been out of the news headlines. It quickly became the largest murder investigation ever conducted in London. Interest reached fever pitch with the arrest of Colin Stagg in August 1993 after a police undercover operation. In September 1994 there was uproar when the case against Stagg collapsed after Mr Justice Ognall ruled that the police had obtained their evidence illegally. Today many people wonder what would have happened if the evidence of the police, that of several eyewitnesses on the Common that day and little Alex had been heard in court.

The search for Rachel's killer continues today, with the police reinvestigating the whole case once more. It became front page news when in late 1995 police flew to New Zealand to interview John Gallagher. Gallagher later returned to the UK and has since been released from police custody.

Now for the first time André Hanscombe, Rachel's common-law husband, has broken his silence about the torment of the intervening years, and what a jury might have heard from Alex, the only eyewitness of the murder, if the Stagg case had been tried.

Chapter One

I WOKE TO THE sound of his voice. He was weeping and moaning. Something in my chest lurched. My eyes shot open. I jerked forward and found myself sitting upright, suddenly wide awake. Alex was stumbling towards me from his camp bed. I reached out and pulled him towards me. Waking brought everything flooding back and what my eyes told me meant it was no dream. It was all true. And everything had changed. For this wasn't our house. And this wasn't my place. Alex was coming to me.

But he never came to me. He went to his mother.

As he stumbled he held my eyes with his. The room was already light and I could see how his face was puffy and bruised. There were cuts under both eyes. He looked deep into me. So many thoughts and so much pain between us.

His needs had to be attended to. Without speaking, he was demanding things from me. But I felt almost like a stranger. It was almost like I was looking at someone else's child. I felt that I hardly knew him. How in God's name was I ever going to be able to give him anything that he needed? Anything to compensate for what he had just lost. And how in heaven or hell would I ever be capable of giving anything which might heal the mental scars inflicted by the evil that he had just lived through?

'There, there,' I tried to soothe him. 'Daddy's here. It's all right.' The words sounded alien to me. The few times I had uttered them before in the night, they had rung hollow. On those occasions I had thought to myself: 'Daddy's here? What does he care?' and I'd soon been obliged to hand him over to his mother.

'Daddy's here!' I pulled him towards me. This time he wasn't strug-gling to get past me to something better. There was no one better for him to get to. He was desperate to roll himself up tight against me and bury himself in my arms.

I don't know how long I had slept. Not more than a couple of hours at most. The sheets were soaked with my tears, there were used tissues everywhere. I had gone to bed late and had lain exhausted and beaten while my mind turned over and over for hours on end. Rachel's brother was asleep on the sofa downstairs. But we still hadn't been able to get through to her parents. They were on a boating holiday some-where on the lakes between Canada and America. We had to get through to them. How could *we* know, and they not know that their daughter was dead? But we had no way of finding them.

I had put Alex in another bed rather than take him to bed with me. I can't explain exactly why I had done this but I hadn't wanted to start off in the wrong direction. I was ready to take him in with me for the whole night if he woke up and if that was what he wanted. He woke up just once and, instead of calling out for Mummy, he called for Daddy. He never had before. Not in nearly three years of life. He had switched seamlessly from one to the other. By the time I got to him he was sound asleep again.

Now, my body felt weak as I pulled him towards me. His sobbing calmed and his tears soon stopped. I told him that I loved him and his grandma loved him and his other grandma loved him and his grandpa loved him and Molly, our dog, loved him and so on and so on through every other member of the family and everyone else that we knew. He lay very quietly. I stroked his hair as I would often stroke Rachel's when she was asleep. My voice was so choked with emotion that it was difficult to get the words out. I felt I was blabbering like a fool. His three-year-old eyes stared into mine, the desperation in them burning into my head. They demanded answers. Answers that I could never give him. I still couldn't understand how he had even been left alive. He was, after all, the sole apparent witness to a murder.

'Everyone dies some time,' I remember saying. I was desperately trying to think of how Rachel would talk to him. She was so clever at putting things in a way that he would understand. I felt impotent. And at the same time terrified of making things worse. 'But nearly every-one gets old and tired before they die,' I heard myself continue.

'Hardly anyone dies when they're young like Mummy.' This was just a terrible, terrible accident. Just look how old Grandma and Grandpa are, and they're not dead yet!'

His mind must have returned to the day before. He looked away. A mental door slammed shut. His body language was clear – he didn't want to remember.

'One day Molly will be too old to run around,' I persisted. 'She'll be tired and will just want to sleep. And one day she just won't wake up any more.' I felt like I was talking to the wall. He fiddled with his blankets as he looked round the room.

Then he said: 'I want to wake up!' He said it quietly, but firmly. Still without looking at me. My head swam. It wasn't the answer I expected to hear. Despite my words I didn't want to go on. And I could only believe he felt the same.

There didn't seem to be anything left for either of us to live for without her. I missed her so much already that I could hardly breathe.

Rachel and he adored each other. It didn't seem possible that he could exist without her. They were always laughing together, up to something interesting, having fun. To me they seemed joined together as one unit. I couldn't imagine how his body could even function without her.

'I want to wake up!'

In that instant a different answer from him would have meant that it was all over. I had only really been waiting for his permission. We would go together. I would kill myself and take him with me. There was nothing left.

'Then you will!' I felt myself being split in two. I heard the words roll out of my mouth as if from a million miles away. 'You won't die until you are very, very old.'

In a split second so many realizations came rushing towards me that I felt close to losing consciousness. I had never fainted in my life but this was the second time in less than twenty-four hours that I had come so close. I could suddenly see that for the poor, innocent, loving child that was Rachel; the poor, innocent, loving child whom I had worshipped and adored; the poor innocent, loving child who had just had everything ripped away from her so brutally, in a manner so vile and cruel and evil; for her the least I could do was to be there for him, for the child that she adored, and to give him all that I could.

But much of me had already left.

It was the least and at the same time the most. For she lived for him. She lived for me too, but it wasn't the same. He needed her more than I did and her giving to him gave her a sense of purpose and worth that she had not found before. And seeing this made me profoundly happy. To somehow make one small thing all right for her through all this horror – and don't ask me how I knew she would know, but I knew she would – then I would have to there for him. As long as I could. As old as I could. He needed me to be the grandfather of his children. If he had chosen to live then he had the right to as full a life as I could possibly provide. And if I really loved her then I would stay with him and not try to find a way back to her. I had to go on.

And I didn't want to.

All of this hit me in the same instant and I felt myself violently jerked back from wherever my despair was taking me and dumped right back into the present. On reflection now I can see that what passed in those few seconds set the future direction of our life together.

While so much was going on in my head part of me was still talking to Alex, still trying to soothe him. He was talking fairly normally but I just knew that there was absolutely no point in me asking him anything directly about what had happened. I could sense his resistance, and I was too charged with emotion myself. The only thing I could do was keep on talking. But I saw something in his posture loosen by the tiniest of amounts. Something in him calmed, even if just by the smallest fraction of a degree. I felt relief. Even if he showed the greatest resistance to talking about what happened the day before at least my first fumbling attempts to reason with him hadn't made things worse. And we had arrived at a decision. There *was* something left. His hunger for life.

We went downstairs. Breakfast had to be prepared. Toast had to be made. Milk had to be poured. A video found, his bottom wiped, a mess sponged up, clothes found in the bottom of the bag that I had packed in a daze from our flat the afternoon before. I went everywhere with him in my arms; he wouldn't be put down. More food. I couldn't touch a thing: my stomach was in knots and I felt I would vomit. If I tried to move as far as the door he would call me back. He had to be in physical contact with me.

5

I sat with Alex on my lap as he watched his video and ate his breakfast. I was thinking about the evening before. Once I had put Alex to bed I had been interviewed by detectives. The same two detectives who had met me at Wimbledon police station. There they had explained to me all they knew as quickly and clearly as they could and I will always be grateful for that. I had had to know, it was my right. The longer they took telling me, the more it hurt. She was mine, Alex was mine. She had been taken away from me: strangers standing between me and the truth would take her away further still.

I felt detached from the world. Nothing around me was solid any more. I felt like my feet would sink through the floor as I walked. But the searing pain inside of me said that it was real. Something was broken. Something was torn away that was never going to be put back again.

Last night when Alex slept the two detectives had a younger officer with them as well. He had not been able to control his feelings, and was in anguish himself. They had gone through lists and lists of questions. Who did we know? Who did Rachel see? When had I left the house? Did we owe anybody money? Did we have any enemies? Could I prove my whereabouts? Did Rachel have any life insurance? Was she wearing any jewellery? On and on and on. My best friend held my hand all the way through. Did I know what Rachel's movements were that morning? What did she normally do? The detectives were struggling with their own emotions and were in tears. That morning they had picked Rachel's mutilated, blood-soaked body off the ground. Now they were confronted with the damage that had been done to her family. That professional police officers should break down because of what had happened to Rachel only served to emphasize the extraordinary horror of what she and Alex had been through. I watched the torment in their faces, trying in vain to guess the even greater depths of psychological damage that must have been inflicted on our child, who was sleeping just above.

Who did she see? What had she done the day before? When was the last time we had gone to the Common together? Had I seen anything that made me suspicious? The detectives asked several times if I wanted to stop then and carry on the next day. But I wanted to get it out of the way and I wanted to give them all the help I could so they could get on as fast as humanly possible and catch Rachel's killer.

The detectives asked for our diaries and address books, details of our bank accounts. What were our movements the night before? they asked. When had we last made love? What contraceptives had we used? What had we done or not done? They explained that they had to know because in cases of sexual assault the defence could always blame any signs found on the victim's body on the partner or boyfriend.

The detectives filled page after page. I signed at the bottom of each one after it had been read back to me. They also wanted me to take part in a press conference the next day to appeal for witnesses to come forward.

But that had been the night before. Now my head was swimming as I moved round this small child, our son, who only hours before had been prised away from the lifeless body of his mother, drenched in blood after witnessing only he knew what. There he sat watching Fireman Sam, chewing his toast. The police had no idea why and how this thing had happened. Only this tiny child knew and he was far from ready to talk about it. She had gone. That was all that was certain.

I stared at what I could see of his face as he sat on my lap. His right eye was tracking across the television screen. What was going on in that head? Would I ever know?

Now was the crucial time to begin the healing. Somehow I had to get as much of the poison of what he had witnessed out of his mind before it clamped shut, leaving him to fight with it alone. It was still all in there. Another shock and it could remain there, possibly for ever. If I could somehow protect him from any more stress he might just relax the tiniest amount and start to talk to me. Begin to let out the horror. But I had some idea of how much a child could keep inside him and for how long. I had been sexually abused by a stranger at the age of six and didn't feel safe enough to tell a soul until I was more than twenty.

From where I sat everything looked absolutely normal. I couldn't see the scars on his face from this angle. But I could feel the difference. He was stressed out and rigid with fear every time he felt me move.

I told myself that I had to isolate whatever had happened. If everything from this day on could proceed as smoothly as possible maybe we could add what was to come to all the wonderful days he had had before and arrive at a sum that could come somewhere near ready to balance against that one day of horror.

But how many good, new days would it take?

At least he had slept well. In fact, four weeks from his third birthday it was only the second time in his life he had made it through the night. He had called out just once, that's all. When he had called out for me and not her. Was it because he was still in a state of shock? Would he soon revert to his usual routine of waking up often in the night? Up until just a few weeks before he had still needed breastfeeding to get him back to sleep occasionally. It had only been a few short weeks since he had been totally weaned.

This morning, he seemed eager to get on with the normal things. He was very demanding. He had always been a fussy child and everything had had to be just right. But now this was exaggerated out of all proportion. His juice had to be in the right cup. Just the right amount of peanut butter on his toast, both his blankets wrapped round him otherwise he would burst into tears and begin wailing and moaning.

I remembered how in the spring, when he was a little more than two and a half, I had taken him out one morning. We had been late back for lunch and he was being difficult. Rachel was aghast. I hadn't given him anything to eat since we had left the house at breakfast time. On top of which we were late for lunch as well. Was I really surprised that he was being difficult? The poor child was starving!

I can still see her face. I didn't understand. I thought he was playing up because he was missing her, and that the best thing to do was get home as quickly as possible. And because he hadn't asked for food it had never occurred to me that he needed something to eat. It had only been a couple of hours since we had left the house. I could wait till we got back so I had assumed that he could too.

Now, wherever she was, I wanted desperately for her to know that I would do a better job. That his every need was being attended to in just the way that she would approve. So I racked my brains to remember all the little things that she would do with him, knowing that if I *could* remember them, I was doing the right thing. I had brought his sheepskin to sleep on, his blankets to hold, his little knife and fork to eat with, his favourite plate, clean clothes. His sheepskin was the most important thing. He had slept with it since the night he had been born in our bedroom. It always came with us when we slept away from home.

An image of her sitting in front of his little chest of drawers lovingly folding his clothes and putting them away flashed into my mind. I fought it off, focusing on the things he liked best: I had brought his teddies for his bed, his Fireman Sam video, his favourite story-books and toys, and his dog was in the garden.

Then I started to make a shopping list in my mind: dried apricots for snacks, those little packets of juice with the straw that he liked, cashews. What else did she get him? Pasta for lunch, yes, veggie-burgers, baked potatoes, cheese on toast. Surely this would give him the message that everything was still there for him – that only one part, even if the most important part, had been ripped away?

When I arrived at the hospital the evening before, I was told that Alex was asleep. I had spent the whole journey between the police station and the hospital visualizing picking him up and carrying him away to some as yet undecided place of safety. But now I was told that there was a child psychologist at the hospital who was on his way to speak to me. I had no idea how long Alex would sleep or how long it would be before the psychologist arrived. The waiting was agony but I was frightened of making things worse by rushing in to him. I didn't know how he would react when he saw the state I was in. But it had taken ages to track down the psychologist, who was in some other part of the building. In the meantime the police rushed me back to our flat to pick up all the things he would need. I had to be smuggled past the newspaper people, just as I had on first arriving at the hospital. I knew right there and then that I would be forced to take Alex out of the country. I had seen how the press latched on to stories like this and never let them go. I knew the lurid, titillating way that things were put. I could see that when the murderer was caught his face would be on the front page of every tabloid every time that something similar occurred. How was Alex supposed to grow up with that? How was he supposed to grow up with people knowing more about him than he did about them? How was he supposed to grow up with parents talking about him at the school gates? 'That poor child, don't you remember what happened to his mother? And he was there too!' How was he to endure what the other children might say to him? All children can be cruel and there was no way of telling how far the normal childhood teasing might go or how painful the jibes might be.

Our flat-mate was there when we arrived. He had come home to find the front door broken down and the flat full of police. They had found the address in our car in the windmill carpark. He was distraught, rambling. 'Why did he have to kill her . . . ?' he was saying. I was asking myself the same question. Surely he had got what he wanted: what was the point in killing her, too? The question was unanswerable.

Journalists had offered our flat-mate money to take photographs of the inside of our home. 'What do you care?' they told him. 'It's no skin off your nose!' Now he was pale and shaken, reeling from emotion after the shock of finding the door broken down, finding the police in the flat and hearing the news of Rachel's murder, and disgusted by the callousness of the journalists on the doorstep . . .

God knows what I must have looked like to him.

I hurriedly stuffed the most important things in a bag, hardly able to breathe with the fear that Alex might wake up without me there. I couldn't spare the time to comfort our flat-mate but was reassured to hear that he was going to spend the night with friends and would not be on his own.

I got back to the hospital: Alex still slept and, looking back, thank God he did. Maybe it provided some relief for his overloaded mind. But who could possibly know for sure? Although I had been occupied with his physical needs I knew that there were other priorities as well. I had to speak to someone who worked with children who had been caught up in violence. I didn't want any academic theories on what the psychological damage might or might not be. I wanted someone who could actually tell me what was going to happen to us.

All the while I was torn between waiting for the child psychologist and wanting to be there when Alex woke up. My mind was weighed down with other concerns: I had to break the news to Rachel's parents. I could only imagine the pain that they would feel when they found out. But it was only fair that they should be told as soon as possible. I had already broken the news to her brother.

He'd arrived at the hospital soon after I had returned from the flat with the police. He had come straight from his office by tube. What an inhuman journey that must have been. Seeing his face made events more real and more undeniable again. But when I saw him I asked myself for a split second whether I had brought him there for nothing. What was he doing here? Everything was fine, wasn't it? But the split second passed. Reality came rushing back. Uttering those words, which I knew would cause him so much pain, was the worst thing I ever had to do.

I forced myself to tell him as much as I knew. He listened calmly. When I had finished he said he felt it best that he be the one to break the news to his parents and immediately set about trying to track them down by phone.

Meanwhile they had finally managed to locate the child psychologist. He came into the waiting room and shook my hand. His eyes never left mine as he told me how sorry he was for what had happened, then immediately predicted that this was going to be worse for me than it was for Alex. At the time I didn't believe him.

He said that I mustn't lie to Alex. I had to tell him that there had been a terrible accident and that Rachel was not coming back. I must not let him believe for a moment there was a chance that he would ever see her again. He must know that she had gone for ever. He went on to say that what children needed most of all after a major shock was a fixed routine. They didn't necessarily need more affection. The most important thing was that they needed to know where they were. They needed a firm base. This was the only way they could begin to absorb the shock. And only then could they begin to build a way forward.

I sat in front of him and tried to stop sobbing for long enough to hear what he was saying. He told me that children were resilient and that they survive and develop remarkably well even after the loss of someone so important in their lives.

What he said made sense but I had known someone who had lost their father at the age of ten and was still showing signs of suffering well into adult life. The psychologist finished by repeating that what we needed most of all was routine and time. It was too early to imagine that things would ever get better but time might make them easier to accept.

The fact that he had given me something practical to focus on made things minutely but tangibly easier. His advice gave me a first firm foothold in a swaying universe.

Very soon afterwards I saw Alex walking down the corridor holding a nurse's hand. I swept up his blankets and strode towards him. I didn't run. I am not sure my legs would have allowed me to even if I had tried. He was very calm and very serious. I never thought to ask if they had given him a sedative. He looked dazed and was very subdued. But in spite of everything he was still looking about him, still taking everything in.

I saw the marks on his face. The signs of recent violence were unmistakable, not only in the cuts and bruises on his face but in the whole atmosphere of the hospital ward. It showed in the behaviour and sounds of the hospital staff at work, the nurse who held Alex's hand, the policeman on duty and even the photographers and journalists locked outside the doors. Everyone was subdued, shocked. Everything was being conducted almost in whispers.

Alex looked relieved when he saw me. As he walked up that corridor he must have been wondering what the hell was going to happen to him next. I picked him up and before my voice gave out I tried to follow the advice I had just been given. 'There has been a terrible accident.' I said, hardly able to look at him. He was so calm. 'Mummy has been killed and she is not coming back . . .' He looked at me steadily, his face just inches away from mine, his eyes never leaving my face. It was as if he was saying: 'I know she's dead. I know she's not coming back.' I persisted: '. . . but we are going on together. Daddy's here for you now and I've got your blankets here and your sheepskin is here and Grandma is here and my brothers are here and your other uncle is here and Grandma and Grandpa will be back soon and we are going to get Molly and then we are going to stay at Grandma's house and we'll get your toys and . . .'

Now, the following day, as he chewed his toast as he sat on my lap, I wanted to know more. What were his chances of living a 'normal' life? How long was a recovery likely to take? Was it a matter of ten years? Twenty years? Five years? Would he be able to go to school? Would he in turn become violent? Would his sexual responses be affected? Would he be damaged for the rest of his life? I felt that the more I knew the more I would be of use to him. Even if I didn't agree with what people told me maybe I could still use their advice to work out a way forward. I was sure of one thing: I wasn't handing him over to anyone to be 'treated'. I had a suspicion of 'experts' and wasn't going to allow Alex to become anyone's guinea pig. Anything that was suggested would be done with me and through me and only if I felt it was safe for him. I was only second best but no one alive knew him better.

12

Chapter Two

AT LAST BREAKFAST was finished and the day had to be prepared for. Rachel and I had often joked that Alex was like a dog. He was so full of energy that he had to be exercised twice a day or he would start bouncing off the walls. And when we did eventually get a dog she never lacked for exercise. Just following Alex's routine was enough.

One of Rachel's old schoolfriends arrived not long after and my mother drove us to Hampstead Heath. There was no question of me driving, Alex would not allow me to put him down. So the two of us climbed into the back.

Because of my mother's second marriage and consequent change of name the press had not yet been able to trace us. The police had made sure we were not followed when we left the hospital the night before. The television news and the London *Evening Standard* had already been full of the story. I knew that the press were watching our flat. I'd heard that reporters had buttonholed parents who were collecting their children from Alex's nursery that afternoon. When the journalists failed to get the response they wanted they had run down the road shouting questions after them. That is the way that many of the parents learnt that Rachel had been killed. I felt grateful that for the moment we were being spared the onslaught. We could leave the house without being harassed. For the moment.

Rachel's brother had left for his parents' house. His elderly grandmother had been feeding the cats while they were away and she was in the house alone. The police had warned him to make sure there was always someone in until his parents got back. If the house was empty, there was a good chance that someone would try to break in and steal family photographs. The press were already ringing the front doorbell continually or calling on the phone over and over again. But the phone couldn't be disconnected in case his parents happened to call.

From the back of the car I could see people going about everyday life. Queuing for a bus, driving to work, buying a newspaper. But all I felt was the cushion of the seat and the armrest sticking into my side. I felt totally disconnected from their world. Yesterday morning I had been doing the same as them. But yesterday morning was a lifetime ago. Worrying about paying the bills, meeting the mortgage. What a pathetic joke! So much wasted time when we had had so little of it. So much wasted time I could never get back.

I thought back to the morning before, when I had been getting ready to leave for work. I had known that something was wrong. I had been feeling strange for a couple of weeks. We both had. I knew that something big was going to change but I didn't know what. So many things had gone wrong for us over the flat. I had the dreadful feeling that any minute the roof was going to fall in on us completely.

Rachel had missed her period. She was fairly certain that she was pregnant but was waiting to have a test. We wanted another child but at the same time our financial situation was so precarious and our life so far out of our own control that the idea frightened us badly. The car had been broken into just the week before and I had freaked out because she had left her pouch in the glovebox with all the car's documents, log book and all. On top of which she hadn't locked the glovebox or put the alarm on. She had spent most of the afternoon sitting in the car until I got home in case the thief came back for that too. Eventually our flat-mate had taken out the distributor leads and a firm had come to fix the window. The incident had left her badly shaken and several times that week I saw her get up and look out of the window to check if the car was still there.

I had been working as a dispatch rider for the last three years. It had started as a way of giving us enough money to keep our flat until we could sell it. Like a lot of people in the 1980s I had bought something to do up, borrowed up to the hilt and then had been unable to sell when the prices slumped. We had already been to court once under threat of repossession and no matter how much I earned we were only just scraping by. The job was uncomfortable and stressful. I was working a lot of hours, and often got home late, wet, dirty, harassed. Then there was always the bike to fix, which ate into the weekend. We didn't feel like we saw much of each other. The day was long and Alex was often asleep when I came home.

But I was always motivated to go. I felt that even if I wasn't home much at least I was giving Alex the best he could have: because I worked Rachel could stay at home with him. And no child could have better than her. For someone who had previously turned her nose up at passing small children as snotty little brats she had turned into a wonderful and creative mother. Using books from the library she would come up with cheap and simple ideas for his development. She looked for toys in jumble sales, they made pictures and patterns out of raw pasta stuck on paper and there was always a drawing for me in the evening of the things they had done that day. No matter how broke we might have been he was learning as fast as anyone could wish for.

And so I worked with hardly a second thought, waiting for the day when we could finally sell our flat and be free to choose a different rhythm of life.

Hardly a second thought – that is, until the last couple of weeks. Suddenly I didn't care any more. I had always tried to get in to work first, always tried to get the best jobs. But that didn't seem to matter now. I was much more subdued about the whole thing. I can even remember saying to another rider 'I won't be doing this much longer.' But I had no real reason to think things were going to change. And the thought filled me with foreboding rather than happiness. It was true that someone had made an offer on the flat and we were beginning to look at other places. But it wasn't the first offer we'd had and was just as likely to fall through at the last minute as any of the others. All I wanted to do was get home as early as I could. I just wanted to be with them.

Rachel would often say to me: 'Don't go! Have day off.' But, as we were paid a bonus for working the whole week from Monday to Friday, a day off was very expensive. Rachel used to tell me that sometimes Alex cried during the day because he missed me so much. This caused me a lot of pain. But much as I would rather have stayed at home with them I considered it irresponsible to do so. I had to be sensible. We would have more time together in the future. Until then we would have to make do with the couple of weeks I took off a year and do as much as we could at the weekend. But I knew how unhappy it made her when I went on those mornings when she had wanted me to stay. It always left me feeling completely torn.

But yesterday morning had been different. I got myself ready for work: leathers on, boots on, radio on, bag – and then sat down again. I had never done that in three years! I just did not want to go. I felt beaten, defeated. I had to fight with myself to get back on my feet again. I was late by the time I finally got my bike started.

First thing that morning we had fought about something stupid. We had immediately made up. But I knew she was still feeling bad so I had gone back to hug her and tell her I loved her, just one more time. I felt she really needed convincing this morning, she seemed really shook up by life in general. How I wished I hadn't gone! I could have ripped off my own arms in remorse. I should have listened to my inner voice. It was the only time I had felt so strongly. I should have listened to myself.

Rachel and Alex appeared at the front door just as I was pulling off. Alex was always excited when my bike was running and he was waving and grinning as he held her hand. She smiled at me and even though she still looked a little fragile she seemed to be feeling better. Then I pulled away.

Then I pulled away. The sun was shining and she stood there dressed in jeans and a simple top, her blonde hair catching the light. The impression of her waving and smiling with Alex, carefree as he held her hand, is burnt into my mind. It was the last time I saw her alive.

In the back of the car Alex asked where we were going. I told him we were going for a walk. He showed no anxiety whatsoever. I watched someone walking in the street with a newspaper. He probably knew all about what was happening in my life right now. The thought just added to the unreality of the situation. He was going about his life carrying mine under his arm. Mine would never be the same again.

On the Heath itself several women walked alone with small children. I wanted to scream, 'How can they? After what has just happened!' I wanted to pick them up and shake them. 'Don't you realize what you are doing?! Don't you realize what has just happened to someone just like you, somewhere just like this?' I half-thought that perhaps, if I explained to them who I was, they would listen to me. But they would have thought I was nuts. When nothing bad has ever happened to you why should you think that it ever will?

Out in the open Alex played quite normally. Shockingly so. Why didn't he break down and cry? I could hardly stop. All the while I was watching his reactions like a hawk. If he showed any anxiety, I would take him away immediately. We played at being trains like in Thomas the Tank Engine and did running races and threw the stick for Molly and tried to recognise letters inscribed on the benches and played all the other usual games that were part of his daily world.

He showed no reaction to being out in the open or to being under the trees. He went under the branches in similar surroundings to where Rachel's body had been found the day before without a backward glance. In my naïve fashion I wanted him to get right back on the horse he had fallen off before he had too long to think about it. I didn't want him to associate the terrible things that had happened to him with the kind of place they had happened in. Otherwise we would never have been able to go to a park or open space again. So far he certainly wasn't giving the impression that he would become agoraphobic. I didn't want to read too much into the first day's reaction but he seemed to be coping far better than I would ever have imagined.

We went to a shopping centre to get some things to keep him amused. We bought a few books and some paper and crayons and things. Things to make, as I knew Rachel would like. We bought a video. I chose it because the blurb on the cover was reassuring. It went something along the lines of: 'A charming and gentle story, for small children that parents can let them watch and enjoy with peace of mind.'

We put it on later in the day. Within several minutes Alex was terribly distressed. He was whimpering in fear, and tears were running down his face. The first story he watched concerned a nation of rhinoceroses waging war on a nation of elephants. The rhinos stormed across the elephants' land tearing down houses and exposing the women and children elephants huddling fearfully inside. Several were being carried off. Alex was terrified by the figures rampaging across the screen. His face became a picture of anguish and fear. I leapt up as best as I could without dropping him and struggled to turn it off. I was shaking with anger. This was just what I was desperate to avoid. Rachel's friend was still with us and we looked at each other in despair.

Just when we were starting to relax a little we got hit by something so ridiculous. Something that should have been so safe.

A little while later I was sitting on the top of the stairs. Alex was on the landing just a few steps below playing with the Hoover. 'You've got a pip in your heart!' he said. 'Have I?' I replied, stunned. Molly had had some kind of seed embed itself in her ears and the lumps had caused her a lot of discomfort. Alex had wanted to know all about it. We had explained how much the 'pips' must have hurt.

He picked up the Hoover and put the end to my chest. 'You've got a pip in your heart and I'm going to get it out!' he declared. I stared at him in amazement. Two more of our friends had arrived and were sitting watching too. I just sat there with the end of the Hoover pinned to my chest while he busily worked away at getting the pip out of my heart.

'I've got to get it out 'cos it hurts!' he told me.

I couldn't for the life of me work out why a three-year-old child should come up with such a thing. I couldn't think of a similar incident in any of his stories or anything he watched that would make him act this way. He had never come out with anything like this in any game I had ever played with him. And, even if it was obvious to him that I was feeling bad, how would he know that it was my heart that was hurting? I was completely blown away and even more choked with tears.

He wouldn't let me move. For what seemed like ages he pinned me in place with the end of the Hoover against my chest while he hummed a Hoover-like noise. He made me lift my shirt up so it would work better and, beaming, he continued to tell me how he was going to get the pip out of my chest.

Whatever he was doing and for whatever reason, it was obviously giving him pleasure. He watched my face carefully as he continued to heal me. For twenty minutes or so he kept me in place. If I tried to get up he made his disapproval so clear that I was forced to sit down again. Finally he seemed satisfied. Beaming at me again, he told me that the pip was now out.

Incredible! For a small child to take you completely in his power and try to make you feel better was something unimaginable to me. But it was perfectly clear that in his way he was trying to do exactly that.

Watching him over the next few weeks I noticed that this was often his reaction to those around him. His way of dealing with others' grieving was the very opposite of what I had expected. He would act the clown. It struck me in fact that he was giving a performance of his normal self but was acting over the top. Alex, but larger than life. He was hamming up being happy and cheerful. His grin was just a little too fixed and his eyes were always checking on the reaction he might be getting.

I was concerned about our friends finding out about Rachel's death by turning on the television or picking up a newspaper. I wanted to spare them that much if I could. I spent much of my time on the telephone that day trying to get hold of them first, but it was almost a hopeless task. The story was now on the front page of every national newspaper. There were some people I just couldn't get hold of. One told me later how he had stood staring at a news-stand in the Midlands asking his companion if he was dreaming. They had both stayed over at our flat only a few days before. Nobody asked my permission for Rachel's name to be released on the day she was killed. And since her parents and family had yet to be informed I found this practice completely beyond my understanding. It was disgraceful and totally unforgivable. Why should anyone have to find out about the death of someone they love by glancing innocently at a newspaper or by turning on the television? There was no need whatsoever to release her name immediately. It caused even more pain than there already was. No consideration at all was given to the people affected by the tragedy. Our lives were taken out of our hands and became public property.

There still was no news of Rachel's parents. By now the police had contacted the FBI and the Canadian police and a manhunt was under way. With so much of Canada's surface area covered with water, they had a huge task on their hands. Her parents had set off by boat with relatives precisely to get away from it all. The boat was self-sufficient as far as sleeping and cooking was concerned and they had no set programme for their trip.

The detectives arrived and brought with them a cardboard box full of cards from well-wishers and some toys that had been donated to Alex. Messages of sympathy had been pouring in from all over the country.

I was genuinely surprised but also deeply moved. The letters were so touching, tears poured down my face as I read them. It was the emotions of others that set me off again each time. I would just get mine in check when I would see the pain that someone else who loved her was going through and I would find myself crying for them as well as for her. To read how complete strangers, people who didn't even know her, were crying too triggered emotions I could never have held back.

The detectives told me that it had finally been decided that the press conference would be put off at least until the next day. Arrangements were also being made for me to formally identify Rachel's body.

I felt so strange. I knew that she was already gone and I would just be seeing the shell. But there was still some part of me that wondered if somewhere there hadn't been a huge mistake. Maybe when I went to see the body there she would be, standing and smiling at me, and we would all laugh about the silly misunderstanding and then all go home together with our arms around each other, me and her and Alex, and we would thank the people for sorting out the mistake, and the next day we would say to everybody: 'Isn't life weird sometimes? You'll never imagine what happened to us yesterday, but . . .'

For a moment I almost allowed myself to get excited. It was almost as if I had a great secret that would make all these grieving people around me jump for joy. They would be cross because I had kept the secret to myself for so long. I looked at the faces of my brothers. Young teenagers now, they had been there the day Rachel and I met. I know how wonderful she had seemed to them. I saw the pain in their faces. She wasn't going to be there tomorrow.

I gave Alex his first bath as a single parent. He began to get rowdy and water started to go everywhere. I tried to calm him down but he gave me the kind of look that children reserve for a substitute teacher when their own teacher is away. A mixture of defiance and mocking. A sort of, 'I'm used to tougher than you!' It was clear that he was going to push his luck as far as he could.

I was beginning to feel that things were getting beyond my control. I was beginning to feel a little out of my depth. A battle of wills was taking shape. It was impressive to see the amount of personality packed into such a little body. Again I felt like a stranger, this time trying to work out what made him tick and what he was going to respond to. I wasn't used to this: I always got him on his best behaviour. Of course he was perfectly at ease with me but he wasn't going to do what I wanted as he would have done for his mother.

I wasn't there all day during the week, and weekends and holidays were usually so taken up with activity that he was worn out by the time evening came. He often fell asleep in the car on the way home from somewhere. And, if he hadn't, there was always Rachel there to sort him out. I felt like a beginner and things were already slipping away from me. The last thing in the world I wanted to do was to act aggressively and shout or smack. But I was physically and mentally drained and things were getting out of my control. Bathtime ended with one very excited little boy.

I was anxious about him going to sleep that night. He was bouncing around like a rubber ball and didn't seem in the least bit tired. This was the first real test of my ability as a single parent. There was no back-up. I wasn't sure how long I could keep up the good humour. I had had my attention totally on him for almost every single minute of the day. Almost everything I had done I had done with him in my arms, and now I was achingly tired. He had sat by the shower first thing, pleading and moaning for me to get out, he had gone with me to the toilet every time, and phone calls had been made with him on my lap complaining that he couldn't hear the television. The day had been long. Now I felt that I had run beyond my distance. I was not at all sure when my legs were going to give out completely.

Fortunately Alex loved stories. His routine had always been a bath to calm him down and ease his muscles (he had had a problem with his legs the year before), and a story in bed to make him drowsy before he got his second wind, and then a song to send him to sleep. I was soon to learn how keeping to a fixed routine was good for us both.

We were nearly at the end of our first day together. Our first day alone without Rachel. I had started the day in complete despair. I couldn't see how I would ever get through it. But up until this moment I had been so engrossed in taking care of so many things for Alex that my mind had been pulled from one task to the next, from one minute to the next, until the day was finally through. I had had very little time to myself to dwell on things.

At last Alex was asleep and the despair was back. Just walking out of his room put my mind back into the vacuum. It wasn't just my mind. I felt physically incomplete. It all came closing in on me. Another wave of pain. She wasn't going to be there when I walked downstairs. I was never going to see her again.

I felt the need to be with adults, to be with our friends. I just wanted to talk about Rachel. And I wanted to hear about Rachel from others. I wanted to drink in everything they had to say about her. She had gone and I would never again have anything new of her. But to hear recollections of others who had loved her, and of friends who had known her before I had, gave me something fresh to savour. I drank in every last word they had to say as they talked through the tears.

We spent a long time talking or trying to talk about what had happened. But no words seemed adequate. It belonged to another world. Something alien, totally beyond understanding.

I tried to explain what the police had told me. Her friends were people who loved her and were in agony too. I felt that they had the right to be included as much as possible, and maybe this would help them with their own pain. For the hardest thing was the feeling of being lost. Lost from everything that was sure. The rules that I thought the world lived by were gone. I had left the romantic world of a life shared, a future to look forward to, hope, the belief that dreams come true if you are patient, work hard and live a good life.

Now I was in the land of nightmares. Nightmares that come true. I had joined the endless ranks of victims named on any television set playing anywhere in the world. Those far-off unfortunates whom I had lived my life next to, saying to myself all the while, 'Those poor people!' while shivering in relief that it wasn't happening to us, and going on my way in the firm belief that it never would.

It was the dark side of a children's fairytale. But the ice and the pain inside me were not going to ease with the turning of the pages and an adult's soothing words.

Don't go into the woods! Something bad will get you.

But weren't we too old to believe in fairytales? Rachel was killed in broad daylight, at ten o'clock on a sunny, summer morning in a London park where people walked their dogs and I had romped around as a child. I had grown up nearby and nearly every other child I had known had played there unaccompanied at one time or another.

It was a place to be avoided at night – but in the daytime? In the daytime it was considered safe. The wardens had seen Rachel walking there alone. Surely if it was dangerous they would have said something to her? She would often stop to let Alex stroke their horses.

I knew now that we had been living in our own version of a fairytale, the good one, where this kind of thing only happened to other people, where no one would ever attack a mother with a young child. And Rachel wasn't small. Surely no one was going to pick on someone who looked like they could put up a fight? You can defend yourself, we had thought; if you really try, you can defend yourself.

We had deluded ourselves with myths. It was easy to do. Rachel was good-looking. Hadn't we read how convicted rapists had admitted to being intimidated by good-looking women and generally left them alone? It was daytime, people are safe in the daytime. . .

Fairytales!

But what was a young mother with a normal, energetic child supposed to do? How could she stay in the house all day? Where *was* it safe for a woman to go? Someone could hold a knife against your child in the street outside your home and force you somewhere against your will without the person next to you even being aware. People break in through the windows of homes all the times. We had both felt the fear; but what were you supposed to do – lock yourself in a cage with a machine-gun?

'You can take sensible precautions but you can't protect yourself from a psychopath.' My own words came back to taunt me, to torture me. It was a phrase I had used several times when the talk between us had turned upon these lines and life had seemed completely brutal and hopeless. Now I was choking on them. I was chilled to the soul and choking on them.

I had spent a lot of time in the United States but had never considered living there because I found it too violent. The irony was sickening.

I should never have gone to work. I should never have let her go to a place like the Common. It was my fault! After all, I was the one who had introduced her to the place. It was where I had often found peace as a child when things weren't going well. Where I had walked and dreamed of a future filled with love and happiness. I had loved the place, and now look what it had done to us.

You can't have anything good in this world. There is always something trying to tear it down and destroy it. She was good, she was kind, she thought of others. It counted for nothing. She was beautiful, but that wasn't her fault.

I could not believe that any particular individual was responsible for what had happened. It was just too far beyond me. I saw it as the doing of whatever forces made the world the way it is today. Children dying of starvation with their parents forced to watch, helpless. Extermination by race in Yugoslavia. World wars, poverty, greed, hate. It was all part of the same.

Only now I was no longer an observer.

To have your wife stabbed forty-nine times, her throat cut and her body sexually assaulted in front of your three-year-old child was something that only happened in concentration camps. Or so I had thought.

Such an unimaginably evil act did not and could not fit in my head. The attack on her had been so sustained and so deliberately cruel that it was beyond the understanding of a normal human being. You would not slaughter a beast in a fashion so cruel. I could not imagine that one human being could do that to another human being, let alone while her child – my child asleep above me – watched. There was nowhere to put it. Nobody could tell me she didn't suffer. Nobody could tell me my child would not have understood what was happening.

I was glad that she was dead. I was glad that she was dead and didn't have to suffer any more. I was glad that she was dead and didn't have to live in this world any more. I was glad that she didn't have to try and live with the wounds that had been inflicted on her. Some things are beyond human capabilities. She wasn't suffering any more. Anywhere she might be now could only be better than this. How could it be worse?

In my mind there was nowhere to go where I could put things to rest. And the mental discomfort was so bad that physically I didn't know what to do with myself. All day long I had had Alex to focus on, just one moment at a time to deal with, but now it was all hitting me hard. Hitting us all hard.

And her parents still didn't know.

To hear her friends talk about the stupid things they had got up to as schoolgirls made me laugh, even through the turmoil and pain. Rachel was someone with a great sense of humour and an almost ever-present smile. She would smile even in pain. Humour was her way of dealing with things. Our midwife had not at first believed that she was in labour when she was expecting Alex because Rachel had still managed to laugh down the phone. 'Women in labour don't laugh!' I remember the midwife saying.

Her humour was very sarcastic; cruel, almost. She would always find something to laugh about in anyone whenever they were out of earshot. She was a natural mickey-taker but in general her targets merited her comments. She wasn't malicious, though. She always used to say that she hoped others got as much fun out of her as she did out of them.

Her sharpest turn of phrase was always saved for those closest to her. There was no question of sparing our feelings. Naturally I was the number one target of fun and derision and often felt that she was running rings around me. I got used to it and tried to let myself be flattered by the attention, even though it wasn't always easy.

Now I could see her, so alive, in her friends' description of what they used to get up to. Their evenings together were full of howls of laughter. They told story after story of mischief and mickey-taking. In spite of the pain, I found myself in stitches. I was suddenly light-headed. Delirious between laughter and pain.

There was a lot more that evening. The laughter was a part of Rachel's spirit that was with us. Often more a smirk than a laugh. Each of us had tears in our eyes. I was crying and laughing at the same time.

I went to bed very late. I couldn't bear the thought of turning in without her. In spite of the wine that I had drunk through the evening my mind would not stop turning. I lay awake for hours picturing what must have happened, trying to somehow be with her when she had needed me most. But no matter how hard I twisted my mind and tried to force the images to make them real, it was too late. I hadn't been there. I had let her down.

I plotted my revenge on whoever had done this. I would do to him what he had done to her. I would do it slower. But the thought brought me no relief. It wouldn't bring her back. And that was all I wanted.

I fell asleep eventually, but woke up soon after, around three in the morning. It was impossible to get back to sleep again. Everything went through my head over and again. Over and above everything was the agony of being ripped away from a part of myself. The disbelief that such a thing could happen pushing vainly against the vast reality of the pain. The sharpness of that pain telling me over and over again that, yes, it really had happened. She really was gone.

It was light before I finally dozed off. It wasn't long before Alex woke up.

I felt Alex lift the duvet and pull himself in beside me. The room was already light and I pretended still to be asleep. He was talking to himself very quietly and I tried to breathe as softly as I could, to catch what he was saying.

'Mine, mine, mine!' was all I could make out. He was patting me at the same time. 'Mine, mine, mine.' And so he went on, patting and murmuring peacefully, while I pretended to be asleep. He seemed perfectly relaxed. Sneaking a look at my watch I worked out that he had kept this up for twenty minutes or so. He wasn't trying to wake me, he was patting very gently. But what he was doing was very considered and very serious. It was as if he was reassuring himself that he still had something. Something that was totally his and that was vitally important to him. I lay there trying not to disturb him. My heart was aching.

At last we got up. He seemed fairly cheerful. He trailed down the stairs behind me carrying his blankets in his arms. No one else was awake. He was still murmuring. Faintly I heard him say: 'Where's Celeste?' I froze on the spot. My heart was in my mouth. I didn't dare turn round. I was terrified that any sudden sound or movement from me would panic him and stifle his fragile attempt to communicate before it had even begun. He and Rachel used to play at being characters from all his favourite stories. One of which was Babar. Babar was king of the elephants and Celeste was his queen. Alex would always be Babar and Rachel would be Celeste. This child behind me wanted desperately to communicate with me, for me to try and help him work things out, but he was unable to ask me directly what was going on. He could only utter what was so painful to him by talking in whispers and riddles. And then only while talking to my back.

'Where's Celeste?' he asked again.

My mind began to race. I was being given an opening but it was absolutely crucial that I didn't blow it.

Downstairs I hurriedly prepared him something to eat. We sat on the floor in the front room where his little plastic train-set was still out from the day before. There was a box of his toys. Before his present passion for dinosaurs Alex had loved to play with a set of plastic animals. There was mother elephant and a baby elephant. I took them both out and put them on the floor. In my head I had solved half the problem, but the second half was more complicated. 'This is Babar,' I said, pointing to the baby elephant. 'Who's that?'

'Me!' said Alex, grinning. He understood the game.

'And this is Celeste,' I said, pointing to the mother elephant. 'Who's that?'

'Mummy!' he said, still grinning and giving every appearance of enjoying the game.

Then came the hard bit. I had to introduce the subject of the killer into the game. 'I know that when Celeste was killed there was somebody else, somebody I don't know.'

I had read an article once about a grandfather who had used some toys to tell his grandson a story. In his story there had been a nasty character who had been the villain of the piece. The story had finished with the villain coming to a sticky end. When it was finished all the toys had been put back on the shelf. But the little boy couldn't forget the story and the toy that had represented the bad man had become an object of fear for him. As time went by he became more and more terrorized by it. Eventually he became hysterical at even the prospect of being left alone in the room with it. Only when the toy had been thrown out could the little boy feel safe again.

I wanted something to represent the man who had killed Rachel, but I did not want something that was going to stay in the house afterwards. I decided to use a piece of paper. I drew a kind of gingerbread man figure with a knife in his hand. 'This is the man that killed Mummy,' I said and placed it on the floor beside the two elephants. Alex followed my hands with rapt attention. 'He is a bad, bad man and I hate him. This is what I want to do with him.' And I grabbed the piece of paper and scrunched it up violently in my hands. Alex was grinning. I jumped to my feet. 'And this is what I want to do with it! Do you want to see?'

Alex scrambled enthusiastically to his feet and followed me out of the room and into the kitchen. 'This is what I'm going to do with him!' So saying, I lifted the lid and threw the ball of paper into the bin. Alex laughed.

He was suddenly very excited and started bouncing around. 'Shall we do it again?' I asked. Alex insisted that we should. We went back into the front room and I repeated the scene, just like the first time. Alex looked positively ecstatic when I scrunched and pounded the picture into a little ball. He skipped after me into the kitchen and squealed as I slammed it into the bin.

The next time when I laid the drawing out next to the elephants I asked: 'What do you want to do with the man who killed Mummy?' Without hesitation he leapt on to the piece of paper, pounded it into a little ball and ran out of the room *on his own* and threw the ball into the bin. I was so proud of him when he came running back in. He had left me without even looking round to see if I was coming with him or not. This was the first time he had felt able to do so since I had collected him from the hospital. He had only been out of the room for a few seconds but in terms of his recovery it was as if he had gone to the moon and back! These were the first few seconds when he had felt confident enough to stand on his own two feet. It was as if he was learning to walk all over again.

Over and over again I drew the same figure and over and over again Alex scrunched it up and threw it into the bin. He did so with relish. His little body was filled with determination and even though he was laughing all the while it was a nervous, hysterical laughter. There was no doubt that he was furiously venting his anger.

I was flooded with happiness. I had found a way to let him express this anger. I felt delirious with relief and with achievement. I could see by his face as we worked away how much this was doing him good. I had found, or rather had been given, a way in. I thanked Rachel, wherever she was, for the inspiration. The poison was beginning to come out. I had no idea how long it would take or if it was even possible to get it all out. I didn't know then whether he would ever be rid of it all, but somewhere was a grain of belief that he would recover in time as long as life would just leave us alone for long enough.

Alex's behaviour altered noticeably that morning. The load seemed to have lightened. For the rest of the day he continued to act over the top but with a little less hysteria and a little more calm. At one stage the room was full of family and friends. The detectives were there too. Alex had his Fireman Sam hat on and he was sitting back in a chair singing the theme song for all he was worth. Over and over again. Everybody was laughing, probably because it was all so insane. It was the last thing in the world you would expect of a child who had been through all that Alex had. It was a surreal moment. The sun was shining through the windows, the flowers were in bloom and it was party time. He was soaking up the attention and beaming with pleasure. He was the sole object of attention for all these adults. He was like a happy drunk.

I felt a moment of spontaneous light-heartedness. Then I was uncomfortable. Of course I was pleased to see him having a good time but I could see that too much of this would not be healthy. Things were going to get distorted. He didn't need to be cosseted, he needed to be among other children where he would be knocked around like everyone else. He should not be treated differently. But this was of course asking virtually the impossible of those around us.

Anyone who looked at him could hardly hold back the tears. Anyone who looked at him could hardly believe that the playful little child in front of them had just been through such an ordeal. That he would never see his mother again. I watched friends leave the room over the first few weeks and break down in tears out of his sight. I preferred it when they cried in front of him. Even if he didn't cry for his mother directly himself, seeing grown-ups crying was at least a way of letting him know that it was all right to feel bad. And that it was all right for him to show his feelings as well. I also thought he had a right to know how special his mother was and how wonderful she had been and how much other people missed her too.

I never wanted Alex to hear me talking in whispers or for things to be going on behind closed doors. Rachel and I had always tried to explain everything to him, even if he didn't completely understand. When he was older we wanted him to be able to talk about and ask questions about absolutely anything at any time. We believed that this should start right at the beginning. I also understood, a lot from my own experience, that children who are victims feel guilty. When I had been young I had always felt that bad things had happened in my life because there was something wrong with me. That it was my fault. I had felt terrible but was unable to talk to anyone about my fear: I didn't think they cared. I was so scared that I would be rejected and sent away to a home. I had read of others who had felt the same unreasoning guilt. Now I was determined to use whatever means I could to prevent Alex from ever feeling the way that I'd felt when I was young.

He would often put his hands on my face and look at me if I started sobbing. And I always tried to say, if I could manage to get the words out, that I was crying because of what had happened to Mummy. Because she had been hurt so much. Because I missed her so badly and I wanted her back but I couldn't have her back. And that I was crying for him because he had had to see such terrible things and his mummy had been taken from him and I couldn't do anything to bring her back for him, either.

He became the centre of everyone's grief. It seemed an incredibly heavy extra load for him to bear. But, with every adult aware of what had happened, how could I have asked them to behave otherwise? They would have been inhuman if they had reacted differently. But I decided to get him back to being with friends of the same age as soon as possible.

Events convinced me that we had no choice but to go somewhere where people didn't know us. Children are very good at seeing how adults operate and then working out a way to manipulate them. Constant sympathy directed at a child growing up seemed like the recipe for all sorts of problems later on. He had to grow up where people would like or dislike him on his own merits, not because of what had happened to him once when he was small. He shouldn't learn to live on sympathy. And neither should I.

Chapter Three

A LEX WOKE UP crying. After the previous days' calm this was to become the daily pattern for nearly the whole of the first year. Just in the time it took to get from my bed to his the sound had scraped my nerves raw. It was a sound between moaning and crying and grizzling. It was very hard to take. It filled me with fear. This wasn't normal crying, but a completely new sound, terrifying in its misery. He was distressed and I wasn't getting through quickly. In these moments he seemed truly broken and deranged. Even his movements were jerky and spastic. This was a child who before had chortled and laughed out loud in his sleep.

I had always thought how amazingly happy he must have been to do that. It was a sound that had filled me with joy and wonder. But now I was in a different world. The room was so empty without Rachel. Instead it was filled with this awful sound: my spirits were at rock bottom. 'Look what you have taken from me!' I screamed silently in my head. 'Look what you have left me with: this broken child!' In an instant I forgot all the positive things from the days before. Against this awful sound they were totally insignificant. I was overwhelmed by depression.

By the time I had picked him up and cuddled him for a while, and gone through what was becoming a familiar speech of reassurance, he was calming down. He spasmed occasionally as he calmed. His eyes were screwed tightly shut. As if he knew what horror the world was going to present him with and he didn't want to see any part of it. When he finally opened his eyes he was very subdued. I took him to the toilet. By the time we were finished he was coping better.

I had gone to bed late again the night before. Again I had drunk a lot of wine. Again we had talked and talked and talked. I didn't want the evening to end. I felt buoyed up by the company. I knew if Rachel had been there she would have had a good laugh. Having her friends there made me feel nearer to her. I was using them like a kind of drug. I didn't want to come down.

Patterns were forming. I would lie awake for a long time, my mind turning over and over. I would fall asleep, wake again between three and four and then find it impossible to get back to sleep. Once again I would turn everything over and over in my mind. I tried to imagine what Rachel must have been through. I was trying to share it with her. My poor baby! So much pain, so much distress, so much fear. Nothing I could do could ease her suffering. Nothing I could do could soothe her pain. She had finished her life alone. Died in fear and distress for what might happen to the child she could no nothing to protect.

There was no one to hold her hand. No one to stroke her head. Just her body destroyed by a maniac after her spirit had already departed. If there was a God then he was obscenely cruel. No reason existed, no justification, no logic. Only agony and suffering. She was just a child. Just a child.

I would do the same to the killer when they found him. I saw myself doing it. But it wouldn't be enough. Nothing I could do to him would make him suffer enough to pay for what he had done. Nothing was enough.

When I woke to the sound of Alex crying it felt like I had finally only just dozed off minutes before.

That morning the police drove us to St George's hospital. I was to identify Rachel's body officially. An autopsy had already been performed and there was a limit to how long her body could be kept unrefrigerated before it began to deteriorate. We were driven round to the back of the building and the car drew up outside the mortuary.

There was another car with us. It contained various police officers. The sun shone through a dirty-white sky. A summer day in London.

We walked through the front door. I could see a table in the room to the right through a gap where the curtain did not fully close. I wanted to go in there but we were shown towards the waiting-room on the other side of the corridor. I had to force myself through the door. She was somewhere near. Strangers had her and I was being forced to wait.

It was very quiet. Oppressive. I was desperate to see her. Surely now it would be confirmed to me, the fact that I alone knew: it wasn't real; she wasn't dead. She would walk out in a hospital gown, the familiar smile on her face.

The delusion faded from my mind. My heart beat even faster. I wanted to scream out. Suddenly I wanted proof that she really *was* gone.

We sat and waited. Hardly a word was said. There was a tank full of ornamental fish. Alex left my lap to examine them. I could smell the ether in the air.

Earlier that morning I had explained to him that we were going to see Mummy's body. I had said that she had really gone and this was just the shell. It wasn't her any longer. It was just like old clothing. He had shown no enthusiasm at the idea of seeing her. He had not looked at me as I had explained to him. But he hadn't cut me off as he had before either by putting his hand over my face or by drowning me out with his own talking. He had let me talk. He had taken in what I was saying.

Now that we were there he showed no curiosity about what we had come to do. He gave no indication that he thought we were going to see her there alive. He asked no questions. He was more interested in the fish.

I sat for what seemed an age. My heart was pounding. My mind, though, was clear and my eyes were dry. It felt like the whole building and everybody in it were focused on us. I felt as if I was living everybody else's nightmare as well as my own.

In fact it was only a few minutes before someone came to say things were ready. The staff were hushed and polite. The curtain was held aside for me. She was there. The staff left Alex and me on our own.

What had I expected to see? Something? Some sign of life?

All I could see clearly was her face. She lay on a table or a trolley, on her back with her hands at her sides. She wore a robe which rose and covered her neck. Her hands were wrapped and bound. They had taken great care to ensure that all of her wounds were covered.

Her face looked like wax. There was no colour in her skin. But it was her face. It had a quality that could never be confused with a dummy. I felt every bump and contour as if it had been years and not days since I had last touched them. I recognized every single particle of skin. The contours under my fingertips felt as familiar as a part of myself. My chest heaved and I sobbed as I stroked her hair. I stroked her cheek. But she was gone. This wasn't her any more. She was somewhere else now. Her skin was hard when I kissed it and ice cold. The colour, or lack of it, said it all.

Tears ran down my face. My chest ached as I sobbed. 'My poor baby.' I would never have her back. Not in this world.

I ran my eyes all the way down towards the bump where her feet were covered and back again. I was hit by waves of shock every time my eyes came back to her face. Like my own face was being slapped. I was being hit by the truth as if confronted by it for the first time.

I stroked her hair as I had when she slept. I felt as if I was looking at my own child. I felt as if I had grown old in the last few days. As if my life had been lived and was already in the past. She looked so young. Her life had only just begun. 'My poor, poor baby. What you must have been through.'

Alex hung back by the curtain. He had followed me in but showed no interest in approaching his mother's body.

'Don't you want to say goodbye to Mummy's body?' I asked, putting my arms out towards him. Reluctantly he came towards me and let me pick him up. I was fearfully conscious of the raw emotion that he was witnessing. I knew that he was still very small. But it seemed right that he should there. There would never be another chance.

He looked sideways at Rachel's body for a moment and then looked away. He showed no signs of fear and no signs of distress and no signs of interest. He just didn't want to know.

'Can we go now?' he asked.

'In a minute,' I replied. 'I want to say goodbye.'

With him in my arms I bent to kiss her forehead.

My mother had been waiting outside. She came in and held my hand. There was nothing that could be said that could take away the pain. She asked Alex if he wanted to look at the aquarium again. He went with her towards the door, but wouldn't go out. 'When are we going?' he asked.

Eventually I kissed her one more time and turned to leave. I picked Alex up. I turned one last time before going through the door. Alex

looked back too. But he was right. She wasn't there. Not on that table.
But I felt her near me. With us.

I realized that she had been with us all the time.

From the hospital we were driven to New Scotland Yard to a press
conference. From the back of the car I could read the newspaper
hoarding outside the tube station. There were just a few words in giant
print. I could read it easily from across the road: 'SEARCH FOR
RACHEL'S KILLER.'

We pulled into the driveway and found ourselves blocked by
another car that was barring the access to the underground carpark.
Stuck outside the main doors, we couldn't go forward and we could-
n't go back. I could see what looked like hundreds of cameramen
inside the glass doors of the lobby.

A van beside us was unloading film gear. The crew had their backs
to us. The press inside were all busy looking into the building and trying to get up the stairs while the child they were all so frantic to get a
shot of was sitting right behind them.

I tried my best to cover Alex's face without upsetting him and I
prayed that nobody would turn round. The detective at the wheel was
losing his temper. He barked at a uniformed officer to get the car out
of our way. Like a scene from a slapstick comedy the obstacle was
cleared while the camera crew were still hard at work with their backs
to us. We screeched down the carpark ramp. As the grille closed
behind us I let out a sigh of relief.

We were led through empty stairwells and corridors. We seemed to be
climbing into the heart of the building but there were no windows to
give any clues. Just the usual cheerless décor and lighting of any government building. It was very much how I imagined a nuclear bunker
must be.

We were shown into an office to wait. Pens were found for Alex.
Paper. Stickers and balloons followed. Colouring books. Biscuits were
offered. Tea. Everyone tried to make us comfortable. Everyone who
saw us immediately recognized us. They looked concerned and
anxious to be as helpful as possible. The more unusually nice people
were to us, the worse I realized our situation must actually be.

A senior officer arrived. He sat on a desk and looked down at us.
Alex froze. The officer began to explain what was going to happen. I

could hardly listen. I could feel Alex's tension. The officer had a nervous smile when he talked. I couldn't see anything to smile about.

I tried not to be aggressive when I asked him if he could get down from the desk. But he was frightening Alex. He was towering above us in a posture that was very threatening. He was only too happy to change his position when I explained why.

He told me that things would be as brief as possible. The idea was to appeal for anybody who had any information, and hadn't already done so, to come forward. Since the day that Rachel was killed a police trailer had been set up in the Common carpark as an incident room. Many people had already given statements. The police wanted to speak to everyone who had been on the Common that morning to clear them from their inquiries. And also to get any new information they might have on the killer: had they seen anybody acting suspiciously? They were eager for anything new. So far they had very little to go on.

He said that the police wanted to keep a good relationship with the press. They were a necessary evil that had to be tolerated. He seemed almost embarrassed to say so. Like it or not, he said, the police relied on the press to get their message over to the public. Many cases had been solved through leads that had come about from press coverage. I found his words chilling. I was amazed to hear a senior police officer suggesting that we should be grateful to the press just for doing what they were paid to do.

I thought of the cases where the gutter press had manipulated information and interfered with juries and witnesses. I was wondering what particular gruesome name they were going to come up with for Rachel's killer when he was caught. 'Ripper'. 'Slayer'. God only knew what. Whatever it was we would have to live with that too for years to come. On top of everything else, that was going to become part of our lives as well.

These 'journalists' must have no feelings, I told myself. We had already had one taste of their harassment. And we were the victims of this crime, not the perpetrators.

Everything was ready as soon as I was able to pull myself away from Alex. Nobody was rushing me.

I had to wait until Alex was suitably absorbed in something. Each time I tried to get to my feet he became upset. Eventually, with several adults working furiously to keep the entertainment going, I managed to creep away. It was a dreadful wrench. I felt I was tricking him. Even if I was only going to be away for a few moments. I was terrified of losing his trust. But this had to be done. They had to catch this 'thing'. I still could not think of Rachel's killer in human terms.

Leaving Alex in my mother's charge I was led by one of what had become 'our' detectives through a door that opened directly behind and beside a stage which filled the width of the room. The room was long and narrow. I was shocked by the number of lenses pointing our way. TV and press. It was very threatening. It was like facing a firing squad.

I don't know how many people were in the room but it seemed like hundreds standing and sitting. Each had a notebook or a tape recorder ready or was hovering behind a lens. There was a general low murmuring but the moment we entered the room everyone focused on us. Flashguns fired and there was a civilized shuffling as people tried to get the best view.

I was ushered behind the desk. The senior officer sat on the front of it and addressed the room. He still had that smile and, true or not, it gave him the impression of enjoying the circus. Rachel and I had seen this very officer in this very room appeal for help when a baby had been snatched some months before. He was beginning to annoy me. Rachel hadn't liked him. We couldn't understand how he had been able to smile then either.

He spoke very briefly and then I was asked to say something. 'Our' detective held my hand tight for support. I managed to get the words out without breaking down. I only did so because I was doing it for someone else. I was doing it for Rachel, and thinking of her gave me the strength to control my emotions.

I said only a few words. But something completely unexpected happened while I did; something that nearly brought me to a stop. Nearly everyone in the room was crying. These hardened professionals, male as well as female, were juggling handkerchiefs with notebooks. I had steeled myself against them before entering the room. I had imagined intrusive questions designed to bring things down to the lowest level. I was watching and waiting for the slightest slur on Rachel's character, primed to let fly at the slightest lack of respect. But I hadn't been prepared for this.

I pleaded for anybody who knew anything at all that could help to come forward. This person had to be found before someone else was killed and another family destroyed. Somebody must know something. I couldn't see how anybody walking along covered in blood in broad daylight could go unnoticed. Alex had been drenched with blood from his chest to his feet.

I wanted Rachel's killer caught before anybody else could be made to suffer as we had. Nothing that could be inflicted upon him – torture, hanging, shooting, being burned alive – could ever make up for what he had done to Rachel because she was never, never coming back. He had put her beyond our reach. Even his total destruction would never change that. The maniac had won. And we had lost. Whatever happened.

But I would do anything I could to stop this nightmare happening to someone else.

'Our' detective gripped my hand all the time. His gesture touched me deeply. In British society it's not a very male thing to hold the hand of another man. I was moved by his sensitivity and compassion. The journalists were still crying.

What had happened to us was so far beyond the norm that it was affecting everybody's behaviour in the most unexpected way. Ours had become a very public mourning.

We had probably been in the room for no more than five or six minutes. I was bustled out before anyone could ask any questions. I was hugely relieved to see that Alex hadn't become a screaming, gibbering wreck in my absence. He was still busy being entertained but instantly he wanted to know where I had been. There were still several adults leaning over him working hard to keep the party going. However, the moment he saw me he latched back on to me. He was put out that I had left him and there was no question of him letting me out of his grip again in a hurry. He had amassed a whole bag full of paraphernalia and was covered in stickers and badges. He insisted that all the grown-ups wear one too. Everyone had to pass his inspection.

The mail from the general public had turned into a flood. Things were being sent from all corners of the country. The response was unbelievable. The fact that people had gone to the trouble of putting pen to paper was touching enough but to send gifts as well showed incredible generosity. The police soon had a room filled with toys which had been sent for Alex.

People had sent things that they had made themselves, things that they had knitted, money, teddy bears, books. Alex and I received the most moving letters imaginable along with the gifts. One mother had written to say that her son had come down to find her in tears. The boy, who was the same age as Alex, had asked her why she was crying. She explained that a bad man had killed the mummy of a little boy just like him. The boy returned upstairs. When he came down a few minutes later he held his favourite teddy bear. 'This is for the boy who lost his mummy,' he said. It had been sent along with the letter.

There were lots of letters from obviously elderly people sending us their love and support. There would often be a postal order for five or ten pounds attached. I appreciated how much such a sum represented to someone living on a pension. Every letter had me in tears.

There were letters from people I had lost contact with over the years. People who were now scattered across the country and even beyond who were thinking of us. There were letters from people Rachel had met on the street. They might only have exchanged a few words but they had remembered her. Someone she might have met in the library while choosing books for Alex, or another mother in the park.

There were cards of love and support from people who lived in Northern Ireland. They expressed their shock. That people who have lived with so much horror every day could be shocked by something that had happened to us knocked me back even further on my heels. What was happening to us?

People sent poems. Two in particular were sent:

Do not stand at my grave and weep. I am not there. I do not sleep.
I am a thousand winds that blow. I am the diamond glints on snow.
I am the sunlight on ripened grain. I am the gentle autumn rain.
When you awaken in the morning hush, I am the uplifting rush of quiet birds in circled flight.
I am the soft stars that shine at night. Do not stand at my grave and cry. I am not there, I did not die.

Anonymous

If the dead can come back to the earth
And flit unseen around those they love
I shall always be with you
And on the brightest day
And the darkest night and when the soft breeze fans
Your cheek
It shall be my breath
For the cool air on your temple
It shall be my spirit

Major Sullivan Ballor
(Written to his wife Sarah during the American Civil War)

It became a daily routine for me to pass the letters around the dining room table. Friends and family shared my own reaction to them. I was always left dizzy by the goodness of people. I wanted to believe the world was bad, to make it easier to accept the bad that had happened to us. But here I was having my eyes forced open to the fact that it wasn't true. I had seen the worst that human beings are capable of. I wanted to hate the world and everything in it. Now, through so many people and so many strangers reaching out to us I was being shown the most unselfish, genuinely pure acts of good that people were capable of as well. Their love and concern succeeded in almost physically buoying me up.

Every day the detectives arrived during those first couple of weeks they had a box of mail under their arm. Every time there was some moving letter to read. People who lived in the countryside offering somewhere for us to stay if we wanted to get away to find some peace; a drawing for Alex from a child who was thinking of him; a book to be read to him.

I have kept every letter and card that we received. We no longer live in the UK but I have no intention of changing our nationality. I have had the chance to travel and see a little of the world and long ago came to the conclusion that people are no more capable of good or evil in one country than another. Times change people, circumstances change people, but the base of human nature stays the same. When Alex is older he will be able to read the things that people sent us for himself. Through them he will be able to see the good that people, and the

British general public in particular, are capable of and the efforts that so many of them went to to help some people that they didn't even know.

It was two days after we had seen Rachel's body. I had finished reading Alex his bedtime story. Quietly I began to sing a song. I stroked his hair. He looked tired and subdued. When I got to the end of the song, however, he was no nearer to going to sleep. He was staring off into space, silently lost in thought. I began another song. I had often come home from work just as he was going to bed and had taken my turn at getting him to sleep. Sometimes he went to bed in a state of high excitement and it took two or three songs to get him drowsy enough to nod off. But I had always managed it, no matter how long it took. I took a kind of foolish pride in the fact that I could at least do this much for my child even if I hardly saw him all day. It pleased me enormously if Rachel said: 'I never thought you'd get him down tonight!'

But tonight my voice was getting hoarse and, despite his calm, there was no sign of him nodding off. I stopped the song. There was no point. He was just staring off into space. 'You're thinking about Mummy, aren't you?' I said. I felt unsure of myself but I just had to do something to reach him. Compared to his normal state he was like a zombie in a trance. And it looked as if he could have lain that way all night without falling asleep.

He lay on his back with his head resting on his chest. Without looking at me he moved his chin up and down just enough to let me know that he meant 'yes'. This one movement revealed all the pain that was concentrated in his tiny body. His sad eyes staring off into space. My heart was breaking for him all over again.

He was staring straight ahead, completely calm and terribly, quietly sad. His eyes, however, were dry. He seemed to be holding everything in: the little nod of his head was the only sign he gave of his distress. It was frightening to see how badly he was really feeling. Every day now he had given the impression of a child searching for every opportunity to play and have a good time. All the while he was hiding all this inside, keeping himself in complete control. Up until now the crying in the morning had been the only sign of the hell he was privately going through. The moment he was truly awake he was instantly back in command of his emotions.

41

This quiet moment of sadness was the first demonstration of anything I could label 'grieving' in the sense an adult might know.

I took a deep breath. 'Your mummy loved you more than anything in the whole world, you know,' I said. He didn't look at me. He didn't move at all. He kept on staring. 'She didn't want to leave you. She would never have left you! She would have done anything in the world not to leave you. But that man killed her. It wasn't her doing. She was taken away from you, she didn't leave.'

The bedroom door slammed loudly.

The sky outside the window was heavy with clouds. A thunderstorm had been brewing since the day Rachel was killed. But up until then there had been no wind.

'She'll always be with you somehow,' I said. 'No matter what. For all your life. All the time you're growing up and even when you become a daddy too. She will always find a way to get through to you.' I watched the side of his face. His expression hadn't changed.

'Some people say that we come back as animals or even as other people,' I continued. 'Mummy always used to say that she was a dolphin before she was born, swimming in the sea. Maybe she'll be a dolphin again, swimming in the sea. She'd like that. Maybe she'll be a beautiful flower. Whatever it is, she will be part of the good things around you.'

She hadn't left him. I had to make him understand. Never, never, never would she have left him, whatever it would have cost her. He had to understand that. 'When the wind blows through your hair it will feel like her stroking your head. And maybe when the sun shines and you feel nice and warm that will be a bit of Mummy trying to make you feel nice.' I didn't really know what I was saying but certain things had to be said. It was what I felt was true. Somehow I could still feel her presence and I knew that the most important thing I could do was to get him to understand that she hadn't left him because she didn't love him. I felt that she was helping me find the words to talk to him in a way that he would understand. She would find a way to him even if it was only through me.

'When we go to the beach and you swim in the sea you'll feel her too.' I was trying to give him things that his imagination could catch hold of. Something that maybe inside him he could feel for himself. 'When the waves push all around you she'll be there somewhere, looking after you. Somewhere with the fishes.' I had the certain feeling that no matter what else happened to him he would never drown. Rachel loved the water, and the sea was wild and another world, and if she could be anywhere to be close to him she could be there.

There was the merest glimmer of a smile. He was taking in what I was saying and somewhere it was striking a chord.

'And when it rains, part of the rain will be Mummy.' I could see from the slightest softening of his expression that the idea pleased him. 'When the rain falls down all clean and new we will think of her. And when it splashes on the ground the sound will be like she's singing to you.'

It began to rain. The window slammed shut as if in encouragement. As if someone was trying to let me know that I was on the right lines.

I wasn't sure what I believed any more. But the idea that someone as vibrant and lively and loud and strong as Rachel could just cease to exist was more difficult for me to accept than the idea that something goes on after we die. I was sure that it was Rachel who was slamming that window. I was sure that she was somewhere safe. But she was angry. She had been ripped away from all that she loved. Before she had even begun.

There was a clap of thunder and the skies opened. The rain came pouring down. But far from being disturbed by the storm, Alex had fallen asleep. His position had hardly changed. He was still on his back but now his breathing was deep and regular and his face was calm. I sat and watched his face.

She had loved him so much. It must have been the worst agony imaginable for her when she realized, as she must have done, that she would be separated from him. Worst of all that she knew that she was dying and she knew he was watching and that he would probably be next and that there was nothing she could do to protect him.

I would have given anything to have taken her place. She was always giving, always well intentioned, always kind. She hadn't deserved to suffer in the slightest way. Let alone this unimaginable horror. Where was the reason in anything? At times like this, I really felt myself looking over a cliff of despair. Everything swirled around my head and I felt nauseous and giddy. She was more use to the world than I was. And certainly more use to Alex. What in God's name was this for? What do we live our lives for?

'We all die one day,' I remember saying. 'And nobody knows what happens to us afterwards. I don't know. No one knows where we come from before we are born either. Maybe we will go wherever Mummy has gone when we die too!'

I couldn't swap places. But I wanted so much for her to know that I would look after him for her. I would bring him up as she would have wanted. It was the one thought that gave me any clarity. It was the only thing that could make any impression on my despair. I wanted with all my being and all my soul to give her some kind of relief from her suffering. And to do this for her was all I could do. And, desperately, I wanted her to know that I was doing it.

The storm broke. It seemed to be just above the house. Our friends, those who had become the 'war party', were downstairs. I couldn't speak to anybody. I was too choked. I walked right past them and out into the garden. I wanted to be in the rain.

The back of the house had been extended into the garden. There was a glass roof and big glass panel windows. The rain was lashing down and the thunder cracked. It was still early, and July evenings are long. The garden was still light. I squeezed out of the patio door and sat on a low garden wall.

I was sobbing uncontrollably. My body was shaking, but I hardly noticed. I was beyond it all. The storm seemed to be crashing all around me and for a moment I left the city and the world of people behind. It was nature that was surrounding me now. More powerful and more pure. Our world was so pathetic and dirty. So shameful.

I felt that I was being cradled by this storm, that it was for me alone. I needed it. It was only just enough to match the depths of my despair. My mind was caving in on itself. Why is the good destroyed? What is the point of so much suffering in this existence? So many people tortured and tormented by life. Human history is just a continuous line of war and cruelty and fear and separation and more war and more violence and more suffering. There are good people, but look what happens. Violence! More pain. And more violence. Whichever way you turn. This is supposedly a 'safe' country. Look what happens!

But the rain was so clean. So much beyond anything human. It was coming down so strong that it felt like it was wrapping itself around me.

Tomorrow I would be taken to where Rachel's body had been found. I had asked to be taken to the spot. I wanted to lay just one flower for her where she had left this existence. But I couldn't see how I could do something so impersonal and artificial as to buy such a thing from a shop.

There were rose bushes lining the garden fence. Most had opened into big blooms and as I looked around, one caught my eye. It was a long bud that had not yet opened. It was not perfectly coloured, part of the pink and red had yellowed and frayed. It seemed absolutely appropriate. I broke it from the bush and went back to sit on the wall. I turned it over in my hand. Distantly I heard my heaving and sobbing begin to quieten but I was still a long way away. I was glad that nobody had come to comfort me. At that moment anybody's presence would have been an intrusion. Right now I wanted to be alone.

But our friends' company had been an enormous support for me. I was able to hurl up everything that I was going through and they made it all right for me so do so. They listened and in turn they voiced their emotions. This did me good to hear: it made me feel that I was of some benefit to them too, that the exchange was going both ways.

I owe everyone around me in those early days a huge debt of gratitude. It was an enormously intense time and I was near breaking point. Of course not everyone could spend every minute of the day with us. But the fact that some could spend so much time with us in the beginning was extremely important. The fact that I could unload so much on to them undoubtedly made a huge difference. I was safe with them. They loved Rachel too. I would have carried on without them, once the decision to carry on had been made, but every little part of the strain that they let me share with them made one more part of me free to do something for Alex. One part less of me occupied with my own survival was one part more of me able to concentrate on his.

Finally I began to feel the cold. There was no point in me getting sick. I would be no good to him like that. I went back inside to get some dry clothes.

The rain eased a little and the thunder began. It seemed to be slowly gathering in power as the night drew in. Often someone's voice would be completely drowned out by it, cut off in mid-sentence. Time and again we were forced to sit and listen. 'It's Rachel,' someone said.

There was an enormous answering roar.

'She's really angry,' said another. Hardly were the words out than there was another roar, even louder than the first. Strangely we were reduced to fits of nervous giggles by the power and timeliness of it.

There was an explosion like a bomb going off around our heads. 'I didn't realize thunder could get this loud,' someone observed, timidly.

I have never been afraid of storms; in fact just the opposite. I have often enjoyed their intensity. But this one did seem to be something apart. Maybe because we were so concentrated upon it; maybe because of our joint state of mind. But it was almost impossible to speak. Each clap of thunder was totally sobering in its violence. And each clap of thunder seemed to have a place in the conversation until there was no place in my mind for anything else. I was in a state that moved from anticipation to humility to nervous giggling at the ever increasing power, shivering and shuddering with each explosion. Each of us appeared to feel the same. Our role was reduced to that of observers, only able to pass the occasional comment. Each time we thought we had heard the loudest crack of thunder, and that the storm really must be overhead, we were surprised with another even louder one. The energy was overwhelming.

Concerned for Alex, I went to check on him but, to my astonishment, he continued to sleep peacefully, unaffected by the storm. In fact his position had hardly changed since I had left him. The three dogs in the house also seemed unusually calm.

Eventually we were forced outside. It was still not quite dark and the power of the storm was too hypnotic to resist. We held each other in the rain like a bunch of pagans, merry now, half drunk with the show that was being put on for our benefit. Filled with exhilaration we savoured each thunder crack. Deep inside ourselves we could feel the after-sound rolling off into the far distance, hanging for an age, doing the tour of the whole planet before its roar completely disappeared.

'Here comes another one.' Another mighty crack took our breath away. It rolled off endlessly into the distance. 'She's doing her best to get through to us!'

'God, she's powerful!'

Another crack. This time the lightning illuminated the descending twilight. The show was wonderful. I was being shown just how much more powerful some things were than our own existence. And that somehow, somewhere, Rachel was still able to pull a few strings. It seemed absolutely clear to us all that this was for our benefit. She was being granted a glorious goodbye. It was the very least she deserved.

For the rest of the night the storm continued to rage above the house. Through the glass roof we could see the rain bouncing and splattering. We were surrounded by water. It was like a storm at sea. It showed no sign of abating and as it grew darker the rain grew heavier.

We kept the lights low and absorbed the spectacle. The rain lashed down against the glass roof and windows. There was water everywhere and regularly lightning lit up the room. Bowls had to be put out to catch the leaks where the water forced itself through the cracks. We got quietly drunk as Alex and the dogs, far from fearful, slept peacefully on.

The next day Alex found the rose that I had picked from the garden. 'This is for Mummy,' I explained. Alex beamed. 'Do you want to smell it?' I asked. I gave it to him to sniff. 'Nice,' he said. It was true, it did smell good. Shop-bought roses often seemed to have no smell at all. I put his hand against his cheek so he could feel how soft it was.

He didn't want to give it back. 'But it's for Mummy,' I explained. He was still smiling, his eyes bright, holding the flower. 'It's Mummy!' he said. 'It's for me.' He was clearly referring to what I had told him the night before. I was, however, certain that this was the flower I wanted to lay. 'Do you want one for yourself?' I asked.

'Yes,' he replied.

We went into the garden to pick one. We found another pretty little rose which was just beginning to open and took it inside. I lifted him up to the sink so he could fill a jar with water. He put the flower in it and set it on the table.

He took great pleasure in showing every new arrival his rose and insisted they smell it and feel its cool, velvety petals. He would inform them that it was 'my mummy!' His interest lasted several days: he would hold it tenderly against his cheek, always smiling what in other circumstances I would have described as a 'happy' smile.

I was a little concerned by what his reaction would be when in due course the flower faded and died. I tried to explain how the petals would turn to earth and feed the next year's flowers in turn. And that they would grow and then eventually drop their petals which would return into the earth, and that more flowers would grow and that things never really disappeared. I didn't know if my words would have any effect on him when the flower actually died.

The flower took many days before it began to fade. I would remember to check on it every few days or so. But whenever I looked at it it seemed just as fresh as the day we had picked it. Then it got pushed to the back of the table and we forgot about it for a while. It must have been a couple of weeks before I thought of it again. By now Alex had forgotten about it too. It had darkened and shrivelled but it had served a significant purpose. I put it out in the garden under some leaves.

Chapter Four

IT WAS TUESDAY morning. Alex had been discovered with Rachel's body the Wednesday morning before. An unmarked police car was taking us all the way across London back to the site.

I had to go.

It was the minimum I could offer in respect and solidarity to be at the last place where she had been in this existence. I had the feeling that when I got to that point then I would be able to say to her that, wherever she had gone, if I could follow then I would follow. There was nothing else in this world that I wanted. But of course she would understand why I couldn't: for Alex. And she would smile, I would be able to see her, and she would say that she would wait. Then something between us would be all right again. The final decision taken by us together. Then, and only then, I would be able to walk away and try to get on with the business of living without her.

I was swinging between the extremes of acceptance of what had happened, that we are not in control of our own or each others' destiny, and a terrible feeling of guilt that it was my fault. I hadn't forced her to understand how dangerous the world was. Sometimes she'd seemed completely oblivious to the way things really were. By going to where she had died I wanted to say to her that, even if I hadn't been there to help her, I hadn't abandoned her. I was here now. Only just behind. Even if it was too late to save her maybe somehow she would understand that I hadn't abandoned her. It was so important to me.

I wanted to get as close to her as I possibly could. I felt that there would be more of her left where she had died than there had been at the hospital where I had seen her body. This was the last time she was

49

a living, breathing being and I was only just behind her. Only just behind. I would have been there for her if I had known.

Known what? Of course, it wouldn't have happened if I had been there.

How could I have let her go? It all seemed so obvious now, after it had happened. So inevitable.

On Wednesday morning, before I left the house, one of the last things she had said to me was: 'I'm so tired. I just want to sleep for ever.' She had seemed so weary, so defeated. 'I just want to sleep for ever.'

Alex was a bouncing ball of energy. His natural curiosity and endless demands for explanations were, as with so many children of his age, extremely draining. On top of which, he was a terrible sleeper. We had been woken up time after time, night after night. On one record occasion I worked out that he woke up every forty-five minutes and took twenty minutes to get back to sleep again. He woke up at least seven times in a row. We took turns getting him back down but even so it was hell. We had seen why sleep deprivation is such an effective torture. Eventually, at five o'clock in the morning, Rachel just sat on the floor unable to get back to bed herself. 'I can't stand the thought of being woken up one more time!' she had said. She looked absolutely exhausted. 'I'd rather not go back to bed at all. There's just no point.' I managed to convince her that any rest was better than none and she finally did go back to bed.

But Alex showed absolutely no ill effects from these disturbed nights. He was thriving. He hardly slept at all in the day. He just didn't need much sleep. We must have heard every well-worn theory imaginable from people around us. Every possible reason why, even if he had never done so in his life, *tonight* he would sleep like a log:

'He's running around like a good'un. *He'll* sleep well tonight!'

'This sea air will do him good. He'll go out like a light later!'

'This country air will do him good. You won't have any trouble getting him to sleep tonight!'

'He seems to like his daddy's beer. There's nothing better for making them sleep.'

'Look at that little one still in the pool! After a swim like that he'll sleep like the dead.'

The worst was: 'Just leave him to cry. He'll be fine! He'll eventually cry himself to sleep.' Neither of us believed that leaving a being unable to understand or fend for itself in distress was the right thing to do. And, even if we had felt differently, Alex had always given the impression, even as a baby, that he was capable of crying to the point where he would have choked himself to death in his distress and frustration.

Rachel and I felt that one of the main reasons why he had been so outgoing was because he always had attention from us when he needed it. It made him the very opposite of clingy. Once his hunger or thirst or discomfort was resolved then he was up and looking for action. Trips to the zoo, days in the country, cold weather, warm weather, bath before bedtime – nothing made any difference. He would still be up several times each night and still show no ill effects the next day. If he did happen to sleep during the day we had to remember to wake him up after twenty minutes. If he slept much longer he could be up till eleven o'clock at night before he began to feel tired again, and bang went our evening of peace.

But even taking all of this into account what she had said had chilled me. 'You don't know what you are saying!' I said angrily. *Be careful what you wish for . . .* said the voice in my head. *It might just come true.*

I hadn't dared repeat it out loud to her. I couldn't stand the thought of anything happening to her.

Not even a week had passed since that morning but our life then seemed a universe away. Here I was being taken to visit the spot where the woman of my life had been brutally murdered. And here was our son on my lap, his scarred face inches from mine.

I had to go for his sake.

There was no question. I needed to know as much of what had happened as possible and I needed to see where it had happened. I needed to be able to understand what Alex had witnessed.

He wasn't yet three. There were still a few weeks until his birthday. But what he lacked in years he more than made up for in personality. Every parent likes to think that their child is a budding genius. He wasn't that, but he did genuinely seem very capable. He would often chat away with the two detectives who had been assigned to us. They had been with us every day and he had taken a liking to both of them. They had young children of their own, and it showed. They were used to the way he operated.

51

They didn't make a fuss of Alex. They didn't make the mistake of paying him too much attention. Very quickly they were able to talk easily with me while I got on with playing with him. He didn't seem at all bothered by their presence. As far as Alex was concerned they spoke when they were spoken to, passed him something if he needed it, and they were a good audience if he decided to sing or perform.

Everyone still had to be extremely careful of what they said in his presence. I went out of my way to hammer the point home. Often he would pick up what someone had said while appearing to be totally engrossed in doing something else. If I happened to mention an exhibition to someone while he was busy playing on the other side of the room, he was sure to take it in. He would not fail to bring up the subject later. 'When are we going to see the dinosaurs?' he would ask. He never missed a trick and I often had to reply to their questions in vague and unspecific ways.

He was soon moving around the detectives as if they were a part of the furniture. One day I noticed him listening to the general conversation with his hand resting totally unselfconsciously on the arm of one of the detectives. This was at a time when the presence of a strange male adult would make him leap into the air with fright.

They were gaining his trust in leaps and bounds. They would often sit back in a low chair, which put their head at the same level as his, as he stood beside them, talking. Or he would have them down on the floor on all fours joining in with whatever he was doing. When Alex asked: 'Do you want to play with me?' the question was purely rhetorical. There was no room for refusal.

Rachel and I had decided that Alex liked adults best anyway. He was never that enthusiastic about other children's company. He didn't seem to play with them for very long. We thought that, because he had had so much adult attention, he probably preferred the fact that they could always come up with something new. He seemed to find other children fun only for a while.

We used to feel that he was directing us in a play. If Fireman Sam was the game of the day then we had to keep in character. We weren't allowed to let the voices drop for an instant. He was completely tyrannical, and temper tantrums would ensue if he was not obeyed. Rachel told me that she got some funny looks pushing a toddler along in the street and talking in a barmy Welsh accent.

So it wasn't surprising to see our nearly three-year-old bringing these two burly detectives to their knees. Whatever his future occupation might be he was going to be the boss. Man management was already approaching an art form.

Our detectives informed me that they had commissioned a psychological profile of Rachel's killer from a researcher at a top university. Apparently this could be done from the evidence of the pathologist's report and the general circumstances of the killing alone.

I had asked them whether they thought that Rachel's killer would be the kind of person who would try and cover his tracks. I had been continually concerned for Alex's safety and we were far from being under twenty-four-hour a day surveillance. I was already behaving as if a psychopath was on our trail. I would not sleep with the window open and I kept the dog in the room. I made sure we were never alone and wanted to know who was coming into the house and when.

In the detectives' opinion, and in the opinion of the psychologist they had contacted, they didn't think there was any danger. They said the killer did not appear to have given any thought to Alex whatsoever. If he had, Alex would already be dead.

This seemed undeniably logical. So many times already I had looked at him and wondered how he could still be alive. But their opinion was only that: opinion. I had to live with the reality and I had to face the possible consequences of them not being right.

In many ways I was still watching Alex as if he was a stranger. I had so much to learn about how he operated. I had only spent this much time with him before on holiday, and of course then I hadn't been in sole charge. I just did as directed, which was absolutely fine.

I had done my share but had not interfered with Rachel's view of things. I was going along with a routine that had already been set. A routine with which the two of them seemed perfectly at ease. Now I was benefiting from all the work she had put in. The fact that he had been dry from a very early age; that he didn't wet the bed; that he was able to ask for the toilet if he needed to go in the night; the fact that he could express himself so well; that he had such a wide vocabulary. The fact that she had interested him so much in books. All the endless journeys that we spent in the back of police cars were made much more bearable by the fact that I could read him stories. He was attentive and nearly always asked for more.

He could concentrate for fairly lengthy periods of time on an activity, whether it was drawing, or painting, or making something out of paper. Obviously the activity had to be changed regularly as with any small child, but the fact that his energy could be channelled positively made life much easier than it might have been.

In many ways he was a real inspiration. He enjoyed doing so many things and dragged the adults along with him. He was directing the show and would have people wearing silly hats and masks and others busy making more. His smile was a real beam of light in so much despair.

But it was so painful for me to look at him. It was so hard to believe that, after the shock he had received, he was even alive at all. To pick my eyes up from whatever he was having me make and see him so busy getting on with things was a kick in the guts. He looked so small and vulnerable, and so alone. I could see the vertebrae of his little back through his woollen jumper and the effort in his shoulders and arms as he applied himself to the task of bending or squashing something. The frown of concentration on his bruised and scarred face. His eyes focused on the job in hand. And so much going on behind them.

The biggest part of him had gone. Where there had always been her leaning over him, sitting beside him, listening to him, talking to him, now there he was, a brave little man, facing the world alone. Even though he was surrounded by people who loved him they had just been part of the scenery before. Myself included. I might have been a more noticeable part of the scenery but I was scenery just the same. I came and I went with the rest of the world. But she was always there, they were always together. Now he had to work it all out for himself without her bubble of protection around him.

He was working things out. He was ready to laugh and play but to me his high spirits were just a good way of keeping the show moving while part of him could sit back and observe and try and work out the angles. The smile didn't always quite reach his eyes.

How could he make any sense of what had happened? But never once did he look around as if he was looking for her. He knew she was gone.

The detectives had considered that today was as good a day as any. The media had been camped out on the Common since the day that Rachel was killed in order to catch their 'grieving lover visits scene of the crime' story. None of us wanted to make it any easier for them than we had to. Meanwhile the authorities in Canada had finally succeeded in tracking down Rachel's parents after nearly a week. Two detectives had flown out with her brother to meet them and to accompany them on their return. They were due back this morning. We hoped that most of the reporters would have got fed up waiting on the Common and would be covering their arrival at the airport.

We were to pick up a friend of Rachel's *en route*, a girlfriend that she and Alex often saw during the day and who Alex was fond of. Another of Rachel's old schoolfriends was already with us. The idea was that we would park the car in a place that Alex wouldn't recognize and another car would take me quickly up to the Common. I would be taken to the spot, left to spent a few minutes there and then be driven quickly back. Meanwhile the girls had everything they needed in the car to keep Alex amused. I didn't like the idea of leaving him but it was unthinkable to take him back to the place where he had so recently been through such an ordeal.

During the journey I had started to explain to him what was going to happen. I was very much aware that the only time that I had left him in six days was for the few minutes during the press conference at New Scotland Yard. I was trying to convince myself that the girls would be able to distract him for long enough for me to return before he became distressed. I had already talked things over with them and had decided that, if he showed too much sign of distress when I tried to leave, then of course I wouldn't go.

But I wanted to.

It was another heavy, muggy day. The sun appeared sporadically but its warmth was oppressive, unpleasant.

'I am going to where Mummy was killed so that I can leave this flower for her,' I had told him. The car stopped in a quiet street behind Wimbledon police station. He had been holding the flower for most of the journey. He already knew what it was for.

'I want to come,' he replied, as lightly as if I was going off to buy an ice-cream. The three other adults in the car went completely silent. I could hear everyone's breathing. I began to feel uncomfortable. This didn't bode well.

'But sweetheart,' I continued, 'I'm going to where Mummy was killed because I wasn't there. You were there and Molly was there but I wasn't there. I'm only going to be a few minutes, I'm going to leave this flower for Mummy and then I'll be back and then we can go home.'

'I want to come,' he repeated even more enthusiastically. It was clear, however, that he understood exactly what I had said. He was looking at me quite happily. The detective in the front looked thoughtful. He was watching events carefully.

I explained to him one more time where I was going and what I was going to do. The answer was the same.

I tried to get this straight in my head. Alex wasn't saying 'I don't want you to leave me on my own', or even 'I don't want you to go.' He was saying that he wanted to come.

I was completely thrown. This was the last thing in the world I had expected. I thought that nothing on earth would have made him want to return to that place. What I had really expected was for him to start to freak out when I tried to get out of the car and that I would not be able to go at all.

I tried to weigh things up. It was for his mother, after all, that I was making this gesture. Surely he had a right to take part in any goodbyes. Which was what this was, after all. If I was sure that he understood what was involved how could I justify not giving him the chance to take part, if that's what he wanted? She had been even more his than she was mine.

He was showing no signs of fear. Maybe it wouldn't cause him any distress to come with me after all. One thing I was beginning to learn was that a child's response was rarely the same as an adult's. It occurred to me that it might even be extremely positive to give him another chance to say goodbye. Maybe this would give him an opportunity to express a little bit more of what he was holding inside.

'What do you think of that?' I asked the detective in the front seat. As he was the father of two small children himself, I wondered what he might be making of Alex's reactions.

'He seems to know what you're going to do,' he said quietly. He paused for a moment. 'He looks like he really wants to come.'

'That's what I think,' I said. 'And if he understands and wants to come then he has to come!' It was a plea more than a demand.

The detective took a deep breath, then smiled in agreement.

'You're going to get a lot of flak for this,' I said. I thought that the general reaction to taking a small child back to the scene of the crime would be extremely critical. I would have thought it completely crazy myself, up until this very moment. I thought that the detective's superiors would want to know what the hell he thought he was doing letting such a thing happen under his nose. And that the next day's papers would surely be full of stories along the lines of: CALLOUS POLICE PROBE CHILD WITNESS WITH NO REGARD TO EMOTIONAL COST.

'I'm used to dodging flak,' he said.

I sat back in the seat. Now Alex was actually smiling at me. It was quite extraordinary. We four adults seemed equally stunned by his behaviour.

'I'll go and organize a few things,' said the detective, climbing out of the car. 'I'll be back in a minute.'

Alex sat completely relaxed while we waited. The detective was back a few moments later. 'I've managed to arrange it,' he said, climbing back into the car.

'Thanks,' I said.

'But apparently there's going to be some press.'

I churned that one over in my mind but didn't respond. I didn't know what 'some press' might involve. We pulled off. Another unmarked police car followed.

As the car began to move my mind was torn in all directions at the same time. I had gone to school in the same road as this police station. Memories came flooding back. I found myself sitting at my old school desk. Everything was fresh. I was really still there. I had simply dozed off and had the strangest of dreams. I could smell the chalk from the blackboard and feel the dread of lessons with my least favourite teacher. I could see the dust caught in sunbeams pouring in through the class-room window and feel the restriction of the tie around my neck. That anxiety was the most important thing in the world. I could see the faces of the others in my class even if I couldn't remember all the names. No, even the names were coming back. I was ten years old. I had seemed so grown up, everything was so important. I was ready for the next lesson now. I just needed to shake my head clear and then I could go on with waiting for the future.

I remembered class trips to the Common in summer. Giggling schoolchildren, I could see their faces clearly, larking about only yards from where the woman of my life was to be slaughtered. I remembered going to the Common for the first time. My grandfather had taken me one Sunday afternoon to the windmill. It was in fact about the only place he had ever taken me. How could I still be bitter about that in spite of everything that was happening to me? We had walked for what had seemed like miles and miles; I had never walked so far. To a child of six or seven the place had seemed vast. We had come back on the top of a double-decker bus. I remembered how thrilled I had been when we had driven down the long hill, only the glass between us and the road rushing up towards us: how it had taken my breath away.

The car pulled up the hill. Later, when I had changed school, I had ridden my bike up this hill every morning. I knew the houses we passed, the trees that lined the road. I had seen them in rain and snow and fog, and thick with leaves in summer sunshine. I had pedalled up, always only just on time. I used to see how late I could get out of bed and still get in on time. I rode my bike up this hill, dreaming teenager's dreams. I would be a famous tennis player. I was hooked on the game, I didn't want to do anything else. I just loved to play. I'd have my name in the papers, not that that bit really mattered to me much. The money would come in handy though, a few million in the bank, not too much. Beautiful women, nice cars, nothing too flash. When I was older and finished playing I would have children. I'd have enough money to stay at home and look after them together with their mother. We would do everything together. They would never be lonely, never know the feelings of isolation that I had.

I remembered how hungry I was to escape, to make my dreams come true. My future was out there somewhere, just out of reach and just out of sight. Whatever it was, it was far from my restricting, tedious, monotonous world so empty of love and attention.

The car reached the top of the hill and continued, with houses on one side and the wooded Common on the other. This was the side of the road I had taken as a teenager towards the centre of London as the world began to open up and my horizons widen. We thought we were pretty cool then, eyeing up the foreign girls with their language-school bags.

The car pulled on to the slip road. There was a police sign

appealing for witnesses. The adjustable date had been set at the 15th of July. Today was the 21st but already years had passed. We pulled up by the windmill. How many hundreds of times had I been here before? Is this what I grew up for? I had travelled all the way round the world and here I was, back where I had started, dragged back to face the futility of my teenage dreams.

A police trailer was parked by the windmill. It was the incident room. There were only a few cars in the carpark: it had been closed to the public. The second car full of plain-clothes officers pulled up beside us. The uniformed officers already on duty were there to let us in. Our detective had explained to me that a spot had been marked by the police to allow well-wishers to leave flowers. I never saw these tributes. The real spot was some distance away. The area was under heavy electronic surveillance and absolutely everybody's movements were being recorded. There was always a chance that the killer would be back to gloat.

We climbed out of the car. The familiar surroundings. Nothing appeared to have changed since my earliest childhood memories. There were puddles on the ground from the recent storm and the day was sticky and warm. It was mid-morning. The girls, together with some officers in uniform, tried to block off the first photographers' approach. There were plenty dotted all around, they'd been staked out for days. Once they had worked out who we were things quickly turned into a stampede. There was none of the sensitivity shown at the press conference – they were too busy rushing to tear off their piece of meat. Bastards! I could just hear them justifying themselves: 'If I don't get the picture someone else will.' I was trying to protect my child but I was completely vulnerable to their sickening assault.

I carried Alex in my arms, talking gently to him all the time, trying to keep him calm. His face was level with mine, obscuring my view. I tried as best I could to cover his face with a baseball cap, which meant that I had one arm underneath him and the other across my face, making it even harder to see. He was no longer a baby and far from light. On the other side and in front of me the detectives and uniformed officers tried to shield us. I could hear the photographers' feet scuffling over the ground, trying the get nearer.

I watched the grass ahead through the gaps in my arm and the gaps between the policemen. Only the sky above my head was clear. At times I stumbled on the bumpy ground, my balance already disturbed by the tunnel vision and my racing pulse.

They weren't making my life any easier. Each photographer had these huge lenses, like a shotgun almost. I felt like a hunted animal trying to protect its young while they closed in for the kill. Do they sleep well at night, these people? Haven't they got children of their own? Hadn't my child been through enough? Yet they were putting him through hell again, totally unnecessarily, for their own selfish interests. It didn't matter how much distress they caused him as long as they got paid. He wasn't even three years old.

The police forced them back like a crowd of football hooligans and managed to give us a little room. But they seemed to consider it their right to do whatever they wanted, no matter who got hurt. I was learning fast how non-existent our rights to privacy were.

What it must have been like for Alex to return to that place with a hat stuck over his face, to have to listen to the sounds of angry exchanges, to feel the anxiety in me and the stress of being hunted I can only imagine. How could such a small child differentiate between the violence of his mother's killer and the aggression with which we were being pursued?

We were walking quickly along a path over the grass, the photographers trying to keep up with us and focus their cameras while the police tried to push them away. Incredibly Alex remained calm. I was blabbering whatever I could in an effort to keep his mind in the present and to reassure him that he was safe and that it wasn't all happening all over again. 'We're going to go to the spot where Mummy was killed and then we are going to leave the flower for Mummy and then we'll be going home. We're not going to be very long and then this afternoon we can go and do something nice and play with your toys and then see Grandma and . . .' As I tried to soothe him my eyes scoured his face, desperately trying to assess how he was coping. I hadn't expected this. I wouldn't had exposed him to this ordeal if I had known.

It took probably four or five minutes to walk the distance. But it seemed an eternity. Everything was so familiar in spite of my distorted view. 'Daddy's with you and the police are here to look after you. The bad man has gone. He'd be very frightened if he saw all of us here,' I told him.

We reached the trees. The police indicated the spot and the officers drew back to a respectful distance to allow us some privacy. I could still hear them struggling with the press.

The spot was only a few yards into the trees, only a few yards from the clearing. Only a hundred yards or so from the carpark. Even though its location had been described to me many times in the last few days it wasn't where I had pictured it. I couldn't imagine how Rachel had got so far from the path. From the path that I had shown her.

The sun was shining now, the trees were green. The grass was lush through the branches. Suddenly the voices were quiet. Only the birdsong and the distant traffic murmured in my ears. The ground was covered with a layer of moss and twigs and broken branches. The world had stopped for just a few seconds. This was a beautiful place. It was a beautiful day. The evil didn't come from this. The evil came from the world of men.

What Rachel must have gone through went graphically through my mind as it did many times a day. It didn't go with the place. I don't know how I thought I would react, but none of the horror seemed to be left. I was crying of course. I was crying for what she had been through. For what they had been through.

'Is this the place?' I asked Alex. He nodded yes. He studied my face, watching my tears. He had none of his own. I leant down and we laid the rose on the ground together. I wondered how long it would lie there undisturbed before a stranger's hand would violate even this.

From my arms Alex looked around while I stood turning things over in my mind. He was still calm. It was very difficult to know what he was thinking.

The ordinariness and the familiarity of the surroundings made things seem even more unreal. I stood motionless. Through the leaves I could see the sun shining. When I managed to focus my eyes on what was in front of me once more I knew that there was nothing left for us. There was nothing left of her here. I had thought that I would be one step closer, but I wasn't. I looked around for one more time but was still left with the same impression. It was a beautiful day.

And this was a beautiful place. And the most insane thought of all was that, in spite of everything, there was still a feeling of peace that hung over the place, just as it always had.

I pushed the branches aside and walked out into the clearing. The photographers had been pushed back up the mound. I wanted to go home. But for us there was no home. Home was with Rachel. The best we could hope for was a little sanctuary.

Our detective checked that I was all right and then started to lead us back along the path to the carpark. I continued to soothe Alex as we walked. 'It's all right now, we're going back to the car now. There's something nice to eat in the car and then we'll soon be home for lunch. . . .' Once more my vision was obscured. Once more I was stumbling down a tunnel, trying to keep my feet as I followed the ground between my arm and the policeman's bodies in front. Once more I was trying to keep Alex safe and out of the sights of the reporters who stalked our every move and burst across our path to fire off another shot.

I wanted to get him away as soon as I could. Rachel and I had seen how the families of victims of accidents or crime were corralled in front of a camera straight after the event. We had been appalled. Maybe those people might have agreed to be filmed, but surely in the first moments of grief no one was in the most lucid state to make such a decision.

When you lose someone you love nothing else matters, least of all your pride. But in these terrible moments we both felt that a victim's grief was being used as thinly disguised entertainment.

Now it was our turn. And worst of all we hadn't even consented to the attention. But we weren't allowed the choice. It was clear that in our 'democratic' society we didn't have the right to privacy. I was learning fast just how non-existent our rights were.

We got back to the carpark and rejoined the girls. It seemed like another world. There was activity and an appearance of normality. Rachel's schoolfriend had intervened in a scuffle between a uniformed officer and a photographer before it came to blows. The officer was upset to the point of tears by the behaviour of the press. 'Why don't you bastards leave them alone?' he had said. At least someone felt the same as me.

A group of men were crossing the carpark towards us as I was try-ing to get into the car. 'André!' I wasn't about to turn round to make any photographer's job easier. 'André!' Something about the voice made me think that maybe it wasn't a photographer. A man with a pointed face and mousy hair walked towards me. Suddenly Alex became hard to hold on to. He was almost climbing out of my arms.

It turned out to be a friend of Rachel's, the father of one of Alex's friends from nursery school. I had never met him but Rachel had talked about him. He stayed home to look after their child and they would sometimes do things together with the children in the daytime. Rachel had met his wife. I had never been jealous of him, only of the time he had free. Rachel always made it quite clear that there was nothing to be jealous of and, anyway, I was perfectly secure in my relationship with her. I still didn't like the idea that he was free to see her when I wasn't so I tried not to think about it much.

I could imagine how devastated he must have been about Rachel's death. We talked for a few moments and I said that I would contact them so the boys could see each other. Alex was still trying to climb out of my arms. I thought that he had had his fill for one day and wanted us to get going so we climbed back into the car and pulled away. Before very long with the rocking of the car Alex had fallen asleep.

The car took us back towards London. We were to be taken to a hotel where we could see Rachel's parents in private. Their plane had arrived from Canada while we were visiting the Common and they were coming straight from the airport. Arrangements had also been made for her parents to meet the senior officers in charge of the investigation. This would of course be followed by the mandatory press conference.

When we arrived we were told that they were already there. I carried Alex through the lobby in his car chair, still asleep. I was shown into a room off a flower-filled courtyard.

Rachel's parents seemed remarkably fresh after their journey. I don't think I really had any picture of what state they might be in but I would not have been surprised to find them on their knees. They were subdued but incredibly in control. The thought that hit me the strongest was how complete they looked. They were so obviously a couple and moved around each other and spoke for each other in the complicity that couples have. In contrast I felt completely alone. I was facing the world with all of that taken away from me. There was no one anticipating the words that I was about to say. There was no one standing beside me. There was no light touch or gesture of support and understanding from someone who was like another part of me. Watching them told me one more time that she was gone.

I had often felt with Rachel that I was looking through the world with two pairs of eyes as if I was looking at the same thing from two separate vantage points. But all that was gone. My vision of the world was limited again. I had lost that other dimension.

I am sure that seeing me made an equally stark impression on them. There was I, alone with the child their daughter had given birth to, a daughter they would never see again. We had been three. One day we would have been more. But now we could only ever be two.

We hugged each other and tears were shed. They saw the cuts and bruises that were still clearly visible on Alex's face, undeniable evidence of the violence that Rachel and he had suffered while they had been so far away. They seemed to be coping with everything just a little too well, but the unreality of the situation and their distance from the events meant that their reaction could never be the same as my own. I had been confronted with events in a way that made them undeniable right from the first moment. I had the feeling that it hadn't really sunk in for them yet. And I was concerned that it was going to hit them hard when it did.

For me Rachel was undeniably missing from my life with virtually every minute that passed. Everything had changed. I was no longer in my own home, she wasn't there to talk to. I was brushing my teeth alone, I was sleeping alone. I was waking without her, I was eating without her. I was making decisions without her, I was looking after her child for every minute of the day without her.

Even though the brutal reality of our everyday existence told me otherwise I was often able to pass long moments at a time where I managed to convince myself that she was still there. At any time of the day or night I could imagine her walking in the door, her smile intact, to say: 'Boo! Got you there, didn't I?' Then I would see Alex's damaged face and my delicious, fragile bubble of self-delusion would burst once again.

If I could still imagine her there then to her parents, who were used to passing weeks without seeing her and to whom she was more often only at the end of a telephone line, the boundary between belief and disbelief could only have been more blurred.

Alex's car seat was propped up on a sofa. He began to stir, and woke up crying and upset. He was going rigid, spastic as he awoke, his body filled with tension and fear. This wasn't the child they had left behind them only a couple of weeks before. He calmed after a little while with the promise of something nice to eat and drink. He was hungry. He was very fond of his grandmother but her presence did not noticeably brighten his mood. I wondered how much, on top of everything else, the morning had affected him.

I tried to tell them everything I knew about what had happened. They had not been well informed and, as was becoming clear, there was nearly always a slightly different version of the events each time they were related. At first I assumed that this depended on the latest conclusions drawn from the pathological evidence, developments that I might not have been informed of. But I began to notice that accounts differed according to who you spoke to.

Life had been taken out of our hands but I was realizing how important it was to try and get a little control back. We were no longer able to influence events except by the smallest of degrees. Giving them the simple facts amounted to only the tiniest of things in the face of all that had happened. But, apart from Alex's survival, tiny things were all we had to hold on to.

I tried to explain how much the media had become involved in everything. Of course they couldn't really appreciate to what extent this was affecting our lives or how much it was to continue to do so. They had the perfectly reasonable idea that if they gave the press a little of what they wanted, a chance to take some photographs, a few quotes for tomorrow's editions, then they would be left alone. They felt that if they didn't do that the papers would hound them until they got what they wanted another way.

I was not at all interested in taking part. I had had more than enough of the press to last a lifetime. A little later we said our goodbyes and left them to it. Alex and I were driven home.

Rachel's parents had flown all the way across the Atlantic just after being told the news of their daughter's murder. They had been in the country for only a couple of hours. They had not even been able to go home yet and, just after their grandson had been made to feel like a hunted animal by journalists, they were having to give a press conference to the same journalists, or their colleagues, in order to give themselves a little peace.

The world was completely mad.

Rachel's father paid tribute to her memory. It was a very dignified gesture. I don't know where he found the self-control to do so. I would never have been capable of the same thing. His words were broadcast on the main news programmes that evening. He also made a plea for Alex to be left alone to try and somehow recover from his ordeal. He asked for our privacy as a family to be respected.

Chapter Five

THE NEXT DAY began like the previous ones. Alex awoke, crying fearfully. I managed to calm him down, eventually. Breakfast was prepared and duly eaten, his appetite, thankfully, had not diminished. Clothes had been found, the detectives had been back to the flat and filled a bag with anything they had thought would be useful, and I had got him dressed.

The sun was shining. It was a lovely summer day. We would be able to go out and burn off some of his energy. Someone had already been out and had come back with the papers. Our visit to the Common had made all of them. In every paper I opened there were shots of my and the detective's faces and then the back of Alex's head or an unidentifiable shot from the side. Then I came to something I had never dreamed I would ever see in a newspaper published in the United Kingdom. There in full colour and totally identifiable was a full-face picture of Alex.

I was reeling all over again. I felt I was just beginning to pull myself up off the floor and climb to my feet and here I was being kicked in the face one more time. Here was my child, the only living witness to an unimaginably savage and vicious murder, revealed for all to see, with the killer still at large, his state of mind unknown.

I was sick with anger and shaking with rage. I was shocked to the core. Even with everything that had happened to us I couldn't quite believe this. I thought that some things truly were sacred, that some lines would never be crossed in this country. I thought that the life of a child, especially this child that the whole nation was focusing on, was something that every single normal person would do everything to protect. I just could not and still cannot believe it. His life was consciously put in danger in order to sell a few more newspapers. After all I had lost, these people were gambling with my child's life as well.

It was only in two papers that his face appeared. Every single editor had had the same set of pictures on his desk to choose from. Of course they all had pictures of Alex's face. With the lenses at photographers' disposal there was no way that I could stop them getting something. But every single editor made the same normal, sane decision and protected Alex's identity. How could they face their own children any other way?

Every single paper except two. Outrage, shame and disgust were words that lost their power in the face of such behaviour. To my mind the people responsible for this had put themselves on the same level as Rachel's killer. Worse, in fact. These weren't apparently homicidal maniacs but supposed 'normal' members of society. I was filled with so much hatred I didn't know who I hated most. They could purposefully put Alex's life in danger while they hid beyond fear of reprisal like the cowardly, snivelling scum they were.

Our much-cherished freedom of movement was put into immediate danger. Up until that moment we had been able to come and go with no real fear of being recognized, and the difference between mine and my mother's married name was continuing to keep the hounds at bay. This tiny breathing space was vitally important to us. Now I had to do something to disguise Alex. *I* could wear sunglasses and a hat but I couldn't put the same restraints on a small child.

A friend of my mother's was volunteered to cut Alex's hair. The photographs had shown him as a curly-haired little angel. Now the curls would have to go. She was reluctant to cut more than the minimum: it upset her to so disfigure him. I knew that his hair would grow back. But this was one more violation – something else forced upon us, taken away from us. But in the balance of things there was little choice. We had to be able to go out and he had to be able to move without being stared at. In the end I took the scissors and finished the job myself. It was unfair of me to impose such a thing on someone else. He finished by looking like a badly shorn sheep. His bruises stood out more under his eyes. I didn't even know how effective his haircut would be in disguising him but I had to do something.

What redress was there for us against the press? They seemed able to do exactly what they wanted with us without fear of control or sanction. For us there was no protection.

As a family we soon became acquainted with the press complaints procedure. It clearly stated that children who were involved in or witness to any crime of a sexual nature were not to be identified. Many weeks later and after letters of complaint written in relation to the rules laid down in this document, Rachel's father finally had a phone call of apology from the editor of one of the papers that had published pictures of Alex's face. This was at a moment when one story after another of newspaper excess was coming to light. Editors in general were fearful that new government powers would be introduced to curb press 'freedoms' in relation to private individuals. They were eager to hang on the to the system whereby they were responsible for regulating themselves and not answerable in law to those private individuals they might have wronged, consciously or otherwise.

It looked as if the editor wanted the matter to stop there. His grovelling apology was given in private of course, far from public hearing. He admitted that he knew that what he was doing broke the rules. Even so he had taken the decision that, in his words, the story was 'too big to miss' – so he went ahead and knowingly broke them anyway.

So there was the bottom line. A set of rules existed but editors were free to break them at will with no fear of sanction under law. It was a case of self-regulation: we were completely at the mercy of their good will. They are far more powerful than we are and in our democracy there is nothing to protect us as individuals against that power. Might is right. It is as simple as that. The rules did little to protect us and against the army of lawyers at their disposal what hope did we have of achieving justice? The only thing we had on our side was the public's support. But how was a family like us, trying to cope with what had already happened, supposed to find the strength to fight these people too? They knew this as well as we did, and played their hand accordingly.

I had to do something. I couldn't leave things the way they were. I was still seething with rage that the press had published those photographs. It wasn't displaced anger. It wasn't me venting my feelings over Rachel's death. Just as a parent can love two children at the same time, you can hate two people for separate and justifiable reasons. In my case

I now hated the editors of these papers as much as the killer.

I couldn't get back at the press but I had to make them understand how I felt. Every time our detectives had come to the house, among the first things they would tell me was which newspapers were requesting to speak to me, or which television or radio station. I had no interest in speaking to anyone individually so I asked if they would speak to the person responsible for such things and organize a press conference on my behalf. They promised to see to it.

Rachel's parents came to visit us. It was another lovely summer's day and all the doors and windows were open wide on to the back garden. Alex was happy to see them; his mood was much better than the day before.

Rachel was only really happy leaving Alex with her mother. She always knew how to play the clown and keep him amused. Alex had a good time with both grandparents. I left them playing with him and slunk off to collapse on a sofa. It was the first time I had felt it was safe to take my eyes off him. I was still not relaxed enough with him out of my sight to sleep, even for a minute. I was still listening and could hear every sound he made. It was a blessed relief just to be able to shut my eyes.

It took him at least four or five minutes to realize that I was gone, but to me it seemed like an eternity. He came in to see where I had got to but then, reassured that I wasn't far away, he allowed himself to be tempted out to play for a little while longer. This time he was away for at least ten minutes, at the end of which I was beginning to feel anxious myself. The umbilical cord was being stretched a little too far. But he was bouncing back in and, even though I pretended not to be interested in him, he refused to let himself be tempted away again. He was pulling at me and there was no chance of lying around any longer.

Alex had found a new game in those first few days. He made himself a tent. He turned over two chairs in what had become his play area and someone had hung a sheet over the top. He would disappear underneath and we could hear him giggling. He would then reappear and seem totally convinced that no one had known where he was.

It became his habit when anybody new appeared in the house to shoot back into the tent. It was always done in fits of giggles. He would reappear only if, and when, he was ready. He gave the impression that he considered this a wonderful game. He was happy to take his snacks and drinks under the tent. He would sit inside with a little toy and play for ages. But he was extremely selective about who he would let in with him. If one of my brothers, for instance, tried to push his way in, then Alex would resist with all his strength and get visibly upset. His space was respected and nobody did force their way. But even when someone asked for permission to come in the request was usually met with violent disapproval.

I was allowed in, of course. His grandmothers were allowed in too, but apart from that, his tent was out of bounds to the whole world. This was very hard on the eldest of my two brothers. Alex was perfectly happy to play for hours on end with him, building train tracks on the floor and making zoos for his dinosaurs, but the moment he disappeared into his tent that was it: my brother was dismissed.

He looked out from his tent and tried to make sense of the world. Nothing was certain, virtually nothing, and everyone and everything else was to be tested and observed painstakingly. Nothing would be taken on trust.

Only a few short weeks before my brother had been the best of friends with Alex, throwing him off the stairs on to a pile of cushions over and over again, and Alex shrieking with laughter. Now he told me that there were times when he would notice Alex staring at him, studying him. So much so that he even asked himself if Rachel's killer had resembled him in some way. This upset him deeply and caused him much heartache. He said that he felt himself being tested methodically. The regard of a small child focused on you so intently and critically can make you feel completely naked. The change in behaviour from unreserved love to one of suspicion was extremely painful to him to accept.

Our detectives had been trying to get specialist counselling for Alex. They made it quite clear that they were more concerned about Alex's well-being than any other consideration and that I would have complete approval of any course of action taken. Anything Alex might say which was of interest to their investigation was secondary.

They put no pressure on me whatsoever. They themselves had hardly any experience with children who had been involved in violent crime: they needed to find out as much as they could as well. Very few children in the United Kingdom, if any, had ever undergone a similar ordeal to Alex. There was virtually nothing to compare his experience with.

I appreciated their approach. I had felt very much at ease with the two of them from early on: it was already more like talking to friends than strangers. They were trying to do the best for us as well as for the investigation. They had been recommended the names of several people who worked with traumatized children and were in the process of contacting them. Meanwhile there was the Child Protection Team, a group made up of police and social workers who were on hand to deal immediately with children who had been the victim of crime. They told me that anything done with Alex would have to be recorded. A procedure had to be followed regarding children's evidence and its admissibility in court. Anything recorded on film would be of more value than anything recorded only on paper.

The importance of Alex's testimony was becoming more and more clear to me. The detectives had asked me several times whether I could add anything that might help in their understanding of what had happened the morning that Rachel was killed. The events had never been out of my mind. I turned them over and over again in my head, trying to picture what must have happened to Rachel and Alex and what Alex must have seen.

One thing had been discussed many times. No one had heard a scream. And yet the attack had taken place in hearing distance of the carpark where there had been people out and about. And when I thought of where Rachel's body had been found in relation to where their usual path would have been I wondered how they had come to be so far off their route.

I told the detectives that I couldn't see how Rachel had got there. Maybe the dog had got lost? Or maybe Alex had been looking for something? Or maybe she had been talking with someone else she knew? Only Alex knew. Only he could tell us for sure.

Within a couple of days the extension of the house was filled with enough video and sound equipment to make a feature film. The technicians had done their best to cover their gear with tablecloths and whatever else was at hand before they left, but they had not really been able to disguise it. There were cameras in the two far corners of the room and strategically placed microphones. The idea was that they wouldn't miss anything if, for instance, Alex decided to head back into his tent while he was talking.

Our detectives arrived one morning and came into the house. They said that they had the two women from the Child Protection Team in the car, as had been arranged, and asked if it was still a good time to bring them in.

Alex was playing quite happily on the floor. It seemed as good a time as any. I assumed they would be using this first meeting to get to know us a little and establish a little trust, and to see how Alex and I operated around each other.

The detectives showed in the two women, who were invited to sit down on a sofa where they could see Alex play. One was a police officer in her twenties. The other, probably in her late forties, was a social worker. The latter had apparently had success in getting young children to talk about their experiences, primarily in cases of sexual abuse. Our detectives sat down out of the way to watch.

Alex promptly turned his back on the newcomers and headed into his tent. Various members of the family came and went, the sun shone through the window, the two women sat on the sofa and Alex continued to play as far away from them as possible.

The younger one attempted to make conversation with me. She hovered on the edge of the sofa. She tried to say hello to Alex and ask him what he was doing. Alex didn't want to know. He didn't even bother to reply when she spoke. The younger one was obviously waiting for the other to take the lead. But the other just sat back in the chair, awkward and quiet.

The supposedly 'experienced' social worker actually gave the impression of being bored, or uncomfortable, with the proceedings. Her expression seemed to say that she would much rather get on with asking him who killed his mother and then get back to the office and type up her report.

But surely that couldn't be the case. Maybe I didn't appreciate their technique. I told myself to give them a little longer. After all, they weren't making enough of an impression on Alex of any kind whatsoever to be doing any harm. And there was always the chance that they were suddenly going to jump to their feet and break out in song in order to break the ice. They surely weren't going to continue like this.

From down on the floor I carried on watching or playing with Alex. Up on the sofa nothing was moving.

This carried on for a while. The gap between them and us was becoming aggravating. Their presence was becoming an intrusion.

Suddenly enough was enough. We weren't achieving anything. Not only did they seem incapable of finding a way to talk to Alex that he would find appealing but it didn't seem to have occurred to them that it might be worthwhile to get down on the floor and join him at his level. They were peering down at him from their position on the sofa. Even sitting back and doing nothing would have been acceptable if I had felt they were observing him properly. But they gave the impression of being ill at ease and out of place. They seemed clueless. Well-intentioned but clueless.

How the hell they had achieved their results with other children I couldn't imagine. And at what cost to the child? At any moment I imagined they would leap up in frustration and say: 'That's fine! You've had a good play. Now tell us about the man who killed your mother so I can fill out my report!'

The detectives were trying to catch my eye. They beckoned towards the kitchen. 'I don't think we're getting anywhere with these two,' began one, when we were out of earshot.

'They've got to go.' I laughed, in spite of myself. Here we were lurking in the kitchen and speaking in whispers. 'They're hopeless!'

'I'm glad you feel the same,' said the other detective, smiling despite his obvious disappointment and discomfort. 'We'll get rid of them. Quietly.'

Back in the extension the detectives whispered something to the two women. I couldn't catch that they said, but soon the women were reaching for their things and on the way out of the door.

It was a relief to have them gone. And in my relief I was actually able to find their ineptitude humorous. However, after some reflection and after talking more with our detectives, I didn't find it funny any more. These people were supposed to walk in when a child was at its most vulnerable; when something had happened to leave that child frightened and insecure. And more often than not when a child was without the protection of any other family member, because it was often that family member who had been the cause of the child's distress in the first place.

74

What possible good were these people to a child in such a situation? It didn't seem that they were capable of relating, or of offering the comfort that was needed. And who was going to prevent them from questioning a child in a way that was not going to cause him or her even more trauma?

I had no reproach for these people as individuals. I was sure that their intentions were beyond question. But, for children in the very first minutes and days after an ordeal, it seems to me that better-trained people needed to be provided. If I hadn't been there, for whatever reason, any attempt that these people made to get information out of Alex would only have caused him distress.

There had to be someone who was not a part of the police but who would be there only for the child, and who was forceful enough, if necessary, to protect that child from questioning. It worried me greatly to think of any child who, at a moment like this, might be left to these people's good intentions.

That night Alex wouldn't go to sleep in his own bed. He wanted to sleep in mine, even when I explained that I wasn't actually going to bed myself yet. He was insistent and I didn't see any point in arguing. I could always move him back again when he was asleep.

When I went up to turn in later on I did just that. But he woke up very soon after and made his way back. Once he was asleep again I put him back in his bed one more time. But again he woke up and made his way back. He wasn't visibly upset but he was obviously in need of reassurance. This time I left him where he was. He had slept for ten nights on his own so far, which was far more than I had expected. I had to accept that things were quite likely to get worse in the short term before they had any chance of getting better. I had to let his needs dictate my responses and not think about any time scale at all for his recovery.

He hardly stirred again that night. In fact he slept till nearly half-past eight the next morning, which for him was an all-time record.

Once awake he climbed into my bed and lay next to me. He was unusually calm this morning. There was no sign of the usual waking terrors. Instead he lay there moaning quietly.

'I can't find my two Baas!'

I was still drowsy.

'I can't find my two Baas,' he repeated.

He had lost his blankets. He must have left them in his bed when he had moved during the night. I couldn't see them in his bed from where I was, and I couldn't see them on the floor where he might have dropped them. Perhaps they were under the covers. I started to pull myself out of bed to go and have a look when I saw that they were right there on the bed with us, just behind him.

'They're there, look!' I said, lying down again. He made no effort to turn and look. 'I can't find my two Baas,' he moaned listlessly.

He lay on his side, looking at me through hollow eyes. It was obvious that he knew exactly where they were. As I lay there I suddenly understood what he was saying. He knew they should be there, just behind him, where he had seen them last. But he didn't believe that they would still be there when he turned to reach for them. He had lost his confidence in the world.

I felt the same.

When you had the world ripped out from underneath you, you question everything. At that moment he couldn't be sure that if he put his foot out in front of him while walking along it wouldn't just sink into the ground and the floor come flying up to smash him in the face.

I reached over for his blankets and put them in his arms. He pushed them away, out of his sight. 'Where are my two Baas?' he said again. There wasn't much to say. I picked them up one more time and again put them in this arms. I held him against me and let my tears run down across my face and his. For both of us, learning to trust the world again was going to take a long, long time.

I left Alex on the toilet seat while I threw something in the washing, or looked for a toilet roll. It had only taken a couple of seconds. He let out a heart-rending wail. 'You said you'd look after me!' he cried.

His scream cut me to the core. It was filled with so much despair and pain. I was instantly choking with guilt and self-recrimination, but I had left him only for a second. I flew back as fast as my legs could carry me: I didn't want his fear to last an instant more. He was immediately calmed by my return and within minutes was talking enthusiastically about the games he would play in the morning ahead. He put the pain away so quickly. His self-control was astonishing. Almost as astonishing as the overwhelming degree of pain that showed through

76

whenever his defences did slip for that instant.

This was a child who, before, could find his way to the toilet on his own in the dark. Such was his confidence that he didn't even need a light. Even in the dark his trust had been total. But now only a few seconds' separation was unbearable for him. Only a few seconds alone was enough to plunge him into terror. He had so little trust left in the world. Or even in me.

My second press conference: this time there were not much more than a dozen journalists dotted around the room. Today was Saturday. If I had been a little sharper I would have realized that this was not the ideal day for maximum impact. The daily papers were resting until Monday while the Sundays were mostly already written.

What could I say that would make them understand? What could I say that would make any difference? The damage was done. In the end I realized that insult or confrontation would achieve nothing at all. In the end I just read out a few lines. I said simply that Rachel's father had asked for our privacy to be respected and for Alex to be protected. I pointed out that he had made this request to a packed room. I said that in spite of this, Alex's picture had appeared in full colour the following day. I said that I hoped that this had been a mistake. I said that I did not expect it to happen again.

My words received a flat reception. But they had been said.

The detectives had been thinking of ways to help Alex to describe the man who had killed his mother. They had managed to track down some dolls which were used in cases of suspected child abuse.

The dolls were like big stuffed toys or puppets. They were recognizably male and female to the point of being anatomically complete. They also came in different ages. There were grey-haired dolls, which obviously represented grandparent figures, black-haired grown-up dolls and child dolls. The dolls came in black as well as white versions.

The dolls were fully clothed but all of their clothing could easily be removed by a child.

Our detectives took Alex and me in their car to Hampstead Heath for our daily walk. Alex was very much at ease with them now as we romped around on the grass for a while so he could burn off some of his excess energy.

When he was feeling a little calmer we all sat down on the grass. The detectives pulled the dolls out of the bag and spread them on the ground. The atmosphere was light-hearted as we each took a doll and had a closer look. It was just as if we were going to start a puppet show. Alex was thrilled at the appearance of all these new toys and eager to join in the game.

Our detectives did something that on later reflection was very effective, and also beneficial to Alex's self-confidence: they asked him for his help.

'We need your help, Alex, because we weren't there. Neither was your daddy. You are the only one who can tell us.'

They began by explaining, as they had several times before, that first and foremost they were policemen, even if they didn't wear a uniform. And, together with other policemen, their job was to catch the bad man who had killed Alex's mummy. As Alex was the only person who was there when his mummy was killed, anything that he could tell them about the man would make it easier to catch him.

Alex responded very well to this approach. He listened attentively, happily even, and watched their faces as they talked. He sat in physical contact with me but was completely relaxed. They began by showing him the dolls which were totally inappropriate as a warm-up, the grandmother doll for example, and asking if it was a woman who had killed Mummy. Alex shook his head and squealed an emphatic 'no'.

One of the next dolls was a black one. 'Was the man who killed your mummy a black man?' Again the answer was an emphatic 'no'.

Alex appeared to be enjoying the game. He seemed to be taking pleasure in being able to help the policemen and in no hurry to finish and get on with something else. By going through the dolls Alex established clearly that the person in question was a young man. His answers were always emphatic and, if the dolls were swapped around and the question put in a different way, his answers stayed absolutely consistent. There was no doubt that he remembered these details clearly.

This was no surprise to me. He had always had a knack of retaining detail. A place or a person or the inside of someone's house was rarely forgotten. After one visit he was usually aware of what the various cupboards in that house contained and was quick to remind the owners on his next visit in case *they* might have forgotten.

We had trouble with establishing the hair colour because the dolls had hair that was either black or grey. They had been conceived for different circumstances. We would have to deal with that separately. The detectives planned to produce a hairdressers' book with illustrations of different styles for Alex to look at.

They moved on to clothing. What colour shirt was the man wearing? Was it a T-shirt or a buttoned shirt with a collar?

The dolls' clothing served for example and if we got stuck for variety we used the clothing that the four of us were wearing for comparison. Alex stated emphatically that the man was wearing dark shoes, not light-coloured trainers, blue trousers, not jeans, a white collared shirt with buttons, worn outside his trousers and, unusually, a belt over the outside of his shirt. This seemed strange to me but Alex was definite about it.

When he was asked if the man had removed or taken down his trousers, Alex said 'no'.

Our detectives seemed quietly impressed with the amount of detail that Alex had been able to establish, and there was little more that could be achieved with the dolls that day. They thanked Alex for the help that he had given them and told him that he was a very clever little boy.

Alex's smile showed that he was pleased to have been able to help these big policemen. He had appeared to take their questioning as a form of game where he had come up with the right answer and where only the right answer would do. And he seemed very sure that the answers that he had given were the right ones.

I felt flushed with pride. He had been so informative and so willing to help. I was filled with optimism that he would be able, one day, to get the whole story out.

During this time Rachel was referred to in virtually every television news bulletin as well as every day's paper. While it was easy to keep Alex from coming in contact with the papers there was always someone who would want to watch the television news, or the news would appear on a television left unattended somewhere in the house.

At first I would ask for it to be turned off. I didn't want Alex to see and there was nothing I was going to learn that I had not been told by the police already.

One morning after I had given Alex his breakfast I switched on to find the screen filled with a picture of Rachel's smiling face. I don't think the sound was even on. It was a very strange moment.

I had spent the whole night either lying awake thinking about her or dreaming about her, I had fed and wiped the bottom of her child, and I turned on the television and there she was smiling back at me. It was as if she was reappearing by magic, reaching out to me, and re-assuring me that things were somehow going to be all right. She was letting me know that she was still around. I just sat and stared.

Alex wandered in. I made no effort to turn off the set.

'Mummy!' he said, beaming. He pointed to the screen.

'Yes,' I said.

He didn't ask why her picture was on the television screen. But then again he had been used to seeing pictures of himself and of us taken with a video camera. The picture was replaced with the face of the newsreader as the programme continued.

I was searching for the right thing to say.

Finally, I said, 'These people are talking about Mummy because everyone is so upset that she has been killed.'

He didn't comment but seemed to be listening while he looked around for a toy.

'Everyone is so upset,' I continued. 'Even people who never met her.'

I got up and turned off the set. 'It was such a horrible thing that happened that people can hardly believe it,' I went on. 'I can hardly believe it still. Everyone is so sad and angry that you lost your mummy the way you did.'

Alex continued to play quietly.

This was one more opportunity to make it clear to him that the horror he had witnessed was not normal. I don't know what exactly I was trying to get over to him. Maybe I was trying to assure him that what had happened wasn't going to happen again; that what had happened wasn't 'life'. What we had had before, together, was 'life'. What had happened to him and Mummy in one day was an aberration.

I suppose I was trying to begin to find a response to the question that he wasn't able to ask. Why?

For it must have been there. Somewhere in his head. Why did this happen? Why me? Why my mummy? What did I do to have her taken away from me?

80

I didn't have an answer. There wasn't an answer. I was beyond even voicing the questions in my own head. There was no point. No sense. No logic. No justice. No fairness . . .

No point at all.

I suppose I was trying to say that if he felt bad then he had a right to feel bad. What had happened was truly terrible and every sane person in the whole country felt bad about it too. It seemed vital that even if he wasn't expressing his feelings himself that he should hear things said by others that he could relate to. When he saw the people on TV reacting to the way his mother had been killed it gave weight to what I was saying. I think in some way he understood.

Sometimes Alex didn't want me to talk about anything. He just didn't want to know. At times like this he would put his hands over my mouth and physically prevent me from speaking, shouting 'Be quiet!' in my ear.

He didn't appear to be distressed at moments like these and his physical efforts to stop me talking were more like a good-natured romp. But my talking was forcing him to look at things which were too fresh and too painful. It was a battle of wills. I could feel how much he wanted to clam everything shut tight and hold it all in. I could feel how much he wanted to ignore it and get on with playing. But I wasn't going to let him. I knew how much harm that would do.

I didn't want to push him to the point where he resented me, though. I was trying hard to find the balance.

I had come to the conclusion that him listening to me when I talked was in itself positive. It meant that he was giving some thought to what I was saying. If he tried to shut me up then I wasn't really achieving anything because that meant he was refusing to deal with things. If I managed to get a nod or a 'yes' then things were going really well indeed. That is why the time spent with the dolls on the Heath had been such a success. It was true, of course, that he had only been expressing the facts of what had happened and not what he was feeling. But at least something was coming out.

There were times when I felt the enormous frustration of knowing that everything needed to find Rachel's killer was locked inside that tiny head. I wanted to be able to look right in and see the film that was playing. I wanted so much to be able to say: 'Look Alex, just tell me

81

what happened the day Mummy was killed.' And it filled me with despair that so much stood between us when we needed to be as close to each other as we could. I just wanted to ask him straight out but I didn't know how many years it would be until I could.

Finding myself thinking this way only made me more protective of him. If I, who was so close to him, could feel so much frustration and impatience then a stranger would feel it even more so. I couldn't bear the thought of someone snapping at him, trying to force him to talk. My resolution to protect him from everyone and everything else that might do him harm was strengthened by these feelings of frustration. I would make sure that everyone – everyone – watched every word they said to him.

Letters and presents were still pouring in from well-wishers. I had asked our detectives not to bring any more of the gifts with them. I didn't think it was a good thing for Alex. They did, however, bring the cards or letters attached to them. When we were more able we would make sure that all the toys and gifts that we could not reasonably keep would go where they were needed. I was sure that this would be in keeping with the spirit in which they were sent.

Every now and then there was something so exceptional that our detectives felt they had to bring it with them. Invariably something someone, either a child or an adult, had made themselves. One day they brought a beautiful knitted puppet which was almost as big as Alex. It was incredibly detailed and life-like. Alex wasn't sure of it when it first arrived. He made his way round it carefully and was very suspicious. Everybody in the house was extremely impressed by it. It was quite amazing. Someone had been to an awful lot of trouble. It was a work of art.

Almost immediately on being presented with it Alex dropped it on a chair and left the room. When he came back he glanced towards it with a face still full of suspicion, then got on with other things. Every now and then he would have a look but it was clear that it wasn't growing in his affections. Eventually somebody picked it up and came towards Alex, thinking he might like to play with it. Alex's face crumpled and he was on the point of bursting into tears when they realized and stopped. In fact the thing was frightening the life out of him. It had to go, which was a shame. But we had to pass it on – straight away. He couldn't stand it being in the house a moment longer.

Every friend or family member who came to the house to see us for the first time since Rachel had been killed, came with a present for Alex in their hands. At first he was thrilled: it was a bit like Christmas all the time. He was given some beautiful toy cars and cranes and teddy bears, some, things that Rachel and I would have considered extravagant and which we hadn't been able to afford anyway. I certainly wasn't going to deprive him of any pleasure but at the same time I was watching carefully to see how things unfolded.

The first toys that he received were played with thoroughly and kept him amused for long periods of time. It was good to see. But I noticed that the amount of time he played with something new diminished in relation to the number of toys he received. He was finding it more than a little disorienting to continually be given something.

I watched him receive his nth beautiful toy car in its shiny box. He was reaching saturation point. He had hardly got the box open before he had lost interest in its contents. But though he was fast becoming jaded, he was still trying to see what people might be holding behind their back for him when they arrived at the door, before he had even said 'hello'. I couldn't really miss the point. Enough was enough.

I had to ask people not to bring things with them any more. Or, if they did, to bring something small and inexpensive. I got into the habit of intercepting people before they saw him, taking anything that they might have for him and hiding it in a cupboard. As time went on the steady stream of presents eased and became instead an occasional gift. I would being something out every few days or so if I thought it appropriate. That way Alex had something fresh when he was ready to appreciate it. I began to forget that there were still things in the cupboard and sometimes it would be weeks and weeks before I thought of looking again.

Books were an exception. I was more than happy that he should have any books straight away because we read so many stories every day that I was always desperate for something new.

People were only being kind but, just as the psychologist had said to me right at the beginning, he needed a normal routine. And being bombarded with presents every day of the year is not part of a normal routine.

Chapter Six

EVERY DAY WHEN our detectives arrived they would have another list of questions with them. These would invariably be a by-product of my answers to the questions they had asked the day before. Almost immediately after Rachel was killed the police had taken a bundle of our clothing to be examined forensically so that they would be able to rule out any fibres which belonged to us and establish anything else as 'unknown'.

They had spoken to my employers and established my whereabouts at the time Rachel was killed. They had also brought a police doctor to the house to take a blood sample from me. When the needle went in I was ashamed of the fact that I actually felt pain. How could I possibly feel anything after all that she had gone through?

Rachel had often said that she was frightened that something would happen and I would end up in jail. She always asked me to try and keep my temper and not get aggressive with people. From time to time she got pestered and said she didn't want to tell me. She was frightened that I might try to take things into my own hands and 'sort them out'. She said that she couldn't bear the thought of being separated from me if I got into trouble. When I was being treated like a suspect, what she had said kept coming back to me and the lines between reality and imagination were hard to define.

There were times when I felt convinced that the nightmare had yet to unfold completely. There were moments when I was convinced that I had lost my memory in a moment of schizophrenia and that, even though I had no recollection of it, it was really I who had killed her. Now that the police were taking my blood I was soon going to be found out and convicted. Then I would be separated from Alex and on top of all his pain he would grow up without a father, too.

It was only by thinking about the fact that Alex had not said it was me, and that he wasn't frightened or disturbed by me, that I was able to break the momentum of this train of thought. It is quite possible that without him there to reassure me I would not have been able to pull myself back from the abyss.

Like Alex himself, I had lost all trust in reality. I was paying lip-service to it, but that was all. While on the face of it I was giving, or I thought I was giving, the impression of relating to people in a normal way, what was going on in my head was very different. I was constantly waiting for the next explosion to go off in my face. In my mind the fact that our lives had been ripped apart once made it more likely that it was going to happen again.

My lack of trust extended to all my male friends. I was operating on two levels. On one level I was struggling not to give in to my paranoia and attempting to treat them as I knew I should. On another I was wondering who was responsible. They must all have been jealous, a part of me was saying, people are capable of anything. Even of coming back and acting like your friend again afterwards.

I found myself watching Alex's reactions very carefully. Just as I felt myself exonerated by Alex's positive reaction to me, I only allowed myself to rule out of suspicion those to whom Alex reacted positively as well. He was my guide and advisor. He had been there. He had seen it. He was the only one who knew. In his reactions I could have absolute faith.

I was joking around with Alex about a male friend who had done something clumsy or stupid, either banged his head or dropped something earlier in the day. I can't remember exactly what. Anyway, he had done something that adults weren't normally supposed to do.

Alex was sitting on my lap and still giggling about what had happened. He was showing obvious affection for the person concerned. I felt that what I was about to ask was so unlikely that I finally gathered the courage to force out the words. The chance of an affirmative answer was so remote that I couldn't believe my asking would freak Alex out.

But in my present state of mind 'remote' did not mean impossible. My pulse rate was going through the roof.

'"X" is our friend, isn't he?' I said. 'He didn't kill Mummy did he?'

Alex didn't stop giggling. He looked into my face as if I had said the most ridiculous thing possible. 'No,' he said, and carried on giggling about what 'X' had got up to earlier.

But I was now in a state of real anxiety and it took a while for my pulse rate to come back down. I continued to joke around with Alex but I was struggling with my mind, which was going in all directions at once.

The detectives' questions were nearly all concerned with trying to establish what Rachel and Alex had done that morning. They asked me who she might be in the habit of talking to, who she might have seen. They asked me where she might have walked.

I was able to say that, when I had left them that morning, Rachel had had a few things to get at the shops. Then they intended to go for a walk on the Common. The week before they had spent time searching for old golf balls that had been lost in the bushes. So it was likely that they would have been somewhere near the golf course. They would probably have parked in the Windmill carpark. They would undoubtedly have intended to be home for lunch.

This was virtually all I could tell them.

So far they hadn't had any specific information from Alex about what had actually taken place that morning. And there was no certainty as to when, or if, they ever would. So they were trying to build a picture of what had happened by establishing the sequence of their movements as best they could. The police were trying to tie what I had been able to tell them together with the times when witnesses had seen Rachel at the carpark and later walking with Alex. This, together with the time that Rachel's body was found, had given them an approximate series of events.

Even before they had taken me back to the Common with Alex the police attempted to explain to me where Rachel's body had been found. They asked me if it was probable that she would have arrived at this point of her own free will. I had said that it was quite possible that they had chosen a route that passed close by.

The police were still very busy taking statements from all of the people who were on the Common that morning. There had been more than a hundred of them and the police were still hopeful that someone had seen something that would make what had happened suddenly much clearer. With no witness, apart from a child who wasn't ready to talk, their task came down to thoroughly going through every little detail imaginable, both forensically and in the tracking down of people's movements. But so far there was no sign of a murder weapon and no obvious suspect. It was as if Rachel's killer had vanished into thin air.

We were playing with Alex on Hampstead Heath. The same friend was with us that Alex had been giggling about. The same who had been staying with us just the weekend before Rachel was killed. The same who had found out about Rachel's death from a newspaper hoarding.

We were romping around, playing trains. At first our friend was wary of playing rough with Alex, concerned that Alex would be frightened by someone lunging towards him. But Alex showed absolutely no signs of fear. We were both on our hands and knees on the grass trying to catch Alex as he ran between us. Alex was squealing with delight and wanted more and more. We were in the middle of a wide open space that sloped gently away from us. From where we played we could see all the way down the hill.

After romping around for a while we sat on a bench under some trees. We could see far into the distance. We were making Alex guess the letters inscribed on the bench when he suddenly became deeply agitated. His face had crumpled and he looked absolutely terrified. His movements had taken on the spastic quality that they showed when he was first waking up in the morning. I couldn't for the life of me see what had triggered his reaction: there was no one anywhere near us.

'What's wrong, Alex?' I asked, trying to take him into my arms.

He was speechless in his terror and all he could do was point down the hill.

We looked. There was no one within two hundred metres of us. However, when we looked in the direction that Alex was pointing there was what looked like a middle-aged man walking his Alsatian. He was alone; there was nobody else near him. The man was wearing a large overcoat and had a stooped-over, almost crouching kind of walk. It was very distinctive. It was this man that was frightening Alex.

His walk seemed so strange that I immediately thought it must be this which was having such an effect on Alex. I thought that he was frightened by it in the same way that children are sometimes frightened by the distorted faces of old people.

'Is it the man who's frightening you, sweetheart?' I asked him as I buried him in my arms. I couldn't get a response. He was completely terrified.

I too was suddenly very frightened. Frightened for Alex's sanity. This terror had been triggered by something as slight as a man walking a dog. A man so far away that from where we were sitting we couldn't even see his face. So far I had only seen this terror a couple of times, apart from, of course, his first waking every day. Was this a sign that such behaviour was going to become more and more part of our lives?

The man with the dog continued shuffling in our direction. Even though still a long way off it was obvious that his path was going to coincide with where we sat on the bench.

'I want him to go away!' pleaded Alex.

I could have picked Alex up and rushed him to the car, but I wasn't even sure that this would be enough to calm him down. I was also worried about how much of a failure running away might be. And how much it might set us back in our efforts at confidence-building.

'Shall I get him to go the other way?' suggested our friend.

That seemed like a very good idea, even if I wasn't sure how he was going to manage it. He set off briskly to intercept the man with the dog. Meanwhile I did everything I could to reassure Alex that he was safe. 'It's only an old man with a dog, Alex! He's not going to hurt you. And anyway we're here to look after you. You're not on your own now.'

I could see our friend reach the man and his dog. He had obviously said something because the man with the dog had stopped to look up from his crouch. I could see their mouths moving and the man with the dog gesticulating in our direction. I got the impression that he was determined to carry on his route as planned and didn't much appreciate the interference. But our friend persisted, with glances and gestures in our direction to aid his arguments.

With a shrug the man set off again in our direction. Our friend obviously hadn't managed to convince him. But he didn't give up: he jumped back in front of the man and continued to talk to him. Then, suddenly, the man veered off at ninety degrees from his previous route.

'Look, Alex. He's going away,' I said. I didn't know what had been said but I was extremely grateful. Alex watched the man with the dog as his figure receded into the distance. He was visibly calming.

Our friend came striding back. He looked over his shoulder as he reached us to see the fruits of his efforts. 'Well done!' I said.

'I told him the kid was afraid of dogs,' he said. 'I said that he was bitten by one just like his.'

'It seems to have done the trick,' I said. The man with the dog had disappeared into the trees at the side of the road.

'Yeah! Eventually,' said our friend. 'At first his attitude was like: "Well, he's just going to have to get used to dogs again, then isn't he!" I didn't think he was going to turn away. Seemed like he was going to be a difficult sod but something must have got to him.'

Alex had almost completely calmed down. In fact it was hard to tell that there had ever been anything to upset him. He was ready to play again. I, however, felt completely frazzled. I wanted to go home.

I strapped Alex into his seat in the front of the car. Things were progressing to the point where he would let me drive. Only, of course, if he could sit beside me. I heard a faint rustling of sweet papers from our friend in the back seat. He was a big person who needed to eat often. He knew that I didn't like Alex having chocolate at all hours of the day so he was doing his best to be discreet. I didn't think Alex had even heard. As we were pulling off, however, and without even turning round in his seat, Alex piped up: 'I can smell Kit-Kat!' He was spot on.

'Smart kid!' said our friend in the back, with amusement. 'Can't hide anything from you!'

There was a little girl in Alex's class that he was particularly fond of. We had been to her birthday party on the weekend before Rachel was killed. I had spoken to her parents and we had arranged for her mother to bring both her and her sister, who was a little younger, to play with Alex.

This was the first time in more than a week that Alex would be with children of his own age. I had no idea how he was going to react. I didn't know whether the events that had happened or the time that he had spent only with adults was going to affect how he saw his friends.

And it was a first for me: the first time I had made arrangements for him to see his friends. This was Rachel's domain. It was another stark reminder of how much things had changed.

I was looking after someone else's child. And only a few days had passed. Even though in that time our life had been turned completely upside down, some things hadn't changed. One of which was that Alex was more Rachel's than he was mine. All of his reactions, all of his habits, all of his expressions of how things were to be done were the result of his days spent with her. It was as if I was the understudy in the play. I knew all the lines, roughly, and he knew I knew all of my lines, roughly, but we both knew that I was only a stand-in. We knew that I was playing someone else's part.

Someone had let them in and the girls trailed through to where we were at the back of the house, with their mother and nanny trailing behind. We had been getting out the things to do some painting and there was a newspaper on the floor to catch the drips. The newspaper had been carefully edited: there were no pages referring to us.

Alex's friend was in the habit of giving him hugs when they were at school. She was a year older and they sat next to each other in class. This much I knew from Rachel's frequent updates on what they got up to during the day. The girls hesitated for a moment when they saw Alex beside me. I had never thought to ask, but I was sure that their parents had explained that his mummy had been killed. There must have been a lot going through their minds as they looked at him.

Before very long, though, they were all on hands and knees on the floor, sploshing colour across the paper with their brushes, the water in their jam-jars turning muddy brown as they mixed.

Soon the room was filled with the sounds and noises of busy children. They were all getting on with things and getting on with each other as if nothing had changed between the birthday party and now. It did me good to see him like this. It was only rarely that I saw Alex with his friends. At weekends it had been mostly just the three of us. This was the world which belonged to his mother and him. But he was going to need this again on a daily basis. Just like any other child of his own age.

I would have to make a rota and come up with a system so that we could see all of his little friends as often as possible. This wasn't entirely straightforward as we were now on the other side of London from most of them.

Later that day, when they had gone, I sat down to write my list. I put down the names of the handful of children that I knew from Rachel that Alex got on with. These were either children that he saw at school or the children of friends of ours. As I wrote them down I mentioned their names to Alex. Alex seemed fairly interested in seeing everybody but wasn't really paying much attention. As we talked about each one I asked if he wanted to see them. He said 'yes' absent-mindedly to each one as I went through them. Until I reached the name of a certain little boy at his school, whom Rachel would often see with his father during the day. His father was the same man who had come up to us in the windmill carpark on the day that Alex and I had gone to lay a flower where Rachel was killed.

Without looking up from what he was playing with Alex said, 'I don't want to see him.'

There was no accounting for children's whims, I told myself.

One of the senior officers came with our detectives to see me at the house. He was the person who was in charge of the day-to-day running of the investigation and had been one of the first on the scene when Rachel's body had been discovered. He had arranged for swabs to be taken from Alex's body and clothing, which had been drenched in blood.

He said that he wanted to explain in person what was going on, even though he knew that our two detectives were doing so on a daily basis. I think he also wanted to see for himself how Alex was. No effort was being spared to keep the family informed.

Alex had disappeared to the end of the garden and even though there were others to amuse him he wanted me as well. I later learnt that this particular officer had tried to talk to Alex when he was in the ambulance that had been called to the scene. According to the officer, Alex would not respond at all. He wouldn't answer any of his questions and appeared to be cold, as if in deep shock.

Again later, I found out that the officer was sure that Alex had recognized him from that day and was frightened by him. There is no doubt that seeing him again would immediately have triggered his memory of what had happened, and that was why Alex was now at the bottom of the garden.

Ferrying myself between one end of the garden and the other I tried to gather as much information as I could. The senior officer gave me the latest version of the attack that Rachel had suffered, as best they could reconstruct it from the pathologist's report. He seemed able to tell me which wounds were inflicted in which order. The first were what were described as 'defence wounds' in Rachel's hands, which she had put up to protect herself.

All the while that he was telling me this I was praying that she had been killed by the first blows and that she had suffered as little as possible. The pathologist had reported that several among the first few could have been fatal. All I could see was her suffering. I couldn't do anything to make it all right. And while he spoke I was being made graphically aware of what this tiny child had witnessed. Once again it seemed almost beyond belief that he could be functioning in any normal way whatsoever.

A witness had stated that she had seen a man acting suspiciously only ten minutes or so before the time Rachel was killed. The description that she gave of his clothing matched exactly that which Alex had given using the dolls on Hampstead Heath. Right down to him wearing a white, buttoned, collared shirt outside his trousers with a belt over the top. The officer was convinced that this was 'their man'. He was in no doubt that this man had been wearing his shirt like an apron to protect him from bloodstains. The officer, with undisguised disgust and anger, said that this person had come out that day dressed in a butcher's apron with the sole intention of killing somebody.

The question of Alex being able to identify anyone in the conventional way was raised, either through photographs or by an identity parade itself. I kept my mouth shut because it was not something I had given enough thought to. The police themselves still had no firm ideas on what would be the best way to deal with this situation if and when it arose. The more material evidence that was discovered to link someone to the crime, the less emphasis there would be on any evidence which came from Alex.

Things were already bad enough but there seemed no hope of a quick and successful end to the police investigation. I had not been able to focus my mind upon the way things were unfolding. Alex's demanding daily routine was my first consideration. As far as all other matters were concerned I had still not fully come down to earth. The evil that had been inflicted on Rachel was still so far beyond my comprehension that I had trouble even picturing her killer as a human being. In day-

light hours feelings of revenge were mostly beyond me. I knew that
there would come a time when that would change. I knew also that
with the way things were, and with no target for those feelings, if I
dwelt upon them then they would eat me up. As some kind of defence
mechanism within me had filed them out of circulation, for the
moment at least, I made a conscious effort to try and keep them there.

But the realization of how hard the police's task was, was beginning
to sink in. And each difficulty they came up against I took as another
physical blow.

So far there was no adult witness to the crime. No weapon had been
found. And there was no evidence left by the killer on Rachel's body
which could be DNA tested. We seemed no nearer a solution than we
were on the very first day. This was something that the police were
trying to keep secret from the press in order not to give confidence to
her killer.

On the other hand, all of the police officers with whom we were in
contact went to great lengths to explain the scale of the operation
under way. This was now a massive investigation with over a hundred
officers involved. As well as the trailer on the Common, an incident
room had been set up at Wimbledon police station with telephones
manned day and night for anyone who had information to give. A
computer system had been set up to have all the witnesses' statements
and other information electronically recorded. Experts were com-
paring Rachel's murder with past attacks up and down the country,
looking for similarities with any others under investigation. Several
cases were being closely examined and the senior officer said that he
would be making visits to the relevant police forces himself. Every
known past offender who lived anywhere in the local area was to be
interviewed. This process was already under way.

Every officer was taking this case extremely personally. The shock
that had been echoed by so many people in the country was, naturally,
felt by them too. They all wanted the killer found, and tried, and sentenced and put away for ever. And they all wanted there to be no
doubt that they were convicting the right man.

But for the time being anything that Alex might have to say would
be extremely useful.

The police relayed an invitation for me to take part in a memorial service for Rachel to be held on the Common. A local church had organized it on behalf of residents and riding clubs and other people who used the Common.

It was out of the question. I wasn't ready to go back there again, and couldn't leave Alex, anyway. And I certainly wouldn't take him back with me. It was also hard to understand exactly what this service was meant to achieve. These were, after all, people who didn't even know us. A memorial was by definition a private occasion, a family affair. The last thing any of us would have thought of would be to hold something so public.

But, strangely, interest in the case was still growing. Instead of it dying away, as time passed our lives became more and more public. Two and a half weeks would have passed by the time the service took place and still Rachel's murder was national news.

People just couldn't seem to get her murder out of their mind. In spite of all that we had become accustomed to seeing and hearing, people were still shocked. The way she had died was so hideous, so cruel. I had the feeling that ours was becoming a very public mourning. The whole country seemed to be grieving too. Not for Rachel personally, they didn't even know her, but for what a mother and child represented. There was a loss of hope. When the unimaginable happens it is hard to look forward with anything but a heavy heart. A lot of times you can brush the news aside and put a distance between it and you. But everyone knows a mother with a small child. A wife, a sister, a friend, a daughter, a granddaughter. Something sacred to everyone who cared for their particular mother and child had been violated.

It seemed to me that one of the aims of holding this service was to reclaim the Common for those who used it. In many ways it seemed like an attempt at exorcizing the evil that had passed over it. I wasn't sure exactly how I felt about that. Nothing that anybody could say was going to make things all right. And even though people were taking what had happened to Rachel very personally it still hadn't happened to them. It had happened to us. And by choosing to do this public thing, with the best intentions in the world, they were putting us back in the spotlight, and obliging us to act when we had other more immediate considerations of our own.

I asked a friend if he could contact the organizers and find out exactly what was involved. Within a day or so he had found out that, as we had heard, there would be a walk followed by a brief service. This bothered me. Rachel wasn't religious. I found it intrusive that anyone should consider holding a religious service in her name. Nobody had asked permission. It was true that they were acknowledging that something terrible had happened but I couldn't help but feel that the real motivation was to reclaim the land for themselves.

There was no way I could take part, but I still wanted at least something to come from us. It was suggested that I write a few words and that our friend be there to read them.

Once I had managed to produce something that seemed appropriate, and that met with general approval at home, our friend rang to talk with the priest who would be holding the service. I followed the conversation from another room. Our friend began to read out what I had written for the priest to hear. He had only got through a couple of lines when I could hear that he had come up against the first objection. Our friend was thrown off balance by the reaction at the other end but tried to jump the offending passage and continue further on. After another few lines it was clear that he had come up against another objection. He tried to jump a few lines ahead again but was met with yet another. He was getting seriously bothered and was clearly exasperated.

I couldn't control myself any longer. I leapt up and grabbed the phone. What was the point of going through with this exercise if the family of the victim were give no consideration whatsoever? It was a farce!

The organizer finally agreed that I might have a point. He would read what I had written.

Our detectives had given me the number of one of the child psychologists who had been recommended to them. They said that I could call her whenever I wanted and that she was happy for us to come and see her at her home if I wished to do so.

I think it was with slight trepidation that the detectives handed over the number, bearing in mind our recent experience with the Child Protection Team. But I still remembered how helpful the psychologist had been at the hospital where I picked up Alex. And there was no doubt that we needed help.

I phoned one evening when Alex was asleep. The voice on the

other end was very warm and down to earth. She listened while I explained some of the things I had been trying with Alex. She seemed very interested by the progress we had made. I asked her how she would hope to proceed. She said that it was important to find a way that a child could use to tell his story, whether through toys, or drawing and painting pictures, or by relating to other stories he or she might know. It all depended very much on the child.

She said that there were children who came back to see her regularly, maybe every year or so, through their childhood. She would often ask them to draw her a picture. The picture would often have something to do with the original event or trauma but the story that the child told was always that much more advanced than the last time. The child would be looking back at an original event that remained unchanged in their mind. But the child was able to describe the event with greater maturity and the information that they could give was that much more detailed on each visit.

This seemed to reinforce what had already been said: that there was no reason why Alex should not one day be able to describe everything that happened to him in perfect detail.

She said that if I wanted more than this elementary advice it would be easier to meet face to face so she could explain more. I agreed, and a time was decided.

We were at Rachel's parent's house when the memorial on the Common was reported on the news. I was stunned to see that hundreds of people had attended. The sight was deeply moving. It was like the sending off of a famous statesman. There were people on horseback and a long procession walking across the park.

I wasn't sure exactly what I had expected, but it wasn't this. In fact I had been so wrapped up with Alex that I had hardly given it any thought at all. In truth I found it hard to fit any of this in with us, with Rachel and Alex and me. It was impossible to understand the connection between what I saw on the screen and our previous life. It was as if Rachel's picture had been mixed up with someone else's and there had been a big mistake made somewhere along the line.

I had often thought that with all of Rachel's charisma and presence, she had everything it took to become a star in whatever field she might have chosen to conquer. But she had never wanted to be one. Now the camera panned over the faces of complete strangers marching solemnly to mark her death. It was such a contrast to what might have been. The fame she had never sought was hers now, reflected in the faces of the crowd.

But I couldn't tell myself she wasn't dead. That their grief made her somehow alive again. I still knew that much was real. But it was hard for me to work out what Rachel's life had to do with all this. The limits of reality and unreality shimmered and swayed in my head. I couldn't make a logical whole of things. My eyes still watched, but my mind had turned away.

Chapter Seven

THE CHILD PSYCHOLOGIST lived an hour's drive from my mother's house, so books had to be arranged and snacks and drinks for the car. There was no question of Alex allowing me to drive for so long; I would be required to entertain him.

Eventually we came to the village. We pulled up at a house in a quiet street and emptied out of the cars. Rachel's parents, my mother, our two detectives and Alex and myself. The child psychologist came out to greet us in the road and quickly showed us into the house. I don't think her neighbours were aware of her work but she was conscious of our problems with the press and didn't want to take any chances that we might be recognized. She was concerned this and any future visits should be conducted in as much privacy as was possible.

We were shown into the front room and invited to sit down. There were toys and other interesting things spread around the room, all within easy access of little hands. Just like a page out of 'Goldilocks and the Three Bears' there was a little chair for Alex to sit in that was just his size, and the wooden coffee table was at his level so he could draw or play on it. Once we were settled, the child psychologist knelt on the floor.

Everything was set up to put children at their ease, by someone who cared for, and was interested in them.

The child psychologist introduced herself and told us about her work. Child trauma, accidents, violence and death were things she was used to dealing with. She was talking to us adults but in her conversation she was also including Alex, who was busy exploring the contents of the table-top. Without seeming slow or awkward she used simple works to describe complicated things, in a manner which fitted well with the vocabulary of a child of Alex's age. Even though he was making himself busy, he was quiet and it was clear that he was taking in what was going on. She wasn't talking down to him. Literally. This made it much easier for him to absorb what she was saying. The contrast with our visit from the social worker couldn't have been more marked. This woman knew what she was doing.

She told us that if Alex was able to talk about what had happened then, above all other considerations, this would be good for him. In her experience, children who had gone through trauma could often describe much of what had happened almost straight away. But what they could describe was limited by the child's vocabulary and by their understanding of the world at the time. She said that as children progressed through childhood they would often feel the need to bring that trauma to the surface and look at it again, but with a vocabulary and an understanding of the world which was that much more mature. It was as if they had to pull it out of where it had been put away, try to come to a new understanding of it and then, when, and if, they were comfortable with it, they would put it away again.

This could happen at various stages of childhood and there weren't necessarily any obvious triggers or landmarks. It could happen at any time. She said that it might well be a number of years before Alex would be able to give an accurate description, in the conventional sense, of the man who killed his mother. This in no way meant that he wouldn't be able to recognize this man right now if he saw him. But as time went by he would be much more likely to be able to come up with details which could help to pinpoint someone.

The long-term effect of what Alex had seen and experienced were another matter entirely. It depended very much on what happened to him from this moment on. She said often these effects could not be fully assessed until much later. Only time would tell.

This wasn't a subject we could really talk about in detail as Alex, judging from the tilt of his head, was listening to everything that was being said.

She asked us if we had been advised in any way about the likelihood of Alex being eligible for compensation from the Criminal Injuries Compensation Board. It was a subject that I knew absolutely nothing about, although it had been mentioned in the course of conversation with one police officer or another.

She said that she could recommend a lawyer who she had worked with before. He had handled compensation claims on behalf of children with whom she had been involved. She promised to give us his details before we left. In cases like ours, where there might be compensation, she often advised an interim payment to be made in the short term but for the balance of the award to be decided when the child's case was looked at again several years later to allow the full effects to be properly taken into consideration.

I wondered how you could possibly compensate a child for his mother being killed. I knew that there were actuarial tables, in which prices were laid down for the loss of an eye or the loss of a limb. But how could you possibly put a value on a mother's life? At least these other victims were still alive.

I knew the ridiculous sums of money awarded in libel cases, when people received huge awards for what were basically hurt feelings. I knew that people could suffer distress and heartache as a result of what was said about them – but they were still alive. How could that possibly compare with all that Alex had endured? And all that he had lost.

But any compensation in a libel case or when someone was injured in an accident was payable by the negligent party. Or more likely by the insurer of those found responsible. In our case it was the state who would compensate us. But the state was not responsible for killing Rachel, and the compensation would probably be nothing like the value of Alex's loss.

It was a strange dilemma. Do you feel grateful for whatever you get, no matter what the amount? Or do you feel that you should be compensated for what the person you have lost is really worth?

The child psychologist raised another issue. One that hadn't occurred to me in exactly her terms. She felt it was very important for Alex as a citizen to know that he had done his duty. He ought to be able to look back, when he was older, and recognize that he had done as much as he possibly could to help the police bring his mother's killer to justice, even if there was never a conviction. The idea that there might not be a conviction was too remote to be contemplated. But to imagine that there was a chance, however slight, that at some time in the future Alex might just come face to face with Rachel's killer in the street, or see him from the top of a bus or from a passing car, was unthinkable. How could he grow up feeling safe and secure like that? What could I tell him about justice and fairness if he grew up knowing that the person he had seen kill his mother was still walking around free?

I couldn't imagine it ever coming to that. I wasn't really expecting the police to have the case all tied up by tomorrow. I was trying, as much as I could, not to think about it at all. But I no longer had the strength to hope for anything good. I was living in a nightmare in which, minute by minute, the prospect of the worst imaginable happening seemed just around the corner. But I was still shaken so deeply, and was in many ways completely detached from the world, that the thought of any other disaster befalling us couldn't frighten me as it would have done before. What could hurt more than the way we were hurting now? I could laugh in the face of nearly anything. Anything, except something happening to Alex.

But for the moment I had the feeling that, with the size and effort of the police investigation, they were, eventually, inevitably going to find Rachel's killer and that my fears that Alex might grow up with him still on the loose were unfounded.

So many people were involved in the investigation and so much detail had already been established about so much that had happened that morning. The police had been able to work out almost exactly how many people had been on the Common, which was an enormous area, and everyone who had been there was being interviewed to find out what their movements had been and what, or who, they might have seen. All of which was then being cross-referenced.

A powerful machine was now in motion. Every detail was being turned over and examined minutely. I was coming to learn that, first, most murders are committed by someone who knows the victim. This I had already heard. Secondly, most cases are solved by a small piece of evidence which comes to light as a result of 'routine' police work. Often cases have turned on the smallest of details which lead to more and more evidence.

Our detectives held the officers in charge of the day-to-day running of the investigation in high regard. They had enormous confidence in them. They referred to them as people who were 'very thorough' and who 'examined every possibility'. This was reassuring to hear. From the way our detectives explained things, we were a long way from the world of eccentric TV detectives solving cases in a flash of inspiration. Surely all this effort would come to something?

As these thoughts flashed through my mind, the child psychologist had been telling us how she had heard about Rachel's murder through the media. And how she had thought: 'Those poor people! What they must be going through right now.' At the time, she had wished that there was something she could do. The police had contacted her soon afterwards and she had been glad of the chance to do something practical to help.

She suggested that this was probably as good a place to start as any. She said that in order to try and put everything in some sort of context it was probably a good idea if each adult speak in turn, and explain a little of how we had each found out about Rachel's death. Alex had been playing quietly and continued to do so as everyone talked. But he was listening hard and taking everything in.

I heard my mother tell of how she had picked up the phone to hear someone wail 'Rachel's been killed!' In the first instant she had thought it was some kind of hoax. Some kind of sick joke. She didn't recognize my voice. I had hardly been able to get the words out. All that she had been able to understand was that Rachel was dead and that Alex was at Wimbledon police station. She had arrived at the police station thinking that Rachel must have been involved in a traffic accident.

Rachel's parents told of how they had arrived back at their family's house in Canada, after several days' boat trip, to find a note pinned to the door. The note asked them to contact the sheriff's office as there was a message for them with news from home. They said that they knew straight away that someone in the family was dead and spent the whole time, between finding the note and someone arriving to break the news, preparing for the shock. And trying to work out who had died. They said that Rachel seemed the least likely of anyone: she had seemed too much alive and too busy getting on with her life. It was Rachel's grandmother, in her eighties, who was their most obvious thought.

I spoke in turn of how I had phoned home to hear a strange male voice answer the phone. I told of all that had happened to me from that moment until I arrived at Wimbledon police station.

The child psychologist was extremely sympathetic as each of us told our story, and the words flowed. Things that we hadn't said because we feared they might sound banal were, it turned out, just what each of us needed to hear. That what had happened *was* 'shocking', 'terrible'. That, just like me, others had thought the world had gone mad. That others hadn't known what to do.

Alex was listening to all of this. I realized that he must have had no idea of what had happened to me that day, before I collected him at the hospital. It had never occurred to me to tell him. But I saw now that he might have a better understanding of just how much Rachel being killed was a shock to all of us. That seeing your mother brutally murdered wasn't usually what happened just before your third birthday.

I could remember swallowing an elastic band when I was five years old. I was sure that I was going to die but too terrified to tell anyone because I thought I would get punished for putting in my mouth in the first place. When I went to sleep that night I didn't think I was going to wake up in the morning.

When I did wake up the next morning of course, I had forgotten all about it. It wasn't until a few days later that I thought about it again. I was then pleasantly surprised that I wasn't actually dead and figured that if I wasn't dead by now then I wasn't going to die anyway and promptly forgot about it all once more. But I hadn't breathed a word to anybody.

I thought that, listening to how terrible the shock had been for everyone else, Alex must feel that the load was spread a little further than just himself and, to a lesser extent, me. It might be one more useful acknowledgement of how much everyone around him was still feeling terrible too. This could only help him come to understand that the pain he had inside him, other people had inside them too.

The child psychologist made no attempts to hold back or hide her own tears as she listened to what each of us had to say. This surprised me a little. I think that, even though it hadn't been our experience so far, I still expected hardened professionals, such as her, to have heard it all before and so be totally immune. It made me realize she was just a normal person, with normal emotions, doing a very difficult job. I wouldn't have had much empathy with her if she had been any other way. And, as a result, she would not have been as effective at what she was trying to do.

I clearly needed to off-load, to be listened to. In spite of how much I had already been able to talk with the people around me it was never enough. I felt the need to talk to different people all the time, to keep talking. But when I had finished talking no one could tell me what I wanted to hear. No one could tell me Rachel was coming back.

What I longed for more than anything was for Rachel to talk to me. My heart ached to hear her voice. To hear the spark she had and, in the way she spoke, to feel everything she felt for me. I missed this more than anything else about her. I could hear her voice in my head, and I was pretty sure that I could guess her reactions to every little thing, but all this was just a shadow compared to her presence itself. I was no longer part of a joint force against the world and everything it threw at us. We could no longer lock the door, pull up the duvet and forget the world outside. I had lost the thing that made me whole. And, surrounded by people, I was totally alone.

Our detectives spoke in turn. As they recounted the events of the day that Rachel was killed as seen through their eyes I realized that they needed to get as much out of their system as anyone in our family. They too had been through a terrible ordeal. They may not have known Rachel before they had arrived at the scene of her murder, but they had come to know her now through us. They had had to deal with my anguish from the very first moments of meeting me. And they had seen all of what we had been going through daily ever since. This must have been putting them under an enormous strain, which they had to cope with as part of their job. Then they had to go back to their own families at night, as if it had just been another day at the office.

I found out later that there was counselling available to police officers. But the policy was that the officer in question had to apply for it, which went on his record. Hardly an incentive for ambitious officers if they risked being labelled 'fragile' as a consequence. Somehow I got the impression that in the tough world of detectives, whatever the pressure you were supposed to be able to 'handle it'.

But everybody has to offload on somebody, eventually. I suppose the weight inevitably falls on their families if they don't want to compromise their chance of promotion. That, or reach for the bottle to ease the pain. Or crack completely. Or perhaps a mixture of all of them. I knew the divorce rate was high. I wondered what the suicide rate was for people who, every day, come up against the worst things that human beings are capable of doing to each other.

In turn each person in the room had a chance to talk. Apart from one.

Each person in the room was shedding tears. All spoke apart from one.

The child psychologist started to talk more directly to Alex. Alex, whose eyes remained dry and whose emotions stayed under tight control. He continued to play with the toys on the table but his playing became more frantic as she talked to him. She spoke kindly but firmly. This was definitely the right approach. He reacted better when people were firm with him. He didn't like wishy-washy people. And he had a way of ignoring them completely if he wasn't interested in what they had to say.

He began to make more noise as she talked to him and was noticeably more agitated. In fact she began not so much by speaking to him as by speaking for him. She was still sitting on the floor and looking slightly up into his face. She was giving him simple phrases that he could relate to. She would say: 'And you were there when the bad man killed your lovely mummy. It's such a dreadful thing to have seen! You must have been so frightened when all this was going on!'

The noise level was rising. Alex was beginning to bang things around. He would only look at her face from time to time. But he made no effort to get away and he wasn't looking to me for reassurance. She continued to talk to him.

'It's such a terrible thing to have happened to your lovely mummy. And there was nothing you could do about it. You must have felt so small and helpless. You must have felt so angry that you couldn't do anything to help your mummy.'

Alex began to bang things around harder now. He scrunched a box of pens across the table-top, his body full of tension. While he was doing this he would look up at her as she spoke. Every time he looked at her he had an expression almost of surprise. It was almost as if he was surprised that an adult should understand how he felt. There was agreement in his look.

'But the bad man with the knife was so much bigger than you and so strong there was nothing that you could do,' she continued. 'You were so small there was really nothing you could have done even though you must have so much wanted to help her, and stop him hurting your lovely mummy!'

I felt that the little phrases she was giving him were also helping him to understand his own feelings better. He just didn't have the vocabulary at nearly three years old to cope with the range of his experiences. It was not something that you brought your children up for.

I was struck by what she was trying to do. And by what she was achieving. It had never occurred to me that he would have felt angry when Rachel had been attacked. Terrified, yes. But it was clear from the look of surprised understanding on his face that this must have been exactly one of the things he had felt at the time.

As she was talking Alex was reliving the events of that day. He gave the clear impression that he could see it all again on the screen in his head. How it felt like to me, seeing my own small child with such unimaginable horror going through his mind, is impossible to describe. I could see by the tension in his body and the distant look on his face that it was all unfolding before him.

But, agonizing as it was to watch, it meant that his memory of that day was on the surface. It wasn't yet buried deep. It meant that there was more chance than I had so far seen, and hoped for, of him getting it all out of his system before it could be put away to rot, and putrefy, and cause God knows what damage as time went on.

I could see that the first steps in his recovery didn't necessarily mean *him* talking. The first step was for him to focus on that day, against his reluctance to do so, and for him to be given the words with which to express what he was feeling. The first step was that he at least listen, and be able to identify with those words. The key was to find the triggers to allow him to relive the event, however terrifying that thought seemed. It was kinder in the long term for him to confront what had happened now, and deal with it with all his family present, than leave him alone out of a natural desire to spare him the pain of facing it. If we let him put it away its power over him might grow and possibly ruin his life.

Just by him listening to us talk about our feelings meant that progress was already being made.

The child psychologist had some little dolls on the table. But, unlike the dolls we had used to help describe the killer's clothing, these dolls were tiny, finger-sized things.

She gave Alex a finger doll which resembled a little boy with brown hair. 'Look,' she said to him. 'Here's little Alex. And maybe one day, when you're ready, you might be able to tell us all about what happened to "little Alex" on that very, very bad day. Your worst ever day.'

Alex took the doll but showed no sign of wanting to talk about anything.

The child psychologist said that she had known children who had found it easier to talk about themselves and what had happened to them through a doll, rather than talk about themselves in the first person. This 'trick' might give him just enough distance from the events that took place to make it bearable to talk about them.

'And I'm sure that he remembers lots about that terrible, terrible day, and the bad man who killed his lovely mummy, because he'd such a clever little boy,' she said.

But Alex's attention had gone. For the last ten minutes he had been completely focused on his memories, but now the curtain had come down again. The child psychologist suggested a break and set about finding some refreshments.

Alex had got up to explore. He reached the doorway to the next room, but wouldn't go through on his own. He came back to tug at me until I got up. There were some more toys and books there, and a door that led into the garden. We went out to look round. I needed some fresh air. I'm sure Alex did, too.

After playing in the garden for a little while Alex was ready to come back into the house. Some biscuits had appeared and something to drink. Alex was perfectly willing to accept the hospitality. By the time he had finished eating and drinking, and the things had been tidied away it was clear that he had reached saturation point. He had had enough for one day. The child psychologist agreed. Another appointment was arranged and everyone said their goodbyes. I thanked her for what she had done and told her that I thought a lot had been achieved. She had given me plenty to think about.

At one stage during the day I had asked the child psychologist if she could tell me a little bit about how a child's evidence was actually used in court.

She told me that the law had recently been changed. Up until now the child's evidence had to be presented 'live'. This was a huge obstacle to overcome. The idea of having to give evidence in a crowded courtroom was intimidating enough for an adult. For a small child it must have been terrifying. And for that child to have to do so in the presence of the person they might be accusing would makes matters a thousand times worse.

It was now easier to admit videos taken of children talking about traumatic events instead of them having to be physically present themselves. The evidence of children over the age of seven would generally be given much more weight than that of a younger child. This seemed the age when it was accepted that a child could distinguish between right and wrong. This age limit struck me as unnecessarily high. But it was up to the judge to decide whether the evidence of a younger child could be heard or not. The he or she would instruct the jury as to how much weight this evidence could be given in their deliberations.

On the way back in the car the idea of giving Alex choices he could relate to played through my mind.

Alex and I were sitting in the back. One of our detectives was driving. The other sat in the front seat beside him.

I took a piece of paper and one of Alex's felt-tips and began to draw some cartoon figures. I drew a fat figure and a thin figure. I showed Alex the sheet of paper.

'Alex, was the man who killed Mummy a fat man or a thin man?' I asked, pointing at each figure in turn.

Alex looked at my drawings and then looked at me. He had the same expression of interest, of 'enjoyment' almost, that he had shown when we had used the dolls on Hampstead Heath. He pointed to the thin man. 'Thin man!'

I could tell by the absolute silence in the car and the tension emanating from back of the heads of the detectives that they were listening with one hundred per-cent attention.

'A thin man like this?' I asked, pointing to the cartoon of the thin man. 'Not a fat man like that?' I pointed to the fat man.

'Thin man, like that!' Alex repeated.

I drew a couple of figures, both of them thin. One just had hair on his head, one had a pony-tail all the way down his back. I showed him the sheet of paper.

'Did the man who killed Mummy have long hair, like this' – I pointed to the paper – 'or short hair like Daddy or . . .' I pointed to one of the detectives' heads. I had hardly any hair; he had a full head of hair. I wanted to be as clear as possible.

Again Alex pointed at the sheet of paper. 'Short hair,' he said.

'Are you sure?' I said. 'Not long hair like –' I named a male friend with a long pony-tail – '. . . or Mummy?'

Alex was sure. 'Short hair.'

He gave every appearance of enjoying the game. 'What can I ask him next?' I asked the detectives.

'Big or small?' said one. 'But then again, everyone's big to a child,' he added. 'It's hard for them to differentiate.'

'How about hair colour?' suggested the other.

I had to think about that one for a moment. What was the best way of putting it? I tried to find some colours in Alex's box and scribbled some more stick figures.

'Alex, did he have yellow hair like Mummy, or black hair like Daddy?' I asked. This time I had drawn three heads. 'Or brown hair like . . . ?' Again I named someone that Alex knew well.

This was a much harder question, and one that perhaps would have to be asked several times, each time giving more subtle choices. It would probably need more than a box of children's felt-tips to get to the point where there was no misunderstanding of what he was describing.

Later that afternoon Alex fell asleep. He seemed very peaceful. But after a while I saw some fluid leaking from one of his ears. I watched his face carefully as I wiped it away. He was still extremely calm. To me this little bit of leaking fluid was an enormous sign. It was the first sign that he had relaxed enough to let the slightest thing out.

I was even more certain that this first session had been valuable for him. I was still struck by how some of the things that the child psychologist had said had produced such a clear reaction in him: she seemed to have tapped into the way he felt about his mother's murder. It had also given me plenty to think about concerning how I should talk to him myself.

A group of mothers from our local area – our previous local area – were organizing a campaign to plant a tree in Rachel's memory. They planned to make it part of a children's playground in one of the parks where Rachel used to take Alex.

I had mixed feelings. Already, within days of her death, some friends of Rachel's had had a bench placed in another park, with an inscription dedicated to her. It was very touching that they should have done so. It was a very moving gesture. But at the same time I didn't want anything connected with Rachel to be on public display: to be exposed in the open like that. I couldn't bear the thought of it being vandalized, as I was sure it eventually would be. There had been desecration enough.

The same applied to the tree the mothers were planning to plant. Perhaps on reflection I should have asked them to dedicate it to victims of violence in general, and not to mention Rachel's name specifically. But at the time it was one of those things that I didn't have the energy to deal with. I tried to accept the fact that they meant only the best and to put the rest out of my mind.

I was busy with Alex's social diary, trying to arrange who we would see for the week ahead. Alex was playing. 'Do you want to see . . . ?' I named the little girl from Alex's class who had come a few days before.

'Yes,' said Alex, without looking up.

'Do you want to see . . . ?' I mentioned the daughter of a friend of Rachel's and mine.

'Yes,' said Alex, still not looking up.

'Do you want to see . . . ?' I named the little boy from his class that Alex and Rachel used to see during the day together with his father.

'No,' said Alex. There was no change of emphasis in his voice. He still did not look up from what he was doing.

Rachel had been pleased when Alex had befriended this particular little boy because, up until then, all of the children that Alex got on with best happened to be girls. The girls were often just a little bit older than him and they always naturally took him under their wing.

Rachel felt it was good that he should have a little male pal. I wasn't concerned one way or the other. My opinion was that children's allegiances changed rapidly. He was bound to go through the stage where girls became something horrible and disgusting, and when he did he wouldn't be seen dead playing with them. I didn't see much point in worrying about him playing too much with them now. So, when Alex said that he didn't want to see this little boy, the first thing that went through my head was that it was because he was a boy, and that Alex had always preferred girls.

This thought was immediately followed by another. The other friends that I had mentioned would more than likely be accompanied by their mother when we saw them. Or a nanny. But certainly someone female. Alex was fearful and mistrusting of all men that he did not know well. I thought that maybe it was the fact that we would be obliged to see the father of his friend which was causing a problem. They were bound to come together.

'Are you afraid of . . . ?' I named his friend's father.

'Yes,' said Alex, still not looking up.

I suddenly thought that the man who killed Rachel might have resembled the little boy's father. I felt everything begin to slow down around me.

'Did the man who killed Mummy look like . . . ?' I named the father of his friend.

'Yes,' said Alex, still not looking up.

I had asked the next question several times when going through the lists of friends and asking Alex whether any of them killed his mother. Even though I thought the chance of an affirmative answer to my question was as unlikely as the last time I'd asked it, the blood was pounding in my head.

'Do you think it was . . . ?' I named the father of his friend.

'Yes,' said Alex, still not looking up.

The world stood still. So much went careering through my mind as I tried to come to terms with the consequences of what Alex had just said.

I was certain that he 'thought' it was the father of his friend. I could tell by his voice, his body language, everything. And I had learnt to trust the detail of what he had to say. This much had been borne out by other adult witnesses. But saying that he 'thought' it was the father of his friend was different from saying that he was 'sure' it was the father of his friend. Even though it had been me forming the questions and him saying 'yes' or 'no' I knew he knew there was a difference. I was frightened to ask him any more. I needed to think.

I tried to picture what Alex would have been able to see. I tried to think of someone coming upon them quickly, of there being a struggle. It wasn't difficult to imagine how hard it would be for

anyone to recognize someone's face immediately in those conditions.
A face that was distorted by frenzy. And what if the attacker did resemble the father of his friend? For a small child, in all the movement, in all the horror, it must have been difficult for him even to focus on in his terror. If there was a resemblance between the killer and (. . . .), why shouldn't Alex think that the killer was one and the same as the only person that he knew who looked like him? Could a young child understand, in the same way as an adult, how some people could look extremely similar without being the same person? When I tried to think back to my childhood and how my mind had worked I doubted that he could.

Alex's reaction in not wanting to see the father of his friend was understandable enough if Alex only 'thought' that he looked like the man who killed his mummy. Who would want to spend any time in the presence of someone whose very appearance could terrify so much?

Alex had moved on and had become engrossed in playing with something else. For the moment the subject was closed. Despite my misgivings over whether Alex could tell the difference between (. . . .) and the killer, I went through all the details of everything the police had told me about the attack on Rachel. At the same time I tried to remember everything that Rachel had told me about her friendship with this man.

I wanted to speak to our detectives. I had to wait until they turned up later in the day. They were going to drive us to our next appointment with the child psychologist.

I sat down with them before we left and explained to them what had happened in my conversation with Alex. I told them how much I believed what he was saying. But at the same time I tried to stress how much I felt that he might only have been describing someone with a resemblance to the man who killed his mummy. That he was not necessarily trying to say that this was the man himself.

They listened almost without interruption. Then they said that what Alex had come out with was very interesting in the light of how the investigation was progressing. They said that the father of Alex's friend was someone who was being looked at very closely. The police had been contacted by different members of the public who remembered having seen a man answering his description in Rachel's company at the local swimming pool and at the children's playground on various occasions. This wasn't exactly news; I'd told the police about Rachel's friendship with (. . . .) some time before.

But then the detectives asked me if I remembered him coming up to Alex and myself in the Windmill carpark on the day that they had taken us back to the Common. I said that I did. They explained that he had been taken there to show the police where he had walked on the one occasion that he and his son had gone there with Rachel and Alex.

I remembered the time they were referring to. Rachel had, of course, talked to me about it. She had thought it a good idea if they went together to walk the dogs. We had just bought a big old estate car and all the dogs could go easily in the back. The other family had two of their own, and ours in particular always needed a lot of exercise.

The detectives asked me if I had noticed Alex's reaction when he had seen (. . . .) when we'd gone back to the Common. This threw me. I didn't remember Alex having any reaction whatsoever. I only remembered the stress of the situation in general, and then trying to work out who the stranger was calling my name while I was trying to get Alex away.

I thought back harder. Then I recalled Alex trying to climb out of my arms. But that was only because he had had enough and wanted to go, wasn't it?

The detectives said they had noticed that Alex had become visibly distressed while I had been talking to his friend's father. They too had seen him trying to climb out of my arms. But they had come to a different conclusion: it had struck them immediately that it was the very presence of his friend's father which was causing Alex's distress.

I asked them if they had established this person's whereabouts at the time. They said that his wife had confirmed that he was at home with her, and that they had got up late. Something about the way they related this information told me they considered this less than conclusive proof. For them he was a major suspect.

Events were unfolding fast around me. It all seemed so obvious and so convincing when put into a certain context. It was easy to follow the logic once someone had pointed it out. I had lead in my stomach and felt like vomiting. How could (. . . .) appear so normal and be capable of such a thing? It couldn't be possible. How could he walk up

113

to me afterwards if he had done such a thing? But then someone who was capable of this was capable of anything.

We spent the afternoon with the child psychologist. Out of Alex's earshot the detectives and I tried to explain to her what Alex had said, and to whom he had been referring. The session turned out to be a short one. The detectives wanted to talk things over with the child psychologist on their own in order to work out the best way forward.

The one thing that was decided was that they would arrange for her house to be wired up and fitted with concealed cameras as quickly as possible. They were concerned that anything Alex might say from this moment on should be properly recorded.

Chapter Eight

MY LIFE HAD totally stopped. I had no wife. I had no home. I had no car. I had no job or income. I had a child who had watched his mother being slaughtered in front of his eyes, and who had had God alone knew what damage inflicted upon him as a consequence. And her killer was still just walking around free. I was completely removed from the realities of my previous life. I was completely reliant on those around me. Materially, I was as helpless as a baby. I was beyond caring. The moment-by-moment answering of the demands of this small child took nearly all the attention that I had. With this alone the days began to pass.

In what was now 'my previous life' I had worked as a dispatch rider. But now my motorbike was parked in the back of a police station on the other side of London. I had worked for several firms. The lifestyle and attitude was always mercenary. Everybody was out for themselves, and the goal was to get the best jobs and to have made as much money at the end of the day as possible. It was a very competitive world, and the effects of the recession were being felt hard, making it more competitive still.

There was absolutely no security. You worked completely on your own. If you had an accident and couldn't work, then that was just too bad. At some of the companies there was a riders' room where at least you could get out of the rain or the cold for a few minutes. But not always. Most of the time you were out on the street, whatever the weather. If you didn't work you didn't get paid and if you didn't work all week you didn't get paid nearly as much. There were no paid holidays and no contributions to your pension. It was dog eat dog.

However, there was in the main a solidarity between riders and a kind of code of behaviour. If you broke down anywhere there would always be another rider, whoever they worked for, who offered to lend a hand or to radio for help. But as a rule, it was a world which was about as unsentimental as you could get.

A few days after Rachel was killed I received a letter from the company I had been working for. To my astonishment they were writing not only to express their sympathies but also to say that, for the present, they would be continuing to pay me. It was a gesture that I never would have expected and that I was very grateful for. It was the only money I had.

Their letter was extremely moving. And not just because of the practical help they were offering. There was other news as well. It told of how riders from other companies were stopping off at the office to leave donations for Alex's welfare. People had been coming in off the street in tears to make some kind of gesture, to try and reach out and help in their turn.

Once again this was a powerful demonstration of how intrinsically good the majority of people are. In my despair and rage at the world there were always these continued and totally unexpected gestures. Because of them, I couldn't allow myself to sink into bitterness. I couldn't say that the whole world was bad when people were capable of such kindness and generosity. I couldn't say that humanity was rotten when people were in pain for a child they didn't even know.

Everyone showed so much concern for Alex. For a brief moment in time he became a personification of all the victims of horror worldwide: a totally innocent being who had had inflicted upon him blind savagery and cruelty. All of this kindness and generosity affected me greatly. There was a black hole of despair that I wanted to fall into. I wanted to wallow in bitterness. But the strength of all of these gestures combined held me back, almost physically, from falling.

I was conscious, virtually from the beginning, of how fortunate we were to be receiving all of this support. I was suddenly aware of how important it was for people in pain to know that someone cares, and that someone wants to make them feel better, even in the smallest way.

I had never had much experience with death before. In the few times that anyone I knew, even vaguely, had lost someone, I felt awkward about talking to them. I thought that if I said the wrong thing I would make matters worse. And anyway how could anything I would say help in the face of what they must have been going through?

Now that I was on the other side I could see things differently. Even for someone to say that they didn't know what to say was extremely touching. To know that they were thinking about us was enough. I wasn't weighing this sympathy against what I'd lost. The gesture stood on its own. I was moved every time. And every time that a stranger took the time to make such a gesture I would think again of how hard it must be for those who were suffering their own pain alone.

Much later I attempted to reply to everyone that I could. But there were many letters and cards with no return address. And there were labels that had become separated from the gifts to which they had been attached so I wasn't completely sure who to thank for what. On behalf of Alex and myself I thank everyone who made the effort to reach out to us and would like to say once again how much it helped.

There was something in the letters people wrote, and the things that I heard said which made me feel that Rachel's murder was almost too much for *them* to take. It was as if, for some of them, their reaching out to us was something they had to do in order to try and find a little comfort for themselves in their own lives. It was as if they felt that this poor child who had been left behind had to have *something* good, no matter how small, to balance against all that he had suffered in order that they themselves could look at the world again without total despair.

I still don't know where the idea came from, but we went back to spend a night at our flat. A couple of friends had volunteered to keep us company and the police had promised to keep an eye on us.

The police had arranged for the door which had been broken down that afternoon to be put back straight away. But, understandably, it was impossible for our flat-mate to live there any more so he had stayed with friends since the day when Rachel was killed. The press had laid siege to the place from the very first moment and he had been harangued each time he had gone in or out. He had obviously been considered a suspect, as I had myself. He had almost immediately been ruled out, but he had not had an easy time because of it. The place had been left empty.

It was so strange to turn the key in the lock. The door was exactly the same as the old one only it looked and smelt brand new. It was difficult to keep hold on reality, accept what had happened as final. Wouldn't she be just behind this door? Surely not that much time had passed?

But when the door swung open the flat was completely empty. Empty and lifeless. Looking around the empty rooms gave me the same impression I always had whenever Rachel would take Alex to stay with her parents. I hated coming back to the flat at the end of the day when they weren't there. All the noise and life had always gone with them. The place was like a tomb without them. I used to find myself at a complete loss for something to do. It gave me the creeps. The thought would cross my mind that this is what life would be without them. I would shake my head to chase the thought away. When they returned I was always so glad, and so relieved, to have them back again, safe and well, and the place full of life again.

Surprisingly, everything was neat and tidy. I think I expected the place to resemble a bomb-site after all the activity that had gone on and all the comings and goings by police and forensic officers.

The tape on the answer machine, however, had been filled with calls from reporters on the day that Rachel's body had been found. But at the beginning of it was a piece of tape where Rachel had accidentally left the machine running while she talked with one of her girlfriends. A few seconds filled with carefree laughter.

It was late in the afternoon when we arrived, and more friends turned up as the time went on. The evening was fast turning into a wake. It hadn't been planned that way but that is what it inevitably became.

It wasn't long before I broke down. But there was always someone to hold my hand. There were so many memories going through my mind. Rachel had come crashing into my life one day, and since the first time that she had walked through this front door we had hardly spent a day apart. It was almost four years to the day.

This was the room where Alex was born, at half-past seven on a Friday morning a few weeks short of three years before, after three and a half days of labour that stopped and started. It had been the hottest week of the summer. One of those rare London summers where the heat and the haze held in by buildings and pollution builds up, day by day, week by week. The summer seemed already to have gone on for months. The days were breathless. Not enough air had moved to disturb a single leaf on the trees in front of the window.

We had gone through a long-drawn-out process to ensure that our baby was born at home. Even so, we were aware before Rachel went into labour that, if things went wrong, she might well end up in hospital for the delivery. But we were both hopeful and, because of all that we had read and all that we had heard in the months before, we were confident, too.

Rachel was terrified of hospitals and I felt much the same. Strangely enough, this had been one of the first things that we had talked about on the day we met. We had both been inspired by documentaries showing film of women giving birth in water-tanks. We had both laughed about how corny it all sounded. But it seemed to beat the hell out of the alternatives. Both of us had agreed that if a baby could be born in a peaceful environment with soft lights and music playing and the mother free to move and take any position she felt comfortable with, and if things were safe for both the mother and baby, how could anyone prefer to give birth in a scrubbed white sterile room, flat on their back, with bright lights shining in their faces and strangers in masks constantly coming and going?

People had often said to us since, when the subject came up, that they would be scared by the idea of being at home to give birth, and that they would feel safer in hospital knowing that they were being taken care of, with doctors and equipment to help if things went wrong. It was exactly all those doctors and equipment that Rachel would have been scared of. For her there was no contest.

If the last part was planned, however, the first part certainly hadn't been. Rachel's pregnancy was due to a pill failure when we had been together for only a few months. But even in that short time it was clear to both of us that this was the 'real thing'. We were both absolutely certain that we were going to spend the rest of our lives together. Finding out that Rachel was pregnant, however, was still a huge shock. We weren't ready for that. Rachel was only just twenty, and our lives were far from stable financially, and Rachel hadn't finished her degree. It wasn't good news.

Together we went for Rachel to have a proper test, although the predictor kit she had got from the chemist came up positive every time.

I had to wait outside the room while Rachel went through the procedure and talked with the nurse in charge. We had felt like a couple up until this moment but now things had changed completely. I was on the outside in more than just a physical sense. Things had gone very black. There was suddenly a distance between us. Rachel was going through a lot of silent reflection. This wasn't happening to my body. I felt like I was just a passenger. It wasn't my life and career that was going to be turned upside down. I wasn't going to be the one who was absolutely obliged to look after this child for the next twenty-odd years.

Not that I had any intention of deserting her. But, whatever her decision might or might not have been, we were still in a very serious situation. I could see that from her point of view she hardly knew me. I had the intuition that what Rachel felt was that, fine, we had passed a wonderful moment together but it was too good to last. And now the chips were down I was going to use this as an excuse to bow out. She felt that she didn't really deserve to be that happy for long. It had been too good to last.

But I loved her more than ever. And I was in complete turmoil because I felt completely useless. I couldn't prove my feelings to her, and saying the words out loud just rang hollow in my ears.

The test had come out positive. There was no denying it. The journey back on the train was bleak. It was drizzling and grey and cold outside. I felt, from the way that she was talking and the way that she looked, that she had already made her decision. I was trying to put both sides of the argument but I felt that I didn't really have the right to try and influence her against that decision if she was really sure. I didn't have the right to screw her life up for her. In reality there was only one practical solution. We weren't ready to have children, but the whole idea of Rachel having to go through an abortion was grim. The short time we had shared together up until now had been filled with laughter and love and happiness. Now we had come down to earth with a crash.

Within a few days it was definite. I phoned a close friend with the idea of asking him to lend us the money until we could pay him back. When he answered the phone I broke the news to him that Rachel was pregnant.

'Congratulations!' he said.

I was completely thrown. There was no trace of irony in his voice.

He was genuinely happy to hear the news. This was the last thing I expected to hear him say and my emotions were so confused that I could hardly speak. Eventually I managed to explain to him that we had decided not to go through with the pregnancy. That, when we weighed things up, the most sensible thing to do was to have an abortion.

He was surprised. 'Why would you want to do that?' he asked. It was clear that he saw us, together, as something that was going to last. He couldn't understand why we didn't see what a good thing this was for both of us. But he said that we were obviously both upset and suggested that maybe we ought to think things through one more time before we finally committed ourselves. He was trying to say that we didn't have to rush into anything we might regret later.

As the conversation continued I realized that all our reasons for not having the baby were very practical and calculated, but left only feelings of gloom and depression. Every time we dared voice the possibility of keeping the baby I felt my heart leap. And I could see a gleam in Rachel's eyes which told me that hers did the same. But we both quickly quashed our feelings and chastised ourselves for having our heads in the clouds. We told ourselves that we were being irresponsible.

But we knew that we were going to have children together one day. And suddenly I felt sure that we should go in the direction that made our hearts leap. We really loved each other. We would find a way to overcome our problems. For surely it was going through difficulties that brought people together. While still talking on the phone I came to a decision for myself. I wanted this baby, for us, if it was at all possible. That's how *I* really felt. And the moment I reached this realization I felt a huge sense of relief. A stupid grin broke out on my face.

I still knew that I hadn't the right to convince Rachel to change her mind. But somehow I knew that she really wouldn't need that much convincing.

As I put the phone down I did my best to hide my grin. My mood had changed from complete depression to mad elation in the course of only a few minutes. But I was well aware that Rachel was as depressed as she had been when I had picked up the phone. And that the decision to go through with things was still hers and not mine. I had to be very careful in what I said.

'Well?' she said.

'What if we have the baby?' I said.

'We can't!' she exclaimed, sadly, her face full of anguish.

'They don't cost much to feed,' I said. It was the first argument that came into my head, and probably the most feeble. 'And they're easy to carry around!' I added, which didn't sound any more convincing. I could no longer hide my grin. 'And every time we think about you having an abortion the future just seems totally grim. But every time we think about having the baby I can only see us doing things full of joy and fun.' Her face was still filled with anguish. 'I know it's crazy!' I added.

'It's completely mad,' she said. But, in spite of the anguish, the trace of a smile appeared on her face for the first time in what seemed like years.

In her heart of hearts Rachel really did want to keep the baby but her head was trying to stop her jumping after a foolish and irresponsible dream. It hadn't taken much to undermine the conviction either of us had in our original decision. Just one phrase from a friend.

But now that we dared to look at the possibility of having the baby for the first time instead of treating the situation as a disaster, the floodgates of imagination were thrown wide open. Suddenly we could think of a thousand reasons why we *should* have it. We were going to have children anyway, so what if it wasn't exactly when we would have planned it? What if something happened which meant that neither of us could have children again and we let this chance go by? If it was breast-fed then it would cost hardly anything to feed for ages; it wouldn't take up any space in the beginning; we would soon sell the flat and then we would have a bit more money . . .

On and on we went. And with each reason that one of us would come up with the gloom and anguish all around us lifted that much more. Soon we were laughing like fools at the idea of us having a baby around. It seemed so hilarious, the thought of carrying a bag around with a living, breathing, pudgy little mixture of the two of us inside. We were both mad. It was a mad, crazy adventure we were about to launch ourselves into together.

But the decision was made – and wouldn't be changed again. And with it the love was back. We were together again.

The only real difficulty left was to find a way to tell Rachel's parents.

From that moment on we threw ourselves into the adventure. Up until then Rachel had always had a haughty, condescending attitude to babies in general. They were smelly, noisy and irritating. But that had been other people's babies, of course. I remembered my two much younger brothers as babies and how I had been amazed by the amount of intelligence coming out of those crying little helpless bundles. I had found them fascinating and had at least handled a bottle and helped change a nappy. Now Rachel was reading with a vengeance everything that we could get our hands on about having babies, about feeding babies, about dressing babies, about carrying babies around and every article was handed on or discussed with me.

The first step was to organize having the baby in the first place. And because Rachel was still sure – in spite of the fact that this was now a reality and not a far-off dream for the future – that she wanted to have the baby at home, we set about finding a way to bring it about.

Our enthusiasm met with nothing but difficulties. Professional reactions ranged from uninspiring to downright obstructive. We went to see local GPs and members of the hospital service. None of them were prepared to even consider the possibility of a first baby being delivered at home. We discovered that there were no medical reasons why a woman in good physical condition, who had no hereditary problems of childbirth in her family, whose pregnancy went smoothly and whose baby presented itself well for the delivery should not have her baby at home. But it appeared that they were going to make sure there would be some mundane practical reasons why it would not happen.

We even discovered that it was our right to have our baby at home if we so wished, and that the authorities were obliged to provide us with a service. But the idea of some sulky midwife or doctor attending the birth of our child virtually against their will was not the most appealing of prospects.

Eventually we tracked down the only GPs in the area who were willing to take on a home birth, but both of them would be away when ours was due. We were out of luck.

After exhausting all the possibilities in our local area we heard of a natural birth centre on the other side of London. The woman who ran the place was a midwife herself. She had plenty to tell us about how she saw women through pregnancy, exercise classes she ran for them and how she helped prepare them for giving birth. She even hired out water-tanks, which was something we were still seriously considering.

She did warn us, however, that every woman had a different idea of what she felt comfortable with. What had seemed a great idea months before often changed at the last minute. It was such a relief to find someone so experienced and positive who could assure us that we were not being totally impractical. Which was all wonderful, except for one thing: we lived too far away to benefit from any of this.

However, she was able to give us the details of an independent midwife who lived very near to us.

A certain weariness about the whole procedure had begun to set in. We seemed to be chasing the elusive pot of gold at the end of the rainbow. But, after a phone call to this latest contact we appeared to be getting much warmer. An appointment was made.

The independent midwife lived only a wet bus ride away. Yes, she did work in the local area. No, it didn't matter that this was Rachel's first baby, as long as there were no obvious medical problems. No, she wouldn't be on holiday when the baby was due. And no, she wasn't grim and uninspiring. Just the opposite.

When we brought up the subject of water-tanks she said that she had delivered babies this way on occasion and that the parents in question had hired the tank themselves. She said that sometimes, however, a labour could start in the tank and finish anywhere else in the house. There was also the chance of the weight of the tank, once filled with water, sending it crashing through the floorboards. She told us that in the majority of cases women gave birth either on all fours or squatting, where gravity naturally came into play to help the baby out. And she said that, if Rachel really felt that she wanted to be in water when the moment came, a bath could serve equally well.

The midwife worked with a partner and between them they took care of all the antenatal tests. Although they worked privately themselves they still worked hand in hand with the local health authority and were connected to a flying team of obstetricians who could be summoned in case of emergency. The mother could quickly be transferred to hospital if there were major complications. We had to pay, of course. But the fee seemed very reasonable when compared to the amount of care involved. So we happily paid a deposit and had nine months to work out how we were going to find the rest of the money.

When Rachel was just over two months pregnant, in the course of the first routine antenatal check-up and with hardly a bump showing, one of the midwives was able to find the baby's heartbeat with a hand-held microphone. It fluttered like a bird and was beating incredibly fast. I was amazed. There really *was* something alive in there.

We felt in safe hands and could relax a little knowing that the arrangements had been taken care of. For Rachel to know that we would only be seeing two people all the way through her pregnancy, right up to and including the birth itself, was very reassuring. The knowledge brought a feeling of intimacy and privacy which we couldn't imagine experiencing any other way.

Telling Rachel's parents that she was pregnant wasn't easy. At first they were extremely disappointed. They had brought Rachel up to be strong and independent. She had done well at school and had been working through a degree in English and History. They knew how much she was capable of. They didn't want to see her tied to a kitchen sink at twenty years old, barefoot and pregnant.

The fact was, however, that just before we had found out that Rachel was pregnant she had let her studies drop. It was nothing to do with her relationship with me; it was more because she had lost motivation. She wasn't at all sure of what she wanted to do and could no longer see the point of going through the motions. She felt that she was wasting her time. Dropping her studies had been very difficult for her and she had been through much heart-searching before coming to her decision.

Rachel had become interested in the idea of getting involved in children's television, either in the making of or the presentation of pro-grammes. This had come about after hours and hours of talking and after throwing around almost every idea possible. But once mentioned the idea seemed to fit the bill. The world being as superficial as it is, I knew that her striking looks and the fact that she spoke well meant that she would have no difficulty in opening the doors. After that she was intelligent enough to make the most of the right opportunities.

But although Rachel seemed to exude confidence from every pore, when it came down to it she wasn't very confident at all. She doubted herself and her abilities to an enormous extent. Nevertheless, she set about researching how to get into television. She had been in the middle of preparing a CV, together with some pictures and an audio-tape of her speaking and had drawn up a list of addresses to contact when we discovered she was pregnant.

Chapter Nine

RACHEL'S PREGNANCY PASSED easily. She suffered from only a little morning sickness in the beginning and seemed to blossom from then on. She had been swimming with her mother only the day before she went into labour. She looked healthy and well, and to my eyes she became more beautiful each day.

We still hadn't been able to sell the flat, though we had come very close. The property market had gone into a slump at the end of the previous year but, because I had done all the renovations myself, we could afford to drop the price and still come out with a profit. One person had been extremely keen and was going to make an offer, but the next day he was told by his employers that he was being transferred to Scotland! Several others came equally close but it felt like we just weren't supposed to move right then. Financially we had to hang on tight until we could get rid of the place.

I had started work as a dispatch rider a couple of months before Alex was due. I hoped that it would only be for a short while: we had the flat on the market with all the agents in the area. Surely it wouldn't be that long until it sold. We were dropping the price all the time. I had started work in spring and hoped to be finished before winter came, at the latest.

The baby was due on a Monday, but there was no sign that he wanted to keep the appointment. By that Monday evening Rachel's impatience was beginning to show. She knelt down before the little chest of drawers she had lovingly filled with tiny clothes and talked to her tummy. 'It's all ready for you!' she implored. 'All we need is you to come out and take a look.'

On the Wednesday evening Rachel's contractions started. When she spoke to our midwife on the phone she was still able to laugh. The midwife told her, 'Women in labour don't laugh.' I had learnt by then that Rachel met almost every event, even the most painful, with a smile. The more painful the event, the more ironic the smile.

The midwife had said that she would come and examine Rachel anyway and was soon at the door. Within a few short moments she was able to confirm that Rachel *was* in labour and that things were already fairly advanced.

I couldn't really quite believe that this thing was going to come out of Rachel's belly. For sure, there was something in there. I had heard its heartbeat and felt its kicks, and even on one occasion watched it turn sideways across Rachel's stomach and push one way with its head and the other way with its feet. This had stretched her skin as tight as a drum across the baby's body and we had been able to make out a shoulder and elbow and bottom and knee. We could make out the profile of its face as well and could almost see the features. It was really weird, just like an alien trying to get out. We could touch it, see most of it, and feel its kicks. But we didn't know its face, and we didn't know its sex. All of which made us feel even more like we were awaiting the arrival of an alien being.

Exciting though it was to see so much of this unborn child, its position was agony for Rachel. It was pushing with all its strength in opposite directions. She wanted me to try and make it turn round. I was hesitant at first: I thought it might be dangerous. But Rachel was in pain – I had to do something to ease her discomfort. I cupped one hand round where the baby's head was protruding, and the other round where its feet were sticking out, and applied a little gentle pressure. It felt so strange. I was holding our baby, and it hadn't even been born. It was reacting to my touch. Now it was the baby's turn to feel uncomfortable from the pressure I was applying on its head and, after thirty seconds or so of my gentle pushing, everything slid back to where it had been before.

Rachel sighed with relief. I felt relieved myself that I had done no obvious harm. It had been really easy to do but the effects on Rachel were dramatic. Where the whole of her front had been taut and bulging out to the sides, now the bulge protruded straight out in front again. Everything was back in its natural streamlined shape. Now there seemed to be room for everything again. And room for Rachel too.

This happened again, but only on a handful of occasions. Each time was equally dramatic and exciting to see. The baby was so alive. We couldn't fail to see just how active it was, and how much it was growing. Each time we could nearly make out its face. Almost, but not quite. We were aching with curiosity to finally know what this person, who was already so much a part of our lives, actually looked like. But each time was as uncomfortable for Rachel. There was only so long she could stand it, before she would want me to turn the baby back the right way.

It was a privilege to be able to help. As a man you don't get to carry the baby and sometimes I felt completely useless and superfluous. I was filled with wonder at the female reproductive machine. It is as close to magic as you can get, to produce another human being out of thin air. For all of those nine months the baby sits there wanting for nothing, completely happy and protected in its own personal flotation tank, getting everything it needs in order to grow healthy and strong. The mother provides everything. In relation to all of that, my fetching the odd pillow here and there, cooking the odd meal and even paying the bills at the end of the month didn't seem much of an achievement.

But here I was, able to hold the baby in my hands and interact with it, because it was responding to my touch, and it would have been impossible for the mother herself to do this: I'm sure that if I wasn't there she would have found a way to manage things but I was no less pleased with my small role.

But on this Wednesday evening I wasn't quite able to believe that, in a matter of hours or minutes, I was actually going to hold this thing. Rachel's contractions came regularly, less than ten minutes apart, and the minutes turned into hours. 'I'm going to be a daddy tonight!' I thought to myself. Or rather, I tried to convince myself that I would. I still couldn't believe it even though faced with the reality of Rachel's enormous belly. I didn't dare say anything to Rachel. She had other things to worry about, and was liable to get irritated. Even her sense of humour had its limits.

After about three hours or so the contractions stopped. And that was it for the night. The midwife went home and at last we got to sleep. I felt disappointed that things had stopped so abruptly. I wasn't going to see the baby tonight after all. But at the same time I couldn't help feeling relieved. I wasn't ready to be a father yet! The dream was suddenly about to become a reality and my head was floating just that little bit in limbo. I didn't know what to expect. It was true that I was slightly anxious that something might go wrong. But that was only a part of it. I was only a little bit frightened. I had tremendous faith in the midwife after all the classes we had been to, and after talking to other parents who had had babies delivered at home by her.

Rachel's contractions woke us up on Thursday morning. This time they didn't last for long. They stopped and started through the day but they weren't of the same intensity as the day before.

Late in the afternoon they started to build up again. This time when the midwife came back she was back to stay.

I had never seen a woman in labour before. I had no idea how physically overwhelming the process could be. The pain involved is part of folklore and something you hear talked about often. I knew that it could be painful for Rachel too, and that there would be very little that I could do about it, apart from provide moral support. But being aware of what was likely to happen was one thing. Witnessing it was another.

I was impressed by how calm she was. I remember thinking that, if it was me, I would have been terrified by the thought of what my body was about to go through, and been reduced to a gibbering wreck. Rachel told me afterwards that she was so taken up with getting through the next contraction that it never occurred to her to think about it that way at all.

The contractions became intense as afternoon turned to evening. Rachel was struggling to handle the pain. She discovered that the most comfortable position was on all fours on a mattress on the floor, with a huge pillow underneath her for support. She would look into my eyes for the whole time a contraction lasted and I would remind her to pant to ease the pain a little. She was completely unable to talk and squeezed my hand till the circulation stopped. All the while she was staring into my eyes, her own wide like a wild animal's, while she panted rapidly.

The contractions lasted a couple of minutes each, with only a few minutes of relief in between for her to try and recover in time for the next one. We went on in this rhythm for what seemed like, and what turned out to be, hours at a time. At first Rachel tried to lie down and rest a little before the next contraction hit but after a while she stopped bothering. She said that it was hardly worth the effort for so little rest, so she just stayed in the same hunched position. Looking upon it as a purely athletic ordeal I could see how a mother might become completely exhausted if this went on long enough. So I tried to gently push her over on to her side and insist that she rest each time. I told her that even a little rest was better than no rest at all and that I thought she should try and conserve every little bit of energy she could. Then, each time she felt a contraction arriving, I helped her back on to her knees and on to her pillow.

Regularly throughout the evening the midwife examined Rachel to check on how much she was dilating. Apparently things were progressing well, but slowly. The midwife spent as much time as she could lying down in another room. She was conserving her strength too. She said there was still no telling how long things were going to take. There was always a chance that it could all slow down, or even stop completely. She advised us to try and take it as easy as we could, when we could.

After a block of a couple of hours the contractions eased away. Those two hours had been taken up in intense periods of activity which lasted only a few minutes at a time. And each few minutes seemed like hours in itself. It had already been a long night.

After half an hour or so things started up again. They followed exactly the same pattern for another couple of hours, before fading away once again. In between, Rachel could talk and smile and act like normal. The midwife confirmed that Rachel was dilating more and more. I could feel the excitement rise inside me. It wouldn't be long before this 'thing' would be tumbling out into view.

Rachel had prepared some of her favourite music beforehand. But now that things had really started this was the last thing in the world that she wanted. She told me afterwards, and it was pretty clear at the time, that absolutely anything that stopped her concentrating on her breathing and looking into my eyes was a huge distraction and irritation. She had to have the lights down low and her pillow and mattress, have me there and know that the midwife was there, and that was it. The odd time when a contraction had hit her before she had managed to get on to all fours and when she had been stuck on her back for its duration, the pain was much more severe and difficult to handle. Then she had found it almost impossible to get her breathing back under control.

But there came a moment, when we were into our third period of activity, and Rachel was panting her way through yet another contraction after what had seemed like already hundreds and hundreds, that I felt myself begin to panic. Apparently things were progressing, but there was still no sign of the baby. How long could she keep this up?

Suddenly I was frightened. This had been going on for too long. I was really feeling for her. Her face was once again wracked with effort, and her eyes were wide as she grimaced in pain. She was really going through it. The whole thing was so physically overwhelming. Christ, I thought to myself, is it always as hard as this? I began to ask myself if I should be starting to get worried now. Taking my eyes from Rachel's for a split second I glanced over to the midwife. She was calmly sitting over by the wall reading a book!

Meanwhile, in the split second that I looked away, Rachel had reached up with a hand and yanked my head back to where she could look into my eyes again.

The midwife's reaction, or rather her lack of reaction, was extremely reassuring. In that one glance her body language alone had told me that there was nothing to be worried about. She clearly had more confidence in Rachel's physical resistance than I did. Her experience told her more about what Rachel was capable of than I could possibly have known.

I wondered all the time how I would handle this if it was me in her place. But I had nothing whatever to compare it with. I had never been through pain like this.

Then, between contractions, Rachel suddenly began to shake violently. She wanted me to hold her still because she couldn't do anything to control herself. Even using all of the weight of my body and all of my strength I was only just able to pin her down. The strength of her shaking was lifting me up in the air as well. I was staggered. I had flashes of some evangelical religious service going through my head where people go into trances and spasms and pass out on the floor. It was the only thing I could compare it to.

This happened another two or three times and lasted for between five and ten minutes each time. I had to use all of my weight and strength to stop Rachel being jerked all over the room. I waited for the shaking to ease enough for me to be able to leave Rachel for a few seconds and went to find the midwife to tell her what was happening. I asked her if this was 'normal'. She was completely unperturbed. 'There's a lot of energy to be given off when two bodies are in the act of separating from what was one,' she said.

It seemed obvious once she had said it. And it made me think once again about how almost 'inhuman' the whole process of childbirth was. Here was this parasite, which had grown from something invisible to the naked eye, sitting inside Rachel's body. It had been feeding off her for all these months and had now grown into this huge lump. Now it was preparing to rip itself apart from its host, push itself out of her body and present itself as an independent intelligent, living creature in its own right. And if it was female it would be able, in time, to go through the whole process again itself. Only this time *she* would be the host and yet another parasite could grow inside of her, and eventually it would rip itself apart and push itself out and present itself in turn as another independent, intelligent, living creature in its own right . . . And if it too was female it could . . . I was beginning to get vertigo, infinity sickness. I tried to clear my head and hurried back to Rachel.

This third period came to its conclusion and the contractions eased off once again. Rachel was very calm and looked completely concentrated on what her body was doing. I was amazed and was filled with respect for her. This was really something else. I had never experienced anything so draining or so intense. There was just us, the night outside the window, a sparsely furnished room and the low light. There was something so primordial about what was happening that we could have been almost anyone, anywhere, at any time. An Indian tepee, an igloo, an African hut, or a pagan one with both of us painted blue.

It now seemed like that we had been in this room breathing together and joined almost as one person for years and years. *Almost* as one person. I was breathing with her and my eyes were locked into hers and I was being swept along by the rhythm. But *I* wasn't feeling any pain. All I could see was the dilation of her pupils and the blue of her eyes. If my gaze wandered for a second she would yank my face back round. The fact that I couldn't share the pain with her was beginning to bother me. I was feeling frustrated and guilty at the same time.

Rachel wasn't complaining in the slightest. I knew with her that this wasn't because she was too proud to or that she was trying to show how tough she was. She just wasn't thinking that way. She was taking every second as it came. I was the one who was suffering with impatience. First, I wanted her out of pain and, secondly, I wanted to see this baby. But as the time went on, and my concern for Rachel grew, the latter became less and less important to me.

Rachel decided that she wanted a bath. She thought it might be refreshing and might make her feel at least a little bit better. I went to run the water and then came back to take her to the bathroom. I helped her into the bath. The midwife came to keep an eye on how things were progressing. 'No enough water!' shouted Rachel, and lashed out with her arm. She caught me in the chest and the blow sent me halfway up the bathroom wall. She had caught me unawares; I was badly winded.

The strength of the blow made me think of the stories you read of the superhuman strength women find in moments of crisis. Of a mother who picks up the front of a car to rescue her trapped child underneath.

I ran more water. Rachel couldn't get comfortable and was struggling with what was going on inside her huge bump. Then she managed to settle for a few moments. 'Too hot!' she shouted, and lashed out her arm again. Even though I saw this one coming I didn't quite believe it could be anywhere near as strong as the first, which was surely only a freak. I was wrong and was nearly knocked off my feet for the second time.

The cold water seemed to calm her. Then: 'Too cold!'

I should have known better, but I got caught anyway. I think I was probably finding some masochistic relief in the fact that I was at last feeling some sort of pain, no matter how little.

I used to tease Rachel regularly about how she had 'beaten' me during her labour. She had no idea afterwards of how hard she had hit me. But the evidence was undeniable: I had the bruises to show.

Rachel wasn't in the bath for long. She was stuck on her back in there and couldn't breathe well. She felt herself being crushed by the baby. I helped her back to the other room, and her mattress and cushion.

It was already past midnight and another set of contractions started, which were as intense as any that evening. We were back into the rhythm and I was pushing Rachel over to rest between them. But, suddenly, something snapped in my head. I had lost it. I had seriously had enough. I managed not to let anything show but my mood had completely changed. I was boiling with anger for this unborn child.

I knew that women die in childbirth. It was rare, but it did happen. For a moment the thought totally obsessed me. I didn't want to lose her. I just wanted her to be all right. I hated the baby. I didn't care about it at all. I looked at Rachel, panting in front of me, grimacing with the effort of controlling the pain, and I just wanted it all to stop.

It was more than I could bear to watch. I wanted it to be me who was in pain, not her. I had to fight my emotions hard so as not to let anything show. Because I knew that, whatever I might have wanted or wished for, there was no getting off the train until we had reached our destination. I wasn't going to do Rachel any good if I panicked. She was relying on me, and I knew Rachel well enough to know that if I let her down now things would be much harder for her. I forced my mind back under control.

Nevertheless, when this set of contractions came to a stop in the early hours of the morning, I found myself completely wiped out. The midwife was with us the whole time now, and, of all things, Rachel had found that the toilet seat was the most comfortable place on earth. I was stretched out on the hall floor, drained of all energy.

Rachel was very nearly fully-dilated and the midwife could feel the top of the baby's head. This finally brought a smile to my face. But I just lay there, completely inert. I felt I should be doing something, or giving some encouragement, but I couldn't bring myself to move. I had peaked too soon. For some reason I had got it into my head that I would see this baby before midnight. At three o'clock in the morning there were still just us three adults knocking around. On the face of things nothing had changed. Rachel was stuck on the toilet, I was flat out on the floor and the three of us were talking as if nothing else was going on at all. For the moment there were no more contractions.

In fact, that was the end of the contractions as we had known them. Rachel was comfortable where she was. The midwife told me not to worry, lots of babies had been born on the toilet. The seat took all the weight and took the strain off the perineum at the same time. We had talked about having a baby born in water but this was ridiculous. But if Rachel was comfortable, that was all that mattered.

The next couple of hours are fuzzy in my head. I don't think much

134

happened. I followed Rachel around the flat in her endless struggle to get comfortable. She returned to the toilet several times before settling in the front room with her pillow and mattress again.

And then the midwife went to fetch her bag of equipment from where she had discreetly stored it out of sight. The sun was coming up, its first rays lightening the drawn curtains.

Rachel was on all fours. I squatted in front of her, half of me trying to give her the words she needed to hear and the other half looking down her back to try and see what was happening at the other end. The midwife was checking to see that everything was presenting itself right when Rachel's waters broke into her face.

Soon the midwife was telling her not to push, but to let the baby come out slowly to keep any tearing to a minimum. I couldn't see all of what was happening. Rachel was panting again and needed to look into my eyes, so I did my best to focus on her while I was itching to see what was happening at the other end. But I could hear. I could hear the baby murmuring.

'Don't cry, little baby,' said the midwife. The baby's head was halfway out and still being squeezed, but here it was *murmuring*. In fact there was only one word for it: it was *singing*! It sounded just like one of the cute creatures in *Gremlins* before it turned into a little monster.

It went quiet, and then murmured again, just as peacefully. Rachel's face was grim with effort. But she could hear too and her grimace was suddenly a mixture of effort and joy. Effort because she still had to concentrate on not pushing. She said afterwards that, at that moment, she just wanted to heave it out and have done with it. She must have felt so good to know that what she was carrying inside her was really alive. And that this was all nearly over.

Soon the baby's head was out and only the shoulders were left. Rachel grimaced and groaned with pain. The joy had temporarily disappeared. The shoulders were harder for her than the head. I could hear the baby slithering and slipping. And then it was out!

The tears were running down my face. This was the best moment of my life.

I lifted my head and, over the top of Rachel's head I was greeted with the sight of a healthy baby boy. But I didn't breathe a word. It looked absolutely enormous. Rachel, from being on all fours, had to lift a leg up over the umbilical cord as she turned herself round.

Then she could finally see that 'it' was a 'he'. Her face exploded in happiness and joy.

Even though the room was warm and there wasn't the slightest draught the midwife had heated an electric pad and covered it with a blanket to catch the baby in. She had always said that she 'caught' babies, she didn't deliver them.

The first thing she did after catching this one, and wrapping him in the pre-heated blanket, was to hand him to his mother.

Rachel said that he looked like a long, skinny rabbit. It was hard to believe that such a big thing had been packed away inside her belly. We could see just how cramped he must have been all these last few weeks. No wonder he had wanted to stretch his legs from time to time. And no wonder he had finally had enough and had wanted to get out of there.

We all agreed there was no mistaking that he was a boy. The thing that struck me most, after how big he was, were the colours. The baby was purple and the umbilical cord was high-tech, matt grey and blue. They were the brand new, spotless colours of a newly opened toy. But the crinkled face of this new toy was the wrinkled face of the world's oldest man, moulded in the softest, most perfect skin I had ever seen. He looked absolutely ancient, and undeniably newborn, all at the same time.

It was a face that demanded respect. It was old and calm and wise. Right then and there the idea that you don't own your children was an undeniable truth. This person had come from somewhere that went further back than the last nine months.

His eyes were scrunched up, but moved under their lids, every now and then opening just the slightest crack and then closing again. This dimly lit room must have been unbearably bright compared to where he had come from. From time to time he would let out that same murmur, but he remained completely calm. There was not the least anxiety in the slightest of his movements.

He smelt so fresh. In the midst of the blood and mucus that came with him this wonderful smell that was so fresh and so clean was completely unexpected. The midwife encouraged Rachel to put him to her breast. He clamped on immediately and began feeding with a vigour and force which was out of all proportion to his tiny size. Suddenly he wasn't the slightest bit delicate.

What was going on went against nearly every image I had ever received of childbirth. Scenes of a stress-filled room, with fear and anxiety on every face, and then an infant being yanked out into the world before being slapped until it screamed, could not have been further away. From that moment on, any time a childbirth scene came on the TV which followed these traditional lines, Rachel and I practically had to turn it off. It distressed us deeply. We knew from our own experience that only in an emergency did things have to be that way.

Almost at once Rachel had the phone in her hand to give her parents the news. Then the midwife clamped the cord and gave me the honour of cutting it. Rachel had warned me, when we had talked about this before, that she wanted me to cut it 'right'. She didn't want a child with a sticky-out belly button. It was only when the time came to do it that we realized that where I cut the cord made no difference whatsoever to how his belly button would look afterwards. The midwife simply tied up the short length of cord that was left, taped it to his belly and told us not to worry if it smelt bad in a few days. It was going to rot and fall off of its own accord. What was left was a matter of luck. However, the midwife reassured Rachel that it was very unlikely that his would be a sticky-out belly button. She looked relieved to hear it.

The delivery wasn't over yet, much to my ignorant surprise. The midwife said that the action of the baby feeding would help to stimulate the contractions again in order to deliver the placenta. Which was, of course, still inside Rachel. When the deflated bag, which had been home to the baby, was finally expelled a little later the midwife advised that we keep it in the fridge for a few days. She said that sometimes a mother had the urge to eat some. I could see that Rachel found the idea sickening. Being vegetarian, I couldn't imagine her ever asking me to make her a placenta sandwich. But I went to find a saucepan and put it in the fridge anyway, just in case. No matter how unlikely it seemed, if she suddenly woke up in the night and felt the urge to eat some, and I had thrown it away, there would be hell to pay.

Then the midwife helped put Rachel and the baby in the bath. I supported him with my hands and floated him in the water. Not surprisingly, after spending the last nine months in the stuff, he looked perfectly at ease. The midwife showed us how to get the baby dry with a hair-dryer, which avoided us having to rub his skin and was more efficient than a towel. He seemed to take real pleasure in the heat and curled up his fingers and toes in appreciation. We had already put oil on his skin to stop him from drying out and now, purple and red, he looked like a cooked chicken.

She warned us that Rachel might still lose some 'clots', which could be as large as a fist or more. This was perfectly normal, she said. They would have been part of where the placenta was attached to the uterus. Soon after Rachel and the baby, still unnamed, were safely tucked up in bed.

Just before the midwife left, Rachel returned from the toilet complaining that she was feeling faint. She walked gingerly into the room and moved towards the bed. There was a sound like a 'sschlopp' and what looked like a piece of liver the size of a dinner plate dropped to the floor.

'No wonder you were feeling faint,' said the midwife.

I cleaned the blood clot up. It was strange to be throwing away what had just been a living part of someone's body. Did I throw it in the bin or flush it down the toilet? The repercussions of throwing it in the bin and the bag breaking open at some poor dustman's feet bothered me for a minute. But flushing it down the toilet seemed such an ignoble end for something that had done such a magnificent job. In the end, regretfully, I threw it in the bin.

We never did get the stain out of the carpet completely. Afterwards we could always see a faint trace. It was a permanent reminder of the morning that Alex was born.

Chapter Ten

OUR MIDWIFE VISITED regularly and when her official care came to an end she became a friend of the family. Tonight, on the night of our return without Rachel, she was at the flat. She had brought her six-year-old son. Alex got on well with him, in spite of the age difference and the fact that her son towered above him like a giant.

Our midwife also ran baby massage classes, and thought that Alex could do with a massage. She had brought some oil and began to explain how I should go about it. Nothing was going to make much improvement to Alex's state of mind, but anything that helped relieve even the slightest part of the tension he was carrying would be a good idea. We went into another room to give it a try. Her son immediately decided that he wanted one too and began playing up until he got his way.

Alex couldn't keep still long enough for me to do anything much. Keeping still was completely against his nature and the moment I put a hand on him he dissolved into giggles. The midwife's son soon got the giggles too and both of them were soon geeing each other on. After the first few minutes it was pretty hopeless, and the two boys were running round the flat playing tag and trying to throw each other to the ground.

By now they had stripped off all their clothes and were covered in oil from head to foot. It was a warm evening and there didn't seem any point in making them get dressed again straight away. Their innocent laughter and fun was so infectious that in spite of everything I couldn't help but smile. It was the kind of moment that Rachel lived for. Those moments of spontaneous high spirits when Alex's desire for fun was unquenchable.

Our two detectives had joined us. As we had already run out of chairs they were sitting on the floor talking among our friends and watching the show as the two boys continued their game of running into the room, throwing themselves on top of one another in the middle of the floor, wrestling for a while and then jumping to their feet and running back out of the room again.

I would get up from time to time and change the music. I put on all of our favourite songs one after the other. Suddenly I was grieving as badly as I had been the very first day. I couldn't hold back the tears. I didn't even try.

We were passing another stage. This was another place where some small part of my imagination could picture her still being alive. Nearly everything that we had shared had been connected with this place. I could still see the traces of the stain on the carpet. It could have happened just the day before. The minute before.

The daily pattern of our lives had been played out here until just a few short days ago. It was so hard to believe that all that was over. So hard to believe that I wasn't going to see her again. It just wasn't getting any easier at all. Now I was sitting in our own home, for the first time since Rachel had been killed, and there was no home at all.

'Home is where the heart is.' But what if your heart is somewhere that you can never be again? There was nothing here for us. No more of her left. I knew that for me, to get up every day in the same place where we had been together, and walk through rooms where we had lived through so much together, was more than I would be able to bear. I was sure I would crack up completely.

I couldn't stand the thought of seeing what had happened to us reflected in the faces of the people in the neighbourhood. With friends it was different. With the people I knew only a little it was much harder to contemplate. The intimacy that you share with friends is only natural. But to have intimacy forced upon you by a tragedy, with people you hardly know, was too painful to bear. I wasn't strong enough for that. I was too raw.

Maybe it was cowardice but I couldn't face a future like that. I would take Alex far away. I knew already that I had to be able to walk out of my own front door without anybody feeling the need to pay me any more attention than they would the next person.

But wherever we went it wouldn't be home. There were some

things that I knew I could never feel the same about again.

The music played on. Music had always been important to both of us. Memories came rushing at me with each song. I could remember how we had said that we would still be listening to such and such a record in our old age. It was so painful but I had to search out every one. I was compelled to do it. As the evening went on I went through every song that I could find that I knew she had loved. And with every one my heart broke into pieces even smaller than before.

On the face of it, it was completely masochistic but I wanted to stick my fingers in the wound where it hurt the most and twist them round. The last thing in the world I could do was forget anything about our life together or even how Rachel had died. And without drugging myself or drinking myself into a stupor I couldn't see how I ever would. Far from trying to forget I often found myself taking the opposite extreme and diving right into the pain itself. In a way I think I was using the pain as a kind of drug. Maybe it was a way of telling myself I wasn't mad, that it really had happened.

'Scotland Yard detectives at naked boys' wrestling orgy,' said one of our friends. 'I can just see it in the tabloids tomorrow.'

I couldn't help but laugh. How could I not help but laugh? How could I feel so many things at the same time?

Alex and his friend's game went on boisterously for hours. Then, suddenly, Alex had had enough. He sat down on the floor and began to grizzle. He was exhausted. I put him in our bed. It looked so big and so empty. And Alex looked so tiny in the middle.

I wondered how he would sleep. I wondered what effect sleeping here would have on him. If he woke up to find everything so familiar wouldn't he think that she would be there too? Would he be able to think that he had dreamed all the badness and that she would be there to comfort him and tell him it was all all right now?

I left the door open wide. The music was still loud but he went out like a light.

There was a song by Marvin Gaye playing in the front room. He had always been a favourite of Rachel's. I couldn't help an ironic smile. How would I stand a chance with her, if I ever got to heaven, with Marvin Gaye already there before me?

I cried for most of that evening. For the last few days I had been fairly calm but tonight I was completely at the mercy of my emotions. I just gave in to them and let the heaving and sobbing have its way.

The grieving was almost as much physical as it was mental and I had made a conscious decision not to try and 'control myself'. Not that I'm sure I could have done. I was frightened that the effort would break me. I knew how people's health could give way after such a shock and I couldn't afford not to be able to give Alex all that I could. I wanted to do everything I could to keep well and yet the best thing seemed to give up completely and let grief run its course. I felt like a drowning man who would never win his fight against the sea. I had to let it take me where it would and grab a breath whenever my head broke the surface.

I was still shocked by the violence of my own reaction. In the first two days I had been unable to stop crying for more than a few minutes at a time, but in the week since then I thought that things had calmed. I thought that things would be a little easier now. But again, this evening, I was being hit by wave after wave of emotion that was as strong as the very first. I would have to think of my own recovery in terms of months, not days or weeks. And more likely years instead of months. I wasn't feeling any better. I didn't expect to feel any better, and I couldn't see how I ever could feel any better. I was never going to forget. This would affect how I saw things for the rest of my life. How could it be otherwise?

But I suppose I somehow felt that my emotions would become less overpowering as time went on. That they must eventually ease in their intensity. So far they hadn't. But it had still been only days.

I decided just to put my head down and try and take it one minute at a time. I wasn't going to ask myself if I was feeling any better. The question was ridiculous. I would only ask myself what was the next thing to do. And with Alex, thankfully, there was plenty to do.

Maybe in a year's time it would be worth asking the question again. Certainly not before. But I was sure that, even then, the answer would still be the same.

For the moment the time just had to pass.

A police officer mounted guard for the night. One of our friends stayed with us too. I couldn't have coped with being there on my own. I needed the reassurance of their presence. I don't know exactly what I was frightened of. I certainly couldn't have stood the aggravation of journalists. We were always on the lookout but, thankfully, none turned up. I had vague fears for Alex's safety, even if logic told me we were perfectly secure.

But I needed help. I was a mess.

Once, long before, I had had a chance encounter with a stranger which had always stuck in my mind.

I was on a ferry crossing the Channel one night at the beginning of summer. I must have been eighteen or nineteen at the time. I had bought a cheap ticket, a young person's special of some kind. The boat was mostly full of students who had done the same and were heading off to the continent during their summer break.

The ship's bar was crowded and I got talking to someone next to me as I bought myself a drink. Or rather, he got talking to me. He must have been a couple of years older than me and struck me straight away as someone very outgoing and friendly. His manner was direct and full of confidence. He seemed to know what he was about.

We had exchanged what must have been only a few polite travellers' questions – where are you headed? how long are you going for? do you know of anything that shouldn't be missed along the way? – then he leant forward and in a low conspiratorial voice he began to tell me the story of his life. I was taken aback; we had literally just met. But he was on a roll – all he needed was an audience and no interruption. I had little choice but to keep my mouth shut and hear him out.

He told me that I probably knew who he was. His face meant nothing to me but I wasn't invited to reply. He carried on without pause, telling me his name, which had a familiar ring but still didn't mean anything specific to me, and then quickly added that his sister had been murdered some time before in what had become very public circumstances. He then proceeded to pour out every detail imaginable about the case so there was no doubt that I knew exactly who and what he was talking about.

He told me where it had happened; he told me when it had happened; he told me how it had happened. He told me that his father was a retired detective who had dedicated his life to solving the case and bringing the culprit to justice as the authorities had so far been unable to do so themselves.

By now I knew who he was talking about. I told him that I remembered the event and said how awful I thought it must have been. He seemed genuinely pleased that I remembered and, what was most disturbing, he actually seemed to relish telling his story and was basking in the light of his secondary 'fame'.

I recalled that this had happened at least seven or eight years before. The story was brought up to date from time to time in the media but as far as I was aware no one had so far been brought to trial.

He continued in the same conspiratorial manner, as if relating secrets of the utmost importance. Without the slightest let-up in intensity he went on to tell me how his sister's murder had ruined the rest of his childhood. And how his father's obsession with solving the case had robbed him of the attention that should have been his. He was clearly very bitter.

I really didn't know what to say. What could I say? I could only sympathize with him. I was more than a little disturbed by the weight of this outpouring from someone I had known only a few minutes. I had learnt his name from his story but he showed no interest in discovering mine. I was relieved when he finally reached the end of his story. Then, after I had expressed my sympathies, and after another few polite sentences of nothing in particular, he turned back to his friends and the session was concluded.

Although apparently still friendly towards me, we hardly exchanged another word during the crossing and he must have been in a different part of the train when the journey continued on the other side. I never saw him again.

But I never forgot him. The memory of that brief conversation came back to me from time to time as the years went past. His intensity had burnt itself into my mind. I had been so struck by the way that this young man, who on the surface had everything going for him, was obsessed to such an enormous extent by something that had happened so long before. I couldn't imagine that anything could so rule someone's life. I knew well enough myself that everyone had problems they needed to talk about at one time or another. But I had never had such an experience with a complete stranger.

His childhood had been ruined. Unnecessarily so, I felt. For even without knowing all the details, I couldn't see how his father could justify ruining the lives of the living by trying to achieve something for those who were dead and beyond caring.

But I was shocked by the undeniable pleasure this man had taken in his secondary fame. And also by the way, the moment his story was told, he could behave as if we had simply been discussing the weather. At the time I had asked myself if perhaps this was his idea of a black joke. Some kind of student's prank. But what he had said rang true. I thought I could even see a resemblance between him and the pictures I had seen published of his sister. In the end it was all too strange not to be true.

The incident came rushing back to me the moment I saw the journalists lined up outside the hospital where Alex had been taken. I would do anything to save him growing up like that young man.

I wasn't going to wear a black suit to Rachel's funeral. She wouldn't have approved. It was hard enough to believe I was going to her funeral anyway, let alone be able to work out what to wear. It was much easier to dress Alex.

The funeral wouldn't have been Rachel's idea. It would have been important for her to have her ashes placed in a beautiful spot by the few people who meant the most to her. And that was exactly what we would do later. It had already been arranged. But today was for her parents. They needed something formal to mark the passage. Rachel would have understood. She had lost a grandmother in the first months that I knew her and she had gone with her parents to the funeral. Nearly all of her family had been there. They were now spread across both sides of the Atlantic and were rarely all together. All had tales to tell of her grandmother. She sounded like a real old character and Rachel had been especially close to her. Rachel had cried all the way through the church service. Even so, she said that it had been a good way to see her grandmother off.

I hardly ever saw Rachel cry. There were times I felt she should have. But she was able to stop herself cold and drag her emotions back under control. The only time I really remember her letting it all out was when her grandmother died. She used to laugh at me because I could easily get emotional watching a film. It was quite usual for me to end up with tears in my eyes. She found it amusing that I showed my emotions so easily. Then again, she used to say that she only enjoyed going to the pictures so much with me because I did.

145

Rachel's grandmother's funeral had been for someone old, and it seemed appropriate to be choosing hymns for her. But the whole idea seemed completely out of place for someone as young as Rachel. Morbid. I respected the fact that for Rachel's parents there was no other way of doing things. But it jarred. It had absolute no connection with the girl I had known or the life we lived. I had never known her put a foot inside a church except on the occasion of her grandmother's funeral and, even though I had been to a religious school, I had no set beliefs and certainly no more time than she did for organized religion.

In many ways it went completely against our beliefs. I couldn't help feeling a sense of sham. This was like people who got married in church just because it looks pretty in the pictures afterwards. I knew Rachel would have said: 'I've lived with my beliefs and I'm prepared to die with them too.' She would be ready to face whatever might come next with the same courage that she lived her life.

Rachel was not particularly daring. I once watched her hesitate for the best part of an hour over whether or not to dive off a rock into the sea below. She had swum out and climbed up about five or six feet to the ledge that I had been diving off all morning. It was perfectly safe and the water was very deep. There were no hidden rocks to bang your head on: I had checked it out first with a mask.

But Rachel wouldn't take my word for it. And even though she could see with the mask for herself that it was safe she still wasn't totally convinced. She hesitated, and hesitated, and was up there for ages. I watched her get to her feet and put out her hands to dive. Over and again she would hover on the edge, just holding on by her toes, only to sit down again and enjoy the sun before she was ready to take another look and try again. Then she climbed to her feet once more and put her hands out again. She was so close to the edge that if the wind had blown she would probably have fallen in. But each time she couldn't quite convince herself. This went on and on. In the end she gave up completely and, face against the cliff, she climbed back down the way she had come and swam back to join us on the beach.

She found it difficult to throw herself off a cliff but she wasn't lacking in strength of character. She had a different kind of courage, one which I found far more impressive. She was able to say whatever she thought at the time to whoever it concerned, regardless of the consequences. She would look you in the eye and let you have it. I thought

146

this was amazing. Not that I always liked what she had to say. But for me it was something that required far more courage than jumping off a cliff into the sea.

She was right, of course. Everyone has the right to their own opinion. And if someone has just given you theirs, no matter who they are, then they should expect you to do the same. But I was brought up not to ask questions and not to criticize. My opinion was rarely welcome or appreciated. And even more rarely solicited. I had tried to overcome this in adult life and tried to say what I thought. And even though I was finding it easier as the years went on I would still agonize over saying anything, and then be full of self-doubt afterwards over whether I had said it right, or even if I should have said it at all.

I came to realize that Rachel went through the same process as well, but that her agonizing and her doubt lasted for much less time than mine, so confident was she that she was doing the right thing. Which was all part of a maturity she had that went beyond her years. I admired her so much because what she did was not out of arrogance. She simply tried to get things straight, and to make sure that things were fair for everyone.

The local police had set up a road block to keep the press at the end of the street. Some of them had even asked if they could be present inside the church to report the service. It was hard to understand such a request. Why would anybody want the press or television intruding on their private grief?

As the car turned the last corner and pulled up by the church I could see what looked like hundreds of reporters on the other side of the road. They had been penned into a field by the police, who were keeping them off the church grounds and out of the road. There were television cameras, photographers on step-ladders, floodlights, the lot. This was totally unbearable. People were killed every day, weren't they? Surely not every one of their families was subjected to this same intolerable attention. I tried to cover Alex's face. I wasn't going to make their life any easier. They weren't helping ours.

Rachel's coffin was unloaded from the hearse. It was tiny: it didn't look big enough for her.

We took our places near the front. The church was already full. As many of our friends were there as possible and, with all the members

147

of family as well, there seemed to be hardly a seat left.

I had told Alex that this was going to be a special party for Mummy, and a chance for everyone to say goodbye to Mummy together. He had accepted this as quite natural. He had never been to a funeral before so how could he know what to expect? But now he looked around and saw almost everyone he knew all together in one place.

Then the organist entered and sat down. The first notes of the music were unbearably loud. We were only feet from the soundpipes and the first notes, played at full volume, struck us like a physical blow. The demented wailing, more appropriate to a horror film than to anything else, shredded my exposed nerves and reverberated within me. Its crescendo was deafening – enough to strike terror into the hearts of adults, let alone children.

It was all I could do not to scoop Alex up and run out of the place. I forced myself to stay and did my best to cover his ears against the noise. Immediately he was upset. How could anyone be so incredibly thick-skinned and insensitive as to play something like that in the presence of a small child who had been through all that he had? Nobody could have been unaware of our circumstances. The media outside had made sure of that much if nothing else.

I tried to jabber nonsense to Alex to keep his mind off the wailing assault on our ears and nerves. But there was nothing I could do to prevent it from upsetting him. He was agitated and unsettled and craned round in my arms to look around the church. I watched his face. He was beginning to grizzle. If it got too much for him we would have to leave. I pulled out the toys I had brought in my pockets but it was hard work to distract him. I had assumed that the service was going to be light and that Alex's feelings and possible reactions would have been taken into consideration. I hadn't expected another ordeal.

Finally the music stopped. It was a huge relief. It was like someone had stopped banging on my head with a hammer. The silence rang in my ears. Things got much easier. Alex calmed down straight away. The church was filled with sunlight. Two butterflies danced through the sunbeams which flooded through the stained-glass windows. They settled on the columns from time to time before fluttering off once again.

Rachel's father spoke. Once again I admired his self-control. I don't know how he managed to keep going. His voice came close to breaking several times but he managed to finish speaking. I had hoped to be able to read out a poem in turn but when the time came I was in no fit state to do so. I wouldn't have got through more than a line without breaking down.

The whole process was disorientating. I didn't know where I was any more. As I looked from the little child on my knee to the wooden box containing his mother's body, nothing made sense at all. I wanted her there to help me understand.

A few of us went on for the cremation once the service was finished. Rachel was a free spirit. It was totally appropriate that her body be transformed into ashes and not buried to rot in the ground.

There was a long wait: it was a busy day for funerals. Thankfully Alex fell asleep in the car.

The weather was a metaphor for Rachel's character. Sunshine and showers. She had been a mixture of extreme moods and emotions with little room for half-measures.

When our turn eventually came I carried Alex inside, in my arms. He was still out cold. He had already sat through one funeral service. What more could another mean to him?

As Rachel's coffin began to move, the music I had chosen started to play. Ironically, it was an organ that played the first few bars of 'Let me wrap you in my warm and tender love'. The moment was completely surreal. Many times I had sung the words to get Alex to sleep while Rachel was busy in the kitchen or even sometimes as she lay quietly beside me. This couldn't possibly be happening.

Another of Rachel's favourite songs played itself out. Then the coffin was gone. All recognizable physical trace of her went with it.

All that was left was to collect her ashes.

Chapter Eleven

THE NEXT SESSION with the child psychologist was spent trying to come up with useful questions. Alex responded best to me so, once I understood what was being asked, I would put the questions to him myself.

I thought this would be the best way, rather than Alex spinning like a top as people all around the room threw questions at him. I thought it would save confusion and stress if it was only my voice that he heard. The child psychologist acted as guide, suggesting ways to put things so Alex understood as well as possible what was being asked.

She was very effective at focusing Alex's attention on the day Rachel was killed.

'I know how much you must remember your worst ever day,' she would begin. 'The police are here to catch the bad man who killed your lovely Mummy,' she continued, 'and to put him in prison where he won't be able to harm anyone else again.'

Alex watched her face as she spoke. The last sentence brought a nervous smile.

The police knew nothing of what happened in the minutes before the attack. They were still in need of even the most basic information that we could supply. So we started with the most basic questions.

'Alex, do you remember who was with you the day that Mummy was killed?' I asked.

'Molly,' he replied, playing with the pencils and toys on the table. There was a thin smile on his lips. He was extremely agitated.

'Alex, did the man who killed Mummy have a dog with him?' I asked.

150

'No.' He hardly looked up from his drawing.

'Did the man who killed Mummy have a bike?'

'No.'

'Was the man who killed Mummy carrying anything?'

'A bag.'

'Alex, do you remember what colour the bag was?'

'Black.'

'What was in the bag?'

'A knife.'

I put many questions to him that morning. Questions which were to be repeated over and over again during the following weeks, mostly by me but on occasion also by the others present. Sometimes by the child psychologist, or by the detectives, or even by Rachel's parents.

In the first few sessions it was often only possible for Alex to concentrate his mind for long enough to answer a handful of the questions that were put to him. Then he would reach the limits of his patience and he simply wouldn't answer any more. He would get on with playing in earnest instead.

The sessions generally lasted for little more than an hour. But much of that time was taken up with playing, serving refreshments, going to the toilet, doing the tour of the house and the garden and all the other normal three-year-old activity.

All of the adults showed great patience and gentleness towards him and it was clear to all present when, in the course of the session, his mind was totally fixed on the day in question. You could almost see the film running back before his eyes.

I tried to avoid giving Alex questions that he could reply to with a 'yes/no' answer. His answers would often give a little more than was demanded by the question itself. This confirmed that he had not only understood the question but that he could remember the detail of events as well.

Once while the child psychologist was talking to him, Alex began stabbing the paper he had been drawing on with a pencil. His movements were manic and there was a glazed look in his eyes. It was terrifying. I asked him to calm down but he turned to me and stabbed the pencil at my face. I told him to stop, which at last he did. But the pieces of paper he had been drawing on were covered with dots, the whole of their surface deeply indented by the force of his actions.

This behaviour absolutely convinced the child psychologist that Alex had seen the attack on his mother. There was no other explanation. He had never done anything like this before in his life.

I found out much later that this way of acting out an event was called post-traumatic play. It was incredibly upsetting to watch. Alex had become really violent. I couldn't help but ask myself if what he had witnessed was going to turn him into a killer too. He had shown only the usual boisterous behaviour of any young child. But this wasn't our child any more. I didn't recognize Alex in the glazed eyes in front of me. And I didn't recognize him in the savagery of his movements. I wanted to pick him up and shake him. I wanted to jerk him back to normal. I wanted to snap him out of it but I knew that over-reacting might cause even more harm. I had to settle for a verbal reprimand.

I didn't understand what was happening to him.

Later I found out that it is a quite common reaction of children who have experienced trauma to want to act out the event itself afterwards. Macabre though it seems, they will turn the event into a kind of game. I heard later of a little girl who had been abducted and assaulted. Thankfully she had been found and returned to her family. Although she had been through a terrible ordeal, often afterwards she would want to play 'kidnap', assigning roles to the people around her whom she would compel to take part. I could understand how her family felt. The event itself is awful enough without having it enacted in front of you over and over again.

During this session Alex had been able to answer a number of questions. A sort of pattern and method had taken shape which promised to be effective as time went on. I thought we were making progress. I was in no hurry. Everything was a question of time.

The next day one of the detectives was at my mother's house on his own. Alex was in a particularly receptive mood and the house was quiet. Alex considered the detective part of the furniture by now and was in no way bothered by his presence.

I asked Alex the same questions that I had before about the father of his friend. Once again, this time in front of the detective, he came up with exactly the same answers. The detective showed no particular reaction to Alex's words, apart from mild interest.

I went back to playing with Alex as normally as I could. This time it was really an effort.

It was Alex's birthday. Nearly four weeks to the day after Rachel was killed. Today was Tuesday but I had decided to celebrate his birthday on the coming Saturday when everyone in the family would be free. But we had to do something to mark the occasion. I wanted to spend it in a way that Rachel would have approved.

The weather forecast wasn't good: thunder and showers were expected. But I couldn't stand the idea of being stuck inside all day. I wanted to take a picnic to a zoo that had been suggested to us where there was a little fairground. It must have been one of the few things that we had not already done all together as a family.

Alex was happy enough to let me drive, as long as his car-seat was strapped into the front right next to me. Together with a friend, we set off for the day.

I was beginning to find thunderstorms comforting. The dark, threatening skies no longer carried any menace. I now found them reassuring and familiar instead.

The zoo was out in the country, north of London, and surrounded by woods. The ground was wet from overnight rain. We had managed to put Alex on a few rides before the first shower of the day came down, accompanied by heavy rolls of thunder from just over our heads. The anvil-shaped clouds reached up grey and black high into the sky. So much for summer.

The weather hardly came as a surprise after the storm we had experienced so soon after Rachel's death. This day of all days she would have wanted to be with him. This was the first major occasion she wasn't there for him. She was missing so much already. Such a display in the heavens seemed only natural. It comforted me to think that she was getting in touch with us again and stopped me from feeling quite so alone as we went through the motions of having a good time.

I felt like a babysitter. It was as if our friend and I were there to fill in for a while. I could only just stop myself from calling out loud: 'It's all right, the joke's over. You can come out now!' I could see Rachel walk out from behind a tree. She'd smile as she appeared, and put her arms round me, and we would walk away together, and she'd gently chastise me for something I hadn't done right with Alex: we would carry on as if nothing had ever happened.

The idea was less strange, less implausible, than the thought that I would never see her again. To never see her again was impossible to accept.

The thunder rumbled even louder overhead and we were forced to shelter in the car while another heavy shower fell. We ate our sandwiches while the windows steamed up and rivulets of water ran down them. Everything was damp. Alex didn't seem to mind. It had made his day just to ride on a pony called Miguel. He was looking forward to having another go as soon as the rain stopped long enough for us to venture out again. His hunger for life was so strong, he was totally taken up with having the best time he possibly could.

I thought back to his last birthday. We had taken him to the seaside. At least his having a birthday in August meant we stood some chance of spending it outside. That day the weather had been fine but only just warm enough to sit around in a bathing suit. We had had such a good time doing hardly anything. A little paddle, an ice-cream, playing on the slides. I was sure I could have spent every day of my life with Rachel and never have had enough. Having Alex just made everything even better. I felt so complete. I knew how rare it was. Any other relationship I had had with anyone, family, friend or girlfriend, had never come close. And the most incredible thing of all was that she felt the same way too.

We used to laugh about how we must have made our friends sick, we were always so much in love. But that was just the way it was. And we were certain that that was the way it was going to stay. We were joined by something indescribable, something so strong. We knew that we were meant to be together. We did have the occasional flaming row, mostly because both of us were so stubborn. We might have made plenty of noise, but that didn't count for much. Those rare arguments did nothing to disturb the depths of our feelings for each other.

On the day when Rachel and I met, I had been looking after my brothers. They were only nine and eleven at the time. The same friend who was with us today had been with us. I had wanted to take the boys to water-slides near the flat and we had all set off together in the car. It was the last Thursday in July and high season. But when we arrived there was a big sign posted across the gate saying they were closed. For just that day. They would however be open again the next day. It was probably the only day of that whole summer that they were closed.

The boys were already hot in the car and I didn't want to disappoint them. So we drove for miles across suburban London to find another pool. This one was open. We were in luck, although I didn't know by how much.

We all had a great time, throwing ourselves down the tubes and running back up to the top again for more. Meanwhile I had passed a few words with one of the female life-guards. At first I was almost reluctant to do so. I was sure the girls got to hear every chat-up line and leery remark possible from the men in the queues filing past them all day long. I was sure they were completely sick of it.

We finished our session and I thought no more of it. She looked too young for me anyway. But when we were swimming in another part of the complex I saw her again. She had changed duties and wasn't far away. I went over to talk to her. She was older than I thought: nineteen, not sixteen, and was obviously very bright. I had just found out that she was only working until term started and that she was studying English and History, when my brothers came to see what I was up to. They couldn't be persuaded to leave us alone and stood staring and craning their heads up to catch every word. I felt extremely self-conscious and felt somehow that I was probably setting a bad example. At the very least I thought they'd helped blow my chances. But against the odds I managed to get a date to see her. I drove everyone home and my friend offered to babysit while I went back to meet her after work.

I was mildly pleased, but not particularly excited. She had seemed charming enough and had talked with obvious intelligence about the degree she was finishing and about other things. But I had found that people were often at their best when you first met them and that things went downhill from there. What could you really tell about someone in a few minutes, anyway?

I was twenty-five and had reached a stage where I was no longer interested in temporary girlfriends. This seemed to be the main subject of conversation at the time with all of my male friends. We were all looking for something more. None of us was really sure what this 'something more' was, but we were agreed that we would recognize it if we came across it. But none of us had – so far.

We would go back through each other's girlfriends to see if we thought that any one of us had actually had this 'something more' in front of him but had been too obtuse to realize it at the time. Then we would take the girlfriends who came at the top of the list to try and work out what little thing they lacked that would have put them in the big league of the 'something mores'.

Then we would wonder if maybe we hadn't seen what we wanted because we weren't ready for it ourselves. If we could get back together with whoever had come closest to having this 'something more', would everything now be different? Maybe now the fact that we were *ready* for it would make the magical difference and this would be all it needed to bring this 'something more' out of the girl in question. We would turn the subject round and round to the point where nothing made sense any more. The whole relationship issue became so complicated that a simple conversation with an unknown woman became a mess of mental checklists and instant predictions of how she might react in a million different situations. It was hard to be spontaneous.

I was sharing my flat with two others at the time. None of us had a current girlfriend so we had invented a little game to keep ourselves amused. Each one of us had chosen the name of a particularly gorgeous film star and had taken to never closing the front door on our way out without a line such as: 'If Kim (Basinger) calls, tell her I'll be back later.' I had had a little trouble coming up with someone, but not wanting to be left out of the game I had picked on Rachel Ward. So for the past six months I had hardly ever gone out of the door without saying: 'If Rachel calls, tell her I'll be back later.'

My flat-mates were away in Spain at the time and when one of them rang the day after Rachel and I had met I calmly announced the news that I had found the woman of my life. 'And just guess what she's called!' When I told him her name was Rachel I got the impression that he thought I was making the whole thing up.

I left my friend babysitting and set off back to the pool. The rush hour was over and the traffic was thinning on the roads. The first few traffic lights were green, which only ever happened to me if I managed to get to each one without someone stopping to make a turn. I felt pleased to skate through them so easily. At least I probably wouldn't be late. The next few lights I came to I also managed to take at green. I started to

smile. I had never got this far before without having to stop. And I was-
n't speeding. Far from it: if I got up to them too fast they were liable to
still be red. But I drifted up to each one easily and then on to the next
and found that it too was turning green just as I arrived. Some I crossed
only just in time but the next one was green again just the same.

I was having a whale of a time. I had never known such a run of
luck. It made me think of tennis matches I had played when every ball
that had touched the net had dropped good for me, leaving my opponent completely stranded. There were days like that, and the luck
never seemed to share itself evenly. When it was my day I would know
almost without looking that the next lucky ball was going to fall for
me. Of course there were just as many days when the ball dropped for
my opponent. But today was my day.

I had never had the same experience with traffic lights. Certainly
not for this long. Even when I took a short-cut through the back
streets, each time I came back on to the main road the next light would
be green. I was beginning to get a real buzz from looking forward to
seeing the colour of the next light ahead. How long would this last?
All the time I was trying to drive easily, without rushing, as this seemed
to be the way not to break the spell.

By the time I had reached the pool I had driven a quarter of the way
round London and had gone through a couple of dozen traffic lights.
Every one had been green (or just!). Even though I was to do the same
route often in the next few weeks it never came close to happening
again.

I pulled into the swimming pool car park grinning all over my face.
I couldn't wait to tell someone how lucky I'd been. I had only just got
out of the car when Rachel appeared. I almost did a double-take. I
hardly recognized her from earlier that afternoon. She was dressed in
jeans and a wrap-around top and it was true that she had had time to
dry her hair, but she looked stunning. She had such bright, intelligent
eyes. And she had the most knock-out smile.

I had to make a real effort not to blurt my words out. Suddenly I felt
physically ill at ease, and she looked so good that I could hardly meet
her eyes. I didn't want to gawp like a creep. I couldn't call it love at
first sight. I had already met her and talked to her for quite a while that
afternoon and had come away only with the impression that she was
charming and that it would be nice to see her again.

But now that I *was* seeing her again I found myself suddenly blown away. It wasn't just the way she looked. I had been lucky enough to go out with some pretty girls before. Some of them had bored me to death after little more than a few minutes. But I had a feeling of complete ease with this girl from the very second that I saw her again that evening. And I felt she was at ease with me too. I knew that I could have been wrong and could have been reading more into things than there was. Only time would tell.

She was a breath of fresh air. Just the way she walked up and said 'hello'. She was so full of life. Hers wasn't the hyperactive nervous energy which people sometimes use to cover their awkwardness. It was a genuine force which was part of her.

I felt so many sensations. So many thoughts went through my head just in the time it took to say 'hello'. I immediately tried to recover my poise and to cover myself against disappointment. But I let myself at least savour the thought that, if this did work out, it could really be something special. I was sure straight away that this was someone I could easily spend a lot of time with. I felt I had already known her for a long time. It was more like I was catching up with an old friend than meeting someone new. In just the first few words I felt that there was a deep understanding between us, almost a complicity, which was rare in itself. And was usually something that only came about after a lot of time spent together.

It was this more than anything which affected me most.

From that moment on, everything she said and everything we talked about confirmed those first, or more accurately, second, impressions. I had my mother's little dog with me and we took it for a walk. Then we sat outside a pub by the river. But what we did most of all was talk.

We talked and talked. For hours. It was so easy to do. It all just flowed out. From both of us.

We talked about how we felt about everything, what we wanted, our childhoods, family, which newspapers we read, what we ate, what we drank, where we had been, where we wanted to go, the children we wanted to have some day. We talked about a thousand different things and I never once felt ridiculous or awkward or misunderstood. And I never felt like I needed to impress or watch that I said the right thing or avoid talking about something else or worry that I might cause offence. We just seemed totally on the same wavelength.

The more the time passed, the more I was filled with a sense of euphoria. I could hardly bear to look at this woman sitting beside me. Not only was I enjoying her company so enormously but she was making me feel better about myself too.

I was trying to keep a little sense of reality. I had to protect myself from disappointment and was telling myself that this was probably too good to be true. This woman was truly amazing. But she was going to be truly amazing with anybody. Just because we were getting along (I couldn't say any more than that for her, I couldn't read her mind) didn't mean anything more than she was enjoying my company. As far as I knew, that was her limit to her feelings.

This wasn't a romance yet. Not by any means. And there was no reason for me to believe that it ever would be.

I was prepared to let myself be enchanted. I had never hit it off with anyone so well in my life. I would try and enjoy the moment for what it was and, when the time came to say goodbye, try not to be too surprised if we both went our own way and never saw each other again.

I could remember before, with other people, how I had been prepared to blind myself to certain things about them in the excitement of the first moments, only to bring them back to mind when things turned sour. I could put up with those things when all was going well but when the passion faded just a little those were the things that would return to bug the hell out of me; even to the extent that there was no way that I would let things last. If I had been honest with myself at the beginning I might not have embarked on the adventure at all. But passion overruled reason. I liked to think I was stronger now. But tonight the question didn't even arise.

Try as I might there was nothing I could see in her that I wasn't crazy about. Which was scary. Perhaps I was sitting next to the human embodiment of all of my dreams come true. Something I had thought of only as a future event, a far-off dream to be fulfilled one day. Another day. Certainly not this day.

I couldn't possibly have found the woman for me! I told myself. At least I tried to tell myself, while all of my senses told me the opposite. I was trying to keep myself from losing all sense of proportion.

If it were true, then this day was going to change my life completely. And when I had got up this morning the day hadn't felt any different from the day before, or from any other day for that matter. And this

159

was so soon, too. I had friends older than me who had been looking for much longer. I had had to learn to wait and fight for everything in my life: I couldn't be about to jump ahead of them in the queue now, in something as big as this.

Surely there should be an earthquake or a comet to let you know that this was really it? To stop you from doing something totally stupid to blow your big chance for ever.

It was a magical night. This much, there was absolutely no denying. The sun had gone down and the moon was out. The lights from the pub garden were reflected in the river that ran past our feet and the shadows of the boats danced while the gentle current rocked the surface. We sat on a pontoon and as the water lapped against the bank, we rocked too. The stars glimmered through the clouds and here I was sitting and talking with this beautiful, wonderful woman. What could possibly be better? I knew that this was one of those rare moments of perfection that I was never going to forget.

Even though we had covered years in each other's minds the time on my watch had only moved in minutes and hours. But suddenly it was late. There was the first awkward moment of the evening. Neither of us wanted to move. Neither of us wanted to break the spell. But there was a last train to catch if she was going to get home. I didn't like the idea of her catching a train so late on her own but she insisted that she would be fine, and that she often did so after going out after work. I offered to drive her to a main station so at least her journey would be cut in half. I felt uneasy and concerned for her safety. But what else could I do for her?

It was difficult. I could invite her home but I knew that that was going to sound all wrong. The last thing in the world I wanted her to think was that I had been turning on the charm all evening in the hope of a quick seduction.

We sat for a few minutes more. Just our shoulders touched. I didn't dare move for fear of spoiling the moment. We hadn't even held hands. Eventually we climbed to our feet. It had got chilly in the damp night air and we both shivered as we made our way to the car.

I walked spellbound. The world was a beautiful, magical, wonderful place where anything was possible. We looked at each other as we walked. I was asking myself if she was real and not just imaginary; everything about her was too perfect to be true. Afterwards she told me that she had been thinking the same.

We found the car. Her teeth were chattering with the cold. I gave her a brotherly hug and rubbed her shoulders through her jacket to warm her up, then opened the doors. 'You know,' I said, over the top of the car before I got in, 'my brothers and my friend are staying the night but there is still a spare bedroom you could have to yourself if you'd rather not get that train alone.'

At one time I would have come out with any line I could think of to make her come home with me. And here I was not wanting her to come at all if it risked spoiling what hadn't even begun. But I had to give her the choice. I was sure she would not have been out so late if she had not been with me. If she wasn't safe, it was my fault. The offer was totally genuine.

After a few moments' reflection she said: 'OK.'

I felt relieved. I had only just found her, I didn't want to lose her. At least I would know that she was safe. And I was elated that I would have even more time with her and that our magical evening was not going to be brought so swiftly to an end.

The boys were asleep by the time we got back. I made us something to eat. We hadn't eaten all evening, apart from a couple of packets of crisps outside the pub, and we were both starving.

It was so weird. We already knew each other so well. I had never known anything like it.

I showed Rachel her room and wished her goodnight. I was head over heels in love but I still hadn't as much as held her hand.

She didn't want me to leave.

We often laughed, looking back on that night, at how we seemed to have rushed into things. But it hadn't been like that at all. Time had shown that we weren't wrong. We stayed together that night and were rarely apart again. In those few hours we had found out more about each other than some people do in months. Maybe more than some people ever do. This was the strange thing: we were both already certain that we had found 'the one'.

There was a quarter-moon that night. The blind was open wide. I remember the way it rose higher across the black sky outside the window and then sank again in an arc on the other side.

'Don't ever leave me,' I said.

'I won't.'

Chapter Twelve

THE MORNING HAD been hot and sticky and unpleasant. The sky was heavy, and thunder threatened. A storm was on the way but for the moment the heat and humidity were oppressive.

I rode with my jacket undone and the zips on my leather jeans open as much as possible to get some air to my skin to relieve the heat. I had learnt to wear my leathers whatever the temperature. They had saved me from serious injury when I had been dragged down the road under a London taxi the summer before.

Since I had left Alex and Rachel on the step outside the flat I had been into the centre of town and then on through the East End of London. The tower blocks and concrete weren't helping to make my mood any lighter. I had turned north and was glad of the prospect of getting out of the city, even though I wasn't going as far as the countryside itself. The houses started to thin out and there was more and more green and open space between them as I crossed the M25 and officially left London.

I always got a buzz leaving London behind. Even in my subdued mood something of the thrill of riding a motorbike returned with the promise of the open road and limitless horizons. I could remind myself that in spite of everything, I was still free. I didn't have to go back to work. I could just keep going. I could open up the throttle and head across the countryside in any direction I wanted. Or I could simply turn my radio off and go home. Rachel would be thrilled if I did.

The reverie would only last a couple of seconds then reality would return. Pissed off though I was, I was doing what I was doing because I wanted to. What I had at home more than compensated for the drudgery and boredom and discomfort. And I knew that if I could just keep going, sooner or later our luck would change. We'd be able to sell up and we would have enough to start up somewhere else in a way that allowed us to see more of each other.

I had already begun to look into the possibility of teaching tennis somewhere warmer. It certainly wouldn't make our fortune but it would give us a lot more time together. I dreamed of being able to have lunch with the both of them every day. Maybe sitting out in the sun in some beautiful, quiet corner.

Rachel hadn't been too keen at first on the idea of moving abroad, but the more we talked about it the more enthusiastic she became. She wanted to be out in the country. She wanted a little garden and her own vegetable patch. She had already talked with Alex about getting him his own pet rabbit and had always talked with affection about carefree childhood days growing up in the country. She had played with her own rabbit as a little girl, taking it for walks on a lead.

To a city child like me it had sounded so idyllic. I had grown up in the streets not so far from where we were living now. I had hated it, even though I had never known anything else. I didn't like the dirt and rubbish in the streets. I didn't like the hot, endless pavements on my walk to school in the summer. I didn't like the drizzle and the grey in winter and the way it was already dark when we came out of school and there was no more time to play outside. I didn't want that for Alex. The thought of him being subjected to the same routines was more than I could contemplate. I wanted better for him.

I had always hated the rain and the cold. When I was at primary school I went to Saturday morning pictures every week as a matter of routine. Crackly old black and white films, the actors with unbearable public school accents, Flash Gordon and an organ playing 'Nelly the Elephant' as a bouncing ball skipped across the screen. The stalls would be a riot of flying popcorn and children shouting and screaming and running through the aisles. It seemed like only one word in three was audible in the chaos and you had to watch out that you didn't get burnt: there was always someone doing their best to light up a cigarette and keep it out of sight under the coats. I would walk back sometimes with a neighbour, often on my own, pockets and mouth full of sweets. As a matter of routine it would be raining each and every one of those Saturdays.

The pictures were the high point. Saturday afternoons I would pray for a break in the rain so I could go and stamp in the puddles with my wellies. But most of the time I was stuck indoors. There was always *World of Sport* on the TV, endless horse races and very little other sport. I hated being confined indoors and longed to be able to get out and play. For years as a child I associated Saturday with rain. Rain and complete boredom.

Maybe I would have felt different if I had grown up in the country too. And Rachel hadn't just had that. She and her brother had spent weeks on end playing on sandy beaches, staying with their grandparents in a south coast seaside resort. Her childhood was so full of love and companionship and fun and laughter. That was what I wanted for our son. I wanted him to have what she had had. I loved to hear about all of the silly little things that they had got up to, the games they used to play, the sweets on the tray in the morning, donkey rides on the beach. It all sounded so idyllic.

To me it was like fiction. A *Janet and John* book come to life. Janet and John at the Park. Janet and John at the Seaside.

But I wasn't jealous. I wouldn't have wanted to go back to being a child again. I was conscious of how it had taught me to value the good things that came my way. Somehow I felt that the contrast made the good things even sweeter. Or at least that's what I liked to tell myself. Logically it wasn't true, because even after all of the good things Rachel had had she was still thrilled by the simplest of pleasures.

She would sometimes say that she had wished we had been brother and sister too and had had the chance to play together as children. But she would soon change her mind when she remembered that we would not have had what we were sharing now if that had been the case. And I would gladly have forsaken the chance to have all that she had had as a child in return for what we were sharing now. What we had was truly special. And I knew it while it was happening. I took nothing for granted. Except perhaps the belief that things were going to last. But I truly believed that Rachel would never leave me. For ever meant for ever. And never in a million years would I be stupid enough to let her go.

I had had trouble locating the last drop. The address was confusing and I had stopped several times and gone into different offices to ask. By the time I finally found the place I was hot and sweaty and irritable. It was a prefabricated unit off the main road. It was lunchtime. I considered this to be half a day's work done and would mentally work out how much I had earned to see if I was going to have to work late to make up for a bad morning. Or if I had made enough to consider getting home at a reasonable time; perhaps even early, if I had done particularly well.

I had to consider how well I had done the days before to check if I was on target for making what we needed to live on by the end of the week. Even if I had done well I had to consider whether I had just been lucky. If so, I should still work as much as I could because there was no guarantee that the rest of the week wouldn't be lousy. If my luck didn't continue, even with a good start, I could still end up not making enough.

On those rare occasions when there was plenty of work around for everyone it was almost a pleasure to watch the number of jobs done mount up and know that we were doing all right. I could tell myself that this week I could relax. As long as the bike didn't break down underneath me. I was always on the lookout for the slightest sign, any noise or wobble to tell me that something needed attention. I needed a good week, every week of the year just to keep our heads above water. There was only the tiniest comfort margin. And plenty of discomfort.

I had had a reasonable morning. Slightly better than average, if nothing spectacular, but enough to take a little pressure off the day. And now I was hungry. I pulled on my hot helmet, its foam lining impregnated with the stench of traffic fumes, and got back on my bike. I rode towards the centre of town looking out for somewhere to buy a sandwich. I was wondering whether to call Rachel first or eat first. I needed to eat regularly, even if it wasn't very much, otherwise I got light-headed. And with a helmet on, a steady dose of diesel fumes, the heat and a heavy radio strapped round my neck, I could soon have a splitting headache.

I cherished the few minutes on the phone with Rachel every day and liked to be in the best mood to enjoy them.

I decided to get something to eat first. But after circling around I couldn't see anywhere that looked promising. And I just couldn't be bothered to go through the effort of stopping and parking to go in and look several times over only to find that there was still nothing that I fancied. So I decided not to waste my time but to head back to London instead and to eat somewhere I knew.

But first I wanted to find a phone.

There was one just off the main roundabout. I pulled a phonecard out of my wallet and stuck it in the machine. I dialled our home number just as I had done hundreds and hundreds of times before. I waited for Rachel to pick up the receiver and tell me the news of the morning. She would probably say 'Hi' and be obviously pleased to hear my voice. Then she would probably let off some steam about someone who had pissed her off in the traffic or how someone had been rude about Alex running round the supermarket or she would tell me that the exhaust was making a terrible noise and sounding like it was going to blow up, or that another bill had arrived that morning that we couldn't pay. Trivial things. But the kind of things that can build into something huge and ruin the whole day, if you are at home without another adult to talk them over with.

She would ask me how it was going, always in the hope that I could say I would be home early that evening, and was rarely able to hide her disappointment if I said that it didn't look like I would.

The phone rang just a few times and then clicked as it was picked up. The word 'hello' stuck in my throat as I realized that it wasn't Rachel at the other end of the line. In the first split second of surprise a thousand thoughts flashed through my mind. A strange male voice said, 'Hello.'

I was electrified. Almost paralysed with terror. Who was this stranger on the end of our phone? What was he doing in our home? I had dialled the right number. There was no doubt about it. The thoughts sped across my mind as I tried desperately to put the pieces back in order. How could there possibly be a strange man in our home? Was he the friend of someone? Was he a friend of our flat-mate? If so, why was he picking up our phone? Where was Rachel? Why wasn't it she who was answering the phone? What had happened to her? Everything was suddenly accelerating. Something was wrong.

'Hello . . . ? Is that André . . . ?' It wasn't the wrong number. All the wheels were turning in my head but this voice didn't fit in any-where. It was older than our flat-mate's. There was something else, too. Its owner wanted something from *me*. He wasn't just picking up the phone to hand over the receiver. I felt overcome by panic.

'Are you Rachel's boyfriend . . . ?'

Who could ask a question like that? Who could be on *our* phone in *our* flat and not know the answer to that? Everything was upside down and my fear was making me angry. I was immediately too far gone to control myself.

'YES!' I shouted back. 'WHERE IS SHE?'

'André, where are you now?' The voice was sympathetic, with no trace of antagonism in spite of my shouting. I was thrown off balance. I was trying to think. 'Don't hang up!' he implored.

There was an undeniable directness and urgency in the tone. This was an official voice. A policeman's voice. God knows why, but I immediately pictured Rachel under arrest and being held in another room. Something was terribly wrong.

Thoughts were shooting through my head but I couldn't make sense of any of them. I wanted this voice out of the way. I wanted it gone. I was filled with fury at this intrusion into our life. How dare anyone keep me away from her, even for a second!

'Who the hell are you?' I shouted down the phone at this stranger. 'What are you doing in my house? Where's Rachel?'

'Where are you, André?' appealed the voice. 'Are you on your own? Please stay on the phone!'

Stay on the phone for what? What was this? *The Twilight Zone?* Were they busy tracing my call while a horde of siren-wailing police cars prepared to descend upon me and bring me in too?

'WHERE'S RACHEL?' I shouted down the line. Why the hell wouldn't he tell me where she was? I was bursting in anger.

'André, are you on your own?' pleaded the voice. I could hear the desperation now, but its owner was trying to deflect my rage. He was playing for time. 'Is there anybody with you?' he asked again.

'WHERE IS RACHEL?' I shouted back. I was furious. I wanted to break the phone. I wanted to climb down the line and put an end to this excruciating performance.

The voice began to break. It said: 'André, I'm a police officer. I have to tell you there's been a terrible accident . . .'

My whole world crumpled and fell apart.

'There's been a terrible accident . . .'

I felt the breath sucked out of me and my insides tighten.

'What's happened?' I just managed to get the words out.

The voice continued to speak: it was on the point of breaking. 'Rachel has been attacked from behind while walking on the Common . . .'

The words twisted inside me with a searing pain. Realization and denial pulled in separate directions. Realization of the consequences of what he had said. And denial that this could ever happen to us.

There was only one reason that we could be going through this performance. The words were hovering on the edge of my consciousness but wouldn't form. Almost as if my will wouldn't let them. And as long as they didn't form I could use my will to keep the unthinkable from becoming a reality.

My head flooded with thoughts and images and I fought with every fibre of my being to hold on to her. I wouldn't let her go.

But I heard myself shouting back: 'IS SHE DEAD?' The words in my mouth were cutting me to pieces. I was shaking as if a fever had gripped me and my heart was pounding in my throat. In my head everything was going in and out of focus. I had to know.

'I *can't* answer that on the phone,' beseeched the voice, distressed and frightened.

She was dead. Otherwise he would tell me she wasn't. He must *know* that he has already told me.

'YOU'VE *GOT* TO TELL ME!' This time my voice was breaking. Didn't he know this was only making it worse? Though I would willingly go through this pain a million times if he would only say that she was all right.

'André, stay where you are,' he tried to say instead, desperate to calm me down. 'Don't move,' he implored. 'We'll get a car to you in a few minutes. Just tell me where you are . . .'

'IS SHE DEAD!?' I shouted again. 'YOU'VE GOT TO TELL ME!'

The human mind is capable of working on many levels at the same time. And in the midst of everything, on one of those levels, I felt compassion for the owner of the voice at the other end of the line. My universe was being torn apart and he was doing everything he could to soften the blow. And he didn't have a hope in hell of being able to do so.

'I *can't* tell you,' he pleaded again.

'IS SHE DEAD?' I shouted again.

'Yes . . .' It was an agonized sound, let out almost against his will.

The pain hit me hard. I was physically crushed by the weight of it.

'No!!' I heard the scream a long way away. As if it came from somebody else.

'I'm so sorry,' he said, quickly. And there was no possible doubt in the world that he was. 'I didn't want to tell you like this . . .' There was pain in his voice. 'But please,' he continued. 'You can't be on your own. We'll get someone to you . . .'

I could hardly hear him.

The fight had stopped. The second before, I had been straining with every fibre of my being and now I had the strength and size of an insignificant insect against the enormity of the universe. A wave of emotion and despair rolled over me in a way I had never experienced. Before the enormity of it I had all but shrunk to nothing.

I saw every moment of my life at the same time. Time concertinaed and every single event came rushing towards me: they were overtaking each other, passing through each other, arriving and then flying away into the distance.

And then the world turned upside down. I could feel the physical pressure on my back and neck.

I didn't even ask myself if I was going mad.

Because madness was all there was.

These were the strangest few minutes of my life. Nothing, nothing, was the same. My eyes and my mind were no longer working the way they had up until that point in my life. Or the way they do now. Sounds were not arriving at my ears in the way they had before.

She had gone and the whole of my life had gone with her. But even more than that, the reality of life itself had changed.

I could hear something laughing at me. Something was holding my life up to my face, all of it, right up until the very moment before. It was grinding my face into it and saying: 'This is the way it is! You were wrong.'

All my beliefs in the good things that life can bring, the idea of time and patience and things coming in order, the idea of working long for something and being rewarded for your effort, the belief that you can change things, the belief that you are capable of achieving anything at all were all being shown to be pitiful.

169

Laughable.

Childish, ignorant nonsense.

Within a split second I heard myself ask: 'Where's Alex?'

I was surely asking the question in vain. He must be dead too.

'He's all right,' said the voice emphatically. I believed him.

I saw Alex in my mind now. I had to be strong for him. He had lost more than me. He was mine now. I was totally responsible for him. I had to get to him as soon as possible.

'He's at Wimbledon police station. Don't go anywhere on your own. We'll get a car to bring you to him. Just tell me where you are . . .'

I gave him the address written on the phone box. I was outside a post office on the edge of a roundabout. It wasn't easy to miss.

'André, please stay where you are,' the voice implored. 'We'll have somebody with you in just a couple of minutes.'

Chapter Thirteen

I HAD TO TELL someone. I immediately thought of Rachel's parents. They were going to be devastated. But they had to know. They would know what to do. They would know how to cope.

But they weren't there! They were on holiday in Canada.

I called my mother. I could only get three words out: 'RACHEL'S BEEN KILLED.'

'Who is this?' came the reply. The sounds that had come out were so contorted that she couldn't recognize my voice.

I put the phone down and collapsed across it. I had been able to make my mother understand that Alex was at Wimbledon police station and that she had to meet me there, and no more.

I was wailing and crying and the pain was too bad to keep still. I staggered across the pavement to throw myself across the back of my bike which was parked in the gutter.

The street was busy with people going about their day. I had to weave through them to get to my bike. Even through my grief I could see that nobody was coming to my aid. Everybody looked the other way and did their best to avoid me. They almost had to step over me to get past. I didn't blame them. I was sobbing and moaning hysterically and must have been a wretched sight. I don't know what I would have done if I was in their shoes.

The image of Rachel was fixed in my mind. I was mouthing nonsense as I tried to cope with the pain. I had totally accepted that she was gone in the sense that I knew that it was undeniably true. Maybe this made the pain worse. I couldn't even begin to tell myself that it wasn't true. I had nothing to put between me and it.

Probably the most insane thing of all was how the people continued to walk on by. I could hear their footsteps even if I couldn't see through the tears. Their world was just carrying on around me while mine had been totally destroyed.

Nothing in their world meant anything to me any more. I was finished with it. I was in agony. I just wanted to die.

I thought of Alex. I pictured his face when he realized that he would never again see his mother. There was nothing left for him, either. These two were inseparable. He couldn't operate without her. It would be too cruel to try and carry on.

We would go together. There was no other way. To carry on living was out of the question. I would do it in such a way that we would painlessly, quietly, slip away together.

No one was coming. I was continually expecting to hear the sound of tyres and a car pulling up beside me. They would only be a few minutes. But the time passed and no one arrived.

I couldn't stay still. The pain was too bad. I told myself I had to wait. I was in no fit state to go anywhere on my own. But the minutes went by and the waiting became unbearable. I had to get to Alex. Rachel would have been distraught at the thought of him being on his own. I had to do what she would have wanted. I couldn't cause her any more pain.

Five minutes. Ten minutes. It was hard to tell, but it was more than it needed to be. If they had contacted the local police station surely it wouldn't have taken more than a couple of minutes for a car to get to me. They couldn't have been sending someone from where they were. That would take hours, not minutes.

I pulled myself to my feet. I had to get to the nearest police station, I couldn't wait any more. I managed to stop crying long enough to ask a passer-by the way. He hardly broke his stride to point up the road and mutter something like: 'It's up there.' Then he hurried past. Heaven help that anything I was suffering from should be contagious.

From where I was standing I could just make out the blue light outside a building further up the road. It was only walking distance. How could they possibly be taking this long?

I had no other choice. I had to get there myself. I couldn't leave Alex on his own. I tried to take stock of my physical state. I was weak and uncoordinated but I thought that if I took it really easily I should be able to make it at least that far without falling off the bike. Then I could forget about it completely.

I climbed on and pressed the starter. I just about had the strength to push the bike off its stand. I pulled away, wobbling unsteadily around the roundabout and turned off towards the police station. It was only a matter of a few hundred metres. I put the bike on its stand, turned off the engine and staggered into the police station.

A couple of people were waiting at the reception desk. There was a young officer behind the desk. After a few seconds he freed the security door to let me through. It was hushed inside, even though far from empty.

'I've just phoned home to be told that my girlfriend's been killed,' I blurted out, fighting hard to choke back the sobs. 'There's a policeman in our flat.'

The officer looked up from behind the desk. He looked bewildered, thrown. I stood there in battered leather trousers, a dirt-streaked T-shirt and a leather jacket. My hair was shorn as it had been since it had begun to fall out a couple of years before. There were tears and snot streaming down my face. I was trying to clear it with my T-shirt.

'They told me to wait . . . that they were sending a car to meet me . . . but I couldn't wait any longer.'

'Just a minute,' he said. He turned away to talk to someone else behind him. He turned back. 'Can you sit down, please, I'll just be a minute.' He motioned towards the wooden benches that lined the walls and looked relieved when I did as he asked.

There were already a dozen other people sitting around the room. No one was talking. The afternoon was heavy and oppressive, the mood reflected in the people's expressions. I sat down in the nearest gap, put my head in my hands and sobbed.

A woman was sitting beside me. 'What's wrong?' she asked gently. 'My girlfriend's been killed,' I blurted out.

There was an intake of breath. 'They shouldn't leave you like this!' she said. I could hear the shock and anger and pity in just those few words. Inside I was desperately grateful for her words of compassion even if I must have looked incapable of taking in what she was saying.

I expected that someone would immediately come to find me and put me in a car. They would have had a message from Wimbledon police station and must already know that it was me they were looking out for. There could hardly be two such instances in the same day.

But again the minutes began to pass and nothing was happening. How could you leave anybody alone in that state I was in, knowing what had just happened? But as that thought went through my mind it was immediately followed by another, which said, how could I possibly expect anything else? In this nightmare all there could be was pain. I was beyond being surprised.

But I couldn't wait any longer. I pulled myself to my feet and crossed unsteadily back to the desk. The young officer was dealing with someone else, but if this didn't take priority what possibly could? He looked up helplessly as I approached. I could tell straight away that nothing had been done.

There was a policewoman behind him now and he turned and said something to her. I couldn't catch what it was. The look she gave me was less than sympathetic. However, they went to the side of the desk and opened the lock to let me into their side of the station. As I came through, both of them kept their distance. I suddenly realized that they thought I was a raving lunatic.

'I've been told what you said when you came into the station,' said the policewoman. 'A police officer would never have told you that on the phone!' Her voice was as hard as nails, the words pronounced with relish. 'We're not allowed to,' she added.

The world was completely mad. I had expected that things would be handled with speed and compassion but instead here I was, on top of everything, having to fight to prove that I wasn't completely insane.

She continued: 'We've been trying to get through to Wimbledon to find out what's going on. But this just doesn't sound right. This isn't the way that we do things.'

'He didn't want to tell me!' I managed to say. 'He didn't want to tell me.'

They weren't sure, either of them. They were hesitating. Eventually they showed me into what must have been an interrogation room of some kind. There was a phone on the table and the policewoman picked it up. It didn't work. She led me into another room and picked up yet another phone. Again there was a problem with it. Time was going past and this was just a shambles. Alex was on his own. I had to get to him.

174

She led me back out into the corridor and wanted me to go back to the public waiting room until they had sorted something out. This was unbearable.

A door opened at the end of the corridor and an officer with grey hair appeared. I assumed from the way they looked at him that this must be a senior officer. He must know what was going on, I thought, and would undoubtedly take charge and sort this mess out.

But he just stood in the doorway and watched.

By now there were several male officers just standing at a distance and watching. I felt like the main attraction in a freak show. I felt completely dehumanized.

Only the policewoman was doing anything. But far from offering help and understanding, she seemed to be relishing the opportunity to display her gung-ho spirit and 'hard as nails' persona. I got the impression that she only wanted to show her male colleagues how capable she was in dealing with a lunatic. And how useless they were in their inability to react.

'I've got to go,' I said. 'You're not doing anything for me.' I had no other choice. These people were going out of their way not to understand. In a minute I could find myself locked up in a cell with no way on earth of getting to Alex.

The officers all looked at the one with grey hair. He nodded in a way that I understood to mean: 'Let him go.'

The policewoman unlocked the door, saying, 'You're in no state to drive.'

I knew that I wasn't. But I had no choice. I tried to take stock of myself once again. I felt a little stronger. I wouldn't ride fast. I couldn't take any stupid risks. I had to keep myself alive for Alex, there was absolutely no way I could afford to take any chances. I had hundreds of thousands of miles under my belt and I had had a couple of minor accidents in that time. I often asked myself how I had survived riding a bike without knowing what I knew now. But even if it took the greatest effort of concentration I had ever made I knew that I would get there in one piece. I had to.

The officers followed me out on to the drive beside the station. All of them, including the senior officer. A couple of police cars were parked outside. The scene was completely surreal, but again, what did I expect?

Again the male officers kept their distance while the policewoman continued to try and convince me not to go. The others remained silent. 'Why don't you wait till we get a car for you?' she said.

The cars were there but I didn't see anybody rushing to get the keys. 'You're not doing anything for me,' I said.

She tried to physically block my bike as the others stood and watched. I pulled on my helmet. She was still in my way. The last thing I wanted to do was to push her. Instead I silently pulled the bike upright and made to climb on. I wanted to make it clear that I was going.

She seemed equally determined to prevent me. Nevertheless, she glanced round to see the reaction of the one with the grey hair. 'Let him go,' he said again.

'It's the least you can do,' I thought to myself.

I pressed the starter and the motor caught. The policewoman moved out of the way just enough to let me roll past and out of the driveway.

I hardly registered the noise of the engine. I was far from the physical world, fighting against madness. But I knew that I couldn't function like that. I struggled to wrench my attention back to what I was doing and what was happening all around me. I had to talk to myself as if I was instructing someone else: first gear, second gear, third gear. Squeeze the clutch, release the clutch. Turn the handlebar, look behind you, put on the indicator, make sure you've got loads of time, accelerate.

But I could still hear the laughter in my head, still hear it mocking me. 'This is the way it is. You thought you were going to escape! You pathetic fool.' The physical world had still not righted itself. Now I have had the impression that I was driving along a wall at ninety degrees to the ground. But it was OK, because the road and everything on it was at the same angle, and nothing was falling off.

Everything was real. I knew it was. I couldn't comfort myself with the thought that this was all an illusion or a dream. This was really happening to me. But I knew at the same time that it was all mad. All of it. Life and everything about it.

I had hours to go until I could get to Alex. An hour and a half at least. It seemed like an eternity. In many ways it was. I was visited by the ghosts of all that I had ever experienced. It was like the whole box of my memory was being emptied out. There were things coming to the front of my mind that I am sure I had never thought of since the day they happened. The weight of all these images was difficult to bear. I thought my head was going to split.

I knew I was in real trouble. All the activity in my head was not making driving any easier. I redoubled my efforts to absorb myself in what my body was doing and in the road and traffic around me.

'Watch out for the bus on the roundabout. That car looks like it will cut you up if it gets half a chance, don't give him half a gap, keep in front of him or get out of his way completely.

'Second gear, third gear, fourth gear. That's enough. Take it easy. Knock off the speed, your reactions are slow, you can't afford to drive that fast. Don't try and overtake all the time, just sit in behind.

'Traffic lights coming up. Brake early and drift through the gaps to get to the front. Don't try and pull away first, that one's bound to want to go well over the speed limit, he'll be pushing you hard in a few seconds. Let him go first instead.'

My mind had settled down to two planes. I was focusing totally on the detail of what I was doing, to such an extent that looking back now I can hardly remember any of the route I took or what I might have passed along the way. Only tarmac and white lines in front of my eyes and the pull of the clutch in my hand. At the same time the wheels were still turning over behind.

I arrived at the Embankment. This meant that I was most of the way there. I can remember staring into the reflections in the darkened back window of a London taxi. I was stopped at the traffic lights and couldn't easily slide past or get into the gap.

I sat behind instead, all the while considering what practical method I should use to kill us both, Alex and me. The time that had passed had done nothing to change my mind. If anything, my resolve had strengthened. There was really nothing worth living for. The world was full of shit.

I had always considered suicide attempts as ultimately sham. An attempt at gaining attention. If you wanted to kill yourself then you wouldn't do it in a way in which you could be discovered and 'saved'. If you really wanted to go, nobody could stop you. What I had in mind was certainly no plea for help. It was nothing to do with anyone else, and no one would even know until it was too late.

I had also considered suicide a form of cowardice but now I was beyond caring. What did I care who thought of me as a coward? There

177

was only one person whose opinion mattered to me. Wherever she was now she knew all the answers. She knew what I was doing, what I was going through. I would only be putting Alex out of his misery.

I was looking out at the queue of traffic, the houses that lined the road and the river that ran along the other side, knowing that I was just about to say goodbye to it all. I looked at the bridges, and at the trees along the bank, and could only feel relief that it was coming to an end. The end of all those hopeless, broken promises.

I wouldn't have to deal with any of it again.

Then I realized that I couldn't do it. I suddenly realized that, what had seemed a lifetime ago, I had promised Rachel that if anything happened to her I would carry on and look after him. The recollection filled me with dread. It was the last thing on earth I wanted to do. But she had made me promise, made me say it out loud.

I had thought she was being ridiculous at the time. But it hadn't been the first or the last occasion that she had insisted on talking the subject through. It had come up regularly and it was always Rachel who did most of the talking. I had found the whole subject totally and unnecessarily morbid. It always made me feel very uncomfortable. I couldn't understand why someone so young and healthy should be so concerned about such a thing. It wasn't something that ever crossed my mind for more than a few seconds and I was the one who was going out every day taking the risks.

I always felt that I would be going home at night. In fact that was how I tried to relieve Rachel's nervousness about me being on a bike all day. 'I always come home at night,' I would say. 'There's nothing to worry about.' There was nothing else to say. There are no guarantees in life. You can be killed crossing the road. Or struck by disease at any time. Life was a risk.

She wanted me to promise her that if anything happened to her I would find someone else. She didn't want me to be alone. She wanted there to be someone to look after me. And she wanted Alex to have a family around him. I said that the chances of finding anyone like her again were about three and a half billion to one. She answered that if I had found her then there must be another one somewhere. I thought she was mad.

I tried to turn it round, not that I had much stomach for it, and ask her what she would do if something happened to me. She said she didn't want another man. She had a low opinion of men in general. I tried to argue that I had also known plenty of women who weren't worth the time of day. The thought of anything happening to me didn't seem to weigh on her. She knew somehow that I would be all right. She said she could see me clearly as a bald, old man.

But she couldn't see herself.

For her there was no future.

One time we had sat in the car and talked while Alex slept. We had been out for the day and it was drizzling outside. We had had a good time. It was still winter but we had been able to get out in the fresh air. We had taken Alex to see some Shire horses. He had been less impressed than we were with how enormous they were in comparison to him. Perhaps as a small child he was used to everything being so much bigger, but to us they had made him look like a toy.

There had been a mini-zoo and Alex was fascinated by some owls in a cage. We must have looked the other way for only a couple of seconds when Alex turned to us screaming and crying and holding one hand in the other.

Immediately we both jumped to the same conclusion – he must have stuck his fingers through the bars of the cage. I managed to prise his hand open and to our huge relief he still had all his fingers. He had a cut on one of them that bore the unmistakable trace of a sharp beak. The cut wasn't deep but he must have come within a whisker of having his finger snapped off completely.

It was a real lesson to us in how quickly an accident could happen. We felt pretty stupid for not taking better care but it hadn't occurred to either of us that he might do such a thing. But then again, we had been lucky so far. He hadn't pulled hot liquid over himself or fallen on any sharp corners or any of the other nasty things that children can do to themselves. So this had given us a shock.

Maybe it was the realization of how close we had come to something horrible happening that explained the subdued atmosphere in the car. Or maybe it was just the rain. Or our financial situation. Or that Rachel was tired. Because I couldn't understand what would make her say what she did. 'What are we going to do?' she had said, her voice full of despair. Which had started a discussion about where we would go and what we would do with our lives once we had sold up and could start afresh.

I was optimistic. I had several ideas about what I wanted to do next but wasn't going to settle on any one in particular. I felt that it was best to see how the land lay when the moment arrived. Rachel, however, was in a black hole.

This in itself did not surprise me. It was part of her nature. It was the other side of the bright sunshine that was so often on display together with that dynamite smile of hers. She could go into a totally bleak, depressed mood. But I had learnt not to panic. It was painful to watch and I felt helpless because I knew that I could do nothing of any consequence to pull her out of it. I could only try and talk her back and then let her get on with it. She always came round on her own. It always passed. And when her smile returned it was like nothing had ever happened.

But at this moment she was on the way down.

'I can't see any future,' she said.

I felt exasperated. What had we just been talking about?

'I mean for me!' she stated.

If there was one thing I wasn't worried about it was Rachel's future success in whatever she eventually decided to do. She was born to shine. She was somebody who everyone seemed to remember and nearly everybody seemed to think well of. The remaining minority usually had had their noses put well out of joint by her sense of fun and forthright manner. But you couldn't please everybody and some were left with plenty to feel jealous of.

I reminded her that she was bright, outgoing, young, well-read, dynamic, intelligent, attractive and that she possessed bucketfuls of enthusiasm and charm. It wouldn't have come as a surprise to me if she had turned out to be the major breadwinner. And I wasn't completely blinded by love in my evaluation of her. All she lacked was a large helping of self-belief.

But anything I had to say left her completely unmoved. Completely. Not the shadow of a smile crossed her face.

'I just can't see anything,' she said. There were tears in her eyes and she was more than upset. She was disturbed. I did my best to comfort her, but her mood had frightened me. And not for the first time.

In some ways I told myself that the way she was behaving was a good sign. It was only with people you really trust that you could express your deepest fears. This was especially true for someone as tough as Rachel. She wasn't the kind of person who anyone expected to be worried by much. I felt privileged that she should feel that she could really lean on me. And I would always do whatever it took to try to help her come round, even though it often felt as if I was achieving nothing at all.

Maybe sometimes we act the most unreasonably when we are in most need of reassurance. I would often be the most rude and unpleasant and obnoxious when I most needed her to throw her arms around me and hold me tight. It was perverse, but she agreed that she did the same. Difficult to recognize, sometimes, when you are the one on the receiving end. Both of us missed the signals at times and it was not surprising that the occasional row would erupt.

On that particular day I thought that Rachel's behaviour was an extension of this. She let herself sink into the blackest of moods because she needed to. And she wanted me to be there for her then too. It was also a test. One that I couldn't afford to fail. It was all part of being in such a deep relationship with someone with such a strong and forceful personality.

But I couldn't understand at all why she couldn't see anything. It was a concept that was alien to me. How could you lose your powers of imagination to such an extent? I could more easily have understood her saying that all she could see was disaster ahead, or that everything was going to go wrong. That much I had no trouble imagining and, like most people, had to spend much of my time fighting off those images and trying to find a little optimism. I just couldn't imagine what she meant by not being able to see anything.

It struck me as a kind of forward-looking amnesia. An imagination power-cut. I was relieved when later in the day she appeared to be more her usual self.

It was during a black moment of despair such as this that she had made me promise. I had done so simply to relieve her mood, never thinking that such a moment would ever arrive. But a promise was a promise. And I couldn't deny that she had known what she wanted. And had planned accordingly. I was trapped. I couldn't break my word. If I hoped to join her by killing myself then I would only be greeted by her telling me that I had let her down. She wanted a life for Alex. A rich life with everything that could possibly be. If I loved her then that was what I would give him. That is what she wanted him to have above all else.

I remembered once when she had gone completely cold. She hadn't appeared to notice but her skin temperature had dropped enormously. I asked her how she felt, imagining that she was suffering from some kind of virus and that she would reply that she felt shivery and cold and that she needed to be covered up. Everything about her was cold, even the inside of her mouth. My heart rate had gone up and I was starting to panic. But I didn't let on. I was worried that I would scare her and make things worse. Mentally she seemed one hundred per cent, but I thought she was dying. I actually said to myself that it was like being in a room with a corpse. The next morning she was still alive. She felt fine. I was so grateful that she was warm again. I told myself I must have imagined it all and put it away never to think about it again. I had been frightened. There are fears that come from loving anyone. Fears about anything happening to them. But there were some things that had been difficult to live with.

At times Rachel had had the most horrific and vivid nightmares. Always involving something awful and bloody happening to her. Once she sat bolt upright in bed in the middle of the night. I woke up straight away. 'Why did you do that?' she asked, looking right at me.

'Why did I do what?' I replied, wondering what terrible act I was about to be accused of. Whatever it was, it was something serious, Rachel's expression was that of someone bitterly betrayed. It turned my stomach to lead.

'Why did you kill me?' she said, looking right into me.

I realized that she must have been having a nightmare. In fact, I could see that she was actually still asleep. I knew that it wasn't a good idea to wake people who were sleepwalking so I said something soothing to get her to lie down. The moment she did so she was immediately fast asleep again. I was left feeling disturbed and badly shaken. I had been accused of something awful and had not even had the chance to talk to her about it. I knew that if I had, we would have found a way to laugh it off.

There were lots of things. Little things that she or I might mention to each other. Similarities in the names and birth dates of past girl-friends or boyfriends. Or even in the places they came from. Often they were the kinds of thing that individually can be shrugged off as coincidence but which, put together, stretch coincidence extremely thin.

182

If we went to the cinema Rachel would never go to the toilets. She was terrified of being attacked from behind. She wouldn't get into the car alone at night for the same reason. She was sure there would be someone hiding in the back who would grab her from behind. Always from behind.

If ever I found myself ensnared in one of her morbid conversations I always tried to bring the subject to a close as quickly as I could. But on this occasion she wouldn't be shaken off. 'Promise me!' she insisted. I tried to laugh it off, but she was absolutely determined and wouldn't give up until she had her way.

I had promised. What harm was there? Nothing was ever going to happen.

The traffic lights changed and the taxi pulled off. I pulled away after it and took every short-cut I knew that would get me across the river and nearer to Alex. I can look back and think of ways that I might have taken but I have very little recollection of the way I actually went. Mechanically I switched back into a mode of self-instruction, trying to tell myself that I was almost there.

I realized that I had nothing to give to Alex. I had no idea whether he had been given anything to eat all day, or even if he would have eaten if anything had been offered to him. He would forgive me if I got there a few minutes later. I knew it was important that I bring him something.

Alex loved grapes. I looked out for a greengrocer's so that I could stop to get him some. I saw one up ahead, and pulled over. I leant the machine over on to its side-stand but I could hardly move. I felt welded to it. It took an enormous effort to swing my leg over and support my weight on my feet.

The situation was totally surreal. I was going into a shop to buy something! This really was insanity. Rachel had been killed and I was going shopping.

There was no one else in the shop, only the woman who worked there. Struggling to get the words out I felt like I was talking to someone from another dimension. They're for my little boy who has just had his mother killed, went the words in my head. I'm just going to pick him up now.

My mouth remained closed as I got out the money to pay her. Once more I saw myself as if from afar. It was like watching some strange and exotic custom from another civilization. It was something that had no connection with my existence whatsoever.

When she looked into my face as she gave me my change it was almost more than I could bear. I could only just manage to hold myself up. The slightest kindness in another human being's eyes was enough to tie me into knots. I managed to get out of the shop without breaking down.

I had to open the box on my bike. My hands felt as heavy as lead as I fumbled with the key. I had one more reason to drive carefully. I didn't want the grapes bruised and squashed for Alex. Rachel wouldn't have liked that. I got back on my bike, reminding myself not to hurry. But in fact I was already moving in slow motion.

I would see him soon. This was really going to hurt.

I was into the last roads now, away from the traffic. I pulled over a railway bridge and into the road where I had gone to school. I had been so far away, travelled halfway round the world, but I was being drawn back into the past. I was ten years old and powerless again. I had never been allowed to leave.

Is this where it comes to an end? Almost back where it all began.

I knew where the police station was. I had walked past it a thousand times. I had had a schoolboy crush on a girl who had lived opposite. A friend had been arrested in the middle of the night for trying to steal the posters outside the cinema and spent the night in the cells.

I dropped over the railway bridge and on to the last few hundred metres of quiet, tree-lined suburban London street. Suddenly I didn't know who I was. Was this my past, my present or future? Had I ever grown up? Or was I still a child whose life was all to come? Everything was so familiar, from the trees to the colour of the bricks in the houses. But surely all this didn't belong in my life now? Not any more. I had gone further than this. Time and sequence no longer made any sense at all.

The road curved to reveal the blue light outside the police station up ahead. Just where it used to be. I tried to prevent myself from accelerating. There was no point in flying under a car at the last minute.

I drove up on to the pavement and put down the side-stand. There was hardly a pedestrian in sight. Everything was quiet. I swung my leg over and got to my feet. Then I turned and walked three short steps, unlocked the box and got out the grapes. I was moving through water, like in a dream.

I had arrived. It had seemed like a thousand miles, a thousand years. It had taken an enormous effort to hold myself together, to keep myself calm, to keep myself functioning. I knew that I could let go just a little bit now. I would never have to do that again. But I still had to deal with whatever I was about to face. Why hadn't they sent a car for me? What was going on?

I walked into the police station and approached the desk. It had changed since I had been here last as a fifteen-year-old to report getting knocked off my bicycle by a reckless driver. Things had moved round and it smelt as if it had recently been redecorated.

I was probably expecting the same treatment that had been handed out to me earlier and I was mentally preparing myself for more confrontation.

I took a deep breath and tried to get the words out without my voice breaking. I knew that I looked a state. 'You've got my son here. I've come to collect him,' I managed to say.

The officer behind the desk reacted as though he was expecting someone like me to appear. Quickly he picked up the phone and in a few seconds a man in civilian clothes appeared on the stairs behind him. He came down and introduced himself as a detective. He invited me through and led me upstairs. It was as much as my legs could managed to make the climb. I asked where Alex was.

'He's not here,' the detective replied.

I had had enough of being messed around. How dare they tell me he was here when he wasn't! And if he wasn't here, where was he?

But before I had the time to open my mouth the detective quickly added: 'He's at St George's hospital.' He must have seen the reaction in my face, and said, 'He's all right, there's a policewoman with him.'

I couldn't see what a policewoman being with him had to do with him being all right or not. It was his mother he wanted. I asked what state he was actually in beyond being 'all right'. The detective told me that he was calm and that he had not been injured.

He showed me into an office where another man in civilian clothes came towards me and introduced himself as a detective. Both of them showed as much kindness as was humanly possible. They showed me to a chair, offered me something to drink or eat. I could only manage

185

water. They found me tissues to wipe my face with and were as sympathetic as they could be. The contrast with my earlier treatment couldn't have been greater.

I let go of any pretence at self-control. I was sobbing helplessly. The two detectives were being as kind as they could, but their physical presence meant that this was no hoax. These strangers were suddenly part of my life. Everything was true.

They began to tell me a little of what had happened. I asked them to tell me everything. I tried to say that it was easier, if you can use such a word in the circumstances, for me to know everything at once.

They told me that Rachel had been attacked with a knife and killed. They said that she had been raped and sexually assaulted.

The pain was indescribable. To have something happen to someone you love is so far worse than to have it happen to you. To have a loved one taken away from you and for them to go through such a thing is the worst imaginable torture. How I wished with all my soul that it had happened to me rather than to this poor child. How could she have endured such suffering? There are just no words. There was something inside me that was on fire. Something was burning and shrivelling. There could be no relief.

My mother arrived soon after. My two brothers were with her, who had been with me the day when Rachel and I met. They had been young boys then, and could hardly help but fall under the magic of her charm. They were both reeling in shock. My mother was as white as a sheet. The detectives did the best they could to provide some comfort for us all. They were running to fetch drinks and provide chairs.

I was anxious to get to Alex. The older of my brothers had decided to go home by train. He was visibly disturbed but he was old enough to make up his own mind. The younger one stayed and came with us in the car to the hospital.

As soon as the detectives had arranged another car we set off to the hospital. 'I have to warn you that there is already a lot of press interest,' said one of the detectives. I had just enough spare capacity in my head to work out that this 'interest' was likely to become a part of our ordeal. The car in front led us through the hospital complex. My suspicions were confirmed a few minutes later when we were forced to use a back entrance and had to be smuggled into the building.

We were shown into a staff entrance and from there to a lift-shaft that was closed to the public. The lift climbed several floors and opened on to a ward which had been placed out of bounds to the public. There were security people posted to keep the press out. It was already like a war.

I looked around for Alex as I came out of the lift. I had no idea where he might be. Perhaps I thought he would be standing there waiting. But apart from the hospital staff going about their duties, the corridor was empty.

What I presumed was the nurse in charge came forward. She said that Alex was in one of the rooms with a nurse and a policewoman. He had only just fallen asleep before we arrived. I asked her what state he was in. She said that he had eaten some biscuits and that he had looked at some books with the nurse and the policewoman. She gave the impression that he had been amazingly calm and together.

It didn't sound like the child that I knew. I couldn't imagine Alex in any circumstances acting calm and controlled if he had been forced away from his mother. Her description frightened me. It was as if he had changed from a child of three to an adult in the course of a few short hours.

Innocence was over. He was such a small child but he had been through more than most adults were ever likely to. His childhood was destroyed. What was left for us now?

Chapter Fourteen

A UGUST: TWO WEEKS after Rachel's death. We went to Brighton for the day. I wasn't about to let up on the entertainments front. It would have been a lot easier if it hadn't been drizzling the whole time. There were roadworks too. Why were there always roadworks on the roads to seaside resorts in the middle of summer? What had been one of our regular trips had taken three hours instead of the usual forty-five minutes.

Alex had a tolerance of about forty minutes, if he was feeling particularly easygoing, and if there was plenty of entertainment. But by the time his period of grace had run out we still had no idea how much of the journey still lay in front of us and had gone too far to turn back. Not that this was even an option. His disappointment would have been far harder to handle than the journey itself. He loved his trips to the seaside. Thankfully we were not alone, and our friend was called upon to read endless stories and join in with Alex's favourite songs.

By the time we arrived it felt as if we had driven halfway across the country. Under the damp, dark skies it could have been November. Only the green leaves still thick on the trees gave the game away.

Everything was familiar, apart from one thing. The pier was still there; the children were still playing on the merry-go-round, Alex included; we even stopped off to have a baked potato in the same old place, Alex eating more than I'd ever seen him eat. But as my mouth began to form the words to speak I realized that there was no one to make the observation to. Who else but his mother would have been interested?

Only weeks before we had all been together in these same

surroundings. Now it was as if a silent screen had slid down to separate us. I still felt she was there, but there was no means of communication. I thought of people who had become obsessed by the paranormal after losing someone they loved. I could understand their frustration. How difficult it was to accept that you could never speak to them again. Just a few words. The simplest exchange of thoughts.

There was a little Postman Pat van on the pier that Alex could get into. I gave him a coin and the truck rolled around as if on a bumpy road while the familiar notes of the theme tune played along. On the seat beside him was Jess, the black and white cat. For a few moments Alex *was* Postman Pat. I watched his face through the windscreen. He giggled with pleasure and his eyes grew wide with excitement. It was the real thing come to life, just for him. He was absolutely thrilled.

To see him so full of joy and happiness would have made Rachel happy for a week. But as I watched, trying to give him all the attention I could, all I could think of was that she wouldn't be there when I turned to look for her. I turned round once, maybe more than once, to convince myself that she really wasn't there.

I had to hold it all inside, take this special moment of his all for myself. But it was too much for one person. The joy on his face was causing me so much pain. I made sure my smile never slipped. I thought of all the other parents who bring up a child on their own. There can never be anyone with whom you can share those little things except the other parent. You can never feel the same way about another person's child.

A few days later, in a wet South Kensington, we met up with the little girl from Alex's school and her sister. We were going to the dinosaur exhibition at the Natural History Museum.

Alex had never been to the museum before and all of the children were spellbound by the diplodocus skeleton which filled almost the whole of the ground-floor gallery. The sheer size of it was hard to believe. How could anything so big ever have been walking around?

There was a queue. Once in we had to follow a fixed route to ensure that everything was seen and nothing missed and to leave room for the people waiting outside to come in behind us.

Alex was more often on his feet now. I had to carry him less and less, but he would still hang on tight to my hand. When he did let go he would never move more than an arm's length away.

The exhibition started off with wonderful skeletons of triceratops and tyrannosaurus and others, all of which seemed almost tiny compared to the giant diplodocus we had queued under. There were all kinds of things to touch and buttons to press. There was a piece of hard, scaly dinosaur skin and even a real tyrannosaurus tooth.

Then the gallery led into the dark. We could hear fearsome screams and roars coming out of the shadows. We carried on into the darkness. I thought that the sound effects were coming from a film show further on. The children moved just ahead of us and we hurried to keep up. The end of the corridor turned sharp right and we were confronted with the source of all those noises.

They weren't coming from a film show. To my absolute horror there in front of us, in living detail, was a life-size, totally lifelike representation of a huge dinosaur, which had been pulled to the ground by a band of smaller predators. In any other circumstances I would have marvelled at the authenticity of the production. Everything was moving: the eyes, the limbs, even the sides rose up and down with each breath. But the smaller dinosaurs were pulling bloody chunks of flesh from the body of the larger dinosaur, which was squealing in pain, its lifelike eyes filled with fear.

Alex and the girls were already there. Their heads only just came over the top of the surrounding barrier and they were looking straight in.

My first reaction was to reach forward and pull Alex away. The room was suddenly hot and oppressive and the sound effects added to the atmosphere of violence and fear. 'What have I done?' I screamed inside. God knows what damage I had caused by stumbling stupidly into this situation. If he hadn't had nightmares so far then this was just the thing to trigger them off! I couldn't believe that I could have been so irresponsible. His confidence was just beginning to grow.

The second he saw what was depicted on the other side of the barrier he would be stricken with terror. In that split second he would be reduced to a quaking vegetable and the long weeks of work would all have gone down the drain. I just managed to stop myself leaping forward and dragging him back.

Thankfully. Because once again his reactions were the opposite of what I would have predicted. Instead of fear he showed a certain detached curiosity. He stood peering over the edge with the others while the large dinosaur continued to squeal in fear and the little ones pulled away with their mouthfuls of dripping flesh.

After a few minutes the children's interest was exhausted and they turned away together and looked for the next attraction.

Alex showed no sign of any reaction to what he had just seen. For the rest of the visit he continued to be totally at ease with the surroundings and with everybody else. His greatest worry came at the souvenir stand where he was concerned that we might go past without buying him at least one or two special little things from all that was on display.

At last he came away, serious but satisfied, his dinosaur ruler and rubber safely in his clutches.

Alex's reaction was, as far as I was concerned, one of the biggest signs so far that he was on the road to recovery. There was no doubt that he was coping better. He was noticeably relaxing his grip on me. And while there was still no way he would let me out of the room he was paying me much less attention and the frequency of his glances to check on my position per minute were reducing all the time.

We could hardly have come across a more graphic representation of violence and distress, yet he had hardly turned a hair. But I couldn't tell whether the fact of witnessing something so terrible had in a way immunized him against any shock that was less than the one he had endured. Or conversely, if the weight of any lesser shocks, added to the original one, might finally tip him over the edge.

I wasn't prepared to take any chances. If I had known how graphic and gory that stand was going to be I would not have let him see it. But he had seen it anyway and appeared to have suffered no ill effects. I decided however that I would still try to protect him from unnecessary surprises. I would deal with the consequences of what managed to creep in round the edges if and when the situation arose.

We were back with the child psychologist the day after the dinosaurs. The audiovisual equipment had not yet been installed.

Once again she was in her usual position on the floor. Alex was sitting at the low table playing with the toys, I was just behind him on the sofa, and the detectives sat back in their armchairs.

We were beginning to know each other well and the conversation was going in different directions between us. The child psychologist had to make an effort to get the focus back on the day Rachel was killed.

'Really, little Alex is doing so well, being able to help the big detectives with their job,' she began. 'He's been able to tell us so much. And he's such a clever little boy, I'm sure there is more he can tell us, too.'

Alex bristled with pride. It pleased him to think that he was able to help these big, strong grown-ups.

No matter what else may or may not have been bubbling under the surface his self-image was very strong. The detectives always had a word of praise for anything that Alex was able to tell them. His body language alone always showed how proud he was to hear how well they thought of him. I had the feeling that this alone was good therapy for him in his struggle to cope with what had happened. Anything that made him feel better about himself, anything that made him feel more secure, made him feel appreciated, could only be good for him.

But the fear that crossed my mind was: would he become so eager for this praise that he might start inventing things just to keep them happy?

The question was always on my mind whenever Alex began to talk about anything to do with his mother's murder in their presence. But I knew that he was too young to lie. It hadn't yet occurred to him that he could manipulate the people around him by playing with the truth. And he didn't have any older brothers or sisters to learn from either. This certainly wasn't a moral judgement: it seemed to me to be a fair observation of the way he operated. But I was constantly on the lookout to try and catch any signs that he had realized that there were other ways of playing the game. So far I hadn't seen any.

His behaviour was bound to change: that was only normal, and probably a sign of intelligence. Everybody learns that there are times when it is better not to tell the truth, even if it is only by not saying anything at all. This change in a child's perception was surely the crux of the issue over the admissibility of children's evidence in the courts.

As was the routine, we started right back from when Rachel and Alex left the car in the carpark and began walking.

'Do you remember getting out of the car with Mummy on that terrible terrible day? The day you probably don't want to think about at all,' the child psychologist asked.

'And Molly was there!' he answered.

He would often give the impression that he was totally engrossed in his play, to the exclusion of all else. But I could always tell that he was taking in absolutely everything that was being said, and was aware of everybody's movements. My impression was borne out by the fact that often, exactly while appearing to be engrossed in getting on with his own stuff and sometimes without even looking up, he would come out with a sentence or a phrase which answered the question precisely. Often in a way that answered several questions at once.

Alex was given heaps and heaps of praise and sympathy, and between his answers he continued playing busily with the contents of the table-top. On the face of it he appeared to be playing normally, if maybe with a little too much intensity. But whenever we reached a point that he must have found more difficult to think about than others his playing got louder. The volume increased gradually until it was a strain to make out what anyone was saying. He was banging and bashing the toys around as hard as he could to drown us out.

If I was putting the question he would sometimes climb up on to my lap and put his hand across my mouth. He would smile as if he was playing a game with me, but he didn't want to hear.

This noise generation was typical of all the children the child psychologist worked with. She said you could always hear the crescendo building on tape recordings of her sessions. There was always the most noise when she was talking about the things which were the most difficult for the child to bear. But this was the most fundamental point of all: did you bow down to a child's desire to stop the pain by ignoring it completely and hoping it would go away? or did you continue to push in the hope of lancing the wound and letting the poison out?

Alex would sometimes look at me in complete confusion, obviously asking himself why I was trying to cause him even more pain. I struggled hard to steel myself against his distress and tried to remind myself over and over of the progress he was making exactly because I kept on pushing. But at times it was hard to balance the equation.

As the sessions progressed the general sequence of events of that day became clearer and clearer. Then it became a question of trying to fill in the missing details. All the details he had provided so far had been extremely accurate. The real problem was keeping his interest and concentration. Things were often repeated over and over, questions asked several times firmly, but gently, before he felt like answering. Then it was a matter of trying not to confuse him, of trying to keep the phrases we used always the same and trying to provide him with questions that he would always clearly understand.

The detectives were searching for a graphic method of presenting things to Alex, bearing in mind the success they had had with the dolls. They were looking into the possibility of having a three-dimensional model made of the exact location where Rachel had been attacked in the hope that it would make it easier for him to understand what was being asked of him.

'Alex, did you see the knife that the bad man used to kill Mummy?' I asked him.

'Yes.'

'We're going to show you some knives so you can tell us which one it looked like.'

The detectives brought in a tray. They presented it to Alex as if it was all part of a party game.

What was I putting him through? What would his reaction be to seeing a knife that looked the same as the one he had seen being used to butcher his mother? Part of me wanted to say Stop! That's enough! I'm not putting him through any more! But another part of me was saying: no matter how painful it is, it is still better to have everything out in the open. Still better that he knew there were no taboos, that there was nothing he couldn't talk about. Nothing he might think I didn't want to hear. Otherwise what choice would he have but to hold it inside and try to deal with it himself?

The child psychologist told us that he was intelligent enough to know that what we were talking about made me upset, that it made his grandparents upset. He may not have wanted to see us upset, much less be the reason for it. There was always a danger that he would be tempted not to say as much in order to spare us. This made us redouble our efforts to make sure he understood how pleased we were that he was being such a big boy and how clever he was to remember so much.

Alex didn't turn a hair when he was presented with the tray. He smiled. I suppose he thought that he was being presented with another chance to prove how clever he was. Although this was exactly the reaction we wanted, it was still completely at odds with the situation.

Why didn't he break down and scream and cry? I asked myself. But as I was seeing more and more all the time, children just don't react like adults.

But my stomach was churning. I felt physically sick. All I could think of was the sequence of events which must have taken place, with a knife like one of the ones in front of us. I could see in graphic detail in my head what must have happened and in my head I could see Alex's face watching it all.

I tried to show no reaction, except to give him a smile of encouragement as he made his choice. Not that he could see my expression anyway as he had his back to me, but I was sure he could pick up my mood.

The detective put the tray down on the table. On it was some ordinary household cutlery, a bread-knife, several large kitchen knives, a penknife and a hunting knife. Alex showed absolutely no hesitation and immediately picked out the hunting knife, whose blade matched the shape of the murder weapon as established by the pathologist after examining Rachel's wounds.

'What did the bad man do after he had killed Mummy?'

'He lay down to look in the water.'

In the beginning there was everything to discover and everything to know. Everything that Alex came up with added to the picture of how the events had taken place. As we went through what had happened Alex would come up with a couple of details here and a couple of details there. This meant that things kept moving along, which helped to keep his interest, and that he had a continuous feeling of achievement when he was able to tell us something we didn't know.

'The bad man washed the blood off in the water,' he volunteered a little later.

There was a stream that ran only a few yards from where Rachel was killed. A witness had reported seeing a man leaning over the stream, apparently washing himself. The time that the witness gave for this sighting was ten or twenty minutes after another witness had reported seeing a man acting suspiciously on the mound less than two hundred metres away. Both witnesses described the man as being dressed in the same clothing that Alex had described his mother's killer as wearing when we had been on Hampstead Heath.

But for one event confirmed, a mystery appeared. There was a pond which Rachel and Alex would undoubtedly have been on their way to visit or on their way back from. But it was too far away to be seen from where Rachel and Alex were found. However, there was a set of Alex's footprints on the ground by Rachel's body and Alex's trousers were soaked with water all the way up to and over the knees.

'He threw the knife in the pond.'

Alex couldn't have seen the man throw anything in the pond unless he had followed behind to watch him. Or, as one of the detectives observed, unless he had been carried off.

But Alex had reached saturation point and was unwilling to answer any more questions. Enough was enough and he had unequivocally pulled down the shutters for the day. But we were making progress. He was revealing more and more. The layers were very slowly peeling away.

I had to remind myself that we weren't there to do the police's job for them. First and foremost what we were doing here was for Alex's sanity. Anything that helped the police in turn was a bonus. But at the same time I was anxious that we be able to give them everything we could so they could put this animal away as quickly as possible.

We were left to ponder over the possible answers to the questions left unanswered. No material evidence had so far been found. Nothing. There was still absolutely no sign of the murder weapon or even of the slightest scrap of bloodstained clothing.

There were moments when being so closely involved in the police's work became too much to cope with. On top of being at Alex's beck and call, and in between the sessions with the child psychologist, and along with the travelling back and forward, I would still spend time each day talking with detectives. Trying to find the answers to riddles, answering questions, then dealing with the questions that my answers inevitably produced. I would become consumed by thinking over anything new they might have told me, any new detail, trying to work out what direction things were going in now. Then I would talk things over with friends, sometimes losing track of who knew what. When Alex had gone to bed there were Rachel's parents to be kept up to date. Sometimes I felt as if, on top of everything else, I was running an information service as well.

At the very beginning of the investigation there was always the hope that this would all be over tomorrow. That something decisive would turn up and the killer would be arrested. Then it would only be a question of waiting for the trial and then he would be put away for ever and then at least the public exposure and constant upheaval would be over. Things wouldn't be any better, but at least it would be the start of trying to put things behind us. It wouldn't be any better, but waiting, with it all still to come, was worse. And because there was always the hope that it would soon be over, it was difficult to know how to pace yourself emotionally. We already knew that even when an arrest had been made there would still be a considerable wait until the trial itself. The High Court was in recess in the middle of summer so the earliest possible date would be autumn of the following year.

There was something about being able to close the book. We knew that Rachel was dead. Some families didn't even have that certainty. I could appreciate a little of how hard it must be for those whose loved ones were simply 'missing'. How could you go forward when there was always the chance, however slim, that your son or daughter or sister or brother was still alive? You would feel like you were in total limbo, your life indefinitely put on hold. Forever waiting for something to happen. Not knowing when or even if it ever would.

The trial ahead formed a landmark in my mind. All those questions – What are you going to do with your life? When are you going to feel any better? When are you going to do something for yourself? – and all of the other, for the moment, unanswerable issues, were put consciously or unconsciously beyond that date. Only afterwards would I really be free to think about living again.

I was always optimistic that the killer would be found, and that he would be put away. So many of the people involved were taking this personally.

I heard it said many times, from all kinds of different people, that it was as if this had happened to one of *their* family. They were totally committed to solving this case no matter what effort might be involved. The thought was always in their minds that this person was still out there, still at total liberty, and there was no telling when he might strike again.

I was told how they broke down the lists of possible suspects. First, they intended to track down and speak to every man who had been on the Common that morning. Secondly they were in the process of going through our address books and diaries and speaking to everyone we knew. They were also in the process of interviewing every past offender who lived in the local area, specifically those who had been involved in crimes of a sexual or violent nature. They had contacted all the police forces up and down the country to see if there had been other similar attacks recorded elsewhere. On top of this they were cross-referencing all the witnesses' statements to extract the maximum of information. Then they were following up on every single phone call that had been received at the incident room, which was still being manned twenty-four hours a day.

No possibility would be left unexamined. They were prepared to grind on and on through all the information until they came up with something. It was hard to see how anything could be missed. It was only a question of time.

From day to day our detectives would tell me who they had been speaking to, or what the latest most hopeful piece of information might be. When they weren't with us they were going through the same daily tasks as the rest of the team. There were regular detectives' meetings in which each would have a chance to hear what the others were up to. All this information was being logged on to computers and the most daunting thing appeared to be simply handling the vast amount of information already collected in a way that allowed everyone to know what was going on so that their work was not duplicated.

When they told me the figures for the number of former sexual offenders who lived within the local area of the Common I was horrified. There were hundreds! When this was added to the number of people who had formerly been convicted of crimes of violence the number was truly staggering. Suddenly the question became not 'Why has this happened?' but 'Why doesn't it happen more often?'

If everyone knew the enormous number of dangerous people walking around, and had described to them what the crimes they had committed actually were, then there is no way that they would let the women or children they love out of their sight, whether it be day or night. These people are often unemployed with plenty of time on their hands to be hanging around parks and school playgrounds fantasizing and planning and looking for victims.

I was so naïve. So incredibly ignorant and stupid. There was no way on earth that I would have let Rachel walk around so carefree if I had known then what I knew now. I didn't own her. And it wasn't for me to say where she should go or what she should do. And I knew that these were the kind of people who could just as easily get in through the window or force the door. But if I had known then what I knew now at least I could have warned her! We had been trying to play the game of safety and trying to be as careful as possible without being totally paranoid. But it wasn't paranoid to be scared when you knew the facts. It was realistic.

It wasn't that we had been happy-go-lucky, thinking that this would never happen to us. Rachel was always very careful about where she went and paid attention to the way she dressed. She would go out of her way not to appear provocative. She would rarely wear anything but trousers if I was not around and would cross the road rather than pass a group of men on their own. She did not consider the Common during the day as a dangerous place, it was as simple as that. If she had done, she wouldn't have gone.

But now I could see that no open space was safe. There was always someone watching, someone looking. It wasn't just paranoia.

Suspicion had fallen upon a man living in the north. As the Common was bordered by a stretch of fast dual carriageway, people could get there from practically anywhere without attracting the slightest attention. This person had previous convictions and was on remand for rape. He was out of prison on bail while awaiting trial, even though he had been positively identified by the victim. He had shown himself to be extremely controlled and clinical in the way that he had avoided leaving any physical evidence which could identify him through DNA testing.

The person who had attacked Rachel had also been extremely careful. As it now transpired, Rachel hadn't been raped. She had been sexually assaulted. Consequently there was much less chance, if any, of leaving evidence. Alex had confirmed that the killer had not removed or lowered his trousers.

The detectives said that there was not much to link the northerner with Rachel's murder. Whoever had attacked Rachel had wanted to kill her. The rest was secondary. But this man was still stalking women on open ground or at night, even while on remand.

The thought was terrifying. Here was another tragedy waiting to happen. I asked the detectives if they couldn't stop him. But apparently he wasn't breaking any laws. There was absolutely nothing they could do. On at least one occasion the detectives following him had thought that he was right on the point of attacking someone. Our detectives didn't say as much but I had the feeling that they would have been glad if he had done. At least that way the police would be on the spot to jump in and save the poor girl, and also to catch him in the act. But the idea was so awful, the risks so great. The poor girl could be dead in seconds, before the police had a chance to intervene.

There were several arrests in the first few weeks. Each time we would be notified beforehand to avoid us having to find out through the press. Often this was the only way that the police could interview an unwilling party in order to eliminate them from the enquiry. Each time we were told the likelihood the police felt that this was their man. Each time the likelihood was extremely low.

Some of the arrests became very public affairs. For instance by the time the police vehicle carrying the northern stalker had reached the police station a crowd had gathered. It was common knowledge that he was being linked to Rachel's murder. I watched the scene on TV. The crowd booed and jeered and shouted, and hammered on the police van with their fists. If they could have got their hands on him they would have lynched him. I knew it was highly unlikely that this was our man. But I felt no sympathy.

The police had had their hand forced by the press. Some journalist had found out that the northerner was under suspicion. The police were still gathering evidence and their job was much easier because this person was walking about totally unaware that he was being watched. He had been slowly revealing things about himself that it would have been hard to prove if he hadn't been under surveillance. But the journalists wanted their scoop. They told the police that if an arrest wasn't made in the next few days then they were going to publish the story anyway.

Our detectives' professional reserve didn't hide what they thought of the press. It was terrifying to think how the press could have compromised the chances of successfully prosecuting Rachel's killer. Although the northerner was an unlikely suspect, *they* didn't know that.

One of the senior officers had been to the south-west where a girl had been found stabbed to death on open ground some weeks before Rachel had been killed. The local police already had a very likely suspect. In fact the case was already being prepared for trial. He hadn't fallen under suspicion until after Rachel's death, so he was still a possible. But eventually his movements on the 15th were established by several different people. He couldn't have been in the two places at once. So, as far as they were concerned, he was no longer of interest.

Meanwhile Alex's friend's father (. . . .) was being looked into extremely thoroughly. He had no criminal record or history of violent behaviour. The police were looking for any indication that he might be someone who could have 'snapped' in a jealous fury.

Chapter Fifteen

LITTLE MORE THAN four weeks had passed since the day Rachel was killed. If the pain had dulled it was hardly enough to notice.

It was Saturday. The sun was shining. At least we could have Alex's party outdoors, even if it had rained on his birthday. But before his party there was yet another session with the child psychologist. Alex was coming up with a steady flow of information now and, rather than drag the process out, it seemed better to follow his pace.

The video cameras and the sound equipment had been fitted. They had done a good job in concealing everything this time. The room looked almost exactly the same as it had before. The only sign was that some of the furniture had been pushed together in one corner to hide some wires.

During the sessions I would have to fight my irritation when others were doing the asking. Only a parent can really know when their small child is thinking and about to speak; or thinking and unlikely to speak; or thinking and confused; or only appearing to be thinking and in fact blanking everything out altogether. Sometimes I would feel that the others were cutting him off, or talking when they should have been letting him think a little longer. A child would feel completely swamped if there wasn't someone he trusted deeply there to reassure him in such circumstances.

We had begun to use the name of the father of Alex's friend (. . . .) in our sessions with Alex. Instead of saying: 'Did the bad man speak to Mummy before she was killed?' one of us would ask: 'Did (. . . .) speak to Mummy before she was killed?' Alex responded with immediate enthusiasm.

Over a close period of days we took Alex through what had happened. From getting out of the car, to seeing someone approach them, and to his mother being attacked. All of us used (. . . .)'s name in our questions: What did (. . . .) do next? Or what was (. . . .) wearing? Or what did (. . . .) have in his hand?

He answered readily enough. But curiously enough, he never used (. . . .)'s name himself. Never once did he say specifically: '(. . . .) was wearing a white shirt', for example. He merely responded to us adults when we used the name.

Often the child psychologist would ask: 'Alex, do you know the name of the man who killed your mummy?'

Never once did he give an answer.

Sometimes one or other of the detectives would gently ask the same question. For the first time Alex actually looked up at them and studied their faces. His previous habit had been nearly always to answer while still looking down at what he was doing, or sometimes by looking at me, irrespective of who had put the question.

By now Alex had confirmed that some words had been exchanged with Rachel's killer before she died. But it was impossible to understand whether this was one word or a conversation. Or simply if her killer had said something to her, in passing. Alex had also confirmed that Rachel's killer was wearing the same clothing that he had previously described to us on Hampstead Heath. That is, white buttoned, collared shirt worn outside blue trousers which weren't jeans, and dark shoes.

'He had a black bag.'

The witness who had seen an identically dressed man nearby only minutes before Rachel was killed, had also said that he was carrying a black bag.

'He took the knife from the bag.'

What more proof did anyone need that Alex was telling the truth? Here was all that he was saying being confirmed by adult witnesses. It was only his identification of (. . . .) that was less than decisive. Why didn't he just come out and say: (. . . .) was carrying a black bag. And: (. . . .) killed my mummy!

Alex again confirmed that the killer had afterwards walked away in the direction of the little stream. Still without using the name himself.

'Did (. . . .) run away, or did he walk away?'

'Walked away.'

The killer had lain down to 'look' in the water. From there the killer had got up and walked away towards the cemetery.

Alex had always said 'no' if I asked had Mummy screamed. This helped me to believe that she had died very quickly. The pathologist had always said from the very beginning that one of the very first few blows could have been fatal. But it was only his opinion. I prayed that he was right.

I would often think of the 'defence' wound in Rachel's hand. This was the way the pathologist described the first blow that Rachel had received. She was always cutting or burning her hands cooking. Sometimes she cut them deeply. I had worked in a kitchen while still at school and had learnt to slice properly. I tried to show her what I had been taught. She never paid me much attention but still she would thrust her hands towards me looking for sympathy when she hurt herself. I could remember the pain in her eyes.

I used to hate the way she injured herself. It upset me deeply. It was so unnecessary. But it was the expression on her face: I could picture her face as she put up her hand to take the first blow. The expression of bewilderment and pain. I knew that her first thought would have been for Alex. She would have done anything to protect him. Anything. She had said again and again that she would let someone do anything to her in order to save him. There was no doubt in my mind that, rather than take any chance of picking him up and trying to run away, she would sacrifice herself and give her attacker what he wanted.

Every time she brought the subject up my stomach would turn to ice. Just the very thought that such a thing could happen to anyone was sickening, but to have the woman you love talk about what she would do it if happened to her was unbearable.

Now at his party, Alex threw himself into having a good time.

He still carried the marks upon his face. He was dark and puffy under each eye and the scabs had blackened on the grazing and cuts across his cheekbones.

Because of the public's generosity the choice was not so much what to give him for his birthday but what not to give him. There was no way that I could allow him to have more than the smallest part of all that had been donated. We settled on a few things that Rachel would definitely have approved of. Several of them we certainly couldn't have afforded, but if we could have she would have been thrilled for him to have them.

But like most children he spent more time playing with the boxes and the wrapping paper than with the gifts themselves. Water balloons were the order of the day and he soon lost interest in nearly everything else.

The first tide of mail had begun to ease off but in the week before his birthday well over a hundred cards arrived via the police. It was staggering how many people had registered when his birthday was due and very moving that they had gone to such trouble to write again now, several weeks after the original publicity.

There was a card from the remand wing of a large prison. Its arrival was a reminder of the treatment that inmates reserved for the perpetrators of crimes against women and children. It only confirmed my belief that the best place for whoever had done this was behind bars, for the rest of his life, with no hope of ever being let out. Dying was too easy.

During the day Alex's grandfather asked him if he was happy now that he had told Daddy who had killed Mummy. Alex had said that he was, and we all agreed that his behaviour was noticeably more relaxed and carefree. He looked as though a load had been taken off his shoulders.

Alex was still much calmer the following day. Between what he had told me on his own and the answers that he had given at the child psychologist's he had let go of a huge amount of information. A huge amount of information that he had been carrying on his own during all these weeks. And with it all the ramifications and possibilities and conclusions he must no doubt have been trying to wrestle with. All the while looking out on a world in which he had so recently been so secure, and that he had had so much trust in. And which he was now trying to come to terms with after all of that trust and security had been turned upside down.

I was busy washing the car in the front drive. Alex was keeping a careful eye on me but in between times he was happy to be amused inside the house by his grandmother. After a while they appeared at the door together. Rachel's mother told me that they were off across the road to thank a neighbour for making his birthday cake. I could see the door from where I was standing and watched sceptically as she led him across the empty street. I wondered how far they would get before Alex felt the tug of the invisible umbilical cord that attached him to me and burst into tears and screamed for me to come and get him.

I watched them walk up the garden path and ring on the front door. Already I was impressed. The door opened and, to my amazement Alex walked straight in. It closed behind them.

I stood looking at the closed door. As the seconds ticked away I was the one who was suffering pangs of anxiety. This was the first time he had entered another building without me. It was an enormous step, even if it was with the person that he next trusted the most in all the world. They were inside for only a few minutes. As they made their way back across the street I could see that he was perfectly relaxed. It was another marker along the way.

We were invited to a barbecue that afternoon and it was only at the last minute that I decided to go. I had avoided all contact with people that Alex didn't know. But this was Rachel's father's secretary, not a complete stranger.

He fell asleep in his car-seat on the way there and I tried to get him through the house without disturbing him.

I sat down in the garden with him on my lap. He wasn't amused.

'I want to go back to Grandma's house!' he said firmly.

I didn't.

Everyone was out for the afternoon and I couldn't face the idea of amusing him one hundred per cent of the time on my own from now until bedtime in an empty house. Sometimes the thought was just too daunting. He needed something different every five minutes, a constant change of activity, and the house was becoming a little too familiar. There was more to amuse him here. There was a nice garden and I was sure I could find a cake or an ice-cream somewhere to tempt him with. Molly was already playing with the family dog. There was a goldfish pond and there were also his grandparents to lend a hand.

Alex would not budge from my lap. He wouldn't be tempted by anything to eat and he refused even to look around to see what was going on. If I made an effort to get up he clamped himself to me in terror. There was no way I could sweet-talk him into having a good time. I had some chocolate bars in my bag and books to read, so we camped ourselves out on the garden bench and carried on as if nothing else existed. I tried to get comfortable and make the best of it.

We read through each book several times over and more than an hour had passed before Alex showed any sign of unwinding. It was the little dog that first captured his attention. It began to bounce up and down in front of us and then sprang up on to the bench. This made Alex giggle because Mollie was never allowed on any furniture. He thought the dog was very cheeky.

I carried on reading but now Alex was splitting his attention between listening to me and watching the antics of the little dog. As time passed he was spending more time looking around him than paying attention to the stories. He began to ask questions about what was going on and what everything was for. Apart from the trestle tables loaded with food there was a pile of building sand in a corner at the end of the garden, not far from the goldfish pond. It looked just the thing to play in with the dumper truck he had had for his birthday.

Eventually he loosened up enough to let me carry him round the garden so that he could have a closer look at everything himself. And with another half an hour's gentle persuasion and an ice-cream I managed to get him to put his feet on the ground himself.

After that it was fairly easy. He nearly let me return to the car to get his dumper truck on my own. But not quite. He had to follow me through the house and along the pavement just to make sure. But once back in the garden he played quite happily with it, moving sand about by pulling on the levers in between looking at the fish in the pond. My role was reduced to making sure he didn't put sand in on top of the fish, or fall in himself. Soon he was having a whale of a time, and had completely forgotten his reluctance.

By the end of the afternoon I had to drag him away. He didn't want to leave. But, happy though I was that he should be having a good time, he still needed to get to bed on time. It had been a very full couple of days. If his routine was disturbed he wouldn't get the rest he needed and tomorrow would be hell, especially for me. No matter how late he went to bed he always woke up at the same time the next day: early.

But once he had been fed and bathed and storied he went to sleep quickly. The following morning was a record. When I looked at my watch as he came into my bed it was a quarter-past eight. He had never slept so late. I could only assume that unloading so much of what had happened to him had eased his mind to the extent that he could already sleep more easily.

Three years later I found a picture taken that afternoon at the barbecue.

In my mind I remembered him having a good time, once he had unwound a little. But the photograph shows an anxious and frightened little boy with a badly bruised face, holding his security blankets tightly around him, while sitting bunched up on his father's lap listening to a story.

We went to spend a few days at a friend's house in the country. My younger brother came with us. We had never been before and were more than halfway there when Alex decided he didn't want to go. He was complaining loudly from his car-seat and no amount of stories being read by my brother or anything that I could say would appease him.

Alex became so adamant that I couldn't help but ask myself if our friend looked anything like (. . . .). But I couldn't see any similarity between them at all.

Alex's complaining got so bad that I had to promise him that, if he didn't like it when we got there, we would turn round and go back home again. We had been driving for a couple of hours, and turning round was the last thing in the world I wanted to do. But this was the only thing that would satisfy him. He was instantly appeased and sat back in his car-seat without another word of complaint.

When we got to the house it really was out in the country. There was a wood beside it and fields behind, and a pig-farm out beyond. Apart from the odd passing car there was absolute calm. So different from the ever-present rumble of traffic in London. It was very, very quiet.

There was even a swimming pool. Alex loved the water, especially cold water, which was handy as the pool wasn't heated, and his day was made when a toad hopped across the garden, jumped into the pool and began to swim across. He was enchanted and wanted to get into his trunks immediately and jump in with it. Soon he had forgotten all about wanting to go home and was as relaxed with our friend here as he was when our friend came to visit us in London.

It was good to get away from London. I didn't have to think about the phone ringing, or keeping everyone informed, or speaking to the police or any of the rest of my now daily chores.

Things were tense between Rachel's parents and myself. It was hard for us to relate. My knowledge of her began on the day we met four years before and grew with all the time and experiences we shared together. In many ways their knowledge of her stopped there, at the point where mine began. We didn't really know the same person. My relationship with Rachel was deep and intense and we often said that it was as if we had known each other for ever. She was my best friend, my lover, my wife, the mother of my child. She knew as much about me as there was to know. Our whole lives were bound up together.

Naturally her parents, like any parents, caught only glimpses of all that passed between us. Their relationship with her was still strong, if often stormy, and continued to grow in other ways, especially after the birth of Alex. Rachel spoke to one or other of them virtually every day. But they could never have seen the side of her that I had and sometimes, when I was with them now, it was as if we were talking about two different people. How could I possibly see her the way that they did? Loving her from a tiny baby, watching her first steps, seeing her lose her first teeth and then as she grew into a schoolgirl, and then a teenager, and then a young woman. I could never really share those things with them, just as they could never share what had passed between Rachel and me.

We stayed for a few days. We went to the seaside a couple of times and for the rest just pottered around, finding things to do as we went. It never much mattered where we were with Alex. As long as he had his meals and his bath at the right time and had his stories and songs at bedtime he was always quite relaxed anywhere. And thankfully I never forgot his blankets or sheepskin, and when he had those, any bedroom was fine by him as long as I was sleeping there too.

As we played on the cold damp pebbles at the seashore I suddenly wanted to swim. There didn't seem any point in being at the seaside otherwise. Alex was hanging on to my leg as I tried to get changed, moaning for me not to go in. But his moaning was not quite as determined as he was capable of. Rather than showing genuine distress, it was more as if he was seeing if he could get his own way just for the sake of it. It was a bit like going through the motions. But I was determined that I was going in. My brother and our friend were there to distract him, and Molly was chasing pebbles across the beach.

Nevertheless, he was still hanging off my leg as I stumbled down to the water's edge. I was interested to see just how far he was prepared to go to stop me going in. It wouldn't have been a complete surprise if he had hung on all the way into the sea itself. I had dry clothes for him in my bag if he was really that determined, but *he* didn't know that. He hung on until I had both feet in the water, and then he decided enough was enough. He threw a few lame 'Come back!'s my way but his heart wasn't in it. Already he was making his way back up the steep shingle to see what the others were doing.

I was only in the water for a few minutes. It was cold. But I was savouring one of the very rare occasions when I had myself to myself. It was an enormous relief not to have that little voice chirping continually in my ear, demanding this and asking for that, and crying for something else.

I was almost completely relaxed. But almost as quickly I was anxious to know how he was. I was soon physically ill at ease not to know exactly what he was doing and what mood he was in. Already I wanted that chirpy little voice back again, just so I could be sure that he was all right.

I could see from the water that he was fine and that he was being well entertained. But that wasn't enough: I still had to see properly for myself, and was soon out of the water and back within earshot. This time it was my need, not his. I had been solely responsible for his every whim for what seemed so long now, and we had been through so much, that I was beginning to understand the difference between what it is to be a father and what it is to be a mother.

As a father I was used to drifting in and drifting out. Which is inevitable when you go out to work. Sometimes it would irritate me when Rachel left Alex with me while she got on with something else and I could see that she was still not able to relax completely. She still had to come and check. I found it insulting to be trusted so little. But now I could see how hard it is, when you are so responsible for someone, to switch off even for the shortest time.

We spent the rest of the day at the seaside, wrapped up in jackets against the cold, damp air. The change was definitely doing me good, even though I had broken down the night before. I had felt completely wretched.

Going to somewhere new reinforced the fact that things weren't going to get better. It forced my face right up against it. Because it was only normal to associate changing things with making them better. Nobody chooses to make things worse. Being somewhere nice, doing something nice, makes you think about sharing it all with the people you love. There was only one person I wanted to share anything with, and she wasn't there. So even though it was preferable to be at the seaside, rather than somewhere else, I still wasn't 'happy'. I still didn't feel 'good'. Instead I felt wretched. I felt like shit but I still preferred to be there.

There were different criteria now. Different standards to judge by. I knew that if Rachel had been there and we had all been together then I would have been happy. Still worried about all the usual material problems, but emotionally as complete and content as it was possible to imagine.

The aching loneliness that I had so often known had been a thing of the past ever since we were together. Only once had I ever given that sensation another thought, and that was only a couple of days before Rachel was killed. In a quiet moment at work I had been weighing up my life. There were some things that weren't going well. A lot of things, in fact. But all of that disappeared in an instant when I remembered the old feeling of loneliness. I could hardly imagine it any more. I knew how complete I was now with Rachel. So deeply secure and loved. Just to think how bad I had felt at times before wiped all of my troubles away in an instant. 'I'll never feel like that again!' I told myself. 'We could lose everything, but as long as we have each other and Alex and our health we'll be fine. As long as we are together I can never feel that bad again. Together we would find a way.' It wasn't romantic nonsense or idealistic foolishness. It was absolutely true.

But we weren't together anymore. And now I understand what people meant when they said that losing someone so close was like losing a part of your own body. I felt physically torn apart. Unable to function. I needed my lungs to breathe and my eyes to see but without her to give me what she did I was no longer living. Merely surviving. She wasn't there, and it was only just bearable to do anything at all. Let alone take any pleasure in it. Only just bearable enough not to give up completely.

In many ways it was much easier when I was struggling and fighting. When even the little things weren't going well. Then I didn't expect to feel good. But when Alex produced some splodge of colour and would come to me with his eyes so full of pride at his 'masterpiece', or when it struck me what a lovely little boy he really was as he skipped across the pebbles, it was like having my guts physically twisted one more time. She should have been there to enjoy those moments, she had done so much to bring them about. He should have had her

211

there to enjoy them. And I should have been wallowing in the pleasure of watching that joy shining in her eyes.

The night before I had just wanted to throw my hands up and say
'Enough! I can't go through the rest of my life like this.' I was trying
my best but nothing made me feel any better. Each way I turned it was
the same. I had to find a way of deadening the pain that wouldn't damage either of us, but for the moment I was allowing myself the luxury
of wallowing in despair. And was grateful for the kind of friends who
allowed me to do so.

Alex was soon completely at home in our friend's house. He sat on the
floor with our friend and produced drawing after drawing. 'Mummy
would have liked these,' he smiled, completely unselfconsciously.

We went to visit HMS *Victory* in Portsmouth harbour. It seemed
like a good idea at the time. Alex liked pirates. He was fine while we
walked around outside and while we waited in the queue. But once
we had climbed the entry gang-planks and made our way inside he
quickly became agitated.

We tried interesting him in the cannons, and told him how it had
been little boys who were made to climb the rigging, but he wanted
to leave straight away. It was hardly surprising. The atmosphere was
heavy and morbid. It was saturated with suffering and death and he'd
picked it all up straight away. He was grizzling, disturbed by the surroundings. We couldn't get back by the way we came: the traffic was
moving against us. The ship was unexpectedly large and it took us
some time to find our way off. He moaned into my shoulder as we
climbed dingy wooden staircases and crossed the deck. The damp and
overcast morning did nothing to lighten the effect.

He calmed down immediately we were back on firm ground and
was soon skipping along cheerfully again. We untied Molly from the
bollard – she had been barking from the moment she had spotted us
on deck – and went to the beach instead.

We went to visit an aquarium. Apart from the tanks full of fish and
other exhibits there was a little theatre to one side where a film was
playing. It was all about sharks. It showed a blonde woman who was
often in the water, sometimes in a cage, while the sharks circled closely
around her. There were gory passages when they went into a feeding

frenzy as chunks of bloody meat were thrown into the water, and there were lots of knives and spears.

Alex was fascinated. The theatre was almost empty and I watched him as he moved from seat to seat, backwards and forwards but always taking in what was on the screen. In other circumstances I probably wouldn't have let him watch but nothing in this film was as terrifying as what he had lived through. He appeared to be testing himself, going away and then coming back again to see more. I wondered how much fear he could take.

Regularly he would ask: 'Where's the lady gone?' He didn't seem particularly anxious and was certainly not scared. He just wanted to know what had happened to her.

I presumed that she was absolutely fine and in fact she would always reappear later on as if in confirmation of my words. Our friend made the observation that Alex was definitely trying to work something through. But it was difficult to know exactly what. On the surface he was like any other small child fidgeting around. He looked happy enough and seemed more intent on moving from seat to seat and running in and out of the theatre than actually watching. But he kept coming back. There was nothing I could do, and very little I could say. I could explain to him exactly what the film was about, but in his head it had another significance.

The film was on a loop and played over and over. In between skipping in and out of the main exhibition, Alex must have finally watched it in its entirety.

I was struggling with myself, fighting the urge to pick him up and carry him away. But there was a balance to be found between protecting and smothering. Because this was uncomfortable for me it did not mean that it wasn't valuable for him. It wasn't easy to stomach, watching images of a woman with blonde hair swirling through bloodstained water with knives and spearguns flashing past, accompanied by dramatic music. And there he was, this little boy, sitting and moving and watching, with possibly all that he had witnessed playing through his head. The only thing I could do was sit with him, watching his face and wondering what exactly it was he was thinking, until he finally asked to go.

Alex came away with a little plastic shark's head on a stick. Its mouth opened and closed when you squeezed a handle at the other end. It was the only souvenir he wanted and it came in handy for playing the baddy in lots of his games for many months to come. Until eventually it was so broken that I had to sneak it into the dustbin and hope that it was a while before he missed it and asked me for an explanation.

He stared off into space for a long time that night. His eyes showed no sign of closing after the first song. I knew he was tired. There had been a few nights when, on reflection, I probably tried to get him to sleep too early, just to have some time to myself. But tonight wasn't one of them. He had run around plenty today and between the beach, the garden and the aquarium he had covered a lot of ground. But he was turning everything over in his head, and he couldn't find any peace.

This restlessness was his demonstration of grief. It was my cue to open my mouth. I had at least learnt that much by now.

I began to talk about how much I missed his mummy. I knew now that he found it easier to agree with me speaking my feelings rather than respond when I asked him how he felt. Even when my questions contained all the vocabulary he needed to form an answer.

I talked about how much it hurt that she wasn't there. I talked about everything. How much it hurt that she had died so horribly. And how much it hurt me that she wasn't there to be with him. I talked about how much I missed her. How I missed her eyes and her hair and her skin. I knew it was the same for him. There had been so much physical contact between them. He was so accustomed to her hair falling softly across him or the smell of her when he cuddled up against her. It was always her eyes that shone with so much love when she looked at him and talked with him. And her hands that picked him up when he fell, or stroked his hair.

He was still so small. It was easy to forget after a day spent battling against his iron will.

I talked about how we danced together, she and I, and how much I was in love with her. I talked of how he used to lie between us in bed and how she used to talk about the three of us as her little 'pack'. Had it only been weeks since we had lain together?

Alex nodded and murmured his agreement while I talked. I knew it wasn't hard for him to understand how somebody else could love her as much as he did. Which was a little strange. But it was almost an adult passion they had shared, so much did they take pleasure in each other's company. If I had been of a jealous nature, or maybe a little less secure, there would have been times when I would have almost felt put out. But I was only glad that my child should have so much love in his life.

Eventually he drifted off, his face calm and peaceful. He fell into a deep sleep which lasted well through the night.

I got my first bath the next morning, the first in weeks. After the usual early morning upset Alex was quickly in a better mood. He was having the time of his life running up and down the corridor as the boys entertained him.

Normally, after Alex had his breakfast, I would try to have my shower. He would always follow, and sit on the edge of the shower pleading and crying 'When are you going to be finished?' over and over again. This went on every morning without fail. There was no way on earth I could get him to watch his cartoons or finish his breakfast without me, no matter who else was there to keep him company. He would cry and wail and moan, often getting so far into the shower that he would get his clean clothes wet, and on top of everything else I would have to get him dressed again as well. I tried gentle persuasion and, when he was in his stronger moods, outright bullying, but nothing would get him to leave me in peace for those few minutes a day.

It felt like I had been in that bath for years. Every single second I waited for Alex to appear round the corner and start bullying me to get out. And every single second I was amazed that he didn't. The door was wide open and I could hear him playing busily.

We pottered around that morning doing nothing very much. 'Pottering around': that was one of Rachel's favourite phrases. She would have loved it here, I thought again. Anywhere we could spend our time out in the open air finding things to do. The irony was crushing. That was just what she had been doing the day she was murdered.

We walked through the countryside surrounding the house and picked some early blackberries, pretending tree trunks were the massive legs of dinosaurs. It was a Rachel sort of day. Our friend told us about how the cows from the neighbouring farm had broken into the vegetable patch and run riot. For some reason Alex found this hysterically funny. He threw back his head and laughed and laughed. As he did so I could see his mother in his face. Something about the way his cheeks crinkled up and his eyes shone behind, almost hidden.

Something about the shape of his mouth, and the way his teeth were spaced. Everyone always said how much he looked like me. He was brown and his hair was curly. He was square and chunky too, but apart from that Rachel and I didn't think he looked much like either of us. Certainly not facially. But suddenly I could see a strong resemblance between him and his mother.

I could only just check myself from turning round to tell her so. The reflex was still strong. Old habits die hard.

By the time we had visited the pig-farm and heard about how our friend had worked feeding and mucking them out one summer, half the day had already gone.

We went for a pub lunch not far from the house. Alex was enchanted by a blonde-haired and blue-eyed waitress. She made him go all giggly just by talking to him. It should have been his mother he was playing with. It should have been her that was there to make him swoon all day long, and not for a few short minutes with some stranger. And she should have been there the next day. And the next. And the one after that. And the one after that . . .

The people in the pub were giving Alex so much attention that I asked myself if they had worked out who we were. It happened from time to time. Someone would see me with him, maybe with him dashing around, and whereas before there would have been a comment along the lines of 'He'll sleep well tonight!' now I was given a quiet look of sympathy instead.

It was hard to know how to react. On the one hand it appeared slightly ridiculous and presumptuous to think that someone recognized you (I always thought about the young man I had met on the boat) but on the other hand something about people's behaviour at times made it hard to think otherwise. It always disturbed me. They could well have been the author of one of the wonderful letters we had received, or the sender of some kind of gift. But, even if they were, it was still a problem. They would no longer be looking at Alex as they would at any other child, and that bothered me greatly. I would be watching like a hawk, more attentive than ever, to make sure there was no inappropriate gesture or comment. I didn't want to be rude or ungrateful but the situation was very delicate.

Each time we had one of these encounters I became more and more convinced that we had no choice but to go and live abroad.

Chapter Sixteen

'DO YOU KNOW the name of the man who killed your mummy?'
'Alex, do you *know* the name of the man who killed your
mummy?'

I had been listening to a detective put the question to Alex time and
time again for nearly three hours. Three hours of interrogation for a
child not more than three himself. It sounded like the scenario of my
worst nightmare. Either I was dreaming or I had finally lost my grip
completely and handed him over for them to do whatever they wanted
with him.

But it wasn't either. Near the beginning of the session the question
had been put to him once or twice, much in the same context as it had
the last time. Gently and without pressure. The detective was sitting
back in his armchair, calm and relaxed. He could have been asking
Alex the name of his favourite toy. Once again Alex listened to the
question, but made no attempt to answer.

The child psychologist observed that Alex was studying the detective
very carefully. Every time he asked the question Alex would examine
him closely, or he would momentarily hesitate in his play as if thinking
about something. There was something provocative about his behaviour.
It was as if Alex was encouraging him to ask the question again. There
was a smile on his lips. Behind the smile the concentration was earnest.

It was a very strange thing to watch. It really looked as if Alex
wanted nothing else better than for the detective to ask him one more
time. It was turning into a game and at times Alex was laughing out
loud. But the most he would say in response to the question was 'The
bad man!'

The detective always put the question as gently as possible, and must have tried it with every different emphasis imaginable.

'Alex, do you *know* the name of the man who killed your mummy?'

'*Do* you know the name of the man who killed your mummy, Alex?'

'Alex, do you know the name of the man who killed your *mummy*?'

It couldn't have been very easy for the detective. He had got to know Alex well. But what he was doing now seemed to contradict all the assurances he had given us: Alex would never, under any circumstances, be 'grilled', I had been told.

If I had ever thought that things would come to this then I would never have given my consent. We would never have started with the child psychologist in the first place. After all, it was the police who had recommended her, she could have been serving their interests more than ours. But here was this big detective doing exactly that. And here was I allowing him to do it.

But if anything it was Alex who was doing the grilling. He was testing the detective. He would leave the room, wait a few minutes, then come back in and look straight at the detective, a smile on his face, and goad him into asking the question again.

'Do you know the name of the man who killed your mummy, Alex?'

'The bad man!'

The child psychologist reassured the detective that, whatever it was that Alex was trying to work out with him, it was something very important.

'You know very well that these big detectives are there to catch the bad man,' she said, gently. 'And you know that anything you tell them helps them with their job.'

We all knew that Alex knew as much: there was no doubt at all that he did.

'I am certain that little Alex has something he wants to say to these two big detectives. He has got something on his mind that is just between them.'

I could see that she was trying to figure out a way to unlock this final piece from his head. I had the impression that Alex was paying her more attention than usual as well. This time he was at the centre of things, leading the game. I hardly said a word. There was nothing for me to say. I watched as closely as possible for any sign that Alex had really had enough.

'I can't believe he wants to keep going!' I said several times.

I was amazed that he should be willing to go on for so long. The minutes had turned into hours. We had gone on far longer than in any other session, but it was clear to me that he didn't want to be anywhere else. He was absorbed in this game. He showed no sign of losing interest. As time went on it was we adults who began to fade. I was getting sick of hearing the same question, and the detective must have been just as sick of asking it.

'Alex, do you know the name of the man who killed your mummy?'

No answer.

'Alex, what's the name of the man who killed your mummy?'

'The bad man.'

'It's all right, Alex,' I said. 'You can tell everyone what you've told me.' I was trying to give him permission. But it didn't make any difference.

At times we broke for refreshments. At times Alex and I went to play in the garden. He went to the toilet. He explored the house. But each time he came back again of his own accord. Each time eager for more.

Alex knew the answer to the question, didn't he? He had already told me it. There must have been a reason why he didn't want to say it out loud himself. I desperately searched for an idea of what that reason might be.

'I think he likes you too much,' I said to the detective after a sudden thought. 'I don't think he's convinced that you're tough enough to deal with this monster.' This was after all the most powerful 'thing' that Alex had ever seen. He had been a witness to so much violence and aggression. Alex had had absolutely no experience of such things. I found it hardly surprising that he should be worried for the safety of anyone he cared about, if he thought they risked coming into contact with this thing again.

We all talked about how there weren't just these two policemen, but how there were lots and lots of them. And how they had handcuffs and truncheons and police cars and police vans and cells with thick steel doors and huge locks to put the bad man in so he could never get out.

'You've got to do something to impress him,' I said. 'Haven't you got any handcuffs, or something?'

I had the feeling that although Alex didn't believe that they were capable of controlling this 'thing', he very much wanted to believe that they could. Now it occurred to me that maybe it was his lack of confidence in their abilities that was causing his reluctance.

The detectives took the point and I could see them both start to think about what would be the most effective way to go about convincing Alex that they were capable of doing what they said they could.

But I was beginning to crack. We had been going round in circles for hours. I couldn't accept that Alex wasn't able to repeat to the detective what was, after all, the same answer that he had already given to him at my mother's house, just days before. 'Go on, Alex, it's all right.'

He had never shown any real hesitancy about repeating any answer once it was given out loud for the first time. He had never had any problem in repeating in his own words that the man who killed his mummy wore a white shirt. And he had never shown the slightest sign of changing his opinion.

So why couldn't he repeat what he had already said this time?

With hindsight, of course I can see that I was making a fundamental mistake. The question I had asked him at my mother's house, once on my own and once in front of the detective, had been: 'Do you *think* that (. . . .) killed Mummy?' To which he answered 'yes'. Which wasn't the same thing at all as: 'Do you *know* the name of the man who killed your mummy?'

You could 'think' it was someone without being completely sure. And, because you weren't completely sure, if someone said 'Do you know the name of the person?' you would have to say 'no' because you didn't 'know', you only 'thought'. Or in Alex's case he said it was the 'bad man', which was correct and truthful every time. It was *a* bad man who had killed his mummy.

I lacked the insight to realize that he understood the difference between the two completely. I assumed that, because of his young age, he would think that the two were the same. I never once asked him, or discussed with him, the difference between only 'thinking' it was someone, and 'knowing' it was someone.

The difficulty was quite simply that Alex had pointed his finger in

(. . . .)'s direction completely out of the blue. And with all the weight and all the consequences of this revelation it was sometimes very hard to keep my thoughts lucid. Up until that moment I had had no image in my head of a real human being who could have been capable of inflicting on another the suffering that Rachel had endured. Now I had to come to terms with the idea that it might be someone I had actually known and met.

Alex's answers to everything else had been borne out on every occasion by independent adult witnesses. So how could I doubt him over this one? I *had* to believe he was telling the truth, I had absolutely no reason to doubt him. And I assumed that circumstances would eventually reveal this to be the case. For the moment (. . . .) had an alibi. His wife said that he had been home with her.

But the detectives had told me that he was far from out of their suspicions, with or without whatever Alex might have had to say. It was not unknown for wives to lie in order to provide an alibi for their husbands' crimes.

But by the end of three hours I had had enough. I was worn down and all I wanted was for him to answer the question so the police could get on with sorting this whole thing out once and for all. I decided to try and give him a little help. I thought that he was feeling the weight of actually 'naming' someone. The responsibility. I assumed that once he had been able to voice the name himself, out loud, this would free him from these inhibitions and that from then on he would be able to repeat it in the same way that he was able to repeat all his other answers.

'Alex, do you *know* the name of the man who killed your mummy?' the detective asked for what seemed like the hundredth time.

No answer.

'Alex, I'm going to write the name of the person that you told me on this piece of paper,' I said. 'And you, because you are such a big boy, can read it out to the detective.'

He couldn't yet read. He could recognise a number of letters of the alphabet but was far from being able to put them together to spell anything out.

I wrote a word on a piece of paper, something completely unrelated. I gave the piece of paper to Alex. 'Go and read it out,' I said.

He took it towards the detective, but turned back towards me as he 'read' out the name. '(. . . .),' he said.

It was said in a quizzical voice. It was said looking back at me. But it was said.

I was flooded with emotion. How could the apparently caring father of a small child commit such an unimaginably evil act in front of another small child? I was swamped by so many thoughts, so many unanswerable questions. But even as my head swam I felt surprise at the quizzical tone of Alex's voice. Why wasn't he more vehement? Why was there no anger?

I looked at his face only inches from mine. He looked back through hollow eyes. The smile of amusement that usually came from cleverly answering all the grown-up questions was absent. His face was filled with sadness: there was a visible confusion there.

How could he make sense of our line of questioning? Hadn't *we* wanted him to say (. . . .)'s name? Now he had spoken the name of the man he thought was Rachel's killer, but there was so much uncertainty in his answer that I felt far from certain myself. I still did not have that luxury. I was still not completely sure that Alex had identified the target of my pent-up feelings of rage and violence.

With hindsight I can see that Alex was telling the truth one more time. He had believed that I had written (. . . .)'s name on the piece of paper because I had told him that I had. And I never lied to him. Then, in order to do what I had told him, he had 'read' what was written on the page. His logic was completely consistent. It was mine that was defective.

In no other session did he speak that name. At no other time did he answer the question 'Do you know the name of the man who killed your mummy?' by mentioning anybody's name.

The next morning Alex and I went across the road to see some pets at a neighbour's house. There was a rabbit in the garden and some more exotic animals in cages in the house. But it was the rabbit that Alex was interested in. He had enjoyed looking round but by the time we got back he had begun to grizzle. I tried to appease him with a drink and some food but he didn't want to know. He was miserable.

I carried him to the garden and tried to find something to distract him with. He didn't even want to look. His face was wet with tears and he was crying hard. It was rare when I couldn't find something that would eventually stem the flow. But now I could find nothing at all. I was bouncing him in my arms like a little baby and giving him all the reassurance I could, but he was just getting more and more upset. However much I asked him, he couldn't tell me what was the matter.

I tried to think over what we were doing that could have set him off. This was the behaviour usually associated with a broken toy or a favourite thing getting lost, neither of which had happened this morning. Then I realized.

'It's the rabbit, isn't it!'

Alex's crying checked momentarily. I must have been on the right track. Going to see the rabbit and giving it something to eat was so much the kind of thing Rachel would have done with him. But I wasn't used to him reacting emotionally in any way over anything to do with his mother. So at first I wasn't completely sure that this was what had set him off.

'Did it remind you of Mummy, sweetheart?' I asked. 'That's the kind of thing you would have done with her, isn't it?'

He murmured his agreement, his face full of sadness and tears. I carried on bouncing him up and down.

I wanted to smile, to laugh out loud. It was the relief which came from seeing him cry for his mother for the first time. At last, after all these weeks, there was some small chink in that oh so solid armour. Some small glimpse past the tough little soldier mask that he presented to the world.

'She wanted to get you a rabbit, didn't she?' I said.

He nodded his head slowly up and down as he sat in my arms, his eyes full of tears. My relief passed in an instant. It was replaced by grief. I knew that Rachel wanted to get him a rabbit when he was a little bigger, when we were able to sell up and maybe get somewhere with a garden. He hadn't forgotten a word, either.

We spent a while in the garden. I carried him in my arms as I talked about Rachel. It was always the same: how much I missed her, how much it hurt, how much she would never have wanted to leave us, what a wonderful mother she was to him, and all of the other things that I would always have to say. But these things never ceased to be true. And this time, maybe more than any other, he really needed to hear them. He wasn't calm today, or in control. Nearly everything I said made him cry a little bit more. But he was too small to carry all of that pain inside alone.

We had Rachel's parents house to ourselves. They'd gone out. It was one of the rare occasions that we were alone together, just the two of us. It was good for me. I needed to know that I really could cope with him completely on my own if we were to go and live somewhere new. There would be no one for me to rely on. It was a sobering thought, but, weighed against the problems of staying, it didn't alter my determination to go. Alex was growing fast and logically, as time went by, he would get easier to look after.

He had calmed down and allowed himself to be comforted, but he was far from being in his usual robust form. I offered him a biscuit to keep him going until his lunch was ready. If he got too hungry by the time I put it in front of him he couldn't eat properly at all.

There were at least four different types of biscuit in the barrel, but he wanted one of those which were virtually finished. He wasn't interested in any of the others. I picked up one of the biscuits he wanted and it fell apart in my hand. He started to cry. 'It's all right!' I snapped, irritated, my patience running thin. I started to search through the barrel for another. There wasn't one. It had been the last. It would have been. When Alex realized this he burst into tears. I tried to be firm. 'What's the matter with the other ones?' I said. 'Normally you eat those! Normally you don't like these other ones at all.' Which was true. But, whereas normally he would have moaned for a while and eventually done what he was told, today was not the same. He was inconsolable. None of the other biscuits would do, and nothing else in the house was good enough.

This time I had to give in. I could see that this was all part of the same process that had started with the rabbit. I got his coat on him and manoeuvred him and his blankets into his car-seat. It was raining now; I tried to keep them as dry as possible. We drove into the village, parked in the carpark and, with him in my arms, I ran through the rain. I carried him all round the supermarket (he wouldn't be put down or put in a trolley) and found the biscuit section. By now he had changed his mind about the biscuits he wanted, even though two minutes before the world would have come to an end if he didn't get exactly the ones he had first demanded.

As we waited for our turn at the checkout, him still in my arms, I felt in my pockets. My heart filled with dread once more. They were empty. I had come out without any money.

'I haven't got any money, Alex,' I said. 'We've got to go back to the house.'

His face crumpled once again. His mouth suddenly went rectangular, with four defined corners, just like in a cartoon. He saved this face for special occasions and it was always the prelude to a deluge of tears. Today was no exception.

We had to leave the biscuits where they were, find a way out of the supermarket, run through the rain back to the car where I strapped him back into his car-seat and drove back to the house; then I had to park the car in the drive, unstrap him from his car-seat (there was no way he would have let me leave him in the car, even parked right against the front door with it and the car door wide open and where I would be gone from sight for twenty seconds at the most), carry him through the house, find some money, shut the house, strap him back into his car-seat, drive back to the supermarket, park in the carpark, unstrap him from his car-seat, run through the rain back into the supermarket, find the biscuits again and eventually pay for them, with him grizzling and crying the whole time.

Once he could see that we were eventually going to get his biscuits he managed to calm down. The moment I had paid for them I ripped open the packet and stuck one in his hand. In a matter of seconds no one would have known that anything had ever been the matter.

That evening I found myself sinking into a deeply morbid mood. When was anything ever going to be proved? Everything was so difficult, so contorted and twisted.

There was no doubt from the evidence that Rachel's killer had been wearing a white shirt outside his trousers with a belt on top and blue trousers and dark shoes or that he had short hair which was between blonde and brown. That much was definite.

Alex had said so. And adults had confirmed that there had been someone near the scene just before and just after who answered that description.

Alex had said that he thought it was (. . . .). Why not? The world was crazy enough. People were capable of anything. Even out of the blue. Even if they had never shown any other signs of violent behaviour. The idea that it was (. . . .) was right on the edge of credibility but then, wasn't my whole life now 'just on the edge of credibility'?

Why not him? It could have been a complete stranger. But most murders were committed by people who knew the victim. It was an undeniable statistic. A jealous rage from someone who couldn't accept that a friendship was just a friendship and was never going to be anything else?

I twisted and turned the thing in every direction I could. I just didn't know anything any more. But in the end it didn't matter. The police only needed to find one little piece of material proof to confirm what Alex had said and it was all over. Then I wouldn't have to try and work it out any more. But until then . . . ?

I took Alex to the park to ride his bike the next morning. It's strange what children come out with sometimes. He said he was happy to be three, but he wasn't going to be four. Next birthday he would have his party as usual but afterwards he would still be three.

'I don't want to go to school,' he said.

I wondered where he had picked up the idea already that school could be less than fun.

In the afternoon we went to a nearby swimming pool. Alex loved the water and we had taken him regularly since he was a very small baby. In the winter, when the weather stopped them from playing outside, Rachel took him several times a week. He couldn't quite swim on his own yet, but was full of confidence in his armbands and loved to throw himself off the side of the pool and into her arms as she stood in the water below.

There was a shallow toddlers' pool as well as the main pool but Alex spent most of his time in the main one. The pool was busy and there were toys and big floating things in the water to jump on and off. Alex was quite happy out of his depth and it was a job to keep an eye on him and make sure his adventurous spirit didn't get him into trouble.

We had been in the water playing for some time when he suddenly began jabbering and panicking and acting like he could no longer hold himself up in the water. At first I thought it was part of one of his games and I reached out to prop him up. He clamped on to my arm and pulled himself into my arms where he clung on desperately with all his strength, his limbs suddenly spastic and stiff. He was still jabbering and was absolutely terrified. I had my feet on the bottom and my shoulders out of the water and Alex clung on to my neck for all he was worth. His grip was so strong that he was hurting me.

'What's wrong, Alex? What's wrong?' He was looking up into my eyes, crying and was completely going to pieces. I couldn't for the life of me understand what had set him off. I looking around the pool, searching for clues, but all I could see was the water full of people having a good time.

My eyes scanned the edge of the pool. Then I froze. One of the life-guards who was busy watching the people in the water bore an extremely strong resemblance to (. . . .). He had the same colour of hair, and the same narrow face. The obvious difference was that he was much, much taller.

I felt relief at the same time as concern. 'It's the life-guard who's frightening you, isn't it?' I said.

'Yes!' said Alex, holding me even tighter.

'He looks like (. . . .), doesn't he?'

'Yes!' said Alex again, clinging on tighter.

'But it's not (. . . .), is it?' I said.

Alex managed to turn his head and look at the life-guard, who happened to be looking in another direction. 'No,' he agreed.

'He's too tall, isn't he?'

'Yes,' agreed Alex, this time smiling in nervous relief.

There was no doubt about the resemblance between the life-guard and (. . . .). Now that Alex was more relaxed he was able to study him from the safety of my arms. The life-guard was not only very tall but his hair was long. The resemblance was very strong but Alex knew that they were not the same person.

I told Alex that (. . . .) would be locked in a police cell. I asked if that would make him happy.

'Yes!' he said, without the slightest hesitation.

After a little while in my arms he was able to shake off his fear and get back on with playing again. For the rest of the time we were at the pool Alex didn't give the life-guard another thought.

While we were under the shower at the end of our swim another father came through to stand next to us. His little boy was a few years older than Alex. Alex studied the boy's father, who was carrying some spare weight around his middle, and then, pointing directly at him, announced at the top of his voice: 'He's fat, Daddy, isn't he?'

Later at the house I told Alex I believed him when he said that (. . . .) had killed Mummy. No matter how confusing the situation, I felt it was vitally important that he knew I had confidence in him.

'Why?' he replied.

I was a little thrown. Why should he ask me 'why' I believed him?

I assumed that he meant 'Why did (. . . .) kill Mummy?' How was I supposed to explain to a three-year-old what I couldn't understand myself? The question had been pounding round and round my head ever since the day I had been arranging for Alex to see his friends, and he had first aroused my suspicions.

What amount of jealousy and rage could lead someone to do such a thing? And not to do it in the heat of the moment, but in a way that was meticulously planned and cold-bloodedly organized.

A senior detective had told me that the way the murderer was dressed confirmed how premeditated his intentions had been. He was wearing his shirt over his trousers like a butcher's apron. He was out looking for someone to kill and he had planned exactly how he was going to do it. I wasn't capable of understanding such a mentality. Any criteria I may have had for working out what motivated people were based on how I operated myself. I considered myself sane. I understood, a little, sane people. But this person was insane and I was lost completely.

'Would you hurt me if I didn't give you a toy that you wanted?' I asked Alex.

'No!' he replied.

'Most people are like you,' I said. 'But *some* people, just a few, would try and hurt you if you didn't give them what they wanted.

'Mummy was wonderful,' I went on, 'and (. . . .) wanted her to be with him like she was with Daddy. But Mummy said "No!" and that made (. . . .) so angry he wanted to hurt her.'

I wondered if he would understand. I didn't understand myself, but it was the only explanation I could give.

Alex was helping me feed the cats that evening.

'Who came up to us on the Common when we went to leave a flower for Mummy?' I asked.

'(. . . .)!' he snapped back so fast that it was as if that had been exactly what he had been thinking about before I asked the question.

I felt completely wretched. I had let him down intensely. Had I unwittingly exposed him to his mother's killer? How could he have felt protected after I had done that?

'That was before you had told me that it was (. . . .),' I tried to explain. 'If I had known then I would never have let him get anywhere near you.'

I explained exactly what I would have done to him if I had known.

While talking everything over with Rachel's father one time he put the question: 'Why would (. . . .) assault Rachel after he killed her?'

I didn't have an answer, of course. 'Maybe it was an ultimate gesture of possession. A final humiliation,' I tried to reason. But the words just sounded wrong as they came out of my mouth. Reason had no part in any of it.

We agreed that it was impossible to put yourself inside the mind of such a maniac without being insane yourself.

The police were going to search (. . . .)'s flat minutely. Microscopically. If there was one thing of Rachel's, one hair, one fibre of clothing that did not correspond with the one fleeting visit Rachel had paid to meet his wife there, then there could be no doubt.

Chapter Seventeen

THE NEXT AFTERNOON Alex and I went to Wimbledon police station to meet our detectives. They were going to take us to another police station so that we could visit the cells. Alex was to be shown the police-horse stables afterwards as a treat. While we were waiting to leave, one of them suggested we go and have a look at the cells there, first.

I had never seen a real police cell, except on TV, but the row of cells looked just as I had expected. The nearest empty ones had their doors open and we could see how thick they were. Each cell was furnished with a toilet without a seat, and a solid bunk which was part of the walls and floor, and was painted in some kind of faded white or yellow.

Alex stood next to me, his face filled with excited curiosity. The detective encouraged him to see for himself just how secure the doors really were. He was hesitant to move. But after a little encouragement he edged forward and touched the heavy door. His smile became even brighter. At that moment there came a muffled voice from one of the other cells. They were occupied. I hadn't realized. It sounded like a voice full of despair. It sounded more than a little disturbed. Immediately I pictured a drug addict, or a drunk sleeping off a binge behind the door.

Alex jumped back. I didn't think the occupant of the cell could see Alex, but if he could there was no telling what his reaction might be. He might have taken the sight of a small child parading in front of his cell as an extreme provocation and responded by hurling abuse.

The detective had obviously had a similar thought. He instantly went pale and between us we shepherded Alex out of there as fast as we could.

'That was close!' he said under his breath. 'That could have gone really wrong.' He was clearly relieved that it hadn't, and it had happened too fast for me to think about it. When I did have time, however, I realized that it had been a ludicrous thing to do without first checking that all the cells were empty. But the intention had been good. And, thankfully, no harm had been done.

At the next police station we were led down to yet another block of cells. This time they had been checked beforehand. There was a block of three, much the same as the others, except that the light was coming in from the far end through panels of very thick frosted glass.

I walked into the nearest one. Alex took his time before following me in. He showed no fear after our near miss at the last place and walked with his head craned up to take everything in.

The detective banged on the door with his fist. It let out a dull thud.

'You see, Alex,' I said. 'No one can get out of here, can they?'

Alex nodded in agreement and looked as excited as a child visiting a fairground.

'What about if we slam it shut?' I asked, after we had had a good look round. The interior was almost identical to the last: a toilet bowl without a seat and a solid bunk which was part of the floor and wall.

I had carried in my head the image of a cell door slamming shut. I thought this might have been the best way to demonstrate to Alex just what locking someone up really meant.

The detective beckoned us out and then, with Alex watching intently, swung the door hard. It swung heavily on its hinges and shut with a mighty bang. The echo boomed around us. Whatever its effect might have been on Alex, it was a sobering demonstration for me of what losing your liberty really meant.

Alex giggled.

'Do you want to try, Alex?' asked the detective as he opened the door again. Alex's eyes widened with excitement. Clearly, he couldn't think of anything better. Together with the detective, he pushed hard on the wide-open door. It gathered momentum and slammed shut, once again the boom echoing around us.

Alex was having a whale of a time. He slammed the door again and again. Eventually he had had enough and came away looking ecstatic.

We went back upstairs to the canteen to get something to eat. The detective came to our table a little later with a newspaper in his hands. He said there was something I ought to see.

I opened the paper to the page he had indicated. There was a picture of me and Alex. The same face-on picture that this very same tabloid had published the day after Alex and I had been to the Common. It wasn't in colour this time, and it was smaller. But it was the same picture and Alex was just as easily identifiable.

I felt sick to the stomach, once again. Once again choking on my impotent rage. These bastards could do whatever they wanted with us. The law and the Press Complaints Council and all that went with it were just a pathetic joke. Nobody was going to stop the papers doing whatever they wanted when all they risked by breaking the rules was a gentle slap on the wrist. All they had to do was apologize and then we couldn't take it any further. But the apology could be on one line, buried behind the greyhound results. That was all it took to get them off the hook.

They knew we didn't have a chance of defending ourselves. They knew how much we had suffered. They knew they were potentially putting Alex's life in danger once again, even though the damage they had done the first time could never be undone. Anybody could get a back copy of the original edition and find the picture of him. But what was his life against selling a few more papers, against earning a few more pieces of silver?

They could do what they liked with us and I just had to swallow it. The taste was very, very bitter. I was filled with the same hatred for them as I had for Rachel's killer. At least he had left Alex alive. The paper was doing its best to finish him off.

We went to visit the stables. The horses were massive: Alex looked like a toy in comparison. But he wasn't at all intimidated. He wanted to see in all the stalls and to find out what all of them were called. I had to hold him up of course, so he could stroke their muzzles. He was a bit concerned that he might have his fingers bitten and, in spite of the encouragement of their handlers, he drew the line at actually sitting on one of the horses' backs.

We left with Alex clutching a horseshoe as a souvenir. He was perfectly relaxed and had had a good day out. It was too early to tell if the visit would have the desired effect; if it would inspire Alex with enough confidence to confirm the name that he had had so much trouble in articulating.

'How sure are you about what Alex has told you?' a detective once asked me.

'I'm totally confident about the detail of everything he's ever had to say,' I replied.

'Yes, but do you believe him when he says that it is (. . . .)?' he insisted.

'If he says he thinks it's (. . . .) then I have to believe him,' I answered.

The detective looked thoughtful for a moment. Then he said: 'The question is: if you had a shotgun in your hand and (. . . .) walked in front of you right now, would you pull the trigger?'

I was stunned by being asked such a question by a policeman. It was a very dangerous thing to ask.

I said that, to be one hundred per cent sure, I needed someone else to come up with one piece of material evidence, no matter how small, to confirm what Alex was saying. And that was *their* job. And when they had that one piece of evidence then they would have (. . . .) under lock and key in an instant and the question would be irrelevant.

God knows I had lain awake with revenge running through my head every night since Rachel was killed. But I knew the probable consequences of anything I might do. My conscience would never allow me to do anything that would mean Alex being separated from me. Rachel would never forgive me.

'And anyway,' I told him, 'Alex has had enough tragedy. How could I do anything that might risk me being locked up away from him in prison? How's he supposed to cope with that as well?'

'You wouldn't get locked up,' he replied.

The next session with the child psychologist turned out to be very hard going. Rachel's parents were there, my mother was there, my younger brother was there, the two detectives were there, as well as the child psychologist and myself.

There is a lot to be said for a child being surrounded by the people who love him. But then unavoidably that child becomes the object of everyone's attention in the most intense way.

We had been going over much of the same ground for weeks now. At the beginning there had been everything to learn. Now we were only looking for the final details to finish the picture.

Alex had described the killer's clothing and hair; the fact that he was white and not black; that he didn't have a bike; that he hadn't had a dog with him; and that, yes, it had only been one man. He had told us that the bad man had been carrying a black bag and that he had taken the knife from it; that it was a hunting knife; that he had not lowered or removed his trousers; that he washed himself in the stream afterwards and then walked away in the direction of the cemetery.

Each session always began with one of us asking Alex: 'Do you remember the day that your mummy was killed?' 'Do you remember getting out of the car?' 'Do you remember all that happened next?'

He was answering some of the questions for what felt like the hundredth time. But he did so in order to move the scenario along until we came to a gap in the chain of events that he had so far described. He was a little like the performing monkey or counting horse: repeating the same show over and again, and pleasing the audience each time he was able to add another little trick along the way. But I had the strong feeling that the monkey was tired of the show. The process had come to the end of its effectiveness. Undeniably, in the beginning, everything Alex was able to tell us had made him feel better. But now, with so little left to discover, this seemed like a laborious and tedious way to finish the job.

I felt we were not only playing for diminishing returns but that there was a danger that Alex would reach saturation point and become completely unresponsive. Or worse, that he might start going off in all directions at once, and start reinventing his answers to everything in order to give us what he thought we wanted to hear.

There had never been any discussion about when this was all going to end. I knew that the police and the child psychologist wanted to go on for as long as they could. The police still needed all the help they could get. The child psychologist believed that this was still the best thing for Alex.

I didn't agree. Other members of the family had voiced a similar opinion. In my head I gave it until the end of September, when I planned to take him out of the country for a few weeks' holiday. It was already nearly the end of August. I wanted as much as ever to give them all the help we could but at the same time I couldn't see that there was much else Alex could tell them.

We couldn't continue at this pace. When we came back from holiday we would pull away from the investigation and let the police get on with it on their own. We couldn't solve this thing for them. The price we were paying might be too high.

We stopped for a break after a while. Alex wasn't being particularly difficult. He just showed no interest in talking about anything, or in answering any questions.

When we came back he suddenly loosened up. He started to talk about how his trousers came to be wet from his feet up to his knees. This had always been a mystery. The grass had been wet but the state of his clothing suggested that it was more as if Alex had been standing in water at some stage. Which begged the question: where might he have done so? And was it before Rachel was killed or after? He talked about the dog running off and how he had got wet chasing her through the wet grass. This still didn't explain things completely.

But his little burst of responsiveness only made me feel more sure that the process had reached its end. The amount of time we had spent and the amount of pressure Alex was now under for such a small revelation was difficult to justify. And the thought of sitting through another session and going over the same ground again for maybe nothing at all ever harder.

We went to stay with friends on the coast and Alex saw his first Punch and Judy show. The tent was set up on the beach and a crowd of excited children had gathered in front of it. Alex, however, watched the build-up from the safety of my lap. I knew that he wanted to see what was going on but he was resisting the urge. We were some distance from the stage, but when I tried to stand up and lead him nearer he dug his heels in and began to whine. So I sat back down again and we watched together as the curtains opened in the distance. From where we sat we could just make out the puppets waving about on the tiny stage.

The children were rapt, their eyes glued to the performance. Now Alex was really curious. Curious enough for him finally to agree to us moving close enough to get a proper look. But only on the understanding that I hold his hand tight the whole time.

He remained glued to me while we crossed the sand. We sat behind the last row, him on my lap. At times it was hard to catch all of the dialogue over the children's laughter. But there was no mistaking the policeman's uniform, or the crocodile. Now Alex was eager to see what it was all about.

I was pleased that he had been brave enough just to come and look. It meant so much to me that he should be able to enjoy such a simple childhood treat, that his trauma should not always get in the way. God knows, he deserved all the treats he could get. But my bubble of happiness was quickly burst.

I had simply forgotten what the story was about. Once it began to unfold I realized that it was about as inappropriate for us as any I could possibly have imagined.

Alex sat with his mouth only inches from my ear. He was in a highly excited state. He jabbered questions continuously, firing one after the other at me all the way through the show.

'What's he doing now? Why's he doing that? Why's he hurting her? Is she dead?' He was extremely nervous and was only just able to bring himself to watch. It was touch and go and he needed constant reassurance. I had to keep reminding him that they were only puppets, which he knew very well, and that everything was only pretend. But even so he was still extremely agitated.

As a small child I had spent each appearance of the Wicked Witch of the West, in *The Wizard of Oz*, cowering with fear under the cinema seat. I knew how frightening 'only make-believe' could be for anyone. But I hadn't had to cope with the terrible shocks that were still reverberating through his system.

The puppets clattered through the story. It was extremely violent. But I was looking at it with new eyes. What had before been harmless slapstick had taken on new meaning. I was struggling to explain to Alex the story of a drunken wife-batterer who kills his own child and then gets beaten over the head by a policeman with a truncheon who then locks him up and chokes him to death with a rope – and still make it sound like light entertainment.

There were moments when I thought he was about to burst into tears and scream to be taken away. He couldn't keep still and was climbing all over me. But he was fighting hard against his fear and was determined to overcome it.

There were moments when I wanted to pull him away, when I felt

I had made a huge, stupid, thoughtless mistake. Not for the first time I told myself that this was all it needed to bring on the nightmares. Only the moments when the crocodile stole the sausages were relatively easy for him to watch. And for me to keep him watching.

By the time it was finished I was almost deaf in one ear from him shouting all his questions straight into it, and my neck was sore from where he had clamped on to make sure he was getting all of my attention. I was glad it was over. On final reflection I thought that, in spite of everything, he had actually enjoyed the show. But there was no doubt that it had been a stressful ordeal for him, and that he too was glad it was over. None the less when the curtains closed there was a genuine smile on his face. A relieved smile, but a genuine one all the same.

The friends we were staying with had two empty bedrooms, one next to the other. I would get Alex to sleep quite happily on his sheepskin in one of them and he would sleep through the evening without waking up. When I turned in for the night, however, I would choose the room next door. Both doors were wide open and there was only a few feet between him and me.

Nevertheless, even before I'd have the chance to fall asleep, he would always wake up crying. Maybe it was because he sensed the house go quiet as everyone went to bed, but he would not be calmed until I had taken him in with me. They were only single beds, and with him sprawled out, there wasn't much room left for anyone else.

He would immediately fall asleep again. I would doze off, only to be quickly awoken by him fidgeting and squirming around. Then I would take the opportunity to slip quietly into the other room and fall gratefully into the luxury of a bed all to myself.

But he would soon sense that I was no longer there, and would wake up crying again. And so I would climb back in with him until we both dozed off once more. Then, when he woke me again with his fidgeting around, I would slip away once more. Only to be woken soon after by his crying and once again have to return to comfort him. And so it went on until he finally woke, crying pitifully, in the morning.

After a couple of nights he had worked out the moves and, when he woke to find I wasn't there, he simply got up, without even crying, and trailed into the other room to climb in beside me. I would soon wake up to find him taking up all the bed and get up and creep into the other room and the bed he had just left. After a while he would wake once again and silently track me down, climb in beside me and fall asleep again. Once again I would wake up soon afterward, then head back to the other empty bed. Once again I would soon awake to find him in with me. And so it went on all night long, every night, until the end of our stay.

On the 3rd of September Alex played on the swings in the park. We were talking about nothing very much in particular when he said suddenly: 'The ranger came on a horse!'

His comment came right out of the blue. It bore no relation to anything we were talking about. It wasn't very significant in itself, but it showed just how much the events of that day were present in his mind. Even when it looked as if all he could think about was having a good time. Once again it showed how good his recall was. A ranger had appeared on horseback some time before Alex had been taken away to the ambulance.

Weeks had passed but everything in his head was still crystal clear. The horrors of that day were not beginning to fade.

There was one brighter note. A few days later the boyfriend of one of our friends was about to go off and buy some ice-creams when his girlfriend suggested: 'Why don't you take Alex with you?'

I smiled wryly to myself. Alex had enjoyed making Lego cars with this man and they had been busy making sandcastles together. But the prospect of Alex setting off one hundred metres across the beach on his own with him was absolutely unthinkable.

A few seconds later Alex trotted off with him as if he didn't have a care in the world.

It was unimaginable! But there he was walking and talking together with what was virtually a stranger as they made their way across the sand. On top of everything, the boyfriend had the same name as (. . . .).

We were all amazed. The family we were staying with had seen just how glued Alex had been to me during the few days of our visit. No matter how much effort any of them had put into amusing Alex in order to try and give me a break, he had not let me as much as leave the room without him the whole time we had been there. I was still not allowed to go to the toilet on my own. No matter what he was doing or how fascinated he was by it he would jump up the moment

I went towards the door and would accompany me to the bathroom.

It was hard to know what to think. They must just have hit it off remarkably well. But more than that. Though I had hardly noticed, he must have been gaining imperceptibly in confidence all the time. We were getting somewhere.

Back at my mother's, Alex watched his first feature film. It was *E.T.* And just as at the Punch and Judy show, he sat on my lap and jabbered questions non-stop all the way through. It was amazing that he heard any of the dialogue at all.

It was hard to explain to him what an alien was but he identified the creature as a dinosaur. He wanted to know where was it going? when was it coming back? what were the children doing? why was the creature in the cupboard? who were the grown-ups? and so on and so on and so on. I knew the creature was going to die at some point in the film but I knew it would be coming back to life as well afterwards. I thought this would give me a little room to manoeuvre if he got upset. But I was nervous about what his reaction might be.

He went very quiet when he realized that the creature was dead. The questions suddenly stopped. I wondered if he was going to burst into tears. The pressure was too great for me to stand and almost immediately I blurted out that the creature was going to come back to life again in a minute. But of course the creature on the screen was still dead, whatever I said, and we had to wait anxiously for the plot to unravel for my words to be borne out. Alex remained very quiet and very serious but his eyes were riveted to the screen. His concentration was total.

At last the film wound itself on to the part where the creature revives itself. Enormous relief was written all over Alex's face. The questions resumed at their previous breathless pace and continued until the very end of the film. He had had dry eyes all the way through but the moment the titles appeared he suddenly burst into tears. He was miserable because the creature had flown away. 'I want to see him again!' he wailed.

I tried to explain that he had gone back to his home and his family and that he would be happy now. But there was no stopping the tears, which were probably also a result of nervous exhaustion. I was shattered myself. The last half an hour had been intense and I was extremely glad it was finished.

Alex was at screaming pitch all the time that I was getting him changed and ready for bed. But luckily, when he hit the pillow, he went out like a light. When I went to bed myself, later, I expected to be woken by him screaming in the night. But by the time I had woken up the next morning I had forgotten my previous night's fears completely and Alex had slept like a log.

Alex was invited to a party. It was the birthday of a child he used to see during the day with Rachel. He was not particularly excited about going, but not hostile to the idea either. He fell asleep in the car on the way.

He was still asleep when we got there but started to wake up as I carried him in. I didn't know anybody there, I had never met the children either, and I had a feeling of discomfort which came from knowing that everyone in the room knew all about me, even though I knew nothing about them. They were as kind as they could possibly be, but the situation was disconcerting nonetheless.

We sat in the kitchen, Alex sleepy on my lap, as I waited for him to come round. Meanwhile the children's games continued all around us. Alex took no interest. While he sat there, slumped with his head on my chest, his face full of melancholy, I had the strongest feeling of Rachel's presence. The weeks were turning into months but the sensation I had that she could walk out from behind the door at any moment was as strong as it had been at any time since the day she was killed.

I could see her looking at me across the room. I could hear her voice as a sad smile played across her face for all the time that we had been apart. But she pulled herself together, shook off her sadness and walked towards us. 'Sorry for the mix-up,' she said. 'I'm not dead, really.' Then she smiled a little brighter and said: 'Come on, let's go home.'

The buzz of busy children surrounded us. I didn't know whether it was my mood feeding off his or his mood feeding off mine, but he wouldn't say a word. No one was staring but we were the centre of every adult's attention. I felt like bursting into tears. And to cap it all Alex chose this moment to act like a 'traumatized' child for the first time.

He wouldn't say a word. He wouldn't respond in any way to anybody's attempts to interest him in the games that were going on except by clinging to me even tighter. He wouldn't even answer me except by nodding his head. It was as if he had lost the power of speech. It was so ironic: he had saved himself for a room full of strangers to play the damaged vegetable, unable to cope with the world around him. I could just imagine the parents going away thinking: 'That poor child! He hasn't got a hope.' I wanted to shout out: 'He's not normally like this!' But what was the point?

Maybe he should have been like that all the time. After all, I would not have been surprised by his present behaviour if I had been one of these strangers looking on at us.

He sat on my lap for ages. I thought about leaving but felt that the effort of getting to my feet was likely to be enough to make me burst into tears. It would have been such an admission of defeat. So I sat there feeling miserable. After so much effort we still weren't capable of acting like 'normal' people.

We sat until eventually people started to leave. As the crowd thinned, Alex's mood seemed to improve. Soon there were only a few children left and Alex finally consented to let me carry him into the other room to watch what the boys were doing. When there were only a couple of children left playing on the floor Alex gathered enough courage to get down on his own and explore the new toys. But still, he wouldn't say a word in response to the parents or even the children. By the time we left, probably not more than five words had passed his lips.

A few days later I left Alex for the first time. I had been building up to this moment for a while. He was fine with Rachel's mother, even if his improvement in general could be described as a constant process of several steps forward followed by a big leap back. A childhood friend of Rachel's was staying and Alex was enjoying the company of another young woman of his mother's age.

I told him I was going, and that I would be back soon. This brought an immediate heart-wrenching moan. But I steeled myself and by turning away tried to make it clear that I was going anyway. It was very hard not to think that I was letting him down, and that I was about to cause him pain for nothing.

But something had changed. For the first time since I had left him on the beach to go into the water, several weeks before, there was the feeling that being separated from me for a short while was no longer going to cause enormous anxiety and distress. For a short while, at least, I felt that he was willing to be entertained without me. And what he wanted most was confirmation that he was going to be all right without me. He didn't need me dithering or flapping. He needed me to tell him what was what, and that that was the end of it, end of discussion.

He went through the motions, regardless, producing his most heart-breaking display of pleading with me not to go. I pretended that I was unmoved by his tears. Inside I was badly torn. But his heart wasn't in it, I could see that. And I took comfort in the fact. I had to start stretching the umbilical cord once more. We had to get on.

So I didn't look back. And with knots in my stomach I headed out of the house and towards the car.

I went to see the child psychologist. All the time I was aware of how much Alex wasn't with me. We lived virtually attached. Nothing sounded right without the constant chirping of his voice or the rustling of whatever he might be playing with. It didn't feel right not to be constantly turning my head to see that he wasn't choking on his food or about to pull something heavy down upon his head.

His grandmother knew exactly where I was. She had the phone number. So, in theory, as long as the phone didn't ring I knew he was fine. Which didn't mean that I wasn't continually fighting the temptation to ask the child psychologist every few minutes if her phone was actually still working.

When I got back to the house Alex was eating his tea. He wasn't at all fazed by the fact that I had been gone for two whole hours, and he showed no sign of clinging to me in the fear that I might desert him again. Both his grandparents were there to amuse him now and they encouraged me to leave him for as long as I could. So I went back out for a run in the park while he finished his tea.

It was the first time I had been alone during the day without Alex in nearly eight weeks. It was a strange feeling not to be focused on another being. But my moment of 'freedom' brought me no pleasure. In theory a few moments on my own should have made me feel 'better'. But I didn't feel 'better'. In fact the very thought that I should feel 'better' only plunged me into depression.

I couldn't feel good about anything without her. As I ran I found myself boiling with impotent anger. I felt I was being held down and tormented. There was just nothing I could do. Nothing I could lash out at. But I was so angry. The only thing I could do was not accept. It was my only rebellion. 'Something' had set things up this way. 'Somewhere' the pattern had been set. The rules of the game were beyond my understanding. The only thing I did know was that it was a dirty game. I wasn't the only one suffering. Maybe on the greater scale of things the majority were suffering in some way or another. And those who weren't now were by no means guaranteed an indefinite escape.

'Fuck you!' I screamed. 'Fuck you!' I'd take a chance on blasphemy. If there was a God what was he going to do to me now that he wasn't already doing? I might as well tempt him out of hiding a little. Let me see his face at least!

But all I heard in return was the echo of my own voice, its pathetic weak sound muffled by the damp air. Impotent.

I hoped that I was on my own out in the fields. The irony of a screaming maniac reported seen running across common land didn't completely escape me. The last thing I wanted to do was cause anyone even a moment's fear or distress.

Alex had finished his meal by the time I returned. This time he was much more concerned by what I'd been doing. He had been totally aware of the time that I had been away. And clearly he considered that this much was fine – but enough was enough.

The following afternoon Rachel's friend and Alex's grandmother set off to post a letter. Alex was ready to go with them on his bike. He wanted me to come but we wanted to see if he would be ready to leave me again. I dithered in the doorway without answering one way or the other while they crossed the drive and started up the road. He called back to me to see if I would come but I stayed where I was.

I could hear them chattering as they carried on up the road and I listened out to make sure he wouldn't suddenly become upset. But he sounded quite relaxed. I turned back into the house and fell into bed. I went out like a light and slept for three hours before being woken by their return.

They had turned the trip to the postbox into an excursion and had been to the park with him and walked all over the village. He had been fine without me. His grandmother had told him that I didn't come because I had probably got myself locked in the toilet. So he came bounding into the house to see if it was true. The fact that I had only been asleep was a great disappointment to him.

Chapter Eighteen

IN THE WEEKS SINCE Rachel had been killed I had been 'approached' by virtually every national newspaper and by virtually every news programme asking for an interview.

I had been cynical about the media and its manipulations of the truth even before Rachel's death. But this hadn't been enough to protect me from the shock of being personally confronted with what journalists were capable of. And how far they were prepared to go to get a 'story'. Our own recent and bitter experience had changed my original attitude into one of outright suspicion and complete mistrust.

I was thrown by the way that requests for interviews reached me through the police. The Metropolitan Police had a press officer who was responsible for arrangements between them and the media over press conferences, releases of information and so on. So, in theory, each newspaper passed on their request to speak to the victim's family through this office. But during the first weeks all I heard through the police was that one newspaper in particular wished to set up a trust fund for Alex. Whenever the subject came up it was only one name that was mentioned.

I found it strange. Why was there only one newspaper that was considering offering money to speak to us? Surely the story was of equal value to them all? At least those who were in the habit of paying for these kind of interviews. Either that or this particular newspaper was simply acting out of the goodness of its heart. And no matter how tragic our circumstances I couldn't really believe that was true. Business was business.

But even though I showed no interest in replying to anyone, especially after the way Alex's photograph had been published, I was still regularly getting the word that this same newspaper was anxious to set up a trust for Alex as soon as possible. 'You don't want to take a chance on him losing out!' I was reminded on several occasions.

I was even told that control of the text would be left up to us and that we would be left the final word on what would be included and what wouldn't. A contract would be drawn up to this end. We took legal advice to see how binding this might or might not have been. We were told that, if in the end a newspaper went ahead and published something against our wishes, and by so doing broke the contract, then the only redress we had was to the Press Complaints Council. We couldn't sue them. And the Press Complaints Council could do little more than demand an apology. Again we would be completely at the mercy of their goodwill. No right of redress. In fact, to all intents and purposes, no rights at all. The prospect was hardly reassuring.

As far as television was concerned I had no interest in appearing in any programme. I had a job to do, which was to look after Alex the best that I could. Anything that risked me becoming more easily recognizable would only make our daily existence harder. And on the most practical of levels, my going to be interviewed would totally disrupt his routine.

But we needed the money. I needed the money so as not to be dependent on anyone around us. We needed to be free to be able to get away as I was almost certain we would have to. It wasn't an easy situation.

Rachel's parents were against me taking Alex away. But it was for me to decide, and I needed to be free to do what I considered best.

There was another element. The fact was that the newspapers had been getting plenty of mileage out of Rachel's death. They were making money out of our suffering and none of it was coming to Alex. Alex's life had been put in danger by the conscious decision of newspaper editors, greedy for a scoop, to sell a few more copies. They'd been happy to knowingly break the rules if that was what was needed. But even though we had been wronged, against the rules, we didn't have a hope in hell of obtaining any material compensation for their acts. It was about time that a little of it came our way. They had had enough for free.

I was warned that speaking to one newspaper exclusively was likely to set off a feeding frenzy. Inevitably they all wanted the same story at the same time. Going away for a few weeks straight after anything was published suddenly looked like a very good idea.

I made an arrangement to meet a journalist from the paper. I wanted to do it in the open air so I could walk away easily if it came to it. I arranged a meeting in a central London park on a day that we were meeting up with some of Alex's friends. At least that way he would be happily distracted while I talked privately for a few minutes.

The park was busy but we managed to meet up without too much of a problem. The conversation was fairly brief. The newspaper wanted a story to run for three days and pictures of myself and Alex in which his face would not be shown. They wanted me to sign an agreement that I would not speak to anyone else before or immediately afterwards. The journalist was eager to interview me and promised not to do anything to cause us any more suffering. But what else did I expect her to say?

A sum of money was mentioned. It wouldn't put us in the league of bit-part actresses who had affairs with government ministers, but that was more a reflection on our society's priorities than anything else. I hadn't a clue of what our story was worth and I wasn't about to employ an agent to maximize our potential earning power. The whole business made me sick. It felt so sordid to be disclosing details of my life with Rachel. But it was a necessary evil. At least it would give us enough money to get us through the next year. Maybe that would have given us enough time for Alex to recover to the degree that I could begin working again myself.

I also tried to console myself with the thought that sometimes hearing or reading how people were coping with their problems could be of help to others who couldn't speak for themselves. It was something Rachel and I had talked about. I knew we weren't the only ones suffering in the world. But, in the end, the only thing that mattered was that Rachel would have wanted me to do whatever it took to make sure that Alex and I were all right.

I told the journalist that I wasn't yet completely decided. I said that if we did go ahead I wanted to see the text before it was published, and have the say in what it did or didn't include. At first this was resisted. 'You can trust me!' I was told.

I let that remark go over my head. I insisted, and despite initial reluctance this point was eventually agreed on. I was still aware through all of this that if they didn't keep to their agreement when the time came then there was absolutely nothing I could do about it.

As far as the money was concerned, I said that I understood it was never a good idea to accept anybody's first offer on anything. The journalist agreed to talk it over with the editor. She left on the understanding that I would think things over and then call them back.

The whole thing weighed heavily on my mind as I tried to help give the children a good time. Luckily Alex was soon giggling hysterically as we rowed around the lake. We had left Molly on the bank with one person while the rest of us set off in the boat. But almost immediately we moved out on to the water she started barking madly. Her wail was so pitiful that she must have thought we were abandoning her for ever. Finally she was let off the lead so she could run up and down the bank. But, instead, she jumped straight into the water and set off after us, swimming for all she was worth. The children thought this was wonderful entertainment. In between trying to catch up with us Molly was also snapping at every Canada goose that happened to be on her course. The geese took off, honking and beating their wings and sending water cascading everywhere. With every goose that took offence Alex laughed louder and louder.

But I was concerned that if the dog caught up with us she would try and climb aboard, possibly pulling the whole boat over and emptying us all out into the cold water. So I was rowing away from her as fast as I could. The lake wasn't small and I was worried that she would get so exhausted swimming around after us that she would end up drowning herself.

We managed to get back dry and safe. The dog climbed out, tired, but suffering no ill effects from its marathon swim. We said goodbye to the others, who had to make their way back home across London before the traffic got too thick. It was still early so I took Alex to the swings.

It was mid-September and the leaves were turning brown. The path was thick with the first fall. Alex had had his first spell of conker collecting the year before and was thrilled to come across some lying on the ground as we walked. He bent down to fill his trouser pockets. 'There's one!' I said, pointing to the ground behind him. He turned and his face lit up with pleasure to see such wonderful treasure just lying there on the grass, all for him. 'There's another one!' I said, pointing a little further away.

By the time he had cleared most of the ground around him his pockets were bulging. He bent for the last of them and as he did so a conker he had already collected dropped silently out of his pocket on to the soft grass and rolled unnoticed out of sight behind him. He straightened, grasping what he thought was the last of the treasure and just managed to shove it into a pocket; both of his pockets were now stretched tight as a drum.

'There's one!' I said, pointing behind him to the conker which had just escaped. He turned and was truly amazed to see a conker where a split second before there had been none. He bent to pick this wonder up and, as he did so, another one dropped just as quietly from his overstretched pockets and again rolled unnoticed on to the grass in the other direction to where he was looking. He straightened again, sure that now he had harvested all there was to find, and that he could go home safe in the knowledge that none had escaped him.

'There's another one!' I said, pointing behind him. He spun round, now almost giddy with the motion, to find yet another treasure there before him, his eyes now wide with wonder. Once again as he bent down another conker dropped silently out of his pocket. This was just about as good as it could get. Every time he turned around there was more treasure, and no matter how much he safely stored away in his pockets there was always room for more!

Round and round he turned, time and time again. And every time there was more for him. At first I laughed to see him so thrilled. But almost the instant that my spirits began to lift I was hit by a wave of intense pain. My chest was aching and my eyes were filled with tears. There were so many emotions at once. I was hit by a reaction I was to confront over and again as time went on. This should have been a wonderful moment, but there was only one person who could have appreciated it as much as me. And she wasn't there. She would never be there. Never again for any of these moments. And without her, what should have brought joy only brought pain. I had to put on a mask and smile and make sure that he didn't see what lay behind it. This was one of those rare moments when the last thing in the world he needed was the truth.

★

I had received several letters from friends I had lost touch with over the years. If they included an address I wrote back. If they only included a telephone number I couldn't bring myself to call them. With people who had known Rachel I was fine. With those who hadn't I was lost. I didn't know where to begin. It was all too complicated and too painful. I didn't have the strength to begin rebuilding new relationships. And trying to catch up with those I hadn't seen for so long would have been exactly that.

There was one family, however, who turned out to be living literally round the corner from my mother's house. They had had two children when I knew them, who must have been teenagers by now, but in their letter they said that they had two more boys since. One of them was only a few weeks older than Alex. Alex was in need of playmates, so, reluctant though I was, I eventually convinced myself to call.

We spoke a few times on the phone. It seemed as if a million years had gone by since we had last seen each other. But there was also the impression that nothing had changed at all. We made an arrangement to meet and, a few days later, Alex and I pulled up in the car across the road from their house. I unstrapped Alex from his car-seat. I had already explained where we were going and that there would be another little boy of his age to play with. Alex wouldn't get out of the car.

Our friends had seen us pull up and came out of the house to greet us. We stood in the road talking but Alex still remained inside the car. I tried to pull him out gently but he just gripped tightly on to the steering wheel so I had to leave him where he was. The little boy was standing on the step but his mother came to explain to Alex how much he was looking forward to meeting him. She explained that there were toys too! Alex stood on the driver's seat clutching the steering wheel determinedly. But he was listening.

We stood in the street for nearly a quarter of an hour before Alex finally consented to let me carry him into the house. Inside, the boys' bedroom turned out to be a veritable treasure trove. With four children passing through the house there were all kinds of toys to discover in every corner. At first Alex would only sit on my knee, or kneel beside me in constant contact. He would squeal at the slightest sign that I might move away. But little by little he became more and more absorbed in exploring the wonders all around him.

249

I felt immediately at ease. I was raised as the only child of a single parent. My stepbrothers came from a much later marriage. The atmosphere I had grown up in and the one that reigned in this house were light years apart. It was warm, and full of fun and laughter. It was like a tonic. Rachel loved large families, even if she wasn't sure she wanted one for herself. She would occasionally leave Alex with a childminder who had four children of her own. Rachel marvelled at the way their house was so full of life. I knew she would have been equally impressed by the noise and happiness we found ourselves bathed in and absorbing through every pore.

We were spending so much of our time surrounded by adults and heaviness that this blast of fresh air was just what we needed. It was a shame that we had lost contact; Rachel would have got on with them all so well.

I rang the journalist back to tell her that, as long as there was a formal agreement allowing me to see all of the text, I was prepared to go ahead with talking to them.

I felt bad about the whole business. Going through this performance was the last thing in the world I wanted to do. But if I was to take Alex out of the country I had no choice. There was no other way I could guarantee our independence in the months it would take us to set ourselves up somewhere else. Everyone was extremely polite and kind with me, but I was out of my depth and I knew it.

If they wanted to break their agreement the only card I had to play to protect our interests, if the worst came to the worst, was righteous indignation and public sympathy.

The journalist came to my mother's house when Alex was asleep. I had expected her to have the written agreement ready for me to sign before we went ahead. All she had come with was her notebook and tape recorder and an eagerness to get on with things. I suddenly felt extremely unprotected. I told her that I was still not convinced that more harm than good was going to come out of it. This didn't go down well.

She said that this story was important to her, too! That she was going to do the best job she could, and that she would be giving a lot of her time and effort to cover it. And that, if it wasn't going to go ahead, then it wasn't worth us starting.

I was perfectly happy to believe that she was going to do the best that she could. But for me it wasn't a 'story', or even somebody's week's work. This was our life. I decided that I might as well go ahead. I had so little control anyway. I asked for the agreement to be prepared for the following session and, if I wasn't happy when I read it, I would stop there.

The police had asked Rachel's father if he would take part in a press conference for them. There was due to be a reconstruction of the events leading up to Rachel's murder on television that week. The police had real faith in the power of this programme to stimulate a large response from the public. They knew that there were still people who had been on the Common that day who had not come forward. They still had so little to go on that any new information would help.

Rachel's father had no interest in talking to the press. But, because the police considered that the programme would be extremely useful to their investigation and the more publicity it had beforehand the better its chances of success, he agreed to take part.

We were told that he would be interviewed at New Scotland Yard by one journalist and one television crew only, to make the process as painless as possible for him. A copy of this interview would then be freely distributed between all the news agencies and would be available to every newspaper and TV channel in the hope of raising as much interest as possible in the coming programme.

The next day the interview appeared in one newspaper alone, together with colour reproductions of the family photographs we had originally given the police right at the beginning. It was run as a four-page spread, with the word EXCLUSIVE blazoned large across every page.

It is difficult to explain why this upset me so much. After all, it was only someone apparently breaking their word; no one had died. But I felt so vulnerable that even the smallest kick in the teeth knocked me to the floor. The whole issue was trivial compared with Rachel's death. And, for some time after, just about everything had gone completely over my head. I had felt that nothing could ever scare me again. Nothing could ever be worse than what had happened, so nothing could ever make me worry. Nothing was worth getting upset about again.

But as time went by, and once I began to make a conscious effort to start living again, I found the opposite was true. The fact that something so terrible had already happened only proved to me that the worst does come to the worst, and there was every likelihood that terrible things *were* going to happen again.

My resistance had gone. It had been burnt up. All the layers of skin had been ripped away and, emotionally, there was nothing left to protect me. Instead of minor events paling into insignificance, they added to the pain. I couldn't shake them off. I couldn't find the strength to be positive or optimistic. I felt like every minor problem was insurmountable, as if I had to get over everything, and this new thing too. I felt like I was constantly being driven to my knees. Everything that was out of place, every dispute or broken agreement, every breaking of trust, every misunderstanding or unwillingness to communicate cut me to the core. I couldn't operate like I had before.

This whole episode was so petty and so sordid. So cheap. We were left with the feeling that we were being manipulated. I was sure that there was no bad faith on the part of the police, simply that others who didn't share their outlook had made the most of their opportunities.

I was choking with anger. I believed we had been lied to and messed around by people who were taking advantage of our ignorance and our good faith. Were they only trying to make a quick buck? Was that all someone's death meant to them? Did these people really never stop and think about the pain they might have been adding to those who were suffering already? Or was I just totally naïve?

The journalist returned that night for the second time. This time she had the agreement. I read it through and – bearing in mind that all they were risking was an apology if they broke it – it contained the principles which we had agreed on. Ironically, I still felt relieved to see everything in print, even though in truth it was nothing more than fantasy.

The interviews progressed smoothly. The journalist basically let me talk, and asked a question here and there to keep me going. I was amazed that, in spite of the times I had recounted the same sequence of events to friends and family, I still found it therapeutic to talk it through once again.

They wanted pictures from our family album. I had already given plenty to the police, and these were now in free circulation. Giving any more was not going to make our private lives any more public than they already were. The journalist had been in tears several times since we had started the night before but the pictures we had taken at Alex's birth brought her to a complete stop. She said she was a grandmother herself. She was choked. She said they were beautiful, and that they were a reflection of what birth should be.

All I could think about was how having Alex at home had been the biggest tangible achievement of Rachel's young life. And of how it should have been the first of many wonderful achievements. But there weren't going to be any more. Her life had just been stopped. Dead.

The journalist asked if they could have those particular pictures to run with the articles. I knew that if there was a chance that anybody else would be inspired enough by seeing them to think of having their own baby at home then Rachel would have been proud. She would have wanted other parents to share the wonderful experiences we had. And there was always a chance that this would stir someone's conscience. Someone else might be moved. Someone who was maybe protecting another by not coming forward. There was no telling what would tip the balance enough to overcome such misguided loyalty.

The agreement was clear: the pictures remained my property and were solely for use by the newspaper for this series of articles and no more. I agreed to let them have the pictures, and I resolved to make sure that this part of the story was emphasized as much as possible. It gave me one more reason to justify what I was doing to Alex and myself.

I told the journalist that on reflection I didn't want to go through with the appeal for donations for a trust fund. I felt like we were begging, I found the idea humiliating. I would be happy just with the fee we had agreed. But she told me it was too late: it formed part of the contract I had signed. I didn't feel good about it.

'There are going to be some TV commercials,' the journalist said. I tried to work out how that might affect things. It wasn't unusual for a newspaper to advertise a particular interview they were running. I had seen the kind of thing before and usually it was the person being interviewed who spoke. They weren't asking me to do it. I would never have agreed to take part anyway. So where was the harm?

Chapter Nineteen

THE POLICE HAD asked if I would agree to take Alex back to the Common. They were still keen to discover any detail, no matter how small, which would explain the exact sequence of events that had taken place that morning. The child psychologist thought this was a good idea.

The police asked if I would hand Alex over to the child psychologist's care, and for me not to be there at all. They must have been completely mad.

I said that I might be willing to allow Alex to go but only if I was present. I had been thinking hard. We had, after all, been back once already. There had been no noticeable ill effects despite the attentions of the press. The event hadn't brought on nightmares or any other problems in his behaviour. The child psychologist had told me of other cases where her colleagues had taken children back to the scene of a disaster in which they had been involved. Apparently the only outcome had been positive. For some of the children the visit had freed things up, allowing them to remember or express more than they had been able to before. Alex was younger than these other children, but after much reflection at last I decided to go.

The child psychologist was waiting for us at Wimbledon police station. She climbed into the car along with one of our detectives.

I had been worried about how to tell Alex about what was going to happen. I wanted to give him the least time possible to dwell on the subject. I thought that the best thing was to tell him we were going for a walk on the Common and then drive to the carpark and explain the details there. The child psychologist was adamant that we should explain everything to him before we pulled away.

She was probably right. But for the first time I began to find her presence irritating. Between us we managed to explain that we, Alex and I, were there to help the police, and that we were just going to walk the way that he had gone with Mummy that morning and then we would go home. But there were too many voices. Things were already confused. I didn't like being disagreed with so strongly in front of him: I was the parent, after all. But I told myself that this was hardly the time to stand on my pride.

I drove up to the Common and pulled up in the carpark. There were a couple of unmarked cars there before us and numerous officers in plain clothes, waiting. I turned off the ignition and our detective and the child psychologist climbed out. I undid Alex from his car-seat in the front beside me. He climbed on to my lap. I was very tense. There was so much going on around us.

I was talking gently to Alex again, telling him why we were there, and that all the policemen were there to look after us, and that we wouldn't be there long. I opened the door to get out but Alex wouldn't let go of the steering wheel. There was this whole pack of people, all straining at the leash and wanting to get on with the show. I tugged gently at Alex's arms but he wouldn't budge. I was beginning to ask myself what the hell we were doing there.

This was exactly the reaction I had been expecting from him the last time we came. When he had said he wanted to come I hadn't truly believed that he understood the consequences. I thought that by the time we got to the carpark he would have begun freaking out and that would have been the end of it. This time I had the feeling that it wasn't so much the place itself and all that had happened which was frightening him as much as all of these people milling around. He doubtless remembered the hunting pack of pressmen last time round.

He was hanging on to the steering wheel but he wasn't freaking out. I felt I knew him so well now. I was sure that I understood the exact level of his anxiety. If he had really decided that he didn't want to get out of the car then he would have been kicking and screaming. He was quite capable of such a display in order to get his own way. But he was very quiet, grizzling a little. This was more like he wanted the assurance from me that, if he did come out, he was going to be OK. But even so, as I prised his fingers off the steering wheel, I couldn't help but wonder what my reaction would have been on watching another parent do the same to their child in the same circumstances. I surely would have thought that they were outrageously cruel and insensitive.

We set off along the path that he had taken with Rachel that morning. Alex soon stopped crying completely. One of our detectives and the child psychologist walked with us, the other police were spread out either in front or behind. At first I carried him in my arms but very soon, and much to my surprise, he wanted to get down. He then walked cheerfully along beside me.

We left the carpark behind us and walked along the path. Some trees were on our left. Ahead of us the ground rose into a large mound. As it began to rise we passed the tree where Alex and I had buried a wild bird that we had found and tried to save. I remembered how we had parked our car near the flat the Saturday before Rachel was killed. When we climbed out of the car the first thing we saw was a thrush fledgling squatting in the middle of the pavement. It made no attempt to escape as we moved towards it. Rachel was adamant that we should try and save it. I was hesitant. As a child I had tried several times to nurse wild birds back to health but they always ended up dying. I didn't want to upset Alex by having this one die on us too. I thought it might have been kinder to let one of the cats get in and put it out of its misery. It couldn't have been out of the nest long or one of them would have got it already. Rachel, however, had decided.

I went off to find a box while the two of them stayed with it on the pavement. When I got back they told me it had hopped around a little but hadn't tried to get away. It made a little flurry as I scooped it up gingerly, thinking all the while that it was probably infested with fleas and lice. I dropped it in the box where its bright eye looked up at us. Maybe this one would actually pull through, I thought to myself. Rachel's optimism was contagious enough.

A lot of time was spent in the back yard grubbing in the dirt, trying to find little worms or insects which we duly force-fed the poor creature with the aid of a pair of tweezers. I eventually managed to get one down its throat before it was time to take Alex off to a birthday party. When we got back later that afternoon, however, the worm had been regurgitated and lay on the floor of the box. The bird was still looking up at us with a bright eye, bobbing its head and blinking from time to time. It still seemed strong and showed no sign of dropping dead yet.

I managed to get another insect down its throat later in the day. But by the evening that too had been brought back up. I didn't hold out much hope.

In the morning we were all suddenly surprised by a beautiful burst of song coming strongly from 'Birdie's' cardboard box. Alex was fascinated and wanted the bird to do it again. We didn't have to wait too long before another burst, equally beautiful, came sounding out. If he was strong enough to sing he was probably strong enough to survive. But when we came back from our walk at lunchtime Birdie was lying dead across the bottom of his box.

Rachel and I were choked. It was the second time in only a week that we had to discuss the subject of death with Alex. It seemed extremely unfair to have to inflict such a weight on a small child. The previous time had been when we had hired a dinosaur cartoon for him. There was a passage where a mother dinosaur was leading her baby dinosaur to safety when they were hit by an earthquake and the ground began to break up around them. The mother dinosaur was hit by a boulder and lay dying. The baby dinosaur was nuzzling her and talking to her, telling her to get up. Alex was glued to the screen. He carried on chewing his sandwich as he watched. If he had qualms he wasn't showing them.

Rachel and I just looked at each other. She was biting her lip. I felt my heart breaking in sadness imagining anything that could happen to separate Alex and her. The thought that he could be left orphaned and helpless like the creature on the screen was just too awful to contemplate.

'Switch it off!' I said to her, only half joking. 'I can't take it!'

Rachel had told me later that she couldn't imagine how Alex would survive if anything happened to her. The whole thing left me shuddering in terror just thinking of it. I didn't want to talk about it.

Now we were confronted with something more concrete. And the question of how to explain what had happened to Birdie was less than simple. How do you explain death to a child?

For a start Rachel and I had to get the story right between ourselves. Rachel saw this as an opportunity to try and give Alex a few ideas on how to look at things. She wanted him to understand a little her belief that we are not our bodies, that something goes on even when the shell no longer functions.

Alex hadn't immediately remembered his new friend with the magical voice on our return, but we wanted to tell him before he had time to ask. 'Birdie's dead,' we started, adding quickly, 'He wasn't strong enough to live out of the nest without his mummy and daddy to look after him.'

Alex didn't really react. He took the news in the same way that he might have taken the news that it was raining too hard for us to go out and play.

'He doesn't need his body any more,' Rachel told him. 'The part that's really him has gone somewhere else now.'

She looked at me, not sure if she was making any sense to him. 'What else *could* you tell him?' I said by way of consolation. All this reminded me of something I had read about the questions you could always ask yourself and never come up with exactly the same answer: 'Who am I?', 'Where did I come from?' and 'Where am I going?' It made me think about the fact that we come in alone and we go out alone. I thought that I would somehow find a way to cope with that. When I'd been young I had spent so much time alone. But Rachel? Rachel hated being alone. She often said so. I didn't know how she would ever be able to cope with being separated from us. In this way, even if in no other way, she was too fragile.

But these were just riddles. I would never know the answers to any of them until I was dead and gone. And then if we were wrong, and there wasn't anything else, it would be too late to worry about it. I tried to shake my head and put all of that out of my mind. In the meantime, what were we going to do with Birdie?

Rachel wanted us to bury him. She had buried her pet rabbit after it died when she was little and she thought this would be a good thing for us to do for Alex. She tried to explain a little to him how Birdie's body would eventually rot and how it would turn into food to help the other plants and trees to grow. It was all going over his head; he was more concerned that we put on his Fireman Sam video.

We were going to the Common that afternoon so we decided that would be as good a place as any to bury the bird.

We set off after lunch with the bird wrapped in newspaper, and a little trowel to dig with. When we had left the carpark behind us and found a suitable spot under the canopy of a small tree Rachel left the whole thing to me. Seeing as I wasn't there with him all week this was another good opportunity to do something with him on our own. She watched from a little further up the path where the mound began to rise. She was looking absolutely radiant. Although it had not been the initial impression I had had of her, as time went on I often thought that I had never seen a more beautiful woman. She would always laugh if I said such a thing to her. She was as insecure as most women seem to be about their looks, with an inaccurate view of herself which often made me think of anorexics who look in the mirror and find themselves fat. She could look in the mirror and find herself ugly. And the most painful thing was, she really meant it.

Alex and I pushed last year's leaves to one side and scraped a little hole with the trowel. I put Birdie gently in the hole and together we pushed the dirt and leaves back over to cover him up. Rachel was still standing in the sunshine, watching. There was a friend with us and together we walked through the trees and down to the pond. The Common was full of people out for their Sunday afternoon stroll, the sunshine probably bringing out more than usual.

As I sat on a bench by the pond and watched the others playing with the dog I noticed some youths looking at Rachel. This was hardly unusual in itself but as I noticed them I heard the words *I wonder which one of them is going to try something on?* trip through my head. I tried to shake the thought out of my head just as quickly. Whether it was para-noid jealousy or over-protectiveness, I tried to tell myself there was no need to be so extreme about people only looking at her. Rachel was careful, I told myself, and for a woman she was big and strong. She was as safe as any woman could be.

Looking back I ask myself what was wrong with me that I didn't see things coming. Or, if I had a fear, then why didn't I act on it? I just didn't think it was really going to happen. You ask yourself afterwards how you could possibly miss something which, after it has happened, seemed so inevitable. I don't have an answer. It is very hard to live with.

Alex and I continued past the tree. I didn't mention Birdie and he said nothing to make me think that he was remembering when we had buried the bird together. More than one of the police officers asked out loud: 'Which way did you go next, Alex?' This was really a bad idea. There were too many voices. This was turning into a circus.

Between me talking to him, the child psychologist, our detective and then various other police officers chipping in, the situation was just about impossible.

I talked to him myself, but felt as if I was shouting to be heard above the crowd. Alex was perfectly cheerful but clearly affected by all the people. I could see that he wasn't at all focused on the day his mother had been killed. I was sure he would have the greatest difficulty in answering anything I asked him. The only way to get him out of this state of mind was to give him enough peace and quiet for him to be able to stop thinking about the circus around us. The simple act of walking on the Common itself should have been enough to take care of the rest.

At least he was calm. I couldn't help feeling that, if he could be in the very place where he had seen so much horror and show himself to be reasonably calm and secure, then this was a good sign. He was having to confront his fear, face on. Surely this would lessen the terror of this place for him if he had flashbacks of it in the middle of the night?

We reached the top of the mound. Everyone had quietened down a little. The sun was shining and someone observed that conditions were much like the day that Rachel was killed. Alex wanted to run down the mound with me. I was sure that this was the general direction they would have gone that morning, judging by the sightings of them by witnesses. They could have been retracing the route we had taken with our friend the Sunday before Rachel was killed. But we had still not been able to establish from Alex whether they had made it through the trees and all the way down to the pond and were on their way back when they were attacked, or whether they had still been on their way.

Alex wanted to climb back to the top of the mound and run down again and again. It was mind-boggling how a child was able to think about playing only yards from where he had watched his mother being slaughtered. I was struggling to keep myself together and I found the effort of trying to play with him at the same time almost too much. But he needed these few moments of relaxation if he was ever going to be able to come up with any other information.

'Were you going this way with Mummy that morning, Alex?' I asked, pointing down the slope. 'Were you going to the pond?' It was hard to get a clear answer. Now he was more interested in the blackberries which were beginning to appear in the brambles.

Eventually he seemed ready to follow the path down the mound and under the high canopy of trees. I knew exactly where we were. I had roamed over virtually every inch of the place as a boy. I was having flashbacks of giddy, joyful bike rides through the dust down these very tracks. I had run cross-country here with my school.

Even though he was now more relaxed I still didn't get the impression that he was leading us in any particular direction. It was much more as if he felt obliged to do something. And everybody was only too happy to follow him whichever way he went. I was still bothered by the presence of so many people. It was adding greatly to the stress we were already under and I found it extremely invasive. All I could think about was what Rachel had gone through that day. Everything else was an intense irritation.

Alex led us all the way down to the pond. He would stop and look round from time to time as if trying to find his way. The undergrowth and brambles and ferns had grown up and it was hard to see clearly through the trees for any distance, as it had been at the beginning of the summer.

The whole party at last found itself down at the pond. I still wasn't convinced that this was the way they had actually come. Voices were still piping up from all around us. I wished everybody would shut up and let him get on with it. Alex was becoming more and more confused and I was getting more and more aggravated.

Now we turned back. People were pointing in different directions and one or another went striding off into the undergrowth. There was no way we could see back up the hill through the trees, so much had things grown up. It didn't look the same. How could Alex know his way back from here, especially when his eyes were so near to the ground?

Yet another voice called out 'Which way did you go, Alex?' I was almost at screaming point. Why couldn't they show just the tiniest amount of patience and keep their big mouths shut?

Alex hesitated between two paths. I knew it was hopeless. We were simply going through the motions. Just as he negotiated a shallow ditch he slipped and fell. I saw that he had cut his leg. As I helped him to his feet he looked down at the damage. He saw blood, and his face crumpled. He let out a long wail. It was more than I could take. To see my child's face distorted with pain, to see the tears and the blood and to know what he had already gone through in that place ripped me apart. It was so cruel. How much pain did he have to suffer?

I could hear myself screaming out loud. What were we doing here? Why had I done this to him? I picked him up and carried him off. I was running as fast as possible without bouncing him around more than I could avoid. He was crying because of how much his leg hurt. I was in agony.

We came out of the trees and I could see the carpark a couple of hundred metres ahead. Alex suddenly began crying louder. I tried to go a little faster but he was pulling at me. He wanted me to stop. He wanted to pick blackberries! I felt that we had left insanity a long way behind and come out the other side as I watched him stand there, his weight on one leg and the cut one held tenderly off the ground while the tears streaked down his face as he stuffed blackberries into his mouth.

I was anxious to get away. I was shaking with emotion. The others hadn't caught up with us yet. They must have just allowed us to go. I pulled a handful of berries off the bush, scooped him up and hurried towards the car. I had just managed to shove him into his car-seat, strap him in, and get in myself when the child psychologist appeared with one of the detectives. She was shouting something after us; I wasn't sure what it was and I wasn't waiting to find out. The rest of the circus were coming out of the trees after them. I put my foot down hard on the accelerator. I knew I was giving the impression of a character in some cheap soap opera but I had to get away from there before I went completely mad.

The last thing in the world I wanted was to drive straight into a ditch. I managed to find enough self-control to ease my foot a little off the accelerator, but the engine was still roaring. Alex was crying again. 'Don't drive so fast!' he wailed. I had to stop where the main road crossed our route. When I had pulled across through a gap in the traffic it was clear that no one was following us.

Only a mile or so away I pulled into a quiet carpark. I wanted to get myself together a little before I drove any more. The carpark looked out over an immaculate cricket field. A more serene corner of England would have been hard to imagine. I turned off the engine and burst into tears.

Alex by now had stopped crying. He sat quietly, studying me in between looking out of the window. 'I'm hungry,' he said.

I fished a yoghurt out of a bag and gave it to him with a spoon. He took a couple of mouthfuls and then said: 'Why did you drive so fast?'

'I'm sorry,' I said.

He took another couple of mouthfuls, then said: 'You frightened me!'

'I'm sorry,' I said again. 'I didn't mean to frighten you. I won't do it again.' He seemed satisfied.

I really had had enough. We were going to go completely mad like this. There was no way we could find even the slightest peace. Problems kept arriving as if they were falling off an endless conveyor belt. There was no end to it.

Alex now looked completely relaxed. He had recovered his composure and showed no preoccupation with all that we had just been through. Instead he wanted to talk about what he could see through the window. He recognized the place. I had come here a couple of times to play tennis.

I was badly shaken up. On top of everything I was supposed to review the first part of my interview which was due to be published the following day. And I had to do so before the deadline with the printers. At first I had wanted to actually see it on paper, but this had become so complicated in terms of meeting up at the right time and so on that I had finally agreed to have it read back to me over the phone.

I sat in the car contemplating the prospect. I couldn't have cared less what they printed any more. I just wanted them to pay me so we could get away from all this madness. I didn't expect that I would be any happier, but at least the conveyor belt might stop for just a little while. It was Thursday and we were leaving for France on Sunday for a three-week break. I hoped it would be long enough to avoid the feeding frenzy among the other papers, eager not to miss out on the meal. The storm of attention was likely to be short-lived. I thought would soon blow itself out. I couldn't wait for Sunday to come. I felt like driving to the airport straight away and getting on the first plane going anywhere. I was in no fit state to drive anywhere much, I could only just stop myself from shaking. I decided to drive to some friends nearby, and hoped that they were in.

That night the reconstruction was due to be broadcast. I was late getting Alex to bed and I got downstairs just before it was due to start. One of the adverts for my interview had already been on before I arrived. I could tell that no one in the room had been impressed. I suddenly felt like a Judas who had sold Rachel's privacy for a few pieces of silver. I felt sick.

The programme started. With the help of actors and the statements of the witnesses it related the events of that morning. They showed how Rachel had arrived at the Common and parked the car. And how a man had been seen acting suspiciously by several different people at around this time in the area near to where Rachel was killed. One woman described how she felt this person's aggression was being focused in her direction, another witness said that she had actually been followed for some time by someone of the same description, but that the presence of her teenage son had possibly proved a deterrent.

The police provided an Identikit picture of the man the different witnesses described. They asked for anybody who had seen this person to come forward if they had not already done so. He wore exactly the clothing, and had the same colour and length of hair as Alex had described. He had also been seen bending over the stream, washing his hands, just as Alex had described his mother's killer 'looking into the water'.

This person's route had been traced on to and off the Common before and after Rachel was killed.

The police said, that according to a psychologist's report, the person they were looking for probably lived alone or with an elderly female relative.

As the programme continued the presenters announced that their switchboards were already busy with people calling in. In all, thousands of leads were established and several important new pieces of information came to light.

I sat watching like a zombie. My eyes were open but in reality it was all just washing over me. I felt numb, unable to make any sense of it. All this activity, all these people. I couldn't make the connection between it and us. What we were. What we had been.

When the programme finished, someone switched channels. Almost immediately one of 'my' adverts appeared. In what I considered the worst lurid exposé style of presentation the journalist who had interviewed me threw down all the family photographs I had given her on to her desk, and invited the public to find out the 'truth' about my life with Rachel, 'tomorrow!'

The salacious tone of the advert had nothing whatsoever to do with the text of the article. And for something like that to be programmed on the same night as the reconstruction of Rachel's death was totally beyond me. Was there no respect?

The next day the police confirmed that the public response to the programme had been extremely promising. They had been given more sightings of the man in their Identikit picture on various points on the route he had taken on to and off the Common. Several callers had actually provided names and addresses of people they suspected.

Some of the names corresponded with people they had already been looking at; others were completely new to them. They were very pleased with the success of the programme and hopeful that the investigation would gain new impetus because of it. The one thing that had so far eluded them was luck. All of which had gone to Rachel's killer. Hopefully, now the tide was beginning to change.

I phoned the newspaper to complain to the editor and the journalist about what I considered their offensive advert. I felt I had been misled. Sure I had been told that there were going to be adverts, but I hadn't been told how they would be presented. The journalist said she didn't have any 'power'. The editor said that to their minds the adverts had been perfectly acceptable. He told me I was probably just upset because of everything I had been through.

I realized I was wasting my time. We had completely different views of the world and I was never going to get my point across. I was only a beginner at this game. If I had known better I would have insisted on our agreement including approval of any TV adverts as well as all the spread itself. But I knew that there was always likely to be something else I hadn't thought of. A poster or a radio advert, even. I couldn't win. I had to try and swallow it and put it down to experience.

It was Saturday. Tomorrow we were getting on a plane. It couldn't be too soon. We went to visit our newly rediscovered friends. In some ways it was as if no time had passed at all. We all looked physically older but everything else was exactly the same.

The morning went quickly as we talked, until the children's bound-less energy made it clear that a romp in the park was called for. Their six-year-old was already big enough to be interested in kicking a ball about with me and his father, whereas Alex and the younger one were soon pretending to be trains. By coincidence this was the same open space where I had been taking Alex all the time we had been at my mother's, and where we had talked with our detectives. We could have bumped into one another at any time.

Alex, as was his speciality, was soon directing things. His new friend was an engine like him, and had the right to run around in every direc-tion as long as he came back from time to time. But his friend's mother, who was a carriage of some sort, was not allowed to leave the station without Alex. From time to time Alex would come back from circling around the grass, and collect her. The two of them would chuff around a little and then Alex would take her back to the station and deposit her there. He would look at her very seriously and tell her she absolutely had to stay put. Then, once again, he would run off, cir-cling around, totally carefree.

He was, however, keeping an eye on his 'carriage' from wherever he happened to be. If she tried to move he would shout his irritation until she was back in place.

Later his new friend's mother told me that she had found Alex's game very significant. She said that at first she hadn't really noticed, but as time went on she realized that Alex was talking to her as if she would be in danger if she didn't do what he said. He was so earnest and serious. She had to stay wherever he put her because that way she would be safe. And then he would run off wherever he wanted because he was in no danger. She was convinced that, in his way, he was telling her that she was a woman, a blonde woman too, and that she had to be careful. He could go wherever he liked because he wasn't a target. I had been watching the game while playing football with the others and, judging by what I had seen and knowing Alex as I did, what she said made absolute sense. She was a potential victim and he wasn't. The blonde woman had been killed. The child had been spared.

My mother drove me to the airport. The atmosphere was bad. Everyone was upset by something or other I had said in those articles. The third and final part of the interview was due out tomorrow,

Monday. I had to ring from the airport to hear what was to be printed.

I had hardly changed a word of what had been written. It was too much focused on me for my comfort but it was all accurate. At each question I had swallowed hard and had tried to give an honest answer. My only reference was Rachel: I knew that was what she would have wanted me to do. She would have told me that the truth can never be wrong, and if people are upset by it then that was their problem, not mine.

I had never had the experience of listening to everything I might have said during an entire evening read back to me. It was a strange sensation and it wasn't hard to see the danger of people being carried away with a false idea of their own importance. Real celebrity, where people actually grow accustomed to this, must be very hard to handle.

By the time we had checked in, got Alex something to eat and found a phone, there was hardly enough time to listen to the journalist who read back the whole piece. The noisy airport lounge made hearing almost impossible, and anyway, I was pretty much beyond caring about what it might or might not have included. The last week had taken its toll.

Alex had been on a plane the year before. Like an old hand, he took the whole thing in his stride. I remembered our all-night wait at Heraklion airport in Crete the autumn before, huddled up on a bench outside under the stars with Alex asleep in his pushchair. Our cheap flight had left at an impossible time. We had spent the most idyllic fourteen days of my life. Our days had been split between beautiful beaches and cheap local restaurants. The summer crowds had left and the island was quiet. We had found a sleepy little village where there had been a beautiful stray dog and eight little puppies who had adopted us. They had gratefully benefited from Rachel's leftovers. The mother even followed us on long walks to neighbouring beaches and tried to rescue us from the water when we swam.

It was a strange coincidence that our puppy of unknown father, taken from an animal shelter a few weeks after our return, should turn out to be almost the spitting image of our recent holiday companion.

We had roasted in the sun, and chased brightly coloured fishes in the clear water. We were in love, our child was healthy and happy, it was the nearest thing I could imagine to paradise on earth.

Alex had played all day, either under the parasol or in the sea. He was inexhaustible. A German couple we'd met remarked that with a child like ours life would never be boring, and that it was a good job there were two of us, because it was always going to take two to match his energy levels.

There was one thing which prevented my happiness from being absolutely complete. We had been talking about coming back the next year. But the thought came into my head that wherever we stayed it had to be totally secure to stop anybody trying to get Rachel. I had visions of men trying to overpower her. The images simply flashed into my head from time to time and bore no relation to what we might be doing or even talking about. I tried to fight the images off but they always left me shaken. I never mentioned a word to Rachel, I knew I would frighten her.

We had had beautiful weather and had found a beautiful place to stay. Apart from the savage scenery of the barren inland mountains the island had shown us only its most peaceful side. We had read a little of its ancient reputation as being the home of the gods but we had seen little out of the ordinary.

One day we had been following a deserted sandy path which threaded its way in between some smallholdings and chicken runs. The path was shaded by acacia trees and lined with the occasional black-berry bush. Alex's face was red with juice by the time we broke out into the sunshine as we neared the beach. We heard bleating coming from a field up ahead. As we approached, the bleating grew more ago-nized. It sounded like a young lamb was in real trouble. The noise was heart-wrenching. As we drew closer we could see that one of the sheep in the field had its head stuck in the fence.

I rushed forward to free it, but as I wrestled with the wire the lamb only pushed harder, entwining itself further still. As I struggled I realized that the lamb had no eyes and no ears. Its head was little more than a stump with no features at all. In spite of the afternoon heat the realization made me go cold. The bleating was louder than ever and the animal forced itself further and further into the wire until it drew blood. I started to shiver and my fingers strained against the wire. I couldn't do anything to get the animal out and asked myself what I was actually struggling with. I couldn't even see where the sound was com-ing from.

'Leave it,' Rachel said and turned her back. She couldn't bring herself to look at it. I let go of the fence and we continued quickly on our way. It was a while before the sound of the bleating died away.

It was only when we were completely out of earshot that we could bring ourselves to talk about what we had seen. It was an aberration of nature that seemed all the more frightening for being in the midst of all this beauty. It was a reminder to us that savagery was never far away.

Even when Rachel and I talked about this incident months later we still couldn't work out exactly what we had seen. And we could never work out how an animal born so deformed could have survived to the age it had.

But the rhythm of sun and sand and sea quickly took us over once more. The days passed peacefully, beautifully and each evening found us healthy, tired and happy.

At last the two weeks came to an end. In some ways we felt that we had been away for ever, so great had been the change from our every-day lives. By the time we had taken a bus and taxi back to the airport we had spent almost every penny we had and had to rummage through all our possessions to try and find enough change to buy a drink.

It was all so different now as I strapped Alex on to my lap for the takeoff to France.

She was gone.

Chapter Twenty

WHEN THE PLANE doors opened we were hit by warm, summer air. We had left autumn far behind. As our friend's car carried us away from the airport I could feel the beads of sweat breaking out on my brow and my back become damp. It was a hot day.

I looked out of the window at the streets and houses. We were in another world. I could feel my shoulders begin to unknot. I sighed deeply in relief. So much pressure had been lifted by one short plane ride. The people in the streets were living their own lives with no idea about and absolutely no interest in mine. It was a balm to look at their faces and realize that they were living in another universe from the one we had just escaped from. Our anonymity was something tangible. The further we got from the airport the better I felt. The thin corridor which ran along our flight-line and into the airport building itself had reached its end at the carpark exit. Up until that point I had the feeling that something could suck us back along that line and pull us back. But now we had passed the gate I felt free.

I had vague memories of the tree-lined streets and canals. I had spent a few days here one summer. I would have loved to return with Rachel and stroll around it together. But I could only appreciate it in the most bitter-sweet way. It was beautiful but the experience gave me no pleasure. Instead it made my chest ache with unhappiness. All its beauty only reminded me of who I should have been sharing it with.

We passed an amazingly quiet time. Three weeks away from the constant attention and pressure made me see just how near to breaking point I had been. The last week before we left had been hell on its own. There is a limit to what anyone can take.

The pain of being without Rachel was no less acute. In many ways it grew. Alex and I were doing new things, a new chapter in our lives was beginning and she had no physical part in it. It put a distance between what had been our life before and what our future would inevitably become.

Alex was not in the slightest bit fazed by the change of scenery. He was always ready to play if ever there was the opportunity for having fun. And as there was plenty to see and do there was never much chance of him getting bored. His routine stayed the same. He had his sheepskin and blankets, and slept near me always. He was perfectly at ease. In fact for the first couple of weeks it was far too hot for any covers at all and I had to prise him off his sheepskin soon after he was asleep to stop him from waking up wringing wet. He had his stories and his songs at bedtime and his meals were much the same as at home. After that it was only a question of keeping the entertainment rolling.

Morning was still the worst time for him. In the period between being totally asleep and totally awake the demons played with his mind. It still took as long as ever to get him to snap out of the disturbed state that he woke up in. His grizzling and distress cut me to the bone every single day.

We spent a lot of time on the beach. It was late September and the summer crowds had gone. The resorts were as much ruled by the school calendar as any other holiday place in the world. But their loss was our gain. We and our friends had the beaches to ourselves.

The first day we were almost blown off the beach by storm-force winds, but after that the weather calmed. The days passed by as we pottered about. Paddling in the sea, collecting starfish, making dinosaurs in the sand. Every single thing we did left my chest aching with pain. What should have caused me pleasure had me permanently on the verge of bursting into tears. She wasn't there. Why wasn't she there? Because . . .

I tried hard to be as light as possible for Alex but it was often a struggle. Thankfully I had our friends to talk to and to keep me company when he was asleep. We drank a lot of beer and ate a lot of French chocolate. I had a good chance to look at the way of life that we could expect if we settled here. The appeal of living somewhere quiet was

271

enormous. I didn't want to live in a city any more. A quiet village or little town somewhere. Maybe I could start to teach tennis when Alex was old enough to go to school. There were plenty of areas to choose from, France has a wildness that is hard to find in the British Isles, apart from maybe in the Highlands of Scotland or the Peak District and Lakelands of England. Perhaps the impression of distance and wilderness would stop me from feeling that the whole world was right on top of me.

Alex was funny when anybody spoke to him in French. On the first evening he acted as if he had understood perfectly. It made me think of how a three-year-old must understand half, or even less, of what an adult says to him even in his own language. It must happen so regularly that often they can't even be bothered to say 'sorry?'

After the first day he became much more defensive. He realized that there was a difference. That he *really* couldn't understand. He didn't like me speaking in French and would begin climbing all over me, pawing at me to get attention when I did. If anybody asked him to repeat a word or a phrase like 'bonjour' then he would take great offence and would glare at the offender with his arms folded across his chest and a sulky expression on his face. But he would listen when it was someone else who was talking, and he was getting the attention he wanted. I watched him from the corner of my eye as he wrestled silently with his mouth trying to make himself repeat the words he was hearing around him.

We hired a house right on the beach for a week. The atmosphere was peculiar. The whole resort was empty and only a few houses had not been closed down for the winter. It was like a ghost town. All the shutters on the little villas around us were closed day and night; only the trees and flowers in the gardens showed any sign of life at all. It was as if all the occupants had just been spirited away.

Apart from a couple of blazing hot days the weather was now overcast and cool. It was the equinox and the weather was stormy. But Rachel and I had known worse on the south coast of England in the middle of July. At least we could still get outside for some of the time every day – and this was 'bad' weather.

The days passed. My feeling of relief at escaping from all the attention that had so recently surrounded us stayed with me. It felt like we had been granted compassionate asylum. Walking around I felt free. I felt that, if we could find somewhere quiet for ourselves, and just be able to gently get on with pottering around every day, then we could put ourselves on a firmer road to recovery. If we could live somewhere where nobody knew our history and where no one was trying to track us down. At home we were constantly under siege. People were continually waiting outside the door, or phoning up for interviews, or following us around, or trying to see in through the windows.

I felt I might have some success writing children's stories. With an imaginative child like Alex we lived most of our day in a world of make-believe already. I was convinced that it was as simple as writing down what we were making up. I had already been asked by different people if I would write a book about our experiences. But at the time that was the last thing I wanted to do.

While we were away I began to do some drawings with Alex. I knew that I would need a proper illustrator when the time came but I wanted to give Alex an idea of what our stories looked like on paper. To my surprise, instead of being snotty about our tatty bits of paper taped together, he was pleased to see our storylines taking the same form as any other of his books. It gave me a little hope that writing children's books wasn't a completely unrealistic idea.

We had a little garden to ourselves which was just right for 'pottering' in. Soon Alex had his collection of starfish neatly arranged in a line across the yard. The rest of us were glad when the first shower of rain washed away the smell which had been getting stronger every day.

After the showers there were snails to collect. We had races to see which of them would be the first to get from one end of a branch to another. Alex acquired an old car tyre, which he lovingly rolled from the other end of the beach all the way back to the house and added it to his growing assortment of driftwood sticks: Hosepipe stick, Hammer stick, Sword stick, Socket-wrench stick. He then had all he needed to keep himself amused for hours at a time. So much for expensive toys. When I say 'himself' amused, however, that meant Alex amusing himself and four adults being required to watch attentively.

Autumn suddenly arrived with a vengeance. There was a huge storm and torrential rain which washed whole villages away. The paper showed a picture of a house in the mountains torn in two by the swollen river rushing down a narrow valley. The house had backed on to a river which ran far below its feet. The picture, taken from a bridge

273

nearby, showed how the water, which was usually just a few inches deep, had risen fifteen metres, sweeping away everything in its path. Now a sofa was hanging over the edge where the living room had been sliced in two. Alex recognized the view from the bridge. We had driven over it only days before on the way to visit a dinosaur museum. It was a reminder of just how irresistible were the forces of life and death. And how often they can skim right by you so closely you can feel them. Yet you never question your own good fortune in escaping, so much do you take it for granted that you won't be touched. It made me think how fragile was the fabric of everyone's existence, and not just our own.

We spent the third week in the big city. It was all I needed to be more sure than ever that the city was no longer for me. Even the most beautiful city is full of so much noise and traffic and fumes. Although I was born in a city, it had never occurred to me before how much energy it takes to create your own little bubble around you to protect yourself from the crowds and the bustle and the faces of so many strangers. I had to put my bubble around a small child as well. I no longer had the strength to cope with it.

During a phone call to Rachel's parents I found out that a journalist had contacted them saying that he knew that I had gone off to Marbella with some girl on the proceeds of the deal I had done with the newspapers. I almost laughed.

It was much harder to keep Alex amused in the city. With all the museums and bookshops and sights, this was something of an irony. That was fine for older children but Alex was at his happiest playing in the park and feeding the goldfish in the pond. We needed open space, and lots of it.

By the third week I was feeling stronger and eager to have something of our own again. We needed our own place and our own things around us. At the moment we were camped out like refugees. In the short term it had been the best thing, we had support on hand. But it would soon be time to start out on our own.

I had seen enough to convince me that a move here was the best thing for us. I had thought about Canada, or Australia, but they were so far away. I was not on the best of terms with Rachel's parents at the time but Alex needed as much family as he could get. He had lost enough already, and so had they.

Once we were back in England I realized how distanced we had been from what had gone on before. The police were still very busy following up all of the leads that had come from the TV programme. For the moment we were under no pressure to resume our sessions with the child psychologist. I wasn't at all keen to resume, so this suited me fine.

I had a goal now which went beyond simply watching out moment by moment for Alex's well-being. I had research to do, plans to make. I had to work out where we could move to and come up with some options in case the first choice didn't work out. There were maps to buy and books to read. There was a language to think about as well.

My French was passable, if not as fluent as it once was. But I knew it would come back quickly. As a teenager I had hitch-hiked my way round France playing tennis tournaments, often staying with French families who spoke no English at all. I only had my O-level French, which was pretty useless, and had been forced to learn the hard way. I would often spend all day repeating mentally one phrase which might come up at the dinner table and which I had not been able to cope with the night before, in the hope that this time I would get it right and people might finally understand what I had been trying to say. But I had happy memories of my visits. Being involved in a sport had helped, and I had avoided the big cities, but I had met with wonderful generosity and hospitality wherever I went.

I had to think of how much a handicap it would be for Alex not to understand anything at all. I was confident that he would pick it up quickly: he was a bright child. I was sure that the best thing for Alex would be to keep him busy in his usual routine, so he had the chance to absorb the language naturally.

I spoke to as many people as I could who had brought their children to England from abroad when they were small. One of Rachel's friends from school had come to England from France at around the same age. I spoke to her parents and asked them how she and her younger brother had coped. Rachel's homoeopathic doctor told me about how they had arrived from Romania and put their four-year-old into nursery only a few days after. Everyone's opinion was that small children cope very well with the change. It seemed that the younger they were, the better they coped.

Alex and his new friend were getting on like a house on fire. Suddenly we were visiting their house as often as we could. The boys became inseparable. Alex had discovered *Thunderbirds* and Fireman Sam was now relegated to second place. Alex's friend and his older brother were already hooked, and soon their house was filled with the noise of the three of them crashing about for hour after hour, happily recreating the latest episode they had seen on TV or simply making up their own stories as they went along.

I had never seen Alex play so well with another child. Normally he would be fairly restrained with other children. Often it was as if they were playing round each other. But these two really complemented each other. They would each come up with something in turn to keep the game going, and at the weekend they would happily play from morning until evening when we had to physically separate them before they over-did it and collapsed in tears of nervous exhaustion. Sometimes I would take Alex away in the car and drive him around until he fell asleep just to give them some rest from each other. Knowing he would wake up the moment I tried to move him, I would park and let him doze where he was for half an hour or so before I took him back for more.

If Alex needed to rest, his friend did even more. Physically they weren't much alike. Alex was very robust and strong. He was rarely sick and had never had anything more than a cold. His friend on the other hand had been chronically ill for most of his life. He suffered from asthma so badly that he had often been hospitalized. He had to have his face strapped to a machine in the house twice a day for twenty minutes at a time, breathing in vaporized steroids just to prevent an attack. And twice a day was when he was doing well; otherwise it was much more. But mentally he was bright and observant and, which I found unusual for a small child, extremely gentle and kind. He was very protective of Alex. If Alex pushed him over, whether on purpose or not, he would immediately spring up to say: 'He didn't mean it!' He couldn't stand the thought of Alex being punished. Emotionally he was totally secure, and being brought up as the last child in a house so full of love it wasn't hard to understand why. He and Alex got on so well together. Their two difficulties, one physical and the other emotional, are no barrier to a wonderful relationship.

The only thing that came between them was the fact that Alex's friend spent every weekday morning at nursery. After a few weeks of their playing together his mother suggested that Alex might be ready to start again himself. It was a fantastic school, she said, and the teacher had been running it for over thirty years. Alex's friend's older brother had been there before him. The greatest strength was how well it prepared children emotionally for proper school. The teacher who ran the school was a survivor of a German concentration camp. If anyone could understand a little of Alex's experience it would be her. The only problem was finding out if there was a place for Alex.

Eventually after our friend had spoken to the teacher, and after I had phoned myself, she agreed to take him. Provided that he come one morning so she could see if he would fit in. Our friend was convinced that once Alex took a look at all the good things that were going on then he wouldn't want to be left out of the fun.

I took him one morning to see for himself. Alex's friend, at his mother's suggestion and in order to prime Alex's curiosity, had been telling Alex a little of what he got up to when he was at school. Superficially his friend was very matter-of-fact about it all, but it was clear from his expression and his eagerness to talk that he loved going.

The nursery was laid out on the ground floor and basement of a large house. As we went through the door we were met by the quiet hum of busy children. Alex's friend was in the basement where there was a large sandpit and a whole child-sized toy kitchen. As we went down the stairs we could see his face beaming up. He was thrilled to be able to show his new friend around 'his' school.

It was halfway through the morning, and the idea was for me to leave him until the end of the session and pick him up when they all came out at lunchtime. This was an enormous step: I was leaving him with complete strangers, with only one familiar face. I could see that all the children were having a good time, I knew that Alex had a tremendous appetite for fun, and I knew that the woman in charge couldn't come more highly recommended, but I still felt sick. He had been attached to me for so long now. They took my phone number and told me to go home, and said that if he was really unhappy they would call for me to come and collect him. 'Just make sure you're first at the door at lunchtime to pick him up!' I was told.

Our friend had assured me that they wouldn't leave him crying for long and would call me if he wasn't going to settle. With lead in my stomach I let myself be convinced, and the moment it looked like Alex was absorbed in what his friend was doing they signalled for me to back out of the door.

It was strangely quiet standing on the pavement outside when the front door closed behind me. I could just hear a murmur coming from inside. Gone was the constant chirping and chatter from around my knees. And gone too were the constant demands. It was only when it stopped that I realized how draining it was having him around me all the time. I never really relaxed when I was with him, even when someone else was attending to him. I was always listening out for signs of anxiety.

I walked back to the car asking Rachel if I was doing the right thing. If things worked out then this would be the biggest step so far towards a return to a 'normal' life.

I was flooded with relief to see him coming out with a smile on his face later that morning. His smile was genuine but there was strain behind it. I could see quite clearly that it must have been a real effort for him to fight for himself in there. He admitted that he had had a nice time but he wasn't over-keen on the idea of going back the next day, and I had to harden myself against his protests. I told him firmly that he was going, and that he would have as good a time as he had had today, and then tried to change the subject. He didn't try that hard to make me change my mind.

His teacher believed it was best if the children went every morning of the week without fail, unless there was a serious reason not to. She said that it was the best way to get over homesickness. They would feel more settled than if they came only every now and then. With what I was beginning to learn about the importance of routine in building up Alex's security this made perfect sense. She said that if they did play up it was usually for the parent's benefit, and it was nearly always over quickly when the parent had left. But she would not hesitate to phone if the child was really unhappy.

Just as they were all going in the following morning, Alex suddenly tried to throw himself back towards me, grimacing and pleading for me not to abandon him. But his teacher wasn't having any of it. Small and slight though she was, she got a good grip on his arm and hauled him back in with the others, signalling for me to make my escape. I left, shaking from the violence of our separation.

'He'll be all right,' said our friend. 'I promise you.'

For the first time we had the beginning of a proper routine. I immediately found the couple of hours a day that I had to myself a huge relief. I was feeling the strain of being totally responsible for a child twenty-four hours of the day with no one to hand him over to. I could remember the times I would come home from work and Rachel would thrust him towards me and say: 'Here, you take him, I can't stand him any more!'

But I didn't have that option. It wasn't easy: he was far more demanding than he had ever been before. I tried not to lose sight of the fact that there were plenty of people who had to put up with more than me. That there were plenty of people caring for elderly or sick relatives who didn't even have the hope that things would get better, or the comfort that anyone was interested in the mundane details of all that they had to cope with.

And what about the victims of oppression and massacre and misery in the world outside our protected little corner? I had travelled enough to see children living off rubbish piled in the street who would never get the chance of an education or have the hope of escaping from their pitiful existence. I knew that in many places your loved ones could be taken away in the middle of the night and tortured and killed without the slightest hope of a police inquiry into their disappearance.

At least I had the hope that Alex *was* going to get better as time went on. His life would never be as rich as it should have been, but one day I was sure that he would be capable of experiencing as much happiness as I had known with Rachel. Having the two of them had gone a long way to heal the scars that I bore from my own childhood. My hope was that one day he would have a family of his own and that this would allow him to be complete again.

I was convinced that a child, or anybody for that matter, needed one person he could rely on always to be there for him, always to stick by them, even when they didn't agree with each other, even after they had fought. Someone whose love was unconditional. Of course that person would normally be his mother. But to me it didn't matter if it was the father, brother, sister, uncle, cousin or friend. As long as there was someone. Everyone I knew who had that someone in their life had a sense of security and a sense of self-worth that was extremely apparent. To a greater or lesser extent everyone else was lost. I had had to wait until I was an adult until I felt nearly so strongly about anyone. And it was only with Rachel and Alex that I was beginning to feel a true sense of self-worth.

But it had finished almost as soon as it had begun. Now there was nothing I could do about it except to see that Alex lost as little as possible. His childhood was the most important thing. If I could get it right now, at the beginning, then the rest should take care of itself.

I tried not to think about myself. Doing so only made things harder. My life was broken, I was miserable and wretched with the pain and loneliness that I had thought I would never feel again. But what was the point in thinking about it? I couldn't change anything. And I wasn't the only one. I was coming to realize that no one has a right to happiness. Those who know it for more than a few fleeting moments are the fortunate few. And this is why it is everybody's duty to do what they can to give a little happiness to those around them when the occasion arises.

Alex was playing upstairs with his friend. The house sounded like it was full of children. He came wandering down with a plastic knife in his hand. I went rigid. Rachel and I had agreed that we would never buy him toy guns or knives. At the sight of him with such a weapon so many confused images churned through my head. I could see Rachel being slaughtered with a knife, I could see Alex watching. And now Alex was standing with a knife in his hand in front of me.

It was hard to make out where the past ended and the present began.

'Put that down! You're not allowed to play with those,' I heard myself saying from somewhere far away.

While we were away the police had tracked down a man who fitted their Identikit picture. He was under arrest on a charge of indecency: he had exposed himself to a woman on the Common in the spring. They were weighing up whether or not they wanted Alex to formally identify him. This would be done behind two-way glass if it were to go ahead – and if I agreed.

They were in a dilemma. If Alex positively identified him then they would have to charge him with Rachel's murder straight away. This would then start a chain of procedural events which would affect the timing of the trial and commit them to preparing a prosecution in full straight away. But as yet they had still come up with no material evidence. The circumstantial evidence was very strong but they wanted the maximum time to come up with the best case they could and weren't keen to do anything that would limit their effectiveness in the short term.

They didn't want a confession. They weren't going to try and question this 'suspect' until he 'broke'. A confession could always be denied later as being extracted under pressure.

The detectives described the 'suspect's' disturbed behaviour during questioning. He had broken down in tears and had been ranting as if delirious. They asked me if Rachel had ever been to the Common wearing a red jacket. In his ravings the suspect had claimed that he had seen her there, wearing one, on some occasion. I told them that in all the time that I had known her, Rachel had never owned a red jacket. The police were convinced that they had their man and the original criminal psychologist was too. The suspect matched the profile that he had given the police right at the beginning of the investigation.

In the days that he was held the suspect was positively identified by witnesses as the man seen very close to where Rachel was killed and dressed in the same clothes that Alex had described only a few minutes before the time of Rachel's death.

In the end the police decided against asking Alex to give a formal identification. A positive identification would compel them to make an immediate arrest, for which they were not yet prepared. However they did prosecute the man on the charge of indecency. A few weeks later he was found guilty of exposing himself on Wimbledon Common. There was extensive press coverage of the proceedings at Wandsworth magistrates' court. The following day one of the witnesses phoned and spoke to detectives again. She said that she had seen the coverage of the court proceedings on TV where footage was shown of him walking down the road towards the magistrates' court. She said that up until that point she had been a hundred per cent sure that it was him. But now, after seeing him on TV, she was one hundred and ten per cent sure! She said that he had a distinctive walk that could not be mistaken. This was definitely the man she had seen on the Common.

The suspect was still denying that he was there at that time.

He was now under intense surveillance, his garden was dug up and his flat minutely searched. Nothing was found. But he had had so long to get rid of any evidence.

The police were looking for that white shirt. Despite being identified as wearing it by several witnesses, he denied that he had ever owned one like it. But more witnesses came forward to say that he had been seen at a funeral wearing exactly that kind of shirt. In the meantime the police were still looking for the knife but had little hope of finding it now that so much time had passed.

It transpired that the suspect frequently visited the Common at night. He had boasted to various people that he had hiding places with weapons buried there.

A little while later a man came to the police to tell of a frightening encounter with the suspect. He was a homosexual and one night earlier in the year he had been hanging around at a known gay pick-up spot not far from the Common. He was approached by the suspect, and after a conversation the two of them headed on to the Common. The homosexual said that he was led by the suspect to a specific spot in the undergrowth. The suspect then began digging through the leaves and dirt. He became increasingly angrier as he appeared to be unable to find what he was looking for. After a while he gave up the search and, telling the homosexual that he was no longer in the mood, went on his way.

The homosexual said that he had been extremely frightened and was convinced that the suspect was about to do something violent.

In the months up to Christmas the police continued to follow up on every lead, including those that had come about as a result of the TV programme. It was turning into one of the largest investigations on record. But there was now a definite hope that it was only a matter of time before they found Rachel's killer. They were nearly there. It was simply a matter of tying up all of the circumstantial evidence. They were still looking for that small scrap of material evidence to back up everything else they had established. So far they had not been lucky. Everything had been achieved by sheer graft. It had been an uphill grind.

It seemed almost too much to hope that this part of the nightmare was going to end. Nothing could make Rachel's death any better, but at least there would be the satisfaction of knowing that her killer had been found and put away for ever. That every time I thought of how much she had suffered I would know that he was suffering too. The thought that this constant emotional battering, the result of being involved in all the ups and downs of the inquiry, and the public exposure and harassment from the media that went with it, might actually one day come to an end, gave us some feeling of relief.

We were still under constant bombardment, with phone calls and letters and people on the doorstep wanting a comment on this or that latest piece of information. They didn't care what time of day they rang, whether it was eight o'clock in the morning or eleven o'clock at night. It always began with 'We're sorry to bother you, but . . .'

I could be trying to put Alex in his car-seat to take him to school or bringing him home asleep in the evening but they would walk right up and blurt out: 'André, I'm sorry, but . . .' They never had any qualms about being on private property and always had to be reminded of the fact. I shook with anger whenever one of them approached. I was terrified by the thought that they would come out with some stupid comment in front of Alex. I never said anything more than 'Go away!' I knew by now that they would turn any other remark into a half-page exclusive interview.

But with the trial over and the culprit in jail there would be some peace. It would mark the end of this media circus. Very soon we would have a date, a moment in time, when we wouldn't have to deal with any of this.

I found myself filled with relief that it wasn't (. . . .) they had arrested. Somehow the idea that it was a stranger was slightly less awful. It was marginally less unbelievable to think that it was a complete lunatic rather than someone with a child of their own. There was definitely a resemblance between (. . . .) and the Photofit picture that the witnesses had compiled. And (. . . .) was probably the only person in our circle of acquaintances who did look like this. Perhaps this alone had caused the confusion in Alex's mind.

Alex had never definitely said that (. . . .) had killed his mummy, and the police admitted that they now had no reason to believe that (. . . .) had been on the Common the morning that Rachel was killed. They had gone through (. . . .)'s past minutely and nothing of an unusual nature had come to the surface. In a case as difficult as this, the police remained interested in everyone. But as far as they were concerned, (. . . .) was now listed among the 'highly unlikely'.

Chapter Twenty-one

A LEX WAS ENJOYING himself at his new nursery. He came out beaming every day. It was the best thing for him. After being so much in the company of adults he was back again amongst his peers. And they had no idea that he was in any way different from any of them. He was being taken on his own merit and fighting for himself. Best of all was how much fun there was to be had.

Very early on his teacher made the observation that he was a very well-balanced little boy. Not well balanced 'in spite of' what had happened to him. Just well balanced. She said it was a tribute to the way he had been brought up. It was a fantastic compliment to Rachel. If he was coming out of this well it was down to all that she had done with him.

We were both benefiting enormously from our friend's house full of children. There was so much life and buoyancy flooding through the place. The boys' games spread all over the house accompanied by shrieks of pleasure and enjoyment. These were punctuated by quiet moments spent feeding their faces in an effort to refuel or slumped in a heap on the floor on top of each other watching cartoons on the TV. Alex was enjoying himself to the full. But it was difficult to apply the word 'happy' to a child who woke up in misery and distress every single morning.

My role was now much reduced. I was still in as much demand as ever when he was not at nursery or with our friends. But in their house it was simply a matter of helping to provide snacks and meals and picking him up and dispensing sympathy after the occasional collision. I always had a bottle of arnica, a homoeopathic remedy, for whenever he banged himself. He had had so much of it since he was young that when he saw the bottle come out he would immediately begin to calm down.

The children got along so well together that it was painful to think that I was soon to disrupt their new-found friendship. I was able to leave Alex from time to time with them. Together with the nursery, this gave me some more time to do things for myself. The first couple of times had been a little hairy. I had told Alex I was going to the bank. Apparently he began to ask when I was coming back almost from the moment I went out the door.

On the first occasion he had had to be reassured with constant attention and bribed with the 'goodies' whose location he had long ago worked out. But if a few chocolate biscuits was all it needed to prevent total hysteria, then things had indeed come a long way. By the time I returned our friend was frazzled. Alex had had her running to and fro like a servant for drinks and snacks and changes of games and cartoons and anything else he could think of. It must have been a stressful couple of hours. She was so concerned that he should not be unhappy, and that I should be able to leave him with them without any fear.

I would soon be giving up this new-found privilege. Wherever we were going we would be surrounded by strangers, and among the benefits this would bring there were drawbacks too. There would be no support for me whatsoever in the day-to-day care of a demanding three-year-old. Not only would he be leaving his friends behind: he would suddenly be without any at all.

Several people had made the observation that the thing Alex needed the most was for me to feel as good as I possibly could. If that was true, then there was no way I was going to feel much better here. We were doing as well as we could with our friends but I had a real need for something of our own. I had come up with a short-list of places in France. The most likely looking was somewhere I had never actually been. I was trying to weigh up what we needed the most. We needed to be not too far from an airport, not too far from a big city, somewhere where the climate was noticeably warmer than England, somewhere beautiful. There was no point moving abroad if the weather was going to be just as bad as here.

In the end I wasn't doing much more than closing my eyes and sticking a pin in the map. It made no difference: things would work out the way they would and there wasn't much I could do about it one way or the other. We are all prisoners of our own destiny. How could I see things any other way?

Alex kept picking up that plastic knife. He knew that I disapproved and he was doing his best to keep it out of sight. But whenever I crept up to peep in on them playing I would see it in his hand.

His friend's parents could see the pain it was causing me. Eventually they took me aside. 'You know there's a danger that you could make this worse than it is,' they told me. 'There's a chance that this plastic knife is *just* a toy and he *just* wants to play with it.'

I tried to explain that it wasn't only the fact that he had seen his mother killed with a knife. As if that wasn't enough. There was the fact that his mother hadn't wanted him to play with weapons. I was trying to defend her wishes.

'I've had four children now,' said Alex's friend's mother. 'Before I had them I had plenty of idealistic ideas which I've since had to let go of. I didn't want my little boy playing with guns and knives either. But the thing is, you can't stop them. If you don't give them to them then they play with their friends' or they just make them themselves.'

I knew she was right. Alex often picked up sticks and pretended they were swords.

'We had a child come here for someone's birthday whose mother wouldn't let him eat chocolate,' she continued. 'When she left him here and when he saw all the chocolate cakes and things he went berserk. He didn't want to play any games or anything, he was too busy stuffing himself. He was obsessed!'

I got the point. But I was none the less in an extremely painful dilemma. Rachel and I had agreed that the best way to make something attractive to a child was to ban it. We had always said exactly that. Even if we didn't want him eating too much sugar we would not be the ones to stop him from eating chocolate when all the other children around him were doing that. But this wasn't quite the same.

'If you really don't want him to play with things like that,' she added, 'and that's totally up to you, then you should take him away from the children who do. It's not fair on him to have them play in front of him if he's not allowed to.'

The last thing in the world I wanted was to take him away from the children with whom he was having such a wonderful time, but I couldn't be true to everything all at the same time either. I was fighting back the tears without much success. Up until this moment I had had no problem coming to any decision concerning Alex's upbringing. I always knew what Rachel would have done and I always knew that she would have been right. For the first time I had to admit to myself that she had been wrong, and I had been wrong. But I didn't have her there to talk it over with.

'She never had this,' said Alex's friend's mother. 'She didn't have to deal with him now. Things are changing, he's changing. He's not such a baby any more, he's growing up fast. If she was still here she might well have been telling you exactly that. You have to make the decisions now and you will be right because you know what he needs now.'

I must have looked a real mess because she added: 'I'm not trying to tell you what to do. I'm just trying to give you the benefit of our experience and save you some of this agony.'

Our new routine had a different pattern. The three weeks away had put some distance between us and the circus we had become part of. And Alex's new friend and new school had taken him on from there. He was so taken up with new things, and I was so relieved to see him having a good time, that for a while I no longer bothered to go out of my way to see if he needed to talk about the events of that day. He showed no sign of being as preoccupied as he had been before.

I had decided to let the knife thing go and, as painful as it was, I forced myself to smile as he played and tried to accept that a game was just a game. For the majority of the time he was happy enough just to trail around with it in his hand or tucked into his belt like Peter Pan. The other boys carried their weapons too and I tried to accept it in the same spirit.

But there was the occasional incident where he would lapse into the 'traumatic play' syndrome. He would thrust something sharp towards someone's face while staring at them with glazed eyes. It could be any household object, and it was always directed towards an adult. I would shout at him immediately I saw what he was up to and this was usually enough to make him snap out of his trance. But it happened repeatedly every few weeks or so.

287

Autumn was turning into winter. Even though we had spent Guy Fawkes Night watching fireworks outside in T-shirts the weather soon turned cold. I would often take Alex to the park on his bike to burn off some excess energy. Though his new friend's breathing problems would leave him exhausted after they had been playing together, Alex would often still be bouncing off the walls.

Now I was pushing Alex through piles of fallen leaves and steering him round puddles. I hated the cold. I hated the grey and the fact that the sky was nearly always so dark and so low. I found it oppressive. I felt crushed and hated the idea of being forced to spend so much time inside when I wanted to be out in the open. But every trip out became an expedition, with gloves and coats and jumpers and scarves, as well as the usual drinks and snacks and all the rest of his paraphernalia.

I had to stoop down to pull the rainbow-coloured gloves that Rachel had bought him over his tiny fingers. My chest ached even harder as, in my mind, I saw her face glow with pleasure as she held them up for me to admire.

The gloves had little white stitches which formed the teeth of a crocodile. The thumb and forefinger formed the mouth. I thought about how upset she would have been if his fingers had been cold so I made sure his coat sleeves were pulled down to provide extra warmth. I made sure the front of his coat came high enough up to keep his chin out of the wind and asked myself again for the millionth time if this was all for real.

The parks were often nearly deserted but Alex was happy enough to trundle around for a while. Often he would pedal quietly, hardly saying a word, then he would become curious and want to explore some corner or be eager to try and climb over some obstacle. I had perfected the habit of keeping my voice cheerful while my head spun over and over again through a trail of memories.

She had said that she would love me for ever. And I knew that, for her, for ever meant for ever.

I knew that Rachel would look after us. It was a strange certainty. At the same time as feeling so overwhelmingly lonely I also had an inner conviction that I was never on my own. There would always be someone with me. I would never be on my own again.

My mother called me to say that Alex was awake. I was watching television and he had been asleep for an hour or so. I went quickly into the room assuming that he wanted to go to the toilet. I found him on his bed, cowering in the corner in the dark. His face, full of tears, was twisted in pain. My heart turned to ice: I had never seen him like this. I spoke gently to him but he didn't even see me. He was staring right through me.

He was shaking with fear and his face was a mask of terror. His eyes were bulging and would not focus on me, even though I was now standing right in front of him and reaching out to hold him. I was terrified. He looked like a creature out of a lunatic asylum, rigid, spastic with fear, his face wet with tears.

My soothing words had no effect. And even worse, his eyes still wouldn't focus on me. Not only were they looking right through me but they were tracking something invisible across the room. He was jabbering unintelligibly, moaning, and acting as if he was dreaming awake. Something was happening in front of him that I couldn't see, something was being played out which was so terrifying that his mind was in danger of breaking. Suddenly I knew that he could see his mother being killed. The realization hit me like a sledgehammer and I could almost see and feel what he was experiencing. I almost spun round to follow the direction of his eyes, half expecting to see her being slaughtered in front of me.

It was so hard to stop myself from picking him up and shaking him, from slapping him across the face to make it stop. And I was so full of rage myself. I wanted revenge but there was no one to lash out against. My hands gripped his shoulders, maybe harder than they should. I was pleading with him to wake up, only just managing not to shout at him that it was only a dream, that this was Daddy, not the monster who had ripped our lives apart come back again, that he was safe, that I would protect him.

Maybe it was only five minutes until I got through to him but it felt like years. For those long minutes he was locked in another world and I couldn't get at him. Even when he began to calm down he didn't acknowledge my presence. Instead he suddenly went floppy and his eyes closed. There was nothing to do but lay him back down in his bed. He was asleep. It was still early but I climbed into my own bed and pulled him in with me. He hardly stirred but it was clear that my physical presence was a comfort to him. He snuggled close against me and I could feel his body relax just a little bit more.

He was peaceful for the rest of the night. It took me a long time to get to sleep. Every time he turned I was afraid that it was all going to start again. My mind was in turmoil, filled with images of horror. I fantasized as to what I would do if I ever got my hands on the man who was responsible for this, and was lost in despair at what lay ahead for our child.

I wondered if this was just a passing event, or the beginning of some new pattern. Maybe this anguish had been incubating and for some unknown reason all had remained fairly calm up until now. Maybe now it was going to come spilling out and he would sink into a deranged state for some untold period of time. Maybe it would be months. Or years! Who could tell?

The next night he slept well. I was tense and on edge from the moment he nodded off but even though I was listening out for the slightest warning sign there was no repeat of the night before.

But no sooner had I begun to console myself with the thought that it had just been a freak occurrence when exactly the same thing happened again. Only a couple of days later the sounds of his waking came from the bedroom. I burst into the room to find him again cowering on his bed, spastic with fear. There was the same terror in his eyes, which refused to focus on me and instead looked right through me. Again they were tracking something that was happening across the room and again it was impossible to get him to acknowledge my presence.

I was talking to him, shouting at him, as I took him in my arms, once again choking with frustration at not being able to get through to him. 'Come on, it's me, Daddy! I'm here, it's all right.'

His eyes remained rigidly fixed on whatever was taking place in front of him in his subconscious. He was whimpering in fear, his face wet with tears and crumpled in terror. I kept on at him: 'It's me! You're all right! You're all right!' His arms were stiff and he was trying to push me away. I felt I was battling for his sanity and that he was fighting me hard. Eventually, the storm began to pass. His body became less rigid and he relaxed completely. Soon he was sleeping peacefully. In fact he had probably never woken up.

The next morning, once he was properly awake, I asked him if he remembered what had happened the night before. He seemed to have no idea of what I was talking about. 'Did you have any bad dreams?' I asked.

'No?' he replied, quizzically, clearly wondering why I should ask.

'You've got to talk to me,' I said, studying his face. 'We haven't talked about when Mummy was killed for a long time now. If things are frightening you, you've got to tell me.' He was looking away, proud and independent and almost insulted that I should even consider that something could frighten him. 'When we talk about things we can make them all right,' I continued. 'We can make them less frightening.' I tapped him on the head. 'You're too little to carry everything around in there on your own. Your head's going to break! You've got to share it with me.'

He showed no enthusiasm to talk about it. But I wasn't satisfied. The moment I said the words it struck me as obvious that these nightmares had come about because we had cut off his means of expression. It was right that we had eased up on our sessions with the psychologist: the rhythm we had been following had been too intense, but it was dangerous to stop completely. I had to find a way to give him the opportunity to talk on a regular basis. I couldn't allow him to clam up again.

From then on and for many months ahead, I made it my regular task, from time to time to take him aside from whatever he was doing for a few minutes and to talk a little about how he or I might be feeling. At times it felt awkward, as if I was intruding on him and forcing him to think about unpleasant memories which were the farthest things from his mind. At other times it wasn't even necessary to take him aside because something would happen to bring it all naturally into the conversation. It might have been that we came across a piece of Rachel's jewellery and began talking about when we remembered her wearing it, or, if I had bought it, where I had got it from. It might have been a 'baddy' in one of his programmes that prompted him to say: 'I know what a baddy's like! I've seen one in the trees.'

As long as something was coming out I felt safer. I felt he was safer. Sometimes I would forget and a few days would go by without incident. Then I would suddenly freeze with the realization that I had not kept to my task and, terrified that the nightmares would start again, I would watch for any sign that he was holding anything in that should have been coming out. I would manoeuvre the conversation around to Mummy as soon as possible.

Alex had a way of dealing with any bug he might pick up. No matter whether it was just a cold or flu or stomach bug, or any other childhood bug that was doing the rounds, he would always get a temperature for a couple of days and throw up. Whatever he had, passed quickly. But it was always difficult, if not impossible, to know what he had had. He had been in contact with other children who were going through the usual childhood illnesses but he had never shown the same symptoms as them, even if he had fallen ill at the same time and in theory must have had what they had had.

He hadn't had even a cold since Rachel was killed. His first illness came soon after the nightmares. The first night his temperature went up and he became a little delirious. He began to moan and the moan quickly changed from one of discomfort to one of fear. He started to show all the signs that he had previously displayed, only slightly less intensely. I watched him like a hawk and was again compelled to turn in with him as it was the only way to keep a proper eye on him. My pulse rate was up the whole time, waiting for him to scream out and go rigid with fear. I found it difficult to sit and watch him dealing with God knows what spinning through his brain. Because of this illness I could get through to him even less than I had before.

His illness passed in a couple of days. I spent the nights anxious about a sudden lapse into nightmares and the days being ordered about, sent for one thing after another, while Alex sat in his armchair in front of the TV watching his videos end to end, and moaning and complaining. He was the world's worst patient, unable to put up with the slightest physical discomfort without complaint. If a blanket should drop on to the floor he would whine pitifully until it was back in his hand again. If he was thirsty it would be beyond him to reach out to accept a cup, it had to be put right up against his mouth. If his video came to an end he dissolved into tears.

Fortunately, although he had been even less coherent during his nightmares, they had not been as powerful as the last. By the third day he was smiling again and ready to play. But I was shattered. From that moment, whenever he began to sniffle or cough or his nose began to run, I was afraid of what the night would bring. I would do my best to cover him up and dose him with homoeopathic remedies and try to get him to sleep during the day in an effort to ward off the delirium that I knew would follow.

Very soon after Rachel was killed we had a message from the police saying that someone had offered to send us to Disneyland as a gift. I had at first thought that they were talking about EuroDisney in Paris. But no, they confirmed that the offer was to send us to Florida. It was an incredibly generous offer that seemed larger than life. But so did everything else in our present existence.

It took me a long time to respond. The simple fact was that the whole thing was completely inappropriate. I had enough on my hands. And I wasn't the only one in the family to treat the offer with some suspicion. It would not have been beyond some newspaper to come up with the idea as a way of getting into our confidence. Not to mention exclusive pictures from the hidden cameraman. But after a while it became clear that the offer was genuine, and that it wasn't a newspaper behind it. The gesture was not completely lost on me. It was as if Rachel had found someone to play fairy godmother for us. I had no doubt that it was a direct message from her.

Our detectives asked from time to time if I was ready to reply, but I kept finding a reason not to, apart from sending a word to say thank you. But now Christmas was looming. The idea was so depressing. Rachel was like a big child at Christmas, and for someone with such a cynical sense of humour she had always taken an undisguised pleasure in the whole performance. I had loved to watch how happy it all made her. The thought of buying presents and writing cards without her was unbearable.

Rachel was pregnant on our first Christmas together. Her bump had hardly begun to show. On a mild winter morning we sat on a park bench feeding the ducks, wondering how it was going to be in a year's time spending Christmas with our own child. I was head over heels in love. Every time I looked at her I could hardly believe she was real. The more I looked at her the more I knew that this was the woman of my life. No human being could ever make me happier.

Rachel glowed as she talked about how she thought our baby might turn out. She laughed about how ugly it would be if it was unfortunate enough to inherit all of our own parents' worst attributes. We

293

nearly always referred to the baby as a 'he', sometimes having the presence of mind to add 'or she', but we were both convinced that it would be a 'he'. Neither of us could picture this child being a girl.

Things had happened so fast. But they were wonderful things. I had been so alone for so long, and now my life was joined in the most wonderful way to someone so incredible. And no sooner had I found myself a part of two than I was on my way to becoming a part of three.

It was so much easier to accept your fate when things were going so well. I had always believed that it was possible to find true happiness and I was slowly coming to terms with the fact that I had been right all along. Things had finally started to go right, and from now on they were only going to get better.

This would have been only our fourth Christmas together. Even though we often said that the time had flown by, at other times it seemed as if we had known each other for a million years. Now my last six months alone had lasted a million years. Maybe the best thing would be to spend this first of every Christmas without her as far away from what we had done together as was humanly possible.

I asked the detectives for the details of the people who had made the offer and contacted them myself.

Our fairy godmother had a thick moustache and a Canadian accent. He and the people he worked with had been moved by the circumstances of Rachel's death and had wanted to do something to give the child involved just a little bit of happiness, even if it only last a few moments.

I had had a real struggle with myself before I felt able to accept. The offer was to send Alex and myself and also a friend to help. I couldn't face the trip on my own. Obviously that involved a major expense. In a way I felt it would be disloyal to accept, because a part of me felt that doing so denigrated the five-pound postal orders we had received from the people who could probably not have afforded them at all.

I thought a lot about the parable of the rich man and the poor widow giving alms in the temple. The widow was judged the most righteous because even though she had given so much less, she had given all she could. We had had our share of poor widows' alms and I had accepted them because they were meant to be accepted. Was it right not to accept something simply because it was more?

I finally told myself that I of all people should understand that people are what they are, and have what they have. I was in danger of missing the point. It was the spirit in which things were done and in which things were given that was important. Everyone who had offered anything had wanted to do something to make Alex feel better. And if by accepting this offer I could somehow achieve this, then that was all that mattered. If we stayed in England for Christmas I was likely to be depressed. That wasn't going to be a barrel of laughs for Alex. So maybe this was the ideal opportunity to get away. I let them know that I would be happy to accept their gift.

'Birthdays and Christmas are going to be the worst time, especially the first.' These were words of advice from someone who had lost their father when they were a child. For Rachel, the events fell within only weeks of each other.

I spent her birthday feeling like she had simply come and gone in an instant. I was only just getting used to having her there, only just falling into the routine of birthdays and anniversaries and cards and flowers, only just getting used to the letters of love and appreciation and passion which were knitting together the scars and quenching my thirst for some kind of true feeling of worth. We had our own history which was only just beginning.

Now it was gone.

I was standing on the edge of an abyss. There I was with Alex beside me, his hand in mine. Just in front of my feet everything had been sliced away, all the way down into nothing. There was nothing to get hold of. The idea that she wasn't there was getting no easier to understand or to accept. One minute you can reach out and touch and the next minute there is nothing. Nothing.

I still had as strong a sense of her presence as I always had but I felt like a blind man who cannot see what is in front of him even though he knows with every fibre of his being that there is something there.

The week before Christmas found us waiting in the passenger lounge for our flight to be called. Our fairy godmother with the moustache and the Canadian accent had delivered a Mickey Mouse teddy and all of our tickets and travel passes for a dream holiday in Florida. I was almost getting used to living larger than life, but not so much as to be unaffected by such remarkable generosity from complete strangers.

Suddenly we heard our names being called over the public address system. 'This is it!' said our friend. 'It *was* too good to be true.' We had talked over the prospect of being met by a swarm of photographers after our fairy godmother had tipped them off about our departure in a carefully orchestrated publicity stunt for his company. Paranoia was very hard to control.

Our friend disappeared to check out the situation. He was soon back with the news that we were being invited for a drink in the VIP lounge before takeoff. We were both relieved and ashamed all at the same time.

The trip was the best thing we could have done. The warm, sticky weather and piles of artificial snow made for an as un-Christmas-like effect as I could imagine. Together with the constant and overwhelming entertainment and distraction there was almost no connection with what we had had with Rachel.

There was more than a little sense of a modern-day Lourdes about the place. We were there with the handicapped, the bereaved and the terminally ill. Maybe there was also more than a little sense of paradise on Earth. Everything was there to please you. And providing you with happiness was the number one goal. It was a world apart.

Alex was thrilled to bits. The journey had been hard for him and even harder for me. We had hardly taken off when he had uttered the first 'Are we there yet?'

'No, Alex. We've just had breakfast and we won't be there till after suppertime.'

'Oh,' he replied. He showed no interest in the video screen in the back of the seat in front and wouldn't keep the headphones on to listen to the soundtrack. His spacious seat wasn't comfortable enough for him. He wanted to sit on my lap. He squirmed round to see the people behind. He squirmed round to look out of the window. He squirmed round to see the people in front.

'Are we there yet?'

We were only a few minutes into a ten-and-a-half-hour flight. The plane was full, not a single spare seat to be seen and, even though I had never travelled in such luxury before, the journey was still extremely hard going. He wouldn't concentrate on anything for more than a few minutes and I had to stretch my imagination in order to continually come up with something new. Every few minutes he would pipe up: 'Are we there yet?'

It was the excitement of it all. It was perfectly understandable: he had seen all the brochures and knew exactly where we were going. I consoled myself with the fact that the trip would certainly be worth the aggravation; we had two weeks to recover and he would probably sleep for the whole of the journey back. Even so, it was a long ten and a half hours.

It took him a day or two to recover from the jet-lag, as it did all of us, but by the third day he was already hitting top gear. He was unquenchable and went from steamboat to pirates of the Caribbean and from swimming-pool to water-slide and whale show to stunt man exhibition with exploding aeroplanes and machine-guns and people jumping off buildings and out of windows. We dived under the waves in a submarine and hurtled through space in a rocket. The only time he showed any fear was in the rocket.

When we entered our capsule the doors closed behind us and our seat-belts fastened automatically. There was no way that I could release him from his seat and take him on my lap as he wanted. We were taken on a madcap dash across space by an out-of-control robot in the front of our capsule. The view was displayed on a screen in front of him and our capsule was jerked and thrown around in sync with the action. The effect was extremely realistic. Alex wanted it to stop. But no matter how much he squealed and cried to get out, there was nothing I could do. We couldn't get out, we couldn't make it stop. The ride was out of control. We were strapped in, helpless and uncomfortable, with no other choice but to hold on tight and wait till the end. Looking back, there was a certain parallel with life itself.

We wobbled off, shaky.

'I never want to go on it again!' he exclaimed.

I assured him that he wouldn't have to and he promptly forgot about the whole thing.

And so the days continued. We were picked up, spun round, turned over and thrown about. We ate enormous ice-creams and shopped for souvenirs. Alex got a chance to see just how big an alligator grows and to feed dolphins with fish from his bare hands. I lost some sleep that night over the dolphins. Rachel always joked that she had been a dolphin in another life, and watching them all cramped together in their concrete pool had been a disturbing experience. I fed one or two myself and found their expression less than friendly. Who could blame them? Like a suspicious dog they grabbed their food and were off. There was no sign of the legendary spiritual communication between man and beast.

We had been spoilt rotten, with an unlimited pass to all attractions. This meant that we could pick the best time to miss the crowds without the pressure of trying to jam everything in in one go. We were there on the busiest days of the year but with the Americans' talent for organization we hardly noticed. It was a whirlwind experience with hardly a minute's respite. We two adults were heading towards saturation point after about a week but Alex wanted to go on and on. 'When are we going to see Mickey again?' he would ask several times a day. But he was beginning to jabber with entertainment overload and a day off was in order.

Christmas Day was like any other day except that Alex woke to find that some presents had mysteriously appeared at the foot of his bed. He was in awe of Father Christmas's efficiency in tracking him down so far from home. His face filled with pleasure and excitement; the marks had almost faded from under his eyes. But there was only me to share with him what should have been a few simple moments filled with happiness. It was desperately hard to smile back at him and not to tarnish his pleasure with my own pain. I felt so inadequate. Nothing on earth would enable me to offer him his mother's wide smile, her eyes filled with the adoration which had nourished him for so much of his life. Such a wonderful moment in a child's life is too much for one parent to hold all on their own. I was reminded of the child psychologist at the hospital and his remark that things would be harder for me than for him. What he had said was being borne out by this trip. Alex was taking genuine pleasure in the good things that life still had to offer. I was in agony.

During the second week our friend wanted to go into the village and buy some stamps. He asked Alex if he wanted to go with him. Alex was quite happy to, but I was gripped by paranoia. What if our friend never came back with him? What if he disappeared with him into the distance and I never saw Alex again? I had known him for years but my picture of the world had been altered to such an extent that I had to fight to get the words out to say that it was all right for Alex to go.

Once they were gone I was reduced to a cold sweat. I sat frozen to my seat paralysed. I could hear the birds singing and could see the sunshine on the trees through the window. It was a beautiful day. But terrible things happen on beautiful days.

I was trying to reason with myself for the whole time that nothing was going to happen. That I could trust our friend implicitly. But my mind was filled with images of them disappearing off into the distance for ever. 'I should never have let them go!' I chastised myself over and again.

But I couldn't live like that. I had to get a grip.

What seemed like hours and hours later I heard Alex's voice and their footsteps returning up the path. It had only been twenty minutes. I was flooded with relief. I felt like I had come back to life. When they walked through the door I had to hold myself back from sweeping him up into my arms and never letting him go again. Instead I tried to appear relaxed, as if I had been reading quietly the whole time. I hid my hands under the table to hide their shaking.

Our time came to an end. In many ways I felt I could stay for ever. After all, what was there to go back to? Disneyworld was a drug which gently cushioned me from reality.

But we couldn't hide in fantasy. It had been the trip of a lifetime and Alex had taken enough pleasure in it for both of us, but I was a long way from being able to 'enjoy' anything. I could intellectually appreciate that something was good but the actual experience was like eating when you weren't hungry. And without even being able to taste the food in your mouth. I was simply grateful for anything that wasn't painful.

As predicted, Alex fell asleep soon after boarding the return flight. Which left us free to drink in the knowledge that someone else could entertain him when he woke up in his own bed tomorrow.

Chapter Twenty-two

THE POLICE TOLD me that a certain Sunday newspaper wanted me to speak to them. This had become a regular request. Once again I told them to file the request in the bin where it belonged. But this time they said there was a difference.

'Apparently they have got a picture of you and a blonde woman walking down the road, taking Alex to school. They're going to run it with the caption: ANDRÉ FINDS NEW HAPPINESS! That is, if you don't speak to them first.'

The 'mystery blonde' was our friend, the mother of Alex's new companion. The picture must have been taken on the way to school.

I asked myself when was I ever going to become unshockable? But I *was* still shocked. What made them torment someone in my position? Wasn't I down far enough?

All I could do was laugh. So now I was being blackmailed. Well, why not? Nothing seemed beyond the realms of probability any more. We had had our rubbish gone through, parcels went missing, the car broken into, our friend's car entered and searched (it happened to be unlocked: things were moved around but nothing was stolen, hardly the work of thieves) and we had strong suspicions that the phone was being tapped. What was it all worth to them? Why was there such an interest in Rachel's death? But on reflection I saw that there were plenty of reasons why Rachel's murder was such a good 'story'.

Murder seemed to be a fascinating subject in general. But this time the victim happened to be female, white, blonde, young and attractive. If the victim had been a man or a black woman the interest would have been minimal. Then there was the sexual nature of the crime, which slotted in immediately with the sensationalist nature of so much that is reported in the press. Then of course the fact that a child had been present as the only witness. The fact that Rachel was from a middle-class background and that her father was a company director were additional factors which made the story of wider interest. On top of which Rachel had been killed in a famous place.

The facts were always dressed up a little, but it doesn't take much to change the emphasis. Rachel's father was always reported as a 'company director' even if he was actually unemployed at the time of Rachel's death, and Rachel was always described as a part-time model, even though she had simply done a few test-shots and a couple of afternoons on the catwalk for a charity show, none of which she had ever received any payment for. The continual use of the term 'part-time model' was particularly upsetting because of its more usual association with 'common prostitute'.

It also became clear from the pathologist's report after the first week that Rachel had not been raped. But the words 'rape' and 'part-time model' jump to the eye more quickly than 'full-time mother' and 'sexually assaulted'. I had been told by one newspaper editor to be grateful that we had been put in such a positive light. 'Just think how it could have been done!' I had been told. Meaning that the manipulation of the truth was something that wasn't even worth remarking on as long as it made you look better than you were instead of worse.

The truth is that in the UK, the moment that an event propels you into the public eye, you and your life are considered public property. The tabloids especially have a drawerful of stories at the ready and are always waiting for someone to walk into the frame. What had happened to our lives would keep them busy for years. They had tried me with the 'Grieving lover with dolly-bird on Costa-kiss-and-tell spend-spree!' Now they were going to try 'Grieving lover steals best friend's wife!'

The fact was that here was an industry, a group of profit-making businesses, that wasn't subject to the same laws and controls as any other industry. There were millions of pounds at stake every day but they were expected to stick to a gentleman's agreement not to be naughty boys.

Innocent people were damaged by their products. Granted, most of the damage was emotional and psychological, but in any other walk of life victims would have been compensated by law. The farmer whose pesticides stray into the local water supply and make the local inhabitants ill is liable under law. Why shouldn't it be the same for newspapers? Why shouldn't they be responsible for the damage that their products do, intentional or otherwise?

It was another violation and so much a caricature of newspaper behaviour that it was almost like a spoof. I had to hear the whole thing repeated twice from a detective to really believe it was true. It was laughable. I was quite happy for them to go ahead and print whatever they liked. I would find a lawyer to sue them for all I could and split the proceeds with our friends.

But after talking it over with our friends I could see that, pitiful though the report might be, it was still very damaging. I had almost grown used to having the press's attention directed at us and I would soon be away from the worst of it. Their family had a life in the UK based around their four children. Even though it might be nice to get paid by a newspaper that had printed something libellous, there was no avoiding the fact that their family would get well and truly dragged into the limelight.

It was an awful thought. They would have reporters on their doorstep. At the moment they sat in their cars and watched from a distance whenever Alex and I were there. One particular car would always pull up without fail a few minutes after we arrived. The driver would sit the whole time we were there, which was often hours. The only time he disappeared was to park round the back of the house and try and look over the garden fence. Eventually one day I went out with a video camera and filmed him. They would have loved a 'Grieving lover smashes reporter in the face!' story, I'm sure. I wasn't going to give them the satisfaction of that one, either.

The chances were that our friends' children would be followed to school and the parents of their children's friends pestered for information. The father would be harassed at work, and his colleagues as well. The mother, of course, would be followed everywhere. A legal action could take years to drag through the courts so their discomfort could last a long time. It wasn't worth the money.

After a few days' reflection and a lot of careful thought the answer to the problem became glaringly obvious. The only way to take the shock value out of what someone has to say is to say it first. If we managed to get a story published about our two families' friendship it would become a lot less interesting.

So that was exactly what we did. Through all the piles of requests for interviews we decided on a picture magazine. It wouldn't pay very much but it would be the shortest and least intrusive interview. And hopefully, among those unsuitable for publication there would be some lovely pictures of the children for our private use.

I had finally decided on the place that I had never seen. I had studied the map, read the books and spoken to friends in France. After checking everything against the list of what we needed I seemed to be on the right track. I had no trouble coming to the decision. I believed more than ever that the big things are decided themselves, by forces I could never understand. Often working out the little things could drive me mad for weeks, but somehow I always arrived at the important choices almost straight away.

The problem was finding somewhere to live. I had studied the estate agents' windows while in France in September, trying to get an idea of what we could hope to rent. For the price of a bedsit in London you could rent a whole house and garden in the French countryside. I wanted at least a separate room to write my stories. It looked hopeful.

I had the idea of travelling out with Alex and staying for a couple of weeks until we found a place, and then coming back to load the car up with our few things and drive them down. The general opinion was that this was a lot of upheaval for a small child. It was true that Alex's routine had become fixed, with his week centred round his five mornings at school. He was doing well and showed more and more signs of coming out of himself. His special friendship was blossoming and my decision to let it all drop was made harder because of it.

In the end I decided to pack everything up, say goodbye and go. This would make for one goodbye instead of two. We could stay in a hotel until we found somewhere to rent. I hoped it wouldn't take too long and there was a friend of a friend who had offered to help. But the inquest into Rachel's death was due at the end of January. I was a witness so we couldn't leave until after that.

On the day of the inquest the police offered to send a driver to pick me up. I didn't fancy sitting in the traffic for two hours while my head span round and round. And I didn't fancy being followed home again, either. I said I'd take my bike. Then I would be able to concentrate on driving instead of thinking about who knows what. I would also be free to come and go as I liked.

I was told I would be able to park my bike in the carpark around the side of the coroner's office. There was a direct entrance from there through the mortuary which would save me having to run the gauntlet of press outside the courtroom itself. A detective would be there to make sure I got in without any problems.

I set off in good time. Soon the traffic was thick. It was part of the same route I would have taken if Rachel and I had stayed over at her parents' house and I had come in to work from there in the morning. She would leave later with Alex, after the traffic. But six months had gone by and instead of listening in on my radio for the next job, I knew exactly where this morning would take me.

As I approached the courtroom building I could see a crowd of pressmen on the pavement outside. I turned before passing them and drove into the carpark. There were a few cars but the yard was deserted. I was relieved that I could get in without being hassled, but my pulse was still racing at the prospect of the morning's events.

I parked my bike and, turning towards the door, pulled off my helmet. The door was locked and I rang the bell. A figure partly opened the door and looked down at me with suspicion from the step above. He wore a green surgeon's gown and hat and his mask was pulled down around his neck. 'Hello?' he said, brusquely.

'I've come for the inquest,' I began to explain. 'I was told to come to this door.'

'You'll have to go round the front,' he said.

'But I was told there would be a detective waiting for me here,' I said. I couldn't believe they had forgotten.

'There's nobody here – you'll really have to go round the front.' The door closed in my face.

I was completely thrown. They had told me to come to this door. They had said there would be someone there to meet me. It had been their idea, not mine. I thought about ringing the bell and trying again but a glance at my watch told me that I was in danger of being late. I had little choice but to turn round and go the other way.

I pulled my helmet back on before turning back on to the main road and managed to walk past the first five or ten photographers strung out along the pavement without any of them turning a hair. Then I heard footsteps running behind me. A camera was suddenly shoved in front of my face with the flash going off. This was followed by a surge as the rest of the crowd moved towards me. I was amazed. If it hadn't been suggested I go to the back door then I would never have given much thought to the press outside. Once it had been mentioned of course my paranoia had taken over. But I had thought it was just that: paranoia. I thought I would be able to walk down the road with a motorbike helmet on without being recognized, but they must have been ticking off everyone who went in, and were watching everything that moved so as not to miss out on every available shot.

I was totally pissed off. Even more so when my route through the main door was blocked. 'Get out of my bloody way!' I shouted. The sound was muffled by my helmet and I might as well have been speaking Martian for all the difference it made. Why was it you had to physically push them out of your way to get them to move? Luckily a uniformed policeman opened the door at that moment and helped me get through.

I was shown to a changing-room and found myself in the company of some of the first officers to have arrived at the scene on the Common that day. They asked after Alex. Once again it was obvious from the way they talked how much they had taken Rachel's killing personally. We spoke for a while about the way the investigation was going.

We were called to take our places in the courtroom upstairs. It had the same smell of wood polish as an old church and reminded me of the place where Rachel had been cremated. We sat on carved benches. Wooden panels hung on the walls. Light streamed through diamond-paned leaded windows and the low voices and the general hush of the room full of people added to my impression.

I found myself talking to the man who had discovered Rachel's body. He was upset but more concerned with my feelings than with his own. I could imagine what a nightmare it must have been to come across such a scene. And then to have to live forever after with those terrible images in your head. He had no idea of the personality which had animated that empty shell. To those of us who knew her, Rachel's body was after all just that, a body. It wasn't the person we knew and,

305

as it was the person we missed, the thoughts of what had happened to her body often took second place in our minds.

The coroner conducted the proceedings in a sensitive manner. He had the courtesy to refer to Rachel as my wife, whatever may have been our 'official' status. He read from witnesses' statements in an effort to describe the order of events of that day. Several witnesses including myself were called to the stand to underline what he was reading. This mostly entailed answering 'yes' or 'no' in confirmation of the excepts.

I stood in the witness box with my hand on the bible. It was hard to make any sense of the scene around me. This wasn't my life. This had nothing to do with me. How could I have got here after leaving Rachel and Alex smiling on the step that morning in July? How could so many people be crying?

As I sat back down again I listened to a stranger describe how he had seen Rachel and Alex walking together, playing together as they crossed the Common. What business was it of his what my family were doing?

I listened to a man behind a high desk state that my wife had received forty-nine stab wounds and had been sexually assaulted. I could see Rachel's smiling face and I wanted to shout out: 'It's not true! She's fine! We're fine! This is nothing to do with us!' We had no place in this room full of strangers.

The proceedings were over. Everyone rose. I was back in the room downstairs, pulling on my bike stuff. A senior officer appeared. He apologized for the mix-up on my arrival. He wanted to reassure me that he was convinced that they were looking at the right man. He wanted me to know exactly how they were pursuing their task: his officers were in the first stages of an undercover operation directed at the suspect. This operation had been mentioned to me by our detectives. But one of the words he used chilled me. I was sure that it was a slip of the tongue and that he meant to describe things another way. I was no expert but I knew that a case could be thrown out if the police crossed a certain line. For a moment I was frightened of the consequences. But I reassured myself that they must know what they were doing. I had been assured that everything they were doing, every decision taken along the way, was done under the strictest and highest legal advice.

I was asked by someone if I wanted to make a statement to the press. They must have been joking! My statement would have contained only two words.

One of the policemen had come by bike as well. I waited until he was ready and we went out the back way together. My emotions were a mess and my head was spinning. It was an effort to put one foot in front of another. I was trying hard to pull myself together for the ride home.

As we went through the door we were confronted with a battery of lenses aimed in our direction. Once again it was like walking out in front of a firing squad. They had been kept back in the road by the uniformed police but were climbing over each other for an angle. I held my helmet up in front of my face as I walked and turned my back on them when I reached my bike. I could hear them calling for me to turn round. Fuck them!

And then, like a horde of savages, they began to jeer. The idea must have been to surprise me into turning round. I was taken by surprise but just managed to stop myself from spinning on my heel and giving them what they wanted. The jeering grew louder and louder. It was a bad impression of a pack of apes. It carried the threatening smell of a lynch mob. It was quite terrifying. I felt that if they got their hands on me they would rip me to shreds.

How could they do that? They knew that I had just sat through the description of the woman of my life's cruel and savage death. This was totally obscene. I just could not believe that people could act in such a way in a civilized society. Why are victims treated like this?

I pulled on my helmet but their howling still rang in my ears. It went far beyond a lack of respect. I was being violated. I put the bike into gear and pulled off as fast as I could. I would have been quite happy to run over anyone who chose to get in my way.

There was nothing left to hold us any more. We were leaving nothing but aggravation behind. We would miss our friends. But then again we wouldn't. How could you miss someone you were going to see again?

The morning after the inquest the newspaper I had originally sold my story to three months before published a whole load of photographs, completely breaking our written contract. I complained vehemently, but it was water off a duck's back. They had been published by 'mistake'. Someone had 'forgotten' that they were only to be used once. I wanted to sue but knew I didn't have a hope. It was another violation, another confirmation that we were powerless and insignificant cannon fodder.

What was worse, their sister paper had taken one of our pictures of Alex's birth, again breaking our contract, and had cut it in the most offensive manner. All that was left was Rachel leaning forward, smiling, wrapped only in a bath towel. I was seething with rage. The world was so full of shit! Everything was distorted and perverted. She had been violated again and I had been fooled into helping them do it.

Even the lunchtime TV news the day before had made its contribution. The footage showed me walking up to the courtroom door with my helmet on. Every sound and voice was audible, just up to the moment when I said: 'Get out of my bloody way!' Then the sound went dead. From the camera angle they had chosen you could hardly see that I had to push photographers out of my way just to get through the door.

The media boys were all looking out for each other. Rachel's parents had agreed to speak to them after the inquest. At their press conference Rachel's father was at pains to express that they were sad that their grandchild was leaving the country but that the main reason he was leaving was because of them, the press. If there hadn't been such an unbearable assault on our privacy we might not have considered leaving.

Not one newspaper picked up on these comments. Almost everything else that he said in regard to the police investigation was carried almost word for word in the majority of them. But not one line appeared about the treatment I had received from the jeering mob outside the courtroom. There must have been a journalist from every major paper present, not to mention TV. All of them must therefore have considered this behaviour normal, merited, not even worthy of comment. I wasn't living in the wrong country, I was living on the wrong planet.

We started to load the cars for the journey at three o'clock in the morning, to avoid any unwanted attention. The night was pitch-black. We had made the arrangements through a series of phone calls to and from various public call-boxes.

At six o'clock in the morning I took Alex out of bed and wrapped him up warmly in his car-seat. The cold winter street was deserted as we pulled away, my mother and a friend in the car behind. The night was still dark. I led the way across a central London completely empty of traffic. I was anxious to get across before the rush hour began. Then I remembered that today was Sunday. There wouldn't be any. The sky began to lighten but the streets remained empty.

I ran through the list in my head, wondering what I might have forgotten. I had been packing the car for weeks in my mind, trying to work out the strict minimum that we should take, that we had room for. Alex's train-shaped bed had had to be sacrificed at the last moment, I just couldn't get it in. He hadn't slept in it for six months and I was hoping he wouldn't be too upset.

The only thing of importance that was left behind was Molly. She would have to wait until we had found a place to live. The rest of our lives was packed into two cars. We were driving towards somewhere we had never been. And we weren't coming back.

Alex woke up before we reached the English Channel. He was happy for a while listening to music from one of his tapes. When he became restless I began to make up a story from what we could see as we went along. If I was going to do this seriously I had better get in all the practice I could. He listened quietly but appreciatively, adding the odd comment from time to time. It was nothing in the grand style of things, but his quiet indulgence of my storytelling was an enormous compliment.

I wondered what he was really thinking. He knew we were going abroad. He knew we were going to have a different house and live somewhere new. But did he realize just how far away we would be? Did he really understand that we weren't coming back?

I was frightened by his possible reaction. At the time I would have said that I was trying to keep his morale high with my cheerfulness, but maybe it was more that I was trying to soothe my own nerves.

One of the last things we saw of England was a huge hole in the hillside. It was part of the Channel Tunnel project. Britain would soon no longer be an island. When it was finished we wouldn't be quite so far away.

The sea rose and fell in a large swell as we crossed. Alex complained that he was feeling sick. I took him out on deck. We could see the houses on the French side appear and disappear behind the swell as the boat rose and fell. The sky was grey and overcast. It was drizzling with rain and the houses appeared drab and devoid of colour. The scene was hardly inviting. The last thing I wanted was him throwing up just as the journey really began. That was hardly going to put him in a receptive mood for the start of our new adventure.

We were approaching the port. Calm water from the inner harbour extended strangely between the waves, its surface still as a pond. The boat pulled towards it, rocked a few more times and then settled. Alex immediately looked much better.

As we pulled on to the first stretch of motorway we all kept an eye out to see if we had been followed off the boat. It had been impossible to tell if we had been followed in England. Passing the ticket and customs control points had the effect of thinning out the traffic and for a few minutes there was nothing in the mirror. When the first car appeared behind us with its British registration plate gleaming in my mirror I felt my pulse rate begin to accelerate. They were on to us already! But the car sailed by. Immediately another one appeared behind, but it was soon on his way past us as well. I calmed down a little as it became clear that at the gentle speed we were travelling everyone was anxious to get past as soon as possible. Nothing sat behind us for long.

The cassette player packed up. I had been relying on it to keep Alex amused during what would be a very long drive. A few miles further on, one of the front windows jammed open. As I pulled on to the hard shoulder to try and sort out the problem the wind began to howl and the rain lashed down out of the dark grey skies which suddenly descended on us. As I fumbled around in the fuse box with the cold rain blowing in on Alex I wondered if this was a sign that we were being propelled forward – or being pushed back?

We drove on for several hours. The weather showed no sign of improving. If anything, it was getting worse. The backdrop seen through windscreen wipers seemed to change hardly at all. Grey, wet, cloudy and windy. With the cassette player out of action there was nothing to break the monotonous drone of water surging off the road under the weight of our tyres.

But even the drab surroundings could not prevent me from feeling lighter. We were gone. And as the miles passed the oppressive weight of so much attention directed at us began to slip away. After the first hundred miles it had gone completely. I could literally feel it dropping from my shoulders. We were now in a completely different environment. We were unknown again, insignificant. Nobody who lived in any of the towns or villages we passed had any idea of who we were or what we had been through. There was only the lingering fear that someone might be following.

This lightness was balanced by my concerns for Alex. He was subdued. Thoughtful.

'Why are we going?' he asked.

'We're going where it's warmer,' I answered, putting on my most winning smile. 'The further we go, the warmer it's going to get,' I added for greater effect. 'Then we'll be able to play outside nearly all the time and won't be stuck indoors!'

I could see him looking thoughtfully out of the window at the pouring rain. I didn't feel brave enough to ask him what he was thinking. He looked like a tiny co-pilot in the seat beside me. The effect was reinforced by the boxes piled up behind our heads which turned the front of the car into a kind of aircraft cabin. The instrument glowed in the dull light and the clouds which, apart from the channel of clear road directly ahead, seemed to completely surround us.

I wasn't sure I would have enough arguments to appease him if he really became upset. I didn't know myself what we were going to find when we arrived. I just had the conviction that, whatever it was, it would be better than what we were leaving behind. And that we couldn't – I couldn't – carry on as we were.

I was trying not to make a big deal of it. We were going, and that was that. But I could sense his uncertainty. I thought that the best thing was to carry on as if our expedition was no big thing. But I was sure he understood that we would be far from all our friends and family, that he had no picture of what life was going to be like from now on. I knew it was this which was making him so subdued. But I knew also that the moment he was caught up in new games and activities he would be quick to put anything else behind him. Hadn't he switched his allegiance from Rachel to me in the blinking of an eye?

We reached Paris by midday and found ourselves trying to negotiate the notorious *périphérique*, the road which circles the city. Even

311

with only Sunday traffic on the road it was a hairy experience. There were cars overtaking fast on all sides and the road signs were extremely confusing. We went past our turn-off and had to pull off further on and turn round. For a terrible moment I thought we had lost my mother and friend. Thankfully they soon reappeared beside us. A little while later we managed to find the right exit together.

We stopped for snacks and hot chocolate and stale croissants in a dingy roadside café south of Paris while the rain lashed down outside. Grey. Dark and grey. There was so much water falling. Only the car headlights provided any brightness through the plate-glass windows. Only the yellow beams confirmed that we were actually in France and not somewhere in the north of England. My promise of us being able to play outside was looking pretty thin.

It looked from the map as if our journey had hardly begun. This was a big country. Alex was climbing over the grimy plastic seats and pressing his face up against the condensation on the windows. He was dressed in boots and a big winter coat. He drank his hot chocolate cheerfully enough, although I was alarmed by the amount of sugar it contained. I wondered how he would be able to sit still in the car afterwards. Luckily the cassette player had begun to work again some miles back, so at least there was entertainment for him.

Throughout the afternoon the scene remained the same. Only the road signs and the diminishing distances marked on them gave any indication that we were moving at all. There were hundreds and hundreds of miles still to go and we had driven for hours already. This was the first time I had driven for so long since I had stopped working. I couldn't help feeling glad to have a big warm, dry car around me and not be sitting on a bike struggling to stop the pins and needles in my feet and the numbing cold from spreading up my legs. Not to mention the ache in my shoulders and back from the effort of concentration involved in staying upright on two wheels in the rain for so long. I felt a little disloyal to those who were still doing so. But sometimes I wondered how I put up with all that for as long as I had.

Alex was an absolute angel. He had been in the car for nearly the whole of the day but had not complained once. He was remarkably good. Unnaturally so. So much so that I wondered whether Rachel wasn't having a little influence. I would never have got through the day if he had started to play me up. We would never have been able to cover the distance we had. Unlike the others behind, I had no one to share the driving with while I entertained him, not that there was any room for anyone else, so I was dependent on him being on his best behaviour. Even so, he was outdoing my best expectations for such a small child. He was happy to amuse himself with the few toys he had in the front with him, to listen to his songs and stories and to talk with me.

The idea of an early stopover was welcomed unanimously. But it was already dark by the time we left the motorway and pulled up at a roadside hotel. The rain had stopped.

Our friend sat on the bed with Alex beside him, both of them watching a TV programme they couldn't understand. Our friend had the advantage of at least a rudimentary understanding of French. Yet Alex still appeared fascinated by the moving images of what was obviously junk TV. The room was so male, no sign of anything feminine at all. It was like a scene out of an American road movie. Marginals on the road to nowhere, with all their worldly belongings in the back of a car parked in the street behind. It was a deeply depressing moment. Happy family life was a distant memory, a million years behind.

Chapter Twenty-three

I PAID THE BILL that night and we left before daybreak. We stopped
briefly to pick up croissants and *pain au chocolat* for breakfast on the
move. This time they were delicious. With the new day it was as if we
had really arrived in France. The smells were different. The air was
clean. We were far from the city. All the road signs and advertising
hoardings were in French. I tried to work out the meanings of the
advertisements we passed and noted the small but definite differences
in hairstyles and clothing and make-up of the people in the images displayed on them. There was no way they could have been English.

We drove through a fine mist as the road followed a winding river
on its way out of town. The trees on the far bank cast deep shadows
over the water. Light from the wrought-iron street lights caught the
matching railings which lined the riverbank and reflected on the surface. It was our first glimpse of French rural beauty.

Alex was once again in an easygoing and uncomplaining mood. In
fact I was horrified to reach down some time later and discover that his
bare feet were as cold as ice. The air vent on his side had accidentally
jammed open and his legs were being blasted with freezing air. He
seemed hardly bothered, which was out of character. I stopped quickly
to get him dressed but he seemed unfazed by his cold feet and soon,
properly dressed, was humming away contentedly to his tape. Out of
a generous selection he had settled on only two. I knew the words to
both by heart already as we switched constantly from one to the other.

The sky steadily cleared as the day began for real. The sun shone
through a damp haze for the first time. 'Look Alex, I told you it would
get warmer the further we went,' I said. 'We are going towards the

sun, so it should get warmer and warmer all the time.' I wasn't sure how to get across the geographical principles involved to a three-year-old, so I left it at that.

By the time we made our first real stop of the day it had turned into a bright clear morning. I was eager to get Alex outside to run around for a while and lose some of the stiffness in his legs. With any luck he might doze a little afterwards. No journey goes quicker than when you are asleep. We walked across the tarmac into the services building. Outside the air was cold. Our breath formed clouds in front of us.

From within I could see a climbing frame and a slide on the opposite side from where we had parked. I led Alex out. But instead of our feet falling on to a springy bed of dew-drenched grass they crunched down on to an uneven carpet of ankle-jarring concrete tufts. The ground was frozen hard. We had left the rain behind but, instead of getting warmer, it was getting colder and colder. The toys were too covered in ice for Alex to play on and he was already complaining about the bitter cold. Some outdoor life I was presenting for him! I felt awful. I felt like I was breaking my promises already.

On and on we drove, mile after mile of motorway. The traffic was sparse, even though it was the first day of the week, but we were now far from any major town or city. Our rhythm was set by the regular need to refuel. We began to count the journey more in terms of these stops than by the miles on the map. At midday we pulled off the motorway and headed into a small town to find a supermarket. There was snow in the air. By the time we emerged after lunch the cars were covered with it and there was a thick layer underfoot. I could hardly believe it!

Alex took it in his stride. He didn't seem the least disappointed that our journey towards the sun was fast becoming a disappearance into a winter wonderland. But a look at the map told us that we were now at the highest part of our route. Not only would we soon be leaving the motorway but it should, logically, soon be getting warmer as well. However, it was a lesson that a French winter was not something to be taken lightly.

As the afternoon began we passed frozen rivers and deep drifts of snow. The snow continued to fall and the motorway was covered with slush. We were driving through thick snow clouds and visibility was poor. I was glad that the car had new front tyres but was beginning to wonder if we wouldn't soon need chains. I didn't have any. There was a hairy moment when the lane I was travelling in suddenly came to a dead stop with only the barest warning. Luckily for me there was nothing in the next lane and I managed to avoid piling into the road-works, the car sliding sideways on the slush. My mother at the wheel behind was not so lucky. They only just avoided a collision with a truck coming up fast behind them.

Once we were off the motorway the road began to wind downwards. We were really in the mountains. I could feel the whole weight of the loaded car bearing down on one front wheel at a time as the road turned one way and then the other. We descended for hours. Thankfully the snow was behind us by the middle of the afternoon. In fact we even had a spring-like moment of clear blue sky and unobstructed sunshine. Suddenly we could see for miles. The countryside was rugged and wild. The snow was gone. It was beautiful. It felt as if we had been smuggled out of occupied territory by the French Resistance. A longer, harder or more obscure route was hard to imagine.

It was hard to find refreshments. Villages were few and far between and practically deserted; petrol stations non-existent. The atmosphere was wonderful. Wild and lost. I felt safe, far from the world. Darkness fell while we were still in the mountains. We considered stopping for the night or pressing on. It all depended on Alex. He was still being an absolute angel. I wondered if this was going to mark a change in his behaviour generally, but decided it was better not to reach too hasty a conclusion.

We pressed on. The road was unlit. Village lights twinkled in the blackness around us. As we reached the plain, the lights were now sprinkled further and further away out to the sides. Nothing out there meant anything to me. The countryside was unrecognizable and we were travelling through areas I had never visited. I could only imagine what darkness might contain. The only brightness outside, apart from the spread of our headlights and those of occasional oncoming cars, was the reflection of those lights on the intermittent signposts which loomed up towards us. I had no idea what these villages looked like or what sights would have met us if we had still been there when the sun rose the next day. Whatever they might look like, to me they represented sanctuary. Somewhere out here we were going to find a place where we would be safe and undisturbed. For a while at least.

We had a contact at our journey's end. I had passed on a message that we would probably be there by the following day, but we were ahead of schedule. I hoped that someone would be there for us anyway, and that there would still be a room for us.

There was no sign of life out on the road. Only twinkling lights in the distance. The road never took us through a town. Only through the darkest countryside. It had been lunchtime since we had last seen any signs of activity, so it seemed almost a miracle when we eventually found ourselves on lit streets lined with shops and apartment buildings. A phone box struck me as almost absurdly modern and sophisticated at the end of a journey through so much wilderness. It belonged to a world we had left far behind and had no business being here after we had travelled so far. As the streets grew narrower and the traffic noticeable for the first time we spotted the yellow arches of a McDonald's restaurant and I was brutally reminded that nowhere is that far away from anywhere.

From another incongruous telephone box I called our contact's number. Luckily for us they were home and soon, like a scene from *film noir*, they appeared out of a frosty night, their breath hanging in clouds in front of their faces, and I was able to match faces to what had only been voices.

Their car in front of us led us out into the blackness once again. I had trouble keeping up as they sped away. I hoped we didn't lose the others; this wasn't the pace we were accustomed to. We pulled up some time later in a tiny village. There were friends of friends. French was spoken in the frosty air faster than I could follow. We were led behind some wooden gates and there, in a hidden garden, was our safe house.

We had seen a sign for a pizzeria in the village and, hungrily, we set out in its direction. It wasn't yet ten o'clock. Our new friends looked at us as though we were mad. They said there was no guarantee that the restaurant would be open so late. It was our first clash with country living. I was so much used to London and late-night opening and twenty-four-hour service. But a telephone call was made and we were told that the kitchen would be opened just for us. Apparently this was an astounding piece of good luck.

The next day began cold and grey. The weather had only just changed

317

in the last few days and as recently as a week or two ago the locals had been walking in shirt-sleeves in temperatures in the mid-twenties centigrade. They were sure that this wouldn't last.

Our contact returned some time after breakfast. She turned out to be an absolute dynamo and whisked us from agent to agent and from village to village in our pursuit of a house to rent. In between she found time to scour the adverts in the local paper while she made us all lunch as well. Everything was done at breakneck speed, from driving to talking. My head was spinning in an effort to keep up with what she was saying. I found myself translating always at least two or three sentences back. When she asked me, from time to time, if I understood I found myself gawping like an idiot, waiting for my brain to catch up with the backlog before I could give her an accurate answer.

We saw only a couple of houses that day, neither of which was very appropriate. But I did get a good idea of the local area and spent most of the time just drinking in the surroundings. There were beautiful villages, and some ugly ones as well, there were river rapids and boats and mountains and woods. But most of all there were vines: bare and skeletal in their winter state and cut back to a minimum. Horizontal rows, absolutely straight, ran in all directions with the earth churned over between them. Uphill, across the plains, right up to the houses. Not the tiniest patch of land appeared to be uncultivated.

The water in the village fountains was frozen thick. We walked in heavy winter coats pulled up against the biting wind. Alex was in balaclava and mittens. It had been warmer in England. Much warmer.

On the third day we awoke to an unbroken blue sky. There was a quality to the light unlike any I had never known in England. There were bright winter days in England but here the air was completely clear and overhead there was nothing but deep, deep blue. Nothing. Not the slightest trace of cloud or dust or haze. The colours in the garden were dazzling. Miraculously, there were flowers still in bloom which had so far managed to survive the frost. Their yellow and orange shone out. The unpainted doors in the village, cracked with heat and age, and the occasional piece of half-painted, half-rusty wrought iron, which would have looked tatty somewhere else, were the stuff of picture postcards.

The sun beat down, there wasn't a breath of wind, and we were forced to pull off coats and jumpers in order not to boil completely. It was only February but it was suddenly as warm as an English summer day. If it stayed as warm as this throughout the winter it could almost be paradise.

We had seen a house the day before which would have been perfect. It was right out in the countryside and part of a working property that produced its own wine. It had a tower with what had once been a pigeon-loft and looked right out over the vines and there were chickens in the yard. What better place to find the peace and quiet we needed? But that would have been too perfect. The owners were really looking for someone to work in the fields in return for rent. I was on duty with Alex all day long for the foreseeable future, so we weren't what they were looking for. They didn't turn us down on the spot, but said they would have to think it over. They were probably just being polite. It didn't look too hopeful so we continued to look at houses which we stood a more realistic chance of obtaining.

It was soon time for my mother and our friend to start the journey back. It was a hard moment when their car finally pulled away. There had been moments when I could almost forget what had happened, so caught up was I in the business of making a new start. As they turned the corner and disappeared from view I stood in the road with Alex in my arms and watched them go.

I stood in a strange road in a strange town surrounded by people I didn't know. Everything we owned was packed in boxes in a stranger's garage. I lifted my eyes to the horizon and I didn't recognize the scenery. My child sat in my arms as I choked back the tears.

Their tail-lights disappeared around a corner and they were gone.

What had led us to this? Why was I in so much pain?

Everything came flooding back into my head. Everything. All of it.

The sky was grey and cold once more: there was snow in the air. I was hit by a wave of loneliness. All at once I was more isolated than ever and my face was being pushed up against the reality that the only reason I was standing there in so much pain was because some maniac had walked out of the woods one day with murder in his mind. I could easily have watched the buildings around me melt into water and disappear into the ground. It would have been no more unreal than anything else that had happened to us.

I took Alex to the beach. He showed no reaction to the departure of my mother and our friend. In fact he struck me as incredibly carefree. He was running and skipping across the sand as if he didn't have a worry in the world. The beach was dark and overcast, and cold.

He picked up a stick and wanted me to play sword-fighting with him. We pranced round the beach, clashing our bits of wood together. It did me good to see him so free. It made me lighter in myself.

Alex stopped for a minute and looked back across the beach towards the houses. His face was thoughtful. It was as if he was looking past the houses, back across the hills and mountains and back across all the miles we had covered to get here. He had watched nearly all of them pass by the car window. He had a strong idea of how far we had left our other life behind us. He knew that we were virtually the only ones who even spoke our language.

'I was playing sword-fighting when the bad man came!' he announced, out of the blue.

Reality, memories, descended upon me, crashing down on all sides. I hoped he hadn't noticed the tightness in my throat as I made some banal reply.

'He pushed me in the mud! That wasn't nice!'

I agreed with him as nonchalantly as I could: no, indeed, that wasn't nice. I wanted to say as little as I could so as not to break the spell. I wondered if that would be all, or if there was more.

He continued to play around me with his stick. He was in no hurry to say any more. 'Where were you when the bad man was hurting Mummy?' I asked after a while.

'I was with Mummy,' he said, looking up at me, his eyes shining bright. He was happy to tell me.

It was hard to restrain myself from launching into the flood of questions that still remained only partly answered, to ask him to repeat again those answers I already knew. But the worst thing I could do was push too hard.

'Why does the bad man like you?' he asked.

I was stunned. It was an extraordinary question. I assumed his logic must have been: why hadn't the bad man attacked us when we were all together? Why had I been spared?

'He doesn't like me. He's afraid of me! He would never have attacked Mummy when I was there. He knew what I would have done to him.'

'He had a bag,' said Alex.

'What did he have in the bag?' I asked.

'The knife.'

A little while later he added cheerfully: 'If Thunderbirds were around they would catch him!'

I asked Alex where the man came from. He signalled to his right. 'I saw him. Mummy saw him.'

I asked myself why Rachel didn't run. But how was she to know what was coming? And her first thought would have been for Alex. How she could best protect him. She would sacrifice herself. I could see the look of surprise in her eyes when the first blows fell, the confusion. How could she understand what was happening to her?

'It was black, I think,' said Alex, his expression one of concentration. He was making an effort to remember everything. It was the bag that had been black. He had said as much before; other witnesses had said the same. His expression changed to one of irritation, then of anger. 'He pushed me over!' His voice was filled with indignation.

That night I wrote down everything that he had said to me. It was the 26th of February. Seven months on and the events were as clear as ever inside his head. He was living with those memories every day, mostly on his own. Who could say how many times a day he saw again what had happened? He was alone, pushing it around his head until he found a place for it. Who knew at what price?

The snow fell. The world around us turned white. In between looking at houses we toured all the furniture shops in the local area. Alex wouldn't even have a bed when we eventually found somewhere to live. He was happy running up and down the aisles of the big warehouses, which at the moment was probably the best way of trying to tire him out. Outside it was now perpetual night. The snow clouds were thick and low, and everything was dark.

We ate breakfast at the inn and made picnics from what we bought at the supermarket. Everywhere was practically deserted. Maybe the bad weather was keeping people snug indoors. We would drive out to somewhere pretty for lunch but the cold forced us to eat our sandwiches in the car. Supper was something of a nightmare. It was hard to explain to French people what a vegetarian was. To them it was like a form of illness. Added to which Alex was not at all flexible in what he would eat, even if it didn't contain meat or fish. He wasn't prepared to eat anything that didn't look exactly like what I would have given him at home. The only things I could get him to eat anywhere else-without a blazing row were pasta, pizza and bread. Over the next weeks and months I became used to disapproving looks and muttered comments of: 'What does he eat, that child?' on top of the usual denigrating comments on English cuisine. It was one of the differences between the French and the English. The French were generally much less restrained, almost childlike in their freedom to make personal comments about others in a way that would be considered extremely rude by the English.

I had often observed groups of French people, usually men, listening attentively while one of them gave his or her expert opinion on something or other. The others would listen hard: not so much in the hope of learning anything interesting but, more usually, not to miss the appropriate moment to jump in and announce that their companion was completely wrong. And then launch into a presentation of their own, opposite opinion. This was usually accepted without offence by the original speaker, who would be looking out for *his* opportunity to jump back in again. I had found these conversations, conducted in loud, and what to me were angry voices, fairly alarming during my first trips abroad. But I had soon come to realize that it was actually a form of sport. One that permitted much letting off of steam. Everyone knew the rules, and good humour prevailed.

There was a lot more shouting than I had been used to when growing up in England. As a teenager travelling around I had at first taken this as a sign of a violent people. But despite all the heated verbal exchanges I had observed I never once saw one come to blows. In contrast I had seen people in England at a bus stop or in the traffic or in a bar with their hands round each other's throats after little more than a look. Maybe there was some connection between the Latin's expansiveness, allowing a situation to dissipate in no more than hot air, and the British reserve that let nothing escape until exploding point was reached. I learned to take raised voices in my stride.

The days were passing and we still hadn't found a place to live. We were stuck in one hotel room with a bag of clothes and some toys and books for Alex. The weather was getting worse with every day. I was finding it hard to maintain my morale.

We came out of a furniture warehouse on the outskirts of a nearby town as night was falling. I got Alex into the car quickly, to avoid the falling snow. It was a tricky job to ease the car out of the slush-filled carpark and on to the main road. As we turned a few hundred metres further up the road and began to pull up the ramp into the carpark of yet another store, the motor suddenly died. The car began to roll backwards into the road. I was blocking the traffic and the cars behind began to blow their horns. I tried again and again but it wouldn't respond to the key. I couldn't get it started. It was all I could do to stop myself from bursting into tears.

In the end the little things bring you to your knees. I somehow managed to find the strength to cope with the big things, because I had to for Alex. But it took everything I had. For a simple day-to-day awkward situation like the car breaking down I had no reserves.

Whatever I tried I couldn't get the car started. I turned the key several times but the battery appeared to be dead. I could see the dark and the snow outside and the street lights of a town full of strangers. I asked myself one more time if it was worth going on. It was just too hard. Maybe we should jack it in completely. It didn't seem that life was going to let me achieve even the tiniest thing. Why bother fighting any more? I might as well accept what was glaringly obvious. We weren't meant to have anything.

I got out of the car and looked under the bonnet. The snow fell down my neck. I couldn't see the problem.

'Why aren't we going?' asked Alex, when I climbed back in.

'I can't get the car started.' I tried hard to make my mind focus on what I should do to get us out of this mess. Even the walk to a phone box to call for help would mean both of us getting completely covered in snow. I couldn't leave Alex in the car on his own, but his coat wouldn't keep out the moisture for long. He would soon be freezing. It looked like turning into a long and uncomfortable evening. I turned the key one more time. The engine roared into life.

On the local news that night there were pictures of cars and trucks which had skidded off the very roads we had been driving along that day. The vehicles were in the ditch and the drivers, huddling against the driving snow, were being interviewed. 'On n'allait pas vite!' they were all saying. The phrase was accompanied by an expression of complete surprise that their vehicles should have lost control. I laughed out loud. I had seen how they drove at the best of times. They didn't have the highest accident rate in Europe for nothing. 'On n'allait pas vite!' We weren't going fast!

The newsreader was more generous, putting the accidents down to the severity of the weather and the fact that snow hardly ever fell in the region. This was a rare occurrence, it was repeated.

I sat in our hotel room later that night with Alex asleep in the bed beside me. It couldn't have been more than half-past eight. I couldn't go out. There was no one to watch him. I hadn't anything I wanted to read, there was no TV or radio. Outside it was freezing. We had just a few things scattered round the room. Each of us is a hostage to his own destiny. But at that moment I was conscious of the fact as I never had been before. I turned off the lights and cried into my pillow.

We found a house that suited us well. It was a modern little villa with its own garden completely surrounded by high bushes. It was quiet and would be easy to keep clean. But there was no view, and for a house which was on the edge of so much beautiful countryside, it had no soul. We had still not heard back from the house in the vines and as long as they hadn't said 'no' for definite I was loath to settle for anything else.

Time was passing by. I was beginning to feel like a permanent resident at the inn. For much of the time we were the only guests. We ate supper at a long wooden table while a fire blazed in the grate. Alex played with the cats and busied himself with his drawings. If anybody spoke to him in French he would go quiet and grin. No amount of encouragement or bribery would persuade him to repeat any word or phrase that was said to him. Instead his grin would turn into a bad-tempered pout. 'Boudeur!'★ I wasn't going to put any pressure on him and did my best to look the other way. He would try when he was ready and, knowing him, pushing him too hard would only make him dig in his heels and the whole thing would take twice as long.

Out of the blue came the word that we had been offered the house in the vines after all. I was extremely and very pleasantly surprised. The setting was idyllic but I had not got my hopes up too high. I had

★ 'Sulky!'

secretly fallen in love with the place but had hardly even wanted to admit it to myself. I was trying to protect myself from disappointment. It had seemed too perfect to be true and I had lost the habit of expecting things to turn out for the best.

But the fact that we could make a new start in such beautiful surroundings gave me a real lift. We had lived as refugees for so long now that I was eager to surround Alex with his own things, with our things, and give him a proper base. Not that I could associate the word 'home' with any of this. Home was with Rachel. Anything else was a pitiful imitation.

The first day we were given the key was spent ferrying all of our belongings from our contact's garage to our new house in the vines. Even though it had once been packed into two cars it took me at least three journeys this time to get it all in. Once everything was inside and a neighbour had shown me how to light the oil heating and the door was bolted shut on the outside world I felt we had finally arrived. It was the closest sensation I had so far had to 'happiness'. In truth it was a huge feeling of relief. I had achieved the first part of what I had set out to do: we now had a roof over our head. Maybe we would be allowed to get on with living.

The house was completely unfurnished. Completely. Right down to the empty light sockets and missing toilet seat. There was no kitchen, only a sink and running water. The hot water worked and, most luxuriously of all, there was a bath as well as a shower. Our voices echoed off the walls and high ceilings as we talked. Both of us were grinning and giggling like idiots as we scampered round the empty rooms and up and down the stairs. Compared to our two-bedroom flat in London this was absolutely enormous. We had never had so much space. But then again, there were only two of us now.

Alex went to sleep that night in a camp bed we had been loaned, after helping me put together the bed that had been Rachel's and mine. It was so strange to see it standing in this unfamiliar room. There was so much of her still around us. I could see her face, thrilled with the pleasure of being here all together. The ache I carried with me everywhere bit a little harder. Hurt a little deeper. I was unpacking our stuff, hers and mine. I was running my hands over things that had last been touched by her. Their smell was so familiar, the months were swept away. I could almost feel her hand on my shoulder, see her shadow sweep across the wall, the light catch her hair. Our child slept in the room next door but there was no one else in the house.

Alex was perfectly relaxed. He went to sleep without any problems. There was no sign of the anxiety that being in such an empty, unfamiliar place might have brought on in the most stable of children. I left him breathing easily.

I unpacked the computer we had brought with us and plugged its fax connector into the wall. I was instantly in contact with our friends in London. Outside the shutters there was not a sound. The moment it occurred to me how quiet it was, the silence weighed even heavier. There was nothing outside the window but vineyards and open countryside. But in all this emptiness I could see my friends' words come up on the screen from so many hundreds of miles away.

When I switched the computer off and its fan no longer whirred all I could hear again was silence. Almost in response to it I could feel a quietness inside of me. I had switched down a gear. Inside my chest for the first time something was still.

I forgot about the cold. For the moment everything was perfect. Alex and I walked around, exploring. Everything smelt so clean, so earthy. There was simply no noise, only the sound of birdsong and the scrunch of soil and gravel under our feet. The soil itself looked like sticky sand. When it dropped off our shoes and dried in the house it became just that, sand.

There was no litter, no rubbish apart from empty shotgun shells occasionally dotted around. It struck me as incongruous that people who lived in so much beauty could leave their bright, shiny plastic crap behind them to spoil the scene. It wasn't like dropping a cigarette packet in an already littered city street. That was bad enough, although there was a certain logic, the scene being already dirty and ugly. But I was surprised at my naïvety. People were capable of short-sighted stupidity no matter where they lived.

The snow stayed for a while. The sky remained stubbornly grey. We busied ourselves with endless long journeys to the nearest hypermarket where we bought everything from light-bulbs to food to a fridge to put it in. Alex soon had his bed on stilts and was thrilled to climb his ladder at night to listen to his story. I suddenly had to prepare three meals a day every single day and a new routine imposed itself. I tried to take Alex out for at least a couple of hours' play each day but felt guilty for the rest of the time he had to spend on car journeys to and fro or in the house while I painted or cooked or organized.

I was beginning to find the endless shopping trips tedious myself, trailing around trying to find chests of drawers and tables and chairs. Added to which there wasn't a lot of choice locally and the nearest Habitat or Ikea were two or three hours' drive away. I decided to try and make as much as I could myself. I hadn't made any furniture before but I enjoyed working with my hands.

So now our shopping trips involved searching for bits of wood and drawer handles and tins of varnish. Before long Alex knew the names of all the shops we visited and could even recognize their logos on the roadside signs we passed as we drove along. And even though these were his first few French words his accent was perfect. Much better than mine, because he was imitating exactly what he heard.

With a little new paint around the place the house began to feel more like ours. I was enjoying the obvious Frenchness of the shutters and the window fixings and the way the sound of my guitar echoed through the empty rooms. Every pleasure was accompanied by the pain of Rachel not being there to share it. Outside the windows the yard was dotted with several tractors and other farm machinery. It had been Alex's biggest thrill to sit on a tractor in England. It made his day when a place we visited had one for the children to play on. He would wait patiently while other children took their turn. Here he had them right on his doorstep. There wasn't much need for organized entertainment. He was mesmerized by the comings and goings in front of us and soon knew who usually drove which coloured tractor and what it would normally be pulling behind it.

Most of our stuff was still in boxes. I set myself the task of making one piece of furniture a week and let myself be guided by what was most urgently needed. Our new French friends naturally assumed that, as Alex and I were at present eating off his little red activity table and chairs, the first thing would be a dining-room table. I started on a chest of drawers for Alex's clothes.

It was impossible to venture out without being completely wrapped up against the elements. Alex played on the swings at the beach in boots and coat, gloves and furry hat. But very soon came still days of sunshine and clear blue skies. We were suddenly sitting on the beach in T-shirts and bare feet, digging holes in the sand. His behaviour had changed noticeably. He was so much more relaxed and carefree. There were moments when I could almost have described him as 'happy'. Although 'content' was a more accurate description. There was still too much tension in his face. I moved the workbench outside and set about making drawers with my shirt off and the sun beating down. It wasn't yet the end of February.

The first drawers were a little wonky. But they worked. Alex's room was beginning to take shape and with a few rockets stencilled over sky-blue walls he had a room to himself for the first time. This was the idea. I wanted him to have his own room in his own house, surrounded by his own things. He would soon have his dog again, his grandparents would visit. I was there night and day. Everything was there, everything was as it should be. Only his mother was missing.

Only his mother.

Alex accepted sleeping in his own room without comment. He had always slept in with me until now, but he appeared at ease with his new environment. I always left a light on and he had no trouble finding his way in to me at night. Often I wouldn't even notice him climbing in and would awake to find him fast asleep beside me with an out-stretched hand on my bare skin. Touching my clothing wasn't good enough. He seemed to sleep easily only as long as he could feel my skin there beside him. I wondered if the contact was necessary for him to reassure himself that I was in fact still there. Or even more to feel that I was still warm.

That I was still alive.

That it hadn't happened again.

Routinely we would eat breakfast and then head off to buy the materials we needed for the day. No matter how hard I tried to think of everything so as to avoid a trip every single day there was always something forgotten. Some tool or fixing that proved indispensable. Alex wanted to go to the beach and we would try and stop off on the way back for a couple of hours and play in the sand. The beach was nearly deserted. It was hard to imagine, when people talked about how unbearably crowded it got in the summer. I would spend the rest of the day working at the house. I had something to get my teeth into and I paid no more attention to the time that passed.

Chapter Twenty-four

I SANG ALEX TO sleep at bedtime, as I had all through the first few weeks. I kissed him as he lay sleeping and left him with the door slightly ajar. A little while later, as I sat quietly, I heard him moaning. I thought he must have woken up and went quickly to see if he needed the toilet. I pushed the door open to find him moaning feverishly and thrashing from side to side in his bed. His movements were tense, spastic. I called out his name but he was still asleep.

With panic rising in me I tried to work out what to do. He was clearly in the throes of a vivid dream. I had seen these violent movements before. They were the same as the nightmares he had had at my mother's house. He was talking but I couldn't make out the words. He was terrified but he was still asleep. I put my hands on him and tried to talk soothingly to him. As before, I thought it would be even worse to wake him abruptly. I decided, though, that if he became any more distressed, then I would have to wake him; I couldn't stand to see him like this.

After a few minutes he suddenly calmed, his body went limp. He whimpered and then dropped into a deep sleep. Thank God it hadn't lasted this time.

I stayed with him for a while but he was through the worst and was now sleeping peacefully. Some time later I went to bed myself. Soon after I climbed under the covers I heard him moaning again. I leapt up and ran to his room to find him going through the same movements as before. Once again my heart was beating right up in my throat. It was agony to watch him fighting God knows what unseen demons and know there was nothing I could do to help him. If I woke him up they were only going to come back again the next time he fell asleep. I couldn't keep him awake for ever. I couldn't sleep for him. How I wished that I could! How I wished that I could confront the demons in his place, that he should be free of their torment.

I watched his tiny body thrash around, his limbs spastic and stiff with terror. Three and a half years old and his soul was battling with the worst horrors imaginable. Real horrors. Horrors that he couldn't wake up from and hear his daddy tell him weren't real; that it was all right; that monsters didn't exist. I shook with fury. Blind rage mixed with the excruciating pain that came from knowing there was nothing I could do but watch. I could only fight during the day, that was all the power I had. Then I could give him everything I could to make him strong, to help him cope. During the day I could tell myself that he was all right, that he wasn't suffering. But at night I couldn't lie to myself, I couldn't pretend. He was fighting it on his own and it was taking all the strength he had.

I watched with tears running down my face. I would gladly have killed whoever had done this to us a thousand times over, ripped them apart with my bare hands. It would have been a joy. I wouldn't have turned a hair. But even if I did, it wouldn't stop his nightmares. I would still be left to watch in complete helplessness, forced to acknowledge my complete impotence, complete humiliation. I had no power. I was capable of nothing.

He began to calm again. I tried to talk soothingly to him, tried to stroke him with hands that twitched and jerked and wanted only to tear the killer's flesh apart. Soon he was fast asleep once again. I stayed with him for a while but he was now calm.

At three o'clock the whole thing started again. Again there was no sign of him being awake. When he eventually calmed again I took him into my bed for the rest of the night. He was somehow conscious of the difference. Maybe it was the physical contact, maybe the cycle had come to its end. He moaned again from time to time but that was all.

'Do you remember what you dreamed about last night?' I asked him at breakfast the next morning.

'No,' he answered cheerfully, giving every impression of enjoying his breakfast.

'Are you sure you don't?' I asked as lightly as possible.

'I didn't have any dreams,' he said, dismissing the subject once and for all.

Alex's disturbed dreams became a regular occurrence over the next couple of months, although they grew less intense as time went on. I would listen every single night for any noise from his bedroom. It was impossible to relax completely. Often I would go rushing in to find that he had just turned over noisily and was wrestling to pull his duvet back over him. I was only ever completely relaxed when he was awake the next morning.

The room was flooded with sunshine. Only a few short weeks had gone by since moving in. The snow was long since forgotten. Sawdust hung in the air and not a breath of air moved through the open door. Alex played happily with the toys that he fished out of one box or another scattered across the floor. His big plastic building bricks were the favourite. 'Make me a Thunderbird Three,' he said.

I was continually required to make things to his specification. After which he would usually play happily with whatever it might be for hours at a time. However, Alex was a perfectionist. And quite tyrannical. If I didn't get his model exactly right then he would dissolve into floods of tears. But the problem was that sometimes by the time I had got it right, it had become so complicated that it would fall apart only moments after he started playing with it. He would come running to me, his face crumpled with tears, holding out the broken bits and would soon be screaming at me to fix it. But he wouldn't accept me making it simpler so that it would last longer. It had to be exactly the way he wanted.

This was the hardest part of Alex's behaviour to deal with. Since his mother's death he had developed a habit of creating no-win situations like these. Compromise had become something totally alien to him. He could listen to me read back a shopping list and would hear that we didn't have any grapes. We could have had a house full of other fruit but, once he had heard the word 'grapes' and the idea had entered his head, then he wanted grapes. He would go to pieces, and be unable to think about anything else until we went to the shops to get what he wanted or I had found some major distraction to take his mind off them. He was impossible. But the tears and upset were those of genuine disappointment rather than a tantrum thrown in an effort to get his own way just for the sake of it. He had lost all sense of proportion.

He was equally hard on himself. He would find a stick that looked like the tool for one of his toys. His face would be flooded with happiness at his lucky find. But when he got back to the house it would not do the job he hoped it would or, worse still, it would work on the first go, pleasing him enormously, and then break on the second. At moments like this he was inconsolable. It was hard to watch.

It was difficult to know the best way to react. On the face of it he was simply busy getting on with things and being as creative as any small child could be. But the difference was in his behaviour when whatever he was trying to make didn't live up to his expectations.

As time went on I found myself being less sympathetic. I would try and point out from the start how ambitious he was being, and explain that what he was trying to do was not going to work. When he ignored me anyway and burst into tears when my predictions came true, I would find myself shouting at him to make him snap out of it.

I was forced to do a lot of shouting. To my surprise and confusion it was more effective than my sympathy in bringing him round. But it caused me a lot of guilt. I didn't want to shout at him. Him of all people. I only wished I had Rachel to try and reason it out with instead of having to deal with it on my own.

A lot of shouting was done in public. He would often produce his worst behaviour in a crowded supermarket or in the street, pulling things off shelves or demanding I make him something while I had my hands full with something else. A quiet word of rebuke would bring no response. In fact a quiet telling-off would only inspire him to become even more unreasonable. He didn't think I was serious. He would just smile, and carry on being impossible until I bellowed in his ear and dragged him away from whatever he was destroying, or confiscated the pieces he wanted me to put together. Then he would start crying at the top of his voice and the spectacle would take on even greater proportions. But I could never have felt the same freedom in the UK to treat him as he needed to be treated. I would always have felt people had recognized us and were wondering how I could be so cruel to him.

I found myself having to be harder and harder on him as time went on. It was upsetting to me that he didn't respond to reason. He was intelligent enough to understand when I explained things to him but seemed driven to do the opposite just the same. I appreciated that his stubbornness was a strength that would serve him well later in life, but his reactions were still out of proportion to the situations themselves. Because of his unbalanced behaviour it was even more important that I didn't let him get away with the things he shouldn't.

I found myself pretending to be angry. Doing a lot of snapping at him that was pure pantomime. I had to deal with a lot of guilt, but it was effective. I had hated the way my father had been so hard on me, which made it doubly difficult to react appropriately to Alex. But I was coming to realize that it was the lack of interest and affection that I had been shown which had really been the problem. To have one without the other wasn't parental discipline, it was only a form of control. Its aim was to make a child do what the parent wanted while the parent got on with his or her own stuff. It made me wonder why some people chose to have children in the first place.

I had unhappy memories of my own childhood. In many ways I saw Alex as myself and me as my own father. On a certain level I was reliving my own past. I had lived alone with my father for half of my childhood and I had been miserable. I was so determined not to make the same mistakes he had that sometimes I would be impossibly self-critical.

I was trapped in a terrible situation. I had been determined that my child would never feel unloved or ignored or unappreciated. But now I found myself uniquely responsible for an unbalanced child. As I worked away at making our furniture I had to tell Alex for the first time ever that he had to wait, that I couldn't attend to him right then. Up until that moment he had always had my undivided attention. Before he had seen his mother killed Alex would not have felt unloved or ignored by being asked to play on his own for a while. The vast majority of times he would have done so quite happily. But now there was no one else to distract him even for a minute. He was totally dependent on me for entertainment.

I simply couldn't give him all my time all day long. Some things had to get done. I was often in turmoil, flooded with guilt and self-recrimination. I could see that I had a real problem, too. I couldn't send him away for more than a moment without feeling I was shunning him or abandoning him. I would constantly run through résumés of the day and work out how much time I had spent solely concentrating on him and what we had done together and how much affection I had shown him. In spite of what the child psychologist at the hospital had said, I was sure he needed this attention more than ever. Rachel had told me I was cold but I had learned during my time with her that I lacked the skills to be anything else. I had slowly been learning from her, observing how easily she showed physical affection, how she always made the effort with a smile or a touch to communicate with me or Alex how much she loved us. I could rarely remember being touched or cuddled or kissed as I grew up. I thought I did fairly well, considering. Apparently not. Apparently it had still been a major problem.

Rachel had no such difficulty. Only those problems with her self-confidence. Between us we were just beginning to unravel the knots tied tight within each other.

But the process had been cut short almost before it had begun. Now she wasn't there for me to talk things over with. I was left to tug at the knots alone.

Being so much alone with my child brought many things to the surface in me that I hadn't been completely aware of before. I started observing my own behaviour. I was fine as long as I was giving Alex my undivided attention. If my mind started to wander or if I wasn't being as creative or as interesting as I knew I could be, then Rachel's face would appear. Her expression would always be one of mild disappointment, with an ironic smile which was at the same time a gentle reprimand. 'You can do better than that,' her face would say.

But when I shouted at him I hated myself. I totally and absolutely detested myself. I was filled with self-loathing. I could hear my father.

I had so much hatred for him, more than I had ever realized, and hated any part of myself that resembled him. I began to feel almost schizophrenic: part of me was him. I began to see myself through Alex's eyes. I didn't like what I saw. I hated the bitter, angry face. I had to stop myself begging Alex for forgiveness out loud.

I was unbalanced myself.

But in spite of everything, in spite of all my awareness of the effects of how I had been treated in my childhood, my natural reflex was to get on with whatever I was doing first and to push Alex into second place.

If I was involved with something, cutting a piece of wood or working on something complex, and he came to me asking something, I would immediately snap and tell him to wait or send him away. But it wasn't my own natural reaction. It was my father's voice sending him away without even listening to what he had to say. I was programmed to do the same.

Often I would catch myself and call him back immediately. Now it was my voice as I asked him what he wanted and reasoned with him why he could or couldn't have it. Inside I had disgusted myself. I wanted to be free of these demons. How could I be so weak as to let them have the first say? How could I let this small child have to see they were there? I could see Rachel's face, shocked to see so much harshness in me, angry that I could speak to her child in such a way.

To Rachel there had been no confusion. She was there to give whatever her baby, her child, needed when he needed it. To her nothing was more important. Making a drawer or hoovering the floor or fixing a meal were all things that could be interrupted time and again to answer a question or fulfil a need. Her patience with him was boundless. I would often ask her, jokingly, why she wasn't the same with me.

As the weeks went by my turmoil grew stronger instead of weaker. Maybe it was because my voice echoed through the house in the same way that my father's had when I was a child, strengthening a sense of *déjà vu*. Maybe it was because the peace we found ourselves in gave me more time to dwell on questions that were impossible to resolve, and so deepened my depression. Maybe this was simply the way my psyche had chosen to signal the fact that it was running on overload.

I knew it didn't matter how long it took to make a drawer, he was only going to be a three-year-old once. I knew the questions he had to ask needed answers now, that the time would never be the same again. I knew I needed to look at him, to really see him, to cherish these moments now. That they could slip by and be missed so easily. How long did we ever have? If I didn't understand that concept then who could? But at the same time I was in real danger of repeating my father's mistakes. I was terrified by the amount of effort it took not to. Even though I 'knew' the right things to do I often had to force myself to do them.

I had to fight to ensure that the ghosts of my past did not succeed in stealing what was left of my future. They had had enough of my life already. I wasn't going to give them a piece of my son's as well.

'Il n'est pas à l'école?' The accent was thick but I was able to understand the question. No, he wasn't at school. The questioner clearly found it hard to understand why a child of his age shouldn't be. The school system was completely different in France. There was a free school place for French children from almost the moment a child was dry. The exact age varied from area to area and on the discretion of the school itself. At three and a half, however, there was a place for everyone.

After a few weeks we were taken to the village school for Alex to register. Because we had arrived in the middle of the year he would have to wait until September. I found it strange to see such small children in a formal school environment: none of them were more than five. The children were quiet when we entered the classroom to speak to their teacher, which I found strange as well. But as soon as they saw Alex they began to liven up. I could see by their bright expressions that they enjoyed being there, but there was no doubt that discipline was strict. More so than in an English school. The teacher, however, was charming and we were made to feel more than welcome.

To me it seemed they had a fantastic system. There was even a crèche which operated between eight and nine, and after school between five and six, as well as a canteen for lunch. I could never accept that leaving a small child from eight in the morning to six in the evening was the right thing, but having a system that operated this way gave a lot of flexibility. There was no obligation to leave them every day at this age. For a mother who wanted to return to work, or even for a single parent with no one else to rely on who might be unable to pick their child up at the usual time, it provided a tremendous amount of support.

It was obvious that people found it strange that a man should be alone all day with a small child. But we were out in the country. I hadn't expected the attitudes of people in a rural area to be the same as those in a major city. Here the men were men and the women stayed home to take care of the children.

We were told while we were visiting the school that, although they couldn't take him until after the summer, there was a nursery nearby which could. I wanted to make certain that Alex didn't miss out on school, but I wasn't keen to hurry him into anything that wasn't strictly necessary. For the moment I was happy to have him with me every day. I knew it wasn't going to last for ever.

We had plenty of visitors during the first weeks. They helped us to explore. We had already worked out some of the choicest places to walk but we were continually finding new ones, some of them surprisingly near to the house. There was so much that was stunningly beautiful: the sunsets, the colours in the distant mountains, the river valleys. At times the irony of it all was too much. Time and again I thought of the line from a Neil Young song: 'Live alone in a paradise/ That makes me think of two.'

I liked to be driving back towards the house as the sun was setting. Often we would return just as the last rays lit up the clouds stretching off into the distance. The sky was wide, there was a great impression of space. This together with the absolute quiet made me feel a thousand miles away from the dirt and the grime and ugliness of city life. I felt I could breathe. There was space between me and the next human being which I badly needed. The space was a balm to my exposed nerves.

It was hardly surprising that so many artists had been fascinated by the south of France. There is an intensity and a clarity of light, a light which is always changing, which often brought me to a standstill. At times there was nothing else to do but stop and take it all in. There were rabbits that froze in the beam of our headlights and owls that hooted and screeched in the night and glided silently across the courtyard on outstretched wings.

It was difficult to stop the pain, even with so much. Everything I saw I ached to share with Rachel to the point where the very beauty of it all was a torment in itself. There were no answers to the questions in my head, and no one to turn to who could help me understand any of it.

At times I wanted a big hand to come down and gently gather me up. It would tell me that everything was all right, that I could let go now, nothing bad was ever going to happen again, I didn't have to be afraid any more. But I was afraid. With a deep, dark, overpowering terror that gripped me by the throat and that I had to fight hard to prevent swallowing me up, taking my sanity with it. A force had come into my life and ripped it apart. Now I lived with the knowledge of that force. I knew it was there, just outside the edge. I knew what it could do. Just because it had come once didn't mean that it wouldn't come again. All of my puny mortal strength, all of my plans, all of my care, all the money in the world were nothing against its power. I lived in the knowledge of my own impotence and its all-powerfulness and I hated it. I loathed its twisted game. Each time I felt thankful for some small blessing I thought of what it had done, and what it could do again. I longed to find a way to spit in its face.

My mother and my brother drove out with Molly, our dog, a couple of weeks after we moved in. I was glad of the dog's company. Her presence made a big difference, especially once Alex was asleep and the house went quiet. I stood outside with her in the dark waiting for her to relieve herself and hoping that she wouldn't start the farm dogs barking. Their sudden howling always made me jump. No street lights brightened the night and in the dark the quiet had a sound all of its own.

In fact the night was far from silent. There was the sound of running water, the swish of a leaf. In the distance the almost imperceptible murmur of a generator in some corner of the buildings. Further still a truck rumbled through the night. I relied on the dog's ears to tell me that there was no one else about. My paranoia was ever-present. I wasn't sure exactly who or what might be out in the dark but Alex was asleep in his bed unprotected while I was out there. It was a relief to shut and bolt the solid door once we were safely back inside.

Sometimes at the beginning, before they were used to us, the farm dogs would begin to howl the moment I opened the door. Then Molly would bark madly too, making me jump straight up in the air. For a moment I would be thrown, not quite sure if she was barking at something she had heard, or just in response to the other dogs. But I knew inside that what I was experiencing was simply blind fear. I knew there was really nothing out there. But I did know that one day someone would come walking down that track to find us. And that from that moment on our sanctuary would be so no longer. It was inevitable that with all the means at their disposal, legal or otherwise, one newspaper or another would eventually work out where we were. And then, being the callous, mercenary and unfeeling scum that they were, they would think nothing of violating the illusion of safety I was working so hard to create around my child. Of course, they would be sure to apologize afterwards.

The smell of wood shavings filled the air, sawdust collected underfoot. The sun beat down on my back and the sound of the electric drill bounced off the courtyard walls. Alex sat on the steps, absorbed with the toy in his hand. There was no shade from the plane trees above my head: there were still only buds on the bare branches. The sky was blue and the whole of our surroundings filled with the deepest of colours. It was a strange contradiction – this warmth and summer sky, and the winter bareness of the trees and plants.

Our surroundings were spartan and utilitarian, shed doors thrown open and pieces of farm machinery scattered in all directions. The quiet was interrupted only by the occasional returning tractor and our voices echoed loud in my ears as they rang off the walls. I felt a little as if I had been institutionalized, as if I was in the spacious grounds of some mental hospital undergoing my occupational therapy. It wasn't so far from the truth. I had something which occupied me physically and challenged me mentally. I was in the fresh air, away from feelings of confinement, and I was, for the moment, cocooned from all that went on around us by the very fact of being a complete stranger. I felt a sense of achievement as the days went past. What I had pictured in my head was taking shape in front of my eyes.

I wasn't able to forget. But I could feel the time passing. My belief was still that the best way to cope with the grief was never to expect to feel any better. Only to wait and see how I actually did feel as the time went on. After Rachel had been killed I told myself that at least a year must pass before I could even start to look at myself. Now that more than half that year had passed I couldn't imagine there ever being any difference at all.

I marked the passing weeks by making a table, a stand for the television, another chest of drawers. The future was a bookcase or some shelves for the walls. We slept, ate, bathed. I hung the clothes out on the line. Alex's voice rang out high and clear with an endless string of questions which always began with the word 'why?'

Unpacking the boxes I came across an African statuette that had been given to me. It was a soapstone carving that represented a mother and child and had always been in the flat. I had grown to look upon it as a kind of fertility symbol since the moment that Rachel became pregnant. Much later she had knocked it off its shelf while clearing up. It had snapped in two, cleanly breaking the mother's body and severing the arms where the mother's and child's flowed into one. I thought nothing of it at the time and tried to glue it back together. I turned it over in my hands, my eyes running over the glue that filled the tiny crack which separated the two beings. They were so close together. But no part of them physically touched each other.

I lay awake in bed at night, the house echoing with silence. An owl's screech sounded outside my window and glided into the distance as I went over and over the same thoughts, the same emotions in my mind. I would go over what had happened to Rachel in the greatest detail. We had shared everything since the day we met but I hadn't even had the chance to say goodbye. The wound was tangible, physical. No one else could ever close it. Only time. Only time – and the months that had already passed could have been just seconds. It was quite true: time was totally subjective. A measure of how any one person's experience related to it did not exist.

I felt I could have easily lain there until the end of my life, lost in my thoughts of her, without the need for anything else. I would welcome my death when it came, I could not imagine feeling any fear of it. I had more on the other side than I did here. If we really were reincarnated again and again until we had learnt all the lessons, like the Buddhists said, then I wanted my lessons now. I didn't want to come back.

I would lie still for a long time, feeling my wounds. Sleep always overcame me in the end. The organism's determination for survival was stronger than my own depression.

Our friends were driving down to see us, eager to see how we were fending for ourselves. They were bringing the two youngest boys with them. The oldest were well able to look after themselves.

The day before they were due to arrive it began to rain. It was raining so hard that it almost brought the car to a complete halt on the main road. It was coming down so heavily that the dog refused to get down from the car to pee. The road became a river in a few minutes.

I had heard stories about the rain here, and had seen some of the damage it could do when we had visited at the end of the summer before. But still, coming from England, I didn't think I had much to learn about rain. I had been told that if there was a large puddle in the road it was best to drive round it. There was always a chance that the road had subsided and the puddle was hiding a huge hole. But now the road was completely under water. I pulled forward slowly, hoping we wouldn't disappear any minute. Meanwhile the rain was like a hosepipe being directed on to the windscreen at full blast: so much water was falling out of the sky.

They were due to arrive that day. The rain was falling off the gables, which kept it clear of the windows and walls. We were looking out from behind a waterfall. The noise was tremendous. It poured down all morning long. The vineyard behind the house was now a lake. There was no soil to be seen and the water was rushing off into the drainage channel between us and it. The level in the channel was rising fast, and where before there had only been a trickle a couple of inches deep, now the water was three-quarters of the way to the top. I began to wonder what would happen when it did get to the top and was glad there were two floors to the house.

Literally minutes before they arrived the rain stopped and the sun came out. The light was dazzling as it reflected off the water and the air was full of the sound of it gurgling. Steam rose from the puddles and the air was thick with humidity. The water continued to run off the vines behind the house solidly for the next two days but the courtyard soon showed no sign of the deluge. One of the books I had read before coming had said that the winter and the summer were dry and that all of the rain fell in a short space of time in the spring and the autumn. This year at least, discounting the snow, things were running true to form.

The children went wild over the next few days. This was real Huckleberry Finn country with riverbanks to explore, rocks to scramble over and the sea to jump into. The sea was only for the most hardy. It was still only Easter and the water was far from warm. Alex was thrilled to see his friends and to show them what was 'his'. We had spent so much time in their house, playing with their things, that it was good for him to feel he had something to offer of his own.

The days went fast and soon we were on our own again. I could almost hear the echoes of their voices laughing and playing. This was a place to share, but I could never give him a brother or a sister close to his age. With them gone there was quiet around us like there had never been before. When Alex and I stopped there was nothing moving. No other influence or conversation. Nothing for us to follow or be enchanted by. It was so lonely without her. But loneliness was always the wrong word. Loneliness was when you were on your own and wanted company. We didn't want company. We just wanted her.

When I ran everything through my head to try and work out how to make it better I always came to the same conclusion. There wasn't a way to make it better. We were in the best place we could be. Even being with our friends wasn't enough. It was wonderful for a while but they didn't fill the vacuum. Their presence only served to remind us of what we had lost. The ringing of their laughter drowned out the sound of another voice.

A few days later a helicopter buzzed over the house, spraying the vines. The ground was too waterlogged for tractors. Whether it was the season or because of the rain I wasn't sure but the vines, which were little more than bare sticks, were beginning to bud. Strung out in parallel lines across the countryside the buds quickly became baby leaves, which uncurled around each other, green and succulent, and the colour of the countryside, which had so recently been white with snow, began to change once more.

Chapter Twenty-five

IT WAS TIME to see about getting Alex into the nursery. France being France, there would be bureaucracy to overcome before he would be accepted. There followed trips to the doctor and to the town hall to obtain the relevant paperwork.

Once everything was in order Alex was duly accepted and it was explained to me how things were run. Already he didn't want to go, and the fact that he would be the oldest by nearly a year made it impossible to entice him with the promise of lots of exciting activities. What was going on in school was simply not very interesting compared with what he was used to.

He had started to cling to me as soon as we walked through the door on our preliminary visit. The mere fact that it looked boring would probably have caused resistance enough from him anyway, even without the language and culture barrier to overcome.

Our friendly dynamo had come with us to help with the arrangements. She was a doctor, which undoubtedly helped smooth things through. But it struck us both how the woman in charge, so used to dealing with mothers, found it difficult to direct her comments to me. She clearly found it alien to be discussing such things with a man.

I stayed the whole of the first morning. He remained attached to me the whole of the time. We were almost back to square one.

Really it was only a crèche. The children there ranged from babies up until only the age of three. When we arrived all the children were having a snack. I had packed Alex a yoghurt and he sat on my lap to eat it. He had grown accustomed to people saying in French: 'Hello, how are you, what is your name, how old are you, goodbye', and 'See you later', but he still showed a real resistance to speaking himself. I could see, however, the intensity of his concentration when people talked and I was in no doubt that he was storing it all away and beginning to work out which phrase went where. I often struggled with the heavy regional accent myself and could quite understand his difficulty in understanding these unaccustomed sounds.

The place was modern and immaculately clean; there was no problem with the facilities. There was a large garden and plenty of room for all the children to play. Once they had had their snack there was a session of songs and nursery rhymes with actions thrown in. Alex, with his love of stories, was transfixed by the performance. I was equally fascinated. It was one thing to learn a foreign language perfectly from afar but you would always be a foreigner if you didn't know all the little customs and habits and rhymes and ways of doing things which were universal to the children of that country. I only had to walk into Alex's old nursery in England for the sight of the small wooden desks and dusty smell of paints and the bulldog clips holding the paper on to the blackboards to put me right back into my own childhood. Once I saw the tiny furniture I could remember everything about milk monitors and cleaning the blackboard and what we had watched on TV and how we had played marbles in the playground and what sweets we ate after school and how they were wrapped and trying to look up all the girls' dresses and what football cards were being collected and falling over and smashing my knee, and so much more of all that had filled my world at that age.

It was fascinating to watch the things that made up these children's day and to try and spot the ones which were going to stick with them for ever. It was amusing to think that Alex would pick much of this up himself. He would have an empathy and a common understanding of French people as he grew up here that I could never have. When he was asleep and I tried to follow the comics on TV it struck me how much of the humour turned on a reference to some little childhood detail which made everybody fall about. Even if I could work out exactly what they were saying I still couldn't get the joke.

In the way of children everywhere, the little ones could approximately follow the tune, even if the words were often garbled. They knew all the hand actions though, and the pleasure they took was infectious. Even Alex was grinning broadly on my lap. As well as the older woman who ran the nursery, and who was wonderfully warm and friendly with all of the children, there were a couple of young helpers. There must have been a member of staff for every three or four children. But warm hearts could not make up for lack of inspiration.

One day they were painting. One child had covered most of his piece of paper with blue paint which he had applied in big broad strokes. He was just getting down from the table when one of the younger helpers called him back. 'C'est pas fini!' she exclaimed. It's not finished! I wondered at the insight she must possess to be so sure that whatever he had created was not exactly as it should be. The boy, who must have been about two and a half, climbed back up to his place and once more picked up his brush. I was fascinated to see which master strokes he would apply to finish the picture to the young girl's satisfaction. When she saw that he was ready to continue she pointed down to the bits of paper that were still white and had not yet been painted on. The boy industriously scrubbed on more blue paint until not the tiniest morsel of white paper remained. In so doing he obliterated any resemblance his picture might have had to whatever shape or form he had been trying to recreate.

Once this was achieved the young girl beamed at him in satisfaction and the boy was allowed to get down. 'Maintenant, c'est fini!' she smiled – Now it's finished!

My heart sank. The contrast with the quality of attention Alex had grown accustomed to at his last school in England could not have been greater.

Afterwards the children played outside in the garden. I was further dismayed to see that there was some serious rough stuff and outright fighting which would never have been tolerated at his old school. The children were clearly bored and understimulated. Already I didn't feel too wonderful about leaving him here. However, September was a long way off and, not only did I need to have some time to myself, but the sooner he started to pick up the vocabulary and understanding he needed the easier would be his entry into proper school later in the year.

I wasn't too concerned about the fighting: he was bigger and stronger than the rest and as long as they didn't gang up on him he would be all right. But I was worried about him being bored. Perhaps the fact that they were all younger than him would be an advantage. Their vocabulary and speech would be simpler and easier for him to follow. I had to force myself to look at the bright side.

I was suffering as I sat in the nursery garden. I was painfully aware that even if on the whole Alex might be better off by leaving England, it looked like his time at nursery was going to be worse than if we had stayed. I might be able to reason that in the greater scheme of things he was better off, but logic was one thing and emotion was another. The prospect of him suffering even the slightest extra unhappiness destroyed me.

On top of which I felt particularly out of place as a man in that environment. They couldn't help but make me feel unusual. I was struggling to choke back the tears and hoping that no one would look at me with too much sympathy. I could just about hold back as long as people remained matter-of-fact, but if they showed any real concern I was lost. Being there emphasized even more than ever how much this wasn't my place. This was Rachel's territory. She would have needed me to bounce her ideas off, but she would have decided whether or not he should go.

As I sat there all I could think about was that Rachel was dead, that we had been left behind, and that I had to cope on my own. That she wasn't with us and, when we went back to our new home, she wouldn't be there to greet us. We were alone, there was just the two of us. Our existence was empty.

As we were leaving I spoke for a few moments with the woman in charge. We were able to speak in French without Alex understanding. She asked me gently if Alex knew that his mother was dead. Her question provided the only relief of the day. It reminded me of exactly why we had come so far from home. No school in the UK would ever have needed to ask me. They would already have known enough from the media. I felt justified in having left. Here at least he really could be treated like everybody else.

He reacted as I knew he would the following morning. We had talked it all through and he knew that this time I wouldn't be staying with him. He had accepted this all fairly reasonably beforehand but he wasn't happy. He clung to me as I took him out of the car and carried him through the gate. He clung to me as we hung up his bag and his jumper. When it was time for me to put him down he began to wail. I had to prise him from me. It was hard not to think of how he had been prised from his mother's dead body only months before.

The staff were very sympathetic and did their best to entice him away. He knew I wasn't going to back down, no matter what he tried.

He and I had been through all this once before at his last school in England. If I backed down it was going to be even harder the next time I tried to leave him, for both of us. Better that there was no doubt. There was just the slightest edge in his crying which told me he was already resigned to his fate. It was best not to give him any false hope.

I still wanted to burst into tears myself as I returned up the garden path. He had flung himself against the glass as I left, his face distraught as they gently tried to pull him away. I knew that hanging around would just make their job harder so without looking back again I lengthened my stride until I was out of sight.

I told myself it wouldn't last, that he was just being true to his dramatic nature, but none the less here I was leaving my child, this child, after all that he had been through, in a strange place and in the hands of complete strangers who spoke a language that he didn't even understand.

I spent the morning at home by the phone. When it didn't ring in the first half an hour I knew that Alex had calmed down. Once he saw there was no point in continuing the performance he would turn his attention to finding out how to have a good time. But my stomach was in a knot right up until the moment I saw his expression again for myself and I understood completely why Rachel suffered so often from stomach upsets whenever she left him with anybody.

He was of course absolutely fine when I returned to pick him up. And I was told that his tears had only lasted a couple of minutes. He had amused himself quite happily for the rest of the time, but he had kept himself completely to himself and hadn't played with anyone else. This didn't surprise me: he was hard-headed and independent. Now I was there he was more than happy to show me the toys in the garden and appeared in no particular hurry to leave. The other children slowly drew nearer as Alex and I talked, some with their jaws hanging down. They were fascinated to hear these strange alien sounds coming from our mouths.

Of course he told me later that afternoon that he didn't want to go back. But his heart wasn't in it enough to make a real performance. The next day he even consented to hang up his bag himself. But then he cut off my escape to the door and, hanging from my legs, refused to let me leave. I had to fight him to get the door open and again he had to be restrained so I could leave. I don't think he really hated the place. It was just not what he really wanted.

I was surprised at times that he didn't hate me. In some ways I had been extremely hard on him. There were times when I screamed and shouted and smacked him and threw things around the house. But tiny though he was, he could be a real little sod. He was so often driven by the urge to be impossible. He could never take the easy option. If I said put on the blue shirt he wanted the green shirt. If I said come here he would walk the other way. If I said he could have one of something, he wanted two. If I said not to do something he would immediately do it and look at me while he did so to see what my reaction might be. At times I went completely berserk. Rachel never agreed with smacking children. She had infinite patience and was usually intuitive enough to come up with a method – putting him out of the room, putting his toy on the shelf – that avoided a confrontation. I tended to meet him head on. It was a mistake. I always lost.

He really didn't mind crying, or even getting smacked. What he liked most was pushing me to the point where I exploded. He enjoyed the attention. He understood the reasons I gave him: I explained everything to him, but when he was in that certain mood he wasn't going to stop there. He knew what was coming next, how I would react and there was no mistaking his satisfaction, almost smugness, when I finally snapped. Something in him needed this. Maybe something in the strength of my reactions was what he needed to feel secure.

I was a mess afterwards. I had a lot of hard lessons to learn about being a father and no one to go through them with. I was left to dwell on it all myself. I didn't want this for him. I didn't want him to grow up alone with an angry and bitter father. Not in a million years had I ever thought that history would repeat itself in this fashion. I had wanted brothers and sisters around me. I had wanted to be in the middle of something. Now I couldn't even give that much to my son. The bitter irony mixed with the pain of everything left me reeling sometimes. The madness of finding myself back where I had started. On reflection, I was always walking along the edge of suicide. But I loved him too much. My overwhelming sense of inadequacy would reduce me to tears in the face of the loving look in his eye when he talked to me sometimes. That and the shame of thinking myself capable of doing anything to make his life worse. He deserved so much more than this.

But instead of hating me Alex was becoming more and more

affectionate. If I hurt myself he would come running to kiss better the finger I had banged. He enjoyed lying all over me while he was watching the TV. He began to make me feel positively cherished. He had such an appetite for fun, and a turn of phrase and a logic which could bring a smile to my face even through the blackest moods.

At the end of the year before I had been using the idea of Father Christmas to try and motivate him to behave. Feeling more than slightly dishonest I had explained that he could see when all the little boys and girls were being good and when they were being bad. Alex was very concerned by the idea that those children caught being bad wouldn't get any presents. One evening he had done something he shouldn't have. 'Father Christmas wouldn't like that. He can see what you're up to!' I said.

Quick as a flash he replied: 'The curtains are closed!'

There were other instances of his logic.

Once I told him off for fighting. 'Don't let me see you hit him again!' I snapped.

'You didn't see me!' he replied.

Once I was clearing away the dishes from lunch and making him wait for his dessert.

'When can I have it?' he asked for the hundredth time.

'Later,' I replied for the hundredth time. My head span from his constant nagging. 'If you ask *one* more time again you won't get any!'

He stood there, beaming in anticipation of the ice-cream to come. Unable simply to wait and not risk losing out, he *had* to say something. 'When you've put that plate in, and that one, and shut the door and pressed the button, then I can have ice-cream, can't I?'

He always pushed me right up to the edge.

Paraphrasing something he had heard on TV one day when he was unhappy with the snack I had presented him with, he barked out in his best military accent: 'WHEN I ORDER HONEY AND TOAST I EXPECT HONEY AND TOAST!'

While eating a plate of strawberries he fished out the only mushy one, which he has been eyeing warily. He held out his hand, offered it to me and in his most enthusiastic voice said: 'This is the biggest, *biggest one* for you!'

'When you've got children you'll bring them to see me, won't you?' I said one day.

'No!'

'What! You'll still want to come and see me, won't you?'

'I'll *always* be living with you!'

To his grandfather he said: 'You look ugly without your glasses. Put them back on – There! You look more like my grandpa!'

He was dressed head to foot in Thunderbird costume complete with hat, yellow sash and green wellies. I said to him: 'You'll be bigger than me when you grow up.' Alex beamed with pride and said: 'Lucky my Thunderbird suit will still fit me!'

After dashing about the courtyard he said: 'I don't want to run now. My legs aren't runny any more.'

One day he delighted in pulling a big piece of dry skin off my back. Afterwards he spotted me putting on moisturizer. 'Don't put it on your back 'cos I like pulling the skin off. Molly's got fur and I've got to have *someone* to pull the skin off!'

'Ow!' he said, grabbing his knee. 'I've got pins and onions in my leg.'

There were plenty more. Many of them seemed so unforgettable at the time. Of course, I have forgotten them now and wish that I had scribbled them down somewhere. Nearly every parent could say the same.

In spite of the blackness, some light was creeping in. On the one hand was all the horror that we had been through and its repercussions that hung around us almost like a physical presence. On the other I found myself in the most beautiful and peaceful of surroundings in the company of a fun-seeking, wonderful little child. At times it was hard to make out which life was real. Or which one I fitted into. How could these two universes exist at one and the same time?

The furniture was finished, for the time being. Everything was finally out of boxes. The skies were blue, streaked only with the highest clouds. The sunshine dazzling as it reflected off the sandy soil and the pale stone walls. Lizards scampered away from our feet as we walked. The cicadas began to sing in the plane trees which lined the courtyard and the cedars that climbed the hill beyond. Everything was clear. We could see for miles.

We walked all around the countryside that surrounded us, limited only by the strength of Alex's growing legs. We set off in a different direction each time, always able to see the house above the vines. Some days we could see snow on the distant mountains. We sat and watched falcons hovering motionless overhead while I tried to explain to Alex how incredible it was that they should be able to do so. But he was a little too young to see anything as incredible. To him everything was accepted as 'normal'. Why shouldn't they be able to hover?

The bigger birds of prey however did manage to impress him. When a buzzard pushed off from a nearby tree and glided above us almost in touching distance, its shadow blocking out the sun as it passed, I wasn't the only one to feel my heart beat faster. As it glided majestically away Alex was left giggling with the thrill.

We saw red squirrels that we had never seen in England and I watched a toad as large as a dinner plate crawl across a red-dirt tennis court. Later Alex found a luminous green tree-frog and tadpoles in the water at the bottom of a drainage ditch. All this with the smell of rosemary and pine resin in the air and cherry trees in blossom rising up over the new green of the vine leaves. Once again the line went through my head: 'Live alone in a paradise/That makes me think of two . . .'

There was so much to make someone happy.

I wasn't. But I reasoned that being surrounded by beauty was better than being surrounded by ugliness. For me the greatest thing about being where we were was still the distance between me and the next human being. I had no tolerance left for people's stupidity, no resistance. I wanted to make the minimum of contact necessary for everyday life, and to pass a little time with the people who were kind, and then to leave it all behind, them all behind, and just be quiet. Apart from those closest to me, having to deal with other people was a distraction which stopped me from dealing properly with the pain. It was becoming clear to me that I really wasn't capable of very much. I had spent all my reserves in the months since Rachel's death, and more than anything, I needed to spend time recovering my strength.

There came a moment when I seemed to stop fighting the world. I had been busy being angry in so many directions at once that in some ways the fighting itself had kept me going. There had been one attack after another. There was suddenly the thinnest of buffers between me and the immediacy of it all: the investigation, the media, the disagreements within the family.

There was a turning point when Rachel's parents first came out to visit. They had been totally against me taking Alex away and things had been extremely tense between us. It was another nightmare, for all of us. A lot of anger and ill feeling had gone in both directions. I had no idea how it was all going to end. When they came however it was perfectly clear that they were going to make the best of the situation and give me as much support as they could.

I had contacted the police in England to let them know that Alex was still talking. I asked them what was the best way of recording the information so that it could be used later. They asked if they could come to visit us. It was out of the question. Our santuary was priceless. I said that we had a video camera and they asked if I would film our conversations and pass them the tape. I said I would do my best.

They also told me that the undercover operation discussed with me on the day of the inquest was well under way. A policewoman had replied to one of the adverts the suspect had placed in a contacts magazine. Her letter had been composed with the help of the criminal psychologist who had produced the offender profile right at the beginning of the investigation. Every move was being referred back to legal experts in the Crown Prosecution Service. The police wanted to ensure that every step they took was within the law.

The suspect had taken the bait and written back. The correspondence had continued and the letters had become more and more violent and deviant in their content, with detailed descriptions of specific sadistic sexual fantasies. The criminal psychologist was confident that their author fitted his original profile. According to him there was only a tiny percentage of the male population whose mind worked in this way; maybe only one in two or three million. His profile suggested that the killer would be a man who lived in the local area; he would have problems relating to other people in everyday situations, and he would be sexually inexperienced. His psychological problems would have begun in his early teens and were likely to come to a violent head in his late twenties.

The suspect lived alone on a nearby council estate with his dog and was by all accounts uncommunicative in the extreme. He was a virgin. He was in his late twenties, he had had family problems in his teens. The tone of his letters became increasingly violent as the correspondence went on. From what was known of the suspect it was hard to imagine the chances of two people with such similar psychological profiles being on the Common at the same time. The odds against it were enormous. The psychologist and police became more and more confident that this was their man. But there was still no material proof.

Studies suggested that when the victim was known to the assailant the wounds were inflicted upon the face and front. This was connected with the direct expression of anger. Apart from the wound in her hand all of Rachel's wounds had been inflicted from behind. It was almost beyond doubt that Rachel had been killed by a stranger.

Several witnesses had seen a man exactly fitting the suspect's description in the vicinity only minutes before Rachel was attacked.

Now several more letters had been exchanged between the police-woman and the suspect. There had even been a meeting in a busy London park where she had been wired for sound and undercover officers had waited close by, ready to jump to her defence. I felt extremely grateful to this courageous young woman who was putting her life in danger on our behalf. If this was the person they thought it was, it was impossible to exaggerate the risk she was running, no matter what measures were taken to protect her.

The policewoman wrote to tell him that she had been involved in some kind of pagan sacrifice. That she had taken part in a killing herself. The suspect had insinuated that he, too, had some dark and violent secret.

The police had been set rules by the Crown Prosecution Service for all conversations, whether written or verbal. Every word of these must be recorded in one way or another. They had been told not to encourage the suspect but only to follow his lead. And not to create a situation where the suspect would feel he was being promised sex in return for certain information. It was a fine line to walk.

I was told that as the suspect's conversations grew more violent there had appeared disturbing similarities between his fantasies and details of the attack on Rachel. On one occasion the suspect referred to the position in which Rachel's body was found, specifically the position of her hands. The police found this information extremely significant and, while not proof in itself (the suspect could claim to have simply guessed), they felt it showed more than ever that they were on the right track.

With every new step of their relationship it was the suspect who set the tone of their conversations. The policewoman would send back letters composed with the help of the criminal psychologist and written in the same kind of language the suspect had already used. When face to face, she would bring up the same subjects the suspect had referred to at their last meeting.

It was a vile job. Through the letters, the policewoman found herself caught up in a world of violent sexual fantasy. When I later read these letters, it was clear to me this world was inhabited by the sick and the depraved. I never met the policewoman but she must have had an enormous amount of composure and inner strength to do such a job. I knew that she was married and that she had the support of her husband in what she was doing. He must also have had real concerns for her safety. There had been talk of making her a fine chain-mail suit which could be worn under her clothing. But in reality, if she ever had been attacked, there was nothing that could have protected her except her own quick reactions.

The problem for the police was that they had a limited time before this artificial relationship showed itself to be just that. They would soon pass the point where the suspect would expect the relationship to move on to a more physical level. Already he wanted to take the policewoman on to the Common so that he could demonstrate his fantasies graphically. There was only a certain amount of time the policewoman could put him off before his frustration at her non-compliance would bring the usefulness of their relationship to an end.

The police were talking about the feasibility of protecting her if she were to go on to the Common with him. But there was no getting away from the fact that it was potentially too dangerous and, whatever the outcome, simply not worth risking someone's life for. In the end they decided against it.

To say that all this latest news filled me with optimism would hardly be accurate. Emotionally it had been very difficult all through the time that (. . . .) had fallen so heavily under suspicion. My moods had swung between hope, rage, disappointment and despair. But that, of course, had all come to nothing. Now, with this new suspect, I tried as hard as I could to listen clinically to the cold facts, and attempted to keep my emotions at a distance.

One afternoon in April I sat down with Alex at his little table. The video camera was turned on in the corner. He showed no hesitation in repeating all the information he had shared with me on the beach when we had first arrived. There were even some new details which he had never told me before and which went on to prove once again the accuracy of all his evidence so far. This time Alex described how, after the killer had left, he bent down to pick up a piece of paper which

354

had fallen to the ground during the attack. Alex had thought it was money and had placed it carefully on Rachel's face.

It turned out to be a receipt from a cash machine and the police, confused as to its significance, had kept this detail a secret even from me. As far as they were concerned it was another piece of the mystery, however tiny, which had been unravelled by the only person who could have known apart from the killer himself. But more importantly it was a piece of information that I could not have primed Alex to produce as I had no knowledge of its existence myself.

I prepared to fly back to London with Alex a few weeks later. The trip was principally to hand the original of the tape over to the police myself. I had already sent across a copy, which they had examined at length. They were extremely pleased with it. I left the house at five o'clock in the morning for the drive to the airport. Alex had hardly stirred during the transfer from his bed to the car. The world was ink-black and cold with only the light from the stars to see by. I witnessed a beautiful sunrise over the hills as I drove cross-country, but it gave me no pleasure. My heart was heavy. Out here the emptiness of the wild countryside helped to soothe the pain. Soon we would be back among the noise and the sights and the smells which would bring everything piling back on top of me.

I bought our tickets at the airport twenty minutes before the plane was due to take off. I didn't want our names on a passenger list. I had learnt that these were scrutinized daily by journalists looking for interesting arrivals. As we got off the plane in London I felt a weight descend upon me once more. It was as if we had never been away. As if the new life we had just begun to accustom ourselves to didn't exist. I even began to wonder if our house in France would still be there when we returned. The woman at passport control in London stared long and hard at my picture. 'Why do I know you?' she said. I took a deep breath. It was starting already. Alex was impatient to get going. What could I do? 'Oh, yes!' she said, evidently remembering. She handed me back our passports. 'Good luck,' she said kindly.

Back at our friends' house it was also as if we had never been away. But this time the effect was more positive. Without a second's hesitation Alex and the other children were once again playing their old games. I felt glad to be back on friendly territory myself even though, in less than a day, a journalist was sitting in his car outside the front

355

door again. At least this one was obvious; there could well have been others I didn't even realize were there.

I met two officers at my mother's house. They were happy with the way that the undercover operation had been progressing and were more convinced than ever that they had the right man. We got on to the issue of how Alex's evidence would be presented once the suspect was arrested and the case reached the courts. There was talk of video linking in which Alex would be connected live to the courtroom. I wanted to know whether Alex would be questioned directly by the defence barrister. They said that it was more likely that an independent voice, such as that of a court usher, would relay the question to Alex.

Their undercover operation had now virtually ground to a halt. Another woman had replied to one of the suspect's contact advertisements. She had said he sounded just the man she was looking for and she was willing to give him just what he wanted. Now that this newcomer had arrived on the scene, the suspect had let the policewoman drop.

We had arrived on a Thursday and planned to stay for a week. On the Friday the news was leaked at a press conference that Alex was in the country and that he had come up with new evidence. I was spitting mad once again. Why couldn't people keep their mouths shut until we were safely out of the country again?

On the Monday morning the front-page story of one of the tabloids was their exclusive interview with the police suspect. It was unbelievable timing! The journalists had got wind of attention that was being paid to this particular individual. But because they weren't aware of the extent of the secret operation that was going on they had walked right into the middle of everything and put the suspect completely on the defensive.

I was now in a complete state. I couldn't risk Alex catching a glimpse of a newspaper and seeing what could be the face of his mother's killer. I had no idea what damage that might do to him. Secondly I had promised the police not to let Alex see images of any suspects except in a controlled environment. I hadn't seen any myself, up until this moment.

I had no choice but to cut short our trip. I couldn't risk staying in the country any longer. There was something I had to get done that morning but we were in time for the evening flight. At the airport the man behind the desk told me that it would not be possible to alter my ticket, as I had bought it at the last minute. He told me that a single ticket was more expensive than a return so I was advised to buy a return, even though I couldn't use the other half. I was told that I would only be able to buy a club class ticket, which was about twice as expensive as a tourist class ticket. No reason was offered for this.

I assumed that the aggravation was because the plane was full, yet when we boarded we found only four or five passengers travelling with us. This confirmed what I already knew: the world was completely mad. The seating was identical all along the cabin but a curtain had been drawn behind the first few rows. I had paid almost twice as much as the usual price for the privilege of sitting in front of a curtain on an empty plane.

A thunderstorm raged in the darkness all around us as we flew south. The plane jolted through the turbulence. It reminded me of our descent towards Crete when we had all been together what seemed like many years before. That night the storm had been even more violent. We had watched the lightning through the cabin window as the plane shook around us. Alex had been asleep. Some of the passengers had become upset and Rachel had begun to get scared. But she had reassured herself with the knowledge that, if anything did happen, we would all go together.

Alex wasn't asleep this time. He watched the storm through the window, completely unfazed. He was so much older now, so much more mature. That trip to Crete had been half his lifetime ago.

The plane shook once again. The storm was getting worse. If we were actually going down this time then I wasn't about to argue. I had more to look forward to on the other side. As the plane buffeted about I could only smile. I felt relaxed. But somehow I knew that this wasn't our time.

The plane juddered and rolled on its final descent but the landing was perfectly smooth. Outside there was torrential rain. The doors opened and the unmistakably Mediterranean odours were carried in by the air. We were at a distance from the nightmare again. A weight was lifted from my shoulders. My relief intensified when the long drive was over and I discovered that our house, our refuge, was still standing. That it, at least, had not been an illusion.

It was the middle of the night by the time we arrived and I was surprised to find that the house was now positively hot inside. Summer was on its way.

Chapter Twenty-six

I HAD MY FIRST few swims in the sea. It was difficult, as Alex didn't want me out of his reach. Nursery was one thing but once he was back with me that was it, I was his. When we were out of the house we remained virtually attached. But I insisted on going for my swim. After all, I wasn't even out of his sight. But it is not easy to enjoy yourself with a small child standing on the shore crying and pleading with you to come back. He would not stop his wailing until I was back out of the water. Then, happy that he had got his way, he would turn his attention to the distractions which had earlier failed to entice him.

Alex's reaction to the new friends I was making was one of undisguised hostility. People in nearly every situation were much more friendly towards children than they are in England. Children are tolerated to a much greater degree. The family is all-important, especially so close to the Mediterranean. Virtually every adult we encountered, whether shopping or organizing insurance for the house or simply buying a loaf of bread, would offer him a 'bonjour' and a smile. Alex's reaction would be to pout moodily and hide behind my legs. 'Il fait la gueule?'* was a comment I rapidly became accustomed to.

If anyone we knew a little better offered him a sweet in return for repeating 's'il te plaît' then he would give them the filthiest of looks, cross his arms over his chest and turn in the opposite direction. I wasn't happy about the idea of offering a child a sweet in return for doing anything, but it was meant innocently enough.

I knew from experience that the worst way to try and get Alex to

---

* 'He's sulking?'

do anything was to ask him directly. I had found that the best way in fact was often to ask him to do the opposite. This usually worked a treat. He was so eager to be difficult that he wouldn't stop and think about whether he was being manipulated or not. It was like waving a red flag at a bull. 'You're not allowed in the garden' usually got him out the door in a flash. And 'You're not allowed back in the house under any circumstances' would usually get him back in again. As for French, he would be ready when he was ready. If I bullied him he would only resist. My attempts to encourage him to try a new word from time to time brought no reaction. He simply wouldn't do it. 'I can't!' he would wail if I insisted. So I left him alone.

It was very interesting to watch him with other children of his own age. Alex was now used to French being spoken by the other children but whenever he started to talk to me in English the other child would jolt upright in surprise, its eyes growing round with wonder. The child would invariably ask its parents for some kind of reassurance that this was normal. The parent would usually respond that he was a 'p'tit Anglais'. The child would accept this, though clearly having no idea what a 'petit Anglais' was, and turn back to examining Alex.

Alex would ask me to translate all that was being said but after a few encounters he began to know the routine. 'He doesn't know what I'm saying!' he would chortle, pleased to be the object of so much intrigue.

With the other two children who lived on the estate and with whom Alex played regularly the language barrier didn't seem to cause much of a problem. They were happy to push toy cars around in the dirt together and ride their bikes round the courtyard. The little boy and girl were both almost exactly the same age as Alex, which couldn't have worked out any better. The girl had an immediate crush on him and would jabber away at a thousand words a minute. When it was clear that he couldn't understand she would look at him indulgently as if he was just a little bit simple.

One day I noticed him singing like a baby in the back of the car. I asked myself what it was about the sound that so intrigued me. After a couple of minutes I realized that he was producing the kind of sounds he had made as a baby just before he had really learnt to speak. This time he wasn't rolling the basic English sounds around his mouth. Instead they were French sounds that he was trying out for size. It struck me that he was training his mouth to get the sounds right. It would have been totally true to his proud nature that when he did decide to make an effort to speak he would want it to be perfect first time. He didn't like being laughed at. This was his most detested punishment.

As time went on he began to say a few words. He tried to act as cool as possible when he used them, like it was no big deal, but he couldn't quite hold back his smile of pleasure at getting it right. I gave him loads of praise: 'See! You can do it!'

Progress was still slow but with every day that passed he was filing away more and more. It got to the point where I would be talking to someone in French and saying that we were going to do such and such tomorrow and Alex would then pipe up in English: 'I don't want to do that tomorrow!' I would have to learn another language if I wanted to keep secrets from him.

I made another observation when some English friends of friends visited. These were people Alex didn't know. He came immediately to me and spoke even less than usual. He watched them very carefully, obviously associating them with the ordeal that he had been through. He was happier with the French, although his relationship with the English people we knew well was not affected in any way.

The days were getting longer. All the vineyards were green. Red carpets of poppies appeared across the countryside. I was amazed how many wild flowers covered the ground in such a dry region. I only knew the names of a few. Every few weeks there seemed to be a change of colour, from white to purple to yellow to white again. And now the red of all these poppies mixed among the endless green of the vineyards. Rachel and I were going to get ourselves officially married when we finally sold our flat. She wanted to hold the ceremony in a field full of wild flowers in France, with a few guests and trestle tables loaded with simple food and wine. I could see her in my mind walking through the countryside around us, growing vegetables in her garden and wiping her brow under the hot sun. I knew how much she would have been fulfilled by a simple life with us. She knew how to be happy, how to appreciate what she had.

But the dark shadows in my mind told me that she would have been at risk even here. That she would have stood out in a small community with her striking looks. That something about her upright and confident appearance could bring out the worst in human nature anywhere. I asked myself for the thousandth time: how do you protect anyone? and came to the same painful conclusion. You can't. We all skim along, inches from the line, even those with the safest of lifestyles, and manage to avoid the falling slates and the electric shocks and the contagious diseases and the skidding juggernaut and the homicidal maniac without paying more than the slightest attention to how near to us the danger had passed. I had ridden my bike through high-speed blowouts, ice- and snow-covered roads, howling gales, had been knocked off in busy traffic, run down by a taxi, but still got up to tell the tale. If either of us were to die it should have been me. But I always got a second chance. Rachel found herself in the wrong place at the wrong time but for her there was no second chance. This as much as anything still sucked my breath away. I had never known her be in the slightest danger from anything before. Just once she got a little bit over the line – and it was all over. Why couldn't she have had a second chance?

I could never gaze out at the beauty around us without finding myself lost in questions that had no answer. The sun setting over the carpets of flowers only reminded me of our broken dreams.

I began to run while Alex was at nursery in the mornings. I had always kept myself fit and now it was time to put an end to a year of almost no physical exercise. From where I ran across the vineyards I could see the walls of his nursery. In the house I was always in reach of the telephone. It was some time before I was confident enough to venture far enough away to do the shopping.

I had started on my children's stories, I would do some drawings on the floor and Alex and I would talk through how the story would go. He would then colour in my drawings, usually completely effacing what was underneath. It was a joint effort and it was good for him to see something finished that he had taken part in himself. I read them to him at bedtime and I got a real kick out of it when he enjoyed what I had written. I tried not to feel too hurt when he showed no interest at all.

Sometimes during the day he would start laughing at something I had read out to him the night before. Often he would repeat the lines over and over again. This was beyond my expectations. But often he was laughing at a moment which I had not even considered funny, so I couldn't claim too much credit after all.

I tried to finish one story a month and Alex was always ready to jump up on my knee for the first reading. He was a very demanding audience and each detail that he didn't understand completely had to be minutely explained and the drawings referred to until he was satisfied. He was very serious and I often thought that he wasn't enjoying it, that I hadn't done as well as the last time. But if I asked him if he wanted to stop reading he would virtually always reply with a categorical 'no'.

Alex's imagination was the source of the stories we wrote. In working them right through to the end I marvelled at the ingenuity and the richness of that imagination. And at his recall of detail. He would often remind me that the name for one of the characters was the name that Rachel had given to the dog which had adopted us in Crete. He had been so small but he still remembered details of what that dog had done, what it had looked like and the colour of its puppies.

The undercover operation had come to a halt. The police felt that they had as much as they needed, and the criminal psychologist was concerned that Rachel's killer would be stimulated by the hot weather. If the suspect was the killer they didn't want to take any chances.

The police made their arrest. Immediately afterwards they carried out a minute forensic examination of the suspect's flat. The garden was dug up and the place completely taken apart. They didn't expect to find anything – the suspect had had many months to get rid of any trace of incriminating evidence – but there was always a faint hope that they might.

I felt no joy at the suspect's arrest. If this was the man who had slaughtered the woman of my life, the mother of my child, then at least now he was behind bars. At least now he was no longer walking around, free to do as he chose. At least he would start to suffer a little now. When the trial finally came around and if he was convicted for the rest of his life, maybe then I would experience some feeling of satisfaction. But for the moment the knowledge of his incarceration provided only the tiniest amount of comfort.

It was summer now. Almost overnight, trousers and jumpers had become a thing of the past. It was too hot to wear anything more than T-shirt and shorts. Alex's skinny little legs poked out of the bottom of his shorts and soon burned a deep shade of brown. He looked smaller out of bulky winter clothing. It appeared even more incongruous to hear such complicated speeches and theories coming out of such a tiny body. So much personality and force in such a little shell.

We passed a lot of afternoons at the beach, digging in the sand, playing in the water. Time which in other circumstances I would have considered ideal. It reassured me a little to see how many people around us really appreciated the surroundings they were lucky enough to find themselves in: the grandparents on the beach with their grandchildren; him in his vest and sun-hat, her under her parasol; the children playing contentedly at the water's edge. It was idyllic stuff. A plastic bag filled with mussels strategically placed under the shade of the parasol and a fresh baguette picked up on the way home. A drive through beautiful open countryside where you could see for miles and miles while the sunset flooded across the sky. It was hard to imagine better. Hard to imagine anything more inspiring. In other circumstances. It was hardly surprising that the French films I saw on TV in the evenings dwelt so often on memories of rural childhood.

At times the evening air turned heavy with thunder, a damp heaviness pressing down. Lightning flashed across the sky, making the house lights flicker or cutting the current completely. The dust was pushed down towards the ground making the air thick and abrasive to breathe. Then the rain would begin to fall in large droplets impregnated with dust while the thunder burst overhead.

One hill in the distance seemed to attract the lightning. From the window I could see it strike time and again. Sometimes it would only rain for a few minutes before stopping but the heaviness would hang all through the night only to roll away the next morning to leave the sky once more bright and clear, and the sunshine free to beat down once again.

The Crown Prosecution Service said that they would not take the case to trial unless I signed an undertaking to bring Alex back to the UK to give evidence. We were given some time to consider. They had confirmed that Alex would not be required in the courtroom itself, and that he would definitely not be cross-examined by the defence barrister on the video-link.

It was now early summer. The earliest date they were suggesting for the trial was the spring of the following year. With the chances of the trial being a lengthy one and because of the long summer recess I couldn't imagine it starting before September. September the following year. It was such a long way to go. So much time was going past.

But at least now there was now a definite point ahead of us where so much of the never-ending public attention would finally come to an end. After that point we would be left in peace to come to terms with Rachel's death in our own time. Everyone in the family began to talk in terms of 'after the trial'. In so many ways life had stopped with Rachel's killing. In many ways life was on hold until the trial was past and done with. The wounds would never really start to close until justice was seen to be done.

Until that time all our thoughts were dominated by the approach of this yet to be confirmed date on the calendar. We were waiting.

Our day began to turn around food. We were in the country of two-hour lunch breaks. The French, like most Mediterranean people, marked the middle of their working day with a decent break and a chance to unwind.

Alex was home from school at twelve, and by half-past almost the whole population was sitting down at a table somewhere. It was as if the entire country had come to a halt. The immediate benefit was that we had time to work on Alex's reading at a time when he was still receptive. By the evening he was far too tired to concentrate.

So at midday I too would find myself pouring olive oil into a pan and chopping onions and garlic and sprinkling herbs. It was a shame that nearly everything I cooked had to end up puréed in order to get Alex to eat it. He would eat just about anything as long as it didn't look like what it was. 'I don't like that!' he would say if ever a piece of red pepper or mushroom was not completely unidentifiable, even though he had been eating them since he was a baby. He was very limited in what he would eat willingly and a vegetarian child would not go far on pasta and chips. Soon fed up with the few basic sauces he limited me to, I found myself searching through Rachel's old recipe books for ideas.

I was soon soaking beans and mixing veggie-burgers in an effort to find something to tempt him with that would actually do him good. For a while I tried to offer him a new recipe a week. The problem was that he didn't like anything. Everything was an effort. At times, in a classic battle of wills, I screamed and shouted at him to eat what was

364

on his plate. Some meals ended up on the floor. Some meals were finished alone in his room. Only the dog did well.

I found myself going through cycles of enthusiastically trying new things and never giving the same thing twice in a week and then, worn down by his complete lack of co-operation, it would be back to pasta and potatoes and more pasta. These were about the only things that he would eat at normal speed. Everything else was turned over and examined minutely, then nibbled by the tiniest fork-load. Lunchtime took for ever. It would end with my patience and my temper shredded. Eating at any one else's house was even worse. Nothing was ever right. And if I wasn't in the most determined of moods or simply fed up with shouting at him, bread and ice-cream was about all that would be consumed.

But once the eating was past he would emerge from the deepest of sulks with the brightest of smiles. All unpleasantness was immediately forgotten and the search for fun began. It was like a rainbow after a stormy sky and was in many ways so like his mother. She too would go from the darkest of moods to the brightest of high spirits with hardly anything in between. She had kept me on my toes, and now her child was doing the same.

The 15th of July. One year on.

It was a false anniversary in many ways. Every day was an anniversary of Rachel's death. Every day all the events that had taken place went through my head. A million years had gone by in one. A million years since I held her in my arms, smelt her skin, heard her voice speak my name or her laughter fill the space around me. A million years that Alex and I had been on our own.

Sometimes, no matter how hard I tried to force my powers of recall, I couldn't remember what she felt like. It was like she had never been there. I would be filled with anger and frustration and self-recrimination. How could I forget? How could I be so disloyal? At other moments I could see her standing in front of me, talking with me, in such detail that it was all I could do not to reach out my hand and try to touch her.

The strongest feeling I had was disbelief. It was still so hard to accept that such a barbaric thing had happened. And so hard to accept that someone can be with you, their presence so enormous, right up until one particular second and then they are gone. Death was unknowable.

365

It was beyond my capacity to understand. I found myself looking into the eyes of our dog only to realise that I knew no more about anything than she did. I was only a dumb beast. I had the computer and the dishwasher and the motor car but I didn't understand the simplest and most universal process that happened to all of us. I didn't have a clue. I would find myself in a crowd of people and want to laugh out loud. They were all going to die! Look at them – so smug! Absorbed in chasing God knows what rainbow. Not one of them knew what they had coming to them. Not the smartest person in the world. Just dumb animals, the lot of us.

A thousand times a day I would look at her child, begin to ask myself the same questions all over again and give up before the sentences had even formed in my head. He was so beautiful. I would have loved him just as much even if he weren't. But he was beautiful. And innocent. If we were all still together I suppose I would have accepted someone commenting on how lucky we were to have such a beautiful child, how lucky I was to have such a beautiful wife. But then again, probably not. Those kind of comments had always grated on me. What did it count for anyway? Luck has nothing to do with how much happiness you may or may not be entitled to.

He had her teeth. The gap was more apparent between the front ones. His lips were hers, her smile. His legs were sprouting downwards while his head pushed ever up. His shape was no longer mine. He would have her long legs, not my square build.

Every time I ruffled his hair or took him in my arms and held him I felt so inadequate. He should have been getting so much more than this, so much more than just me. There was so much I couldn't give him. At the same time I knew that he didn't know just how much. I'm sure he knew a bit: I saw how much he enjoyed the company of the women he knew well, how affectionate he was with them. Just the most superficial of comparisons showed the differences. They were soft and cuddly. I was all corners and bristle and gruff voice. But I was his and he knew that. He came from me. I would have given my eyes, my legs to give her back to him.

I would ask myself why I was being punished. Why had she been taken away from us? Why did I have to watch my child suffer? I would ask myself what I had done wrong in this lifetime or any other to merit this. But it wasn't the answer. What had Alex done? What had Rachel done? What had her parents and her family done? How could we all be implicated together and tried by some all-seeing force in any way that made this right?

And hadn't I seen the children crawling across the rubbish dumps in India, destined to a life of never-ending squalor and discomfort and misery? Didn't I know about the millions of people starving to death across the planet? The parents condemned to watch their children waste away before their eyes. The victims of war. In my self-pity I was in danger of falling for the illusion. Happiness was no universal reality. No one's was guaranteed.

I was told that the anniversary had been reported on the evening news. One of the programmes had run some footage of the home video which I had been asked for by the police in the first few days after Rachel was killed. I had given it to them to help to jog the minds of potential witnesses. As far as I was aware, the video was still my property. I certainly hadn't signed anything to the contrary when I gave it to them. Now that their suspect was in jail awaiting trail it had served its purpose. I found it deeply upsetting that it should be used now without anyone even showing the courtesy to ask my permission. And for the sake of mere entertainment.

But to make the upset a thousand times worse the film had been left to run past the section which concentrated on Rachel, which had been shown before. It continued while the camera swung round to Alex and he ran towards the camera. His face filled the screen in giant close-up.

Weren't they ever going to stop? They broke all the rules all the time. They weren't allowed to do that! Their rules said uncategorically that they couldn't do that! Today of all days, all they did was cause us more and more pain. The frustration was unbearable. And of course they would have their pathetic letter of excuse the following day when Rachel's father complained on the family's behalf. But once again the damage had been done. If only they had to take responsibility personally for the 'mistakes' they made. If only they were liable for damages for the harm that their 'work' produced.

I went to bed that night feeling tormented beyond belief. I didn't want to feel sorry for myself, I was sick of talking to all my friends about myself, but the torment just wouldn't stop. If I didn't talk to them, I would explode completely. But all they heard from me was my rage and frustration and misery. That thought alone was almost enough to push me off the edge.

The last Thursday in July. Four years before I had awoken to a morning like any other, little suspecting how much my life was to change before that day was through. The journey from then until now seemed more than a life time. But still I could remember the flowers embroidered on the top Rachel wore and the feel of my old jacket, the pull of my mother's dog on the lead and the lights reflecting in the river that evening as I rocked on a pontoon, shoulder to shoulder with the woman of my dreams.

The joy of those moments I felt as acutely as the pain of her death. I spent the day reeling between the two.

During the first week in August a senior Scotland Yard detective flew out to meet me. I had a long drive to the airport and luckily some friends from England were there to look after Alex while I was gone. The detective had always struck me as someone who got on with his job quietly and with the minimum of drama. I appreciated his manner, and there was no hiding the fact that like so many he took Rachel's murder personally. There was no way I could imagine him or his team making any more effort than they already had to convict Rachel's killer. He had flown out expressly for me to sign the papers the Crown Prosecution Service had supplied. This was my undertaking to bring Alex back to the UK to give evidence.

I met the detective in the airport building. Most of the passengers on his flight had already gone. He carried only a briefcase, as he was going back that afternoon. I showed him to the car and we drove off to find a quiet place to talk. He said it was like being in a spy film. On reflection he was right: meet man in airport lounge with black briefcase, give password and drive to secret location.

We sat on a shady bench by a canal and he brought me up to date with the latest events.

He was not relaxed. The French being as sports-mad as they were, there were plenty of people out for their lunchtime run. Each time someone came past he stopped talking. I was sure we hadn't been followed from the airport and after a while I pointed out that the likelihood of anyone going past who spoke perfect English were extremely slim. They couldn't have given a damn anyway. We were nothing to do with their universe.

He was convinced that they had their man. He was at pains to explain to me, however, that he could not guarantee conviction. He told me that juries were hard to predict and that they sometimes did strange things. Rachel's father had explained to me that they had been told the same thing. We assumed that this was just professional caution. But that was not what I wanted to hear. I wanted to hear that from now on everything was going to be a formality.

He said that Alex's evidence would be vital. Once again he assured me that Alex would be far away from the courtroom, that he could testify from any part of British territory. He said that he was certain that if, when the moment came, Alex could answer as he had done before that the killer wore a white shirt, blue trousers and dark shoes and that he carried a black bag then the jury would be convinced. If he could answer only that much then we should be home and dry. If he didn't say anything then we would all have done our best. Nobody wanted to put any pressure on him. Nobody wanted to cause him any more distress.

I sat there thinking as he talked. What if Alex couldn't say anything when the time came? What if he was too intimidated? How would he cope with the guilt later if things went wrong because of it? How much would he feel personally responsible? If all went well, then fine. Hadn't we spent so much time conditioning him to feel good about making his contribution? I wasn't decided. I wasn't sure. There was still so much to weigh up. I wondered if the detective's caution over the final outcome was a way of motivating me just that little bit more to bring Alex to give evidence.

But there was still time: the trial was still a long way off. If I didn't sign the papers then this 'suspect' would be walking the streets again. If I did sign then he would stay where he was. And at least the wheels would continue to roll. I signed. Soon after, I dropped the man with the black briefcase off to catch his return flight home.

I drove back to Alex with my head full of visions of the trial. I wanted to get on with it. I wanted it over with. I wanted the hurdles overcome and the verdict read out. I couldn't see anything beyond that point but I wanted to get there as soon as we possibly could. And there was still more than a year to wait.

Chapter Twenty-seven

AUGUST WAS AN incredibly busy time. It seemed to me that summer had already gone on for ever. The locals were complaining about what a lousy summer it had been. I thought it had been wonderful. We had been able to get outside every single day for months already. But they were complaining because a lot of days had been cloudy. And if it wasn't the clouds then they were complaining about the wind.

The local weather was greatly affected by the wind. I had once seen a plaque high on a hillside which at first glanced looked like a sundial. On it were marked seventeen different directions and each one had the name of a wind. There were nearby parts of the countryside where the trees were stunted and bent to one side by a local wind which blew for more than three hundred days in the year.

But the dominant wind meant clear skies and sunshine. Sometimes it blew the sand in our faces, but we could live with it.

The locals were equal to the English in their obsession with the weather, perhaps even more obsessed. Maybe because it could change so dramatically and violently. After the first 'Ça va?' the next comment would almost invariably concern the weather. There would be a gaze up at the sky and a knowing word or two of what to expect for the day to come. With the local economy having been dependent on grape cultivation for the last two thousand years, I suppose so much concern was only natural.

We had friends visiting from England who were staying nearby and there were daily trips to the beach. Alex, already a healthy colour as a result of my father's African blood, had turned almost black. We visited new friends and Alex had other children to play with. I tried to let myself go with the flow of it and give the impression of having a good time. Our everyday condition could have been a lot worse.

It was Alex's birthday. We had spent the morning together playing with his pirate ship while the temperature rose outside. Inside, the house was already hot and the stone floors only gave the slightest relief underfoot. I almost felt that I had been doing this for ever, that our life with Rachel had never existed. Rachel had had two birthdays with him. We had had two without her. It hardly seemed possible. He was thrilled with his presents and there was no denying the fact that he was genuinely happy as he played. I had to put on my best smile although my heart felt like lead.

He was so much more grown up than the year before. His legs were so much longer and the roundness and babyishness were nearly gone. At four years old he was a real little man. The bruises under his eyes had finally gone and the whole expression of his face and the way he held himself had changed. He was opening out. Slowly. Since we had been here he had started to unfold. When he was alone with me I could see just how much of the fear and the physical tension had melted away. In the presence of others they were still very noticeable. But on our own that morning I could see the change. Whatever happened from here on in the move to France had served its purpose. The thought gave me a little comfort.

Alex now understood a great deal of what was being said around him. He was able to guess quite well the sense of what had been said even if many of the individual words escaped him. When he was with other children, and when he thought I was out of earshot, I could hear him trying out a phrase or two for size. I was so proud. His accent was perfect, which of course it should have been as he was hearing the real thing every day. It was an enormous relief. It still bothered me deeply that he might be suffering because of the language barrier.

A turning point came when he decided he preferred to watch the cartoons in French on the TV as he ate his breakfast instead of his own videos in English. I was thrilled. He watched them without fail all the way through the summer. He couldn't have understood much of what was said even if he did follow what was going on. I found it difficult myself when I couldn't see people's lips moving, so cartoons were a nightmare.

Children had a vocabulary of their own, which took us both time to learn. And they were more demanding if you didn't get it right. As time went by I found it much more of an achievement to be able to hold a conversation with a small child than with an adult.

The last part of August turned cold. The sky was suddenly grey and covered in cloud. Winter had appeared early. It rained from time to time and the pattern continued into the beginning of September. It was raining on the first day of school. I had been playing down the significance of the big day, but it was now that the language question would really come into play. Nursery had been closed for August and I hadn't bothered to put him back in for the few days of September before real school began.

By now Alex knew a handful of children who would be in school with him. They would all be in class together. As was the custom I accompanied him to school and helped him hang up his bag and coat. He gave me a hug and a kiss outside his classroom and surprisingly enough went off without the slightest word of complaint. I had decided to leave him only for the mornings for the first term. I felt that if he stayed all day not understanding much then he would get bored and that might put him off completely. All-day attendance wasn't compulsory until he was six.

I picked him up at lunchtime and presented him with a new raincoat. (You had to go to the classroom door. The teacher had to see you before the child was allowed to leave, which I thought was a very intelligent system.) But now the rain had disappeared. The sun was beating down and it was summer again. From his smile I knew he had had a good time.

'What did you do this morning?' I asked.

'Nothing.'

'How was it?'

'Fine.'

Much more than that I had to guess. The rest of the week was almost anticlimactic. He was as happy to go off each morning as if he had done so all his life. Sometimes he would even leave me waiting outside the classroom door while he finished off whatever he was busy with. So much for my worrying that he would be bored.

Once more a new pattern began. He was at school every morning except Wednesdays, when there was no school, and three Saturday mornings out of four. I had some time to myself again, although I was always watching the clock. I became a busy little house-person, gauging the success of my day by the tasks I had ticked off my mental list. Clothes washed and hung out to dry, dishes stacked, beds made, floors swept and hoovered, bath cleaned and, most importantly, lunch prepared. I had started playing tennis again and, together with taking the dog for a run, my time was quickly used up. One trip to the hypermarket and the time it took to unpack all the shopping and it was time to pick him up again.

Alex would be ravenously hungry whenever I picked him up and I tried always to have something in the car to offer him even though it was only a few minutes to the house. Otherwise he was unbearably grumpy. On reaching the car he would dig out a tightly folded piece of paper from the bottom of a pocket and hand it to me. This would be the drawing that he had done that morning. He was always deeply satisfied with the quality of his work and had no doubt whatsoever that I would be in agreement with him. There was no denying his strong vein of self-confidence.

We had got to the stage where we knew where everything was that we needed and the days were becoming easy to fill. We settled into a quiet pattern. Time was passing.

Just over the horizon, was the trial. But there was still a year to wait. Until that time there was nothing to do but try to get through each day as it came. Nothing to do but wait.

I tried to content myself with the thought that Alex was now firmly set in a pattern which would bring him almost daily progress. I was managing to finish my children's stories every month, which was an achievement in itself. I tried to tell myself that just to continue as we were was going to bring us to next September the quickest way possible. I told myself to forget about it. But I couldn't.

I did the sums in my head many times a day. I tried to assess how much time we had if we continued living quietly as we were. Our expenditure was at a minimum, I fixed the car myself when I could, we didn't need much heating in the winter, I didn't smoke or go out. Apart from rent, food and electricity we had very little expenses. I told myself that the most important thing was to get through the next year. Alex would then be that much older, that much stronger in himself and that much more adaptable; if I had to spend more time away from him in order to work then at least he would be that much more able to cope. We could hold out for at least that long so I had to try not to worry about things until then. But it was easier said than done.

I had said the same to myself in the weeks after Rachel died. That this first year was going to be the most important year of Alex's life. It didn't matter what amount of compensation he might get when he was eighteen. No amount of money would be able to compensate for his ruined life if he was left permanently disturbed. What he needed more than anything in the world was his father with him for as much of the time as was humanly possible.

It wasn't that I personally would be the remedy to his problems. It wasn't my personality or any abilities or understanding I might or might not have. It was purely and simply that I was the most important organic link he had with any other human being. Someone else's understanding or sympathy might have been a hundred times greater than mine, but I understood beyond a shadow of a doubt that that didn't matter. It didn't matter that I might be completely miserable. It didn't even matter that I might be shouting at him. Taking myself away even for a moment because I didn't want my mood to make him feel worse would have been the worst thing possible. He needed to know that he was still joined to someone. And that someone would always be there, always love him regardless of anything else in the world.

And I began to understand something else clearly too. He would never owe me anything. He had a right to me, to the best that I could give him. I had the right to nothing. As a parent I had to earn everything. I didn't have the right that he should even like me once he was grown up, let alone love me. My role was to give without expecting anything back.

Alex still wouldn't speak French at school. His teacher told me that he showed every sign of understanding but he would hardly say a word. She complained that she couldn't get through to him. I was hardly surprised. Alex already had a lot going on in his life and his teacher didn't as yet have the same references. He might not have been talking but it was clear he was having a good time. If not I would have had to drag him there screaming and kicking each morning. Instead he skipped off perfectly happily, eager to see what the day would bring.

He had been watching French television for a while but he hadn't as yet been hooked by anything in particular. Nothing like the way he was hooked on Thunderbirds. He had the suit, he had all the machines, he was dreaming of Tracey Island for Christmas and drew Thunderbird drawings at school for me. When he was into a thing he was into it in a big way. His teacher would have a tough time finding anything interesting enough to drag his attention away from what it was already happily focused on. I let her remark go over my head.

A few weeks had gone by and I was waiting for Alex outside the classroom when she announced glibly, 'There is too much black in what Alexander draws for me. It worries me. And he still has a problem in communicating. I want to refer him to the school's psychiatrist. Could you give me the details of your doctor?'

I felt our world spinning upside down once again and everything that I had been trying to build up come crashing down around me. The familiar sickness returned to my stomach. Was there to be no peace, even for five minutes?

I kept my mouth clamped shut but inside I was reeling. I said the minimum in the teacher's presence as Alex came out to meet me. I waited until we were inside the car to swear out loud. The school knew nothing of our past, as far as I was aware. All they knew was that Alex's mother was dead. In their eyes they were simply being conscientious. In my eyes it was a potential disaster. The last thing I wanted was him in the hands of some strange psychiatrist, most of all without my presence. I would rather take him out of the school completely.

When I was calm enough to analyse the situation a little better I could see how the issue had come about. As well as Thunderbirds Alex was now into Captain Scarlet. His drawings often contained the two circles of the Mysterons eyes. But the potato-shape figure accompanying them was harder to make out. There was no neck or recognizable head and the legs were two spindly lines coming out in any direction. But if the potato shape was red then it was Captain Scarlet. If it was black then it was Captain Black. And as Captain Black was the main villain, he featured in a lot of the drawings, often on his own. And with Alex if Captain Black had to be black then he had to be very black. Hence the black pen and the black drawings. Hence the mysterious black figure that featured so much in his thoughts.

I could see it from her point of view as well and I had the distinct impression that my explanation would not be satisfactory. As for him having trouble communicating, he had only been in a French school for a matter of weeks. And then only half a day and with two weeks' holiday at half-term. If he had already been conversing fluently in French his teacher would have been a genius. If he was reluctant to try to speak it was because he was proud. He didn't want to make a fool of himself in front of the other children. He would speak when he was sure he had it perfect. That was the way he worked.

I phoned our friend the doctor and told her what had happened. I was furious at nobody in particular, only with the situation itself. I told her that I saw no choice but to take Alex out of the school if his teacher went ahead with her plan. It was the last thing I wanted to do, because I could see that he was making great progress. She did her best to calm me down and assured me that she would speak to his teacher. She said there was no need to panic.

The subject wasn't mentioned again and over the next few days I went out of my way to avoid any conversation with his teacher when I picked him up from school. In fact soon after he contracted a bug that was doing the rounds, and was at home sick. He had started by throwing up in the car. His temperature shot up that night. I knew the scenario by now and was prepared for all that came with it. I knew it wouldn't be pleasant but I expected him to be back on his feet in a couple of days.

This time he wasn't able to shake it off so easily. I had never seen him ill for so long. I was used to two days of drama, and then a third day with him jumping around the house and bouncing off the walls when he was recovering.

The nightmares started again. They were less intense, but I had still had to take him into my bed for the whole of the first two nights. He slept longer between disturbed periods and, as I helplessly watched him fighting his demons once again, his body had been less rigid with fear, his limbs less spastic. I didn't know whether he was becoming accustomed to the apparitions or whether they were really losing some of their power to terrify. But I had taken him into my bed straight away this time. Maybe this had helped to reassure him, even in the depths of his sleep. I just didn't know. Once again I found myself trapped on the outside, powerless to intervene. The apparent lessening of the intensity of his nightly ordeal was my only relief.

But the days turned into a week and he was still showing no sign of bouncing back. We were due to go to the mountains and I was on the point of cancelling the trip. But the mountain air was supposed to be a tonic, so with Alex still feeling really poorly we set off anyway. Luckily he slept all the way up the winding roads and the journey didn't cause him too much discomfort.

I had promised Alex I would take him skiing. We had the mountains virtually on our doorstep and the out-of-season low prices to tempt us. I had only skied once so it seemed an ideal opportunity to try again. He looked like a little garden gnome in all his clothing. The big boots and the skis made him appear smaller than ever. He managed to keep going the whole of the first day despite his tiredness. He looked so sweet in all his gear, and at four years old was probably the youngest child on the mountain. I could hardly look at him. When he was sick or when he was being a complete pain in many ways it was fairly easy to keep going. There was always something to be taken care of. But there on the ski slope I stood back and watched a small child being completely adorable. It should have been a moment to cherish. Instead it was one of complete heartache. These were the moments his mother had been denied.

As I stood and watched him I could feel the violence with which all this had been ripped away from her. There was no way to turn to make the discomfort any less, no place to put the pain I felt. No way of finding any understanding of what had happened. I stood looking out at clean, white snow and picture-postcard peaks as far as the eye could see. Pure and clean and peaceful. The very opposite of the horror and the violence he had survived. There was no way I would ever understand.

I had thought that on top of his illness the exercise would have knocked him out completely. But it was the exact reverse. He got stronger every day. He was running round the restaurant at night while I was falling asleep over my plate. I had to sleep eleven hours a night just to keep up with him. He was soon whizzing down the slopes and weaving in and out of the classes ahead. I was having nightmares of him shooting down the steepest of slopes and disappearing off the edge and out of sight. He was going so fast that Rachel would have had a fit. I wondered if I wasn't being totally irresponsible. But after the first couple of days he hardly ever fell. I was the one who fell in an effort to keep up with him. With his bobble hat and dark glasses he looked like a demented toy in a Duracell advert who kept on going, on and on and on . . .

Alex wanted to make a snowman all week. When a moment came to prise him off his skis he decided that he wanted it to look like Mummy. With a huge smile on his face he trudged off beside me to find a good spot. It was hard not to let my agony show. He didn't stop smiling the whole time that we piled up the snow. It was going to be

Mummy and he wanted to make sure that we would have something for the eyes and the mouth and the nose. Rachel had always said her nose was like a ski slope: the irony was crushing.

By the time we had finished, the snowman was nearly as big as him. He was thrilled. I could find no way to share his joy. It was hard to make my smile reach as far as my eyes. I made the effort because I knew that's what he needed to see. In a moment of weakness I wondered what Rachel would have been going through if our roles had been reversed.

From the moment we returned home Alex's behaviour changed radically. This was soon remarked upon by virtually everyone we knew. The skiing and the time spent at altitude meant that physically he was in great shape. He was bursting with energy and cheerfulness.

At the end of the first week back his teacher remarked to me, with the widest of smiles, that getting him to talk was no longer a problem. Now he talked to her all day. So much so that, when he left, her ears were ringing. His first complete sentence came out of the blue when she had told her colleague that she was going to check on the toilets. 'Hurry up and do a wee, then you can come back and look after me!' he had piped up in faultless French, with perfect local accent.

Instead of hiding behind my legs Alex was almost running up to people to say hello and to talk about what he was up to. At the tennis club where he had previously been climbing the fence and pleading and crying for me to stop playing now he took an interest in all that the other children were doing. 'This isn't the same child!' people said with astonishment.

It was hard to pick out one particular reason why he had changed so dramatically and so instantaneously. He had obviously been storing away all that he had heard for some time now, and had been sifting through it until he was sure of what went where. His confidence and trust in his surroundings and the people around him was building all the time.

He had felt so bad before we went, but was so full of beans by the time we had come back that he was finding pleasure in everything. He had had a wonderful week. Our trip had come just at the right time.

Alex woke up at five o'clock on Christmas day thrilled to find the pillowcase on the end of his bed stuffed with presents. By means of both threat and persuasion I managed to get him back to sleep for a little while longer. This was our second Christmas on our own. His birthday I had coped with fairly well but for me this was the worst day of the year by far.

I had thought it best that we have Christmas in our new home, that this could be the start of a new tradition. Last year in Florida had not been Christmas at all. We had put up a tree downstairs a few days before and Alex had had a wonderful time helping me arrange the decorations and lights. With his obsession for detail he had a question about every tiny thing. Where had it come from? Had I bought it at the shops? If so, which shop? Was it something from when we had Mummy? He made sure that I turned the lights on every single day and discussed all the decorations over and over again.

I so much wanted to enjoy it with him. He was so thrilled by every little detail. While we were busy with the preparations I convinced myself that it wouldn't be too bad, that it was really only one morning out of the year and then it would be over. But once he had gone to sleep on Christmas Eve the house rang with emptiness. My mood plummeted as I arranged his main presents under the tree. My head was full of images of Rachel's face, bursting with happiness to see her child taking so much pleasure in all the activities which she had loved so much herself. But I was standing in an empty room. The only glow came from the lights on the tree. The room was void of human warmth. The tackiness of the tinsel and plastic and shiny paper only added to the emptiness. There was too much of his happiness for an audience of one. But then it must be the same for any single parent, whatever the circumstances.

Without being conscious of the fact, Alex set about distracting me in the most theatrical way possible. The present that gave him the most pleasure was a Queen video. Once his breakfast was over he set about transforming the living room into a music studio. With a tennis racket hung from his shoulder by a shoelace, a toy microphone attached to an electric crane and headphones on his head, he proceed to play all the way through the tape. Even the shutters had to be closed to get the atmosphere exactly right.

Alex wasn't playing at being Freddie Mercury. He *was* Freddie Mercury. In the same way that when he had been Fireman Sam at two and a half years old he wouldn't answer to any other name. If you called him Alex he ignored you. If you called him Sam he turned immediately, beaming in joy at being recognized for who he really was. Nothing had changed with the years, only the character. Now I was called upon to bring out my guitar to play the backing band. There was only one star.

I made a real effort with lunch, a vegetarian roast and all kinds of different vegetables. The dog got most of it, Alex hardly ate a thing. I finished off a bottle of wine but wasn't the slightest bit drunk. I felt completely uncomfortable. I couldn't sit, couldn't stand, couldn't settle. The sensation was close to extreme boredom. I knew that whatever I might do it wasn't going to make me feel better. On top of everything it was pouring with rain and the wind was lashing at the windows. It was strange to see that all Alex wanted and needed was my presence in order to have a wonderful time. I could not wait for the end of the day to come and relieve me of my misery.

Alex had finished his first term on a high. All talk of psychiatrists was forgotten. His teacher said that she didn't want our doctor's details after all. As far as she was concerned he was doing absolutely fine. In fact, she said, he was well on the way to becoming bilingual. From now on I would be taking him back to school after lunch for the afternoons as well. Alex hadn't offered a word of resistance at the prospect.

In the UK, committal proceedings for the suspect, who had been on remand since the previous summer, were due at the end of January. Far from being a formality, the proceedings would be the first major test of the admissibility of the police's evidence. I was told that there would be an 'old-style' committal proceeding where, instead of passing the case on automatically, the magistrate would examine the legality and the strength of the prosecution's evidence himself and decide if there was a case to answer. This procedure had been requested by the defence, who wanted to challenge the investigation that had been carried out by the police. The police themselves informed me that, in their opinion, if the magistrate allowed the evidence then it was a near certainty that the trial judge would do so as well when the time came. A lot was hanging on the outcome of the proceedings.

I wasn't required to return although several principal witnesses were called to give evidence. I followed the outcome from a distance, grateful that I could take Alex to school in anonymity while in the UK the story was once again making front-page news. Rachel's parents were besieged by reporters and bombarded by their telephone calls. I felt almost guilty being able to come and go in complete peace.

The proceedings lasted the best part of a week, at the end of which

I learnt by phone that things had gone as well as could have been hoped. The police were extremely satisfied. The mood was one of optimism. Even though challenged by the defence, the evidence had been allowed through, including all that had been gathered during the undercover operation. There was every reason to believe that all was rolling smoothly towards a final successful conclusion later in the year. I felt the tide turning in our direction once and for all.

I found it quite amazing to hear my child speaking a foreign language fluently. His progress was electric. Now when I picked him up from school he would carry on a conversation with one of his pals over his shoulder in perfect French while continuing another one with me in English. He could go from one to another in mid-sentence without losing his thread in either. The two languages were developing at the same time but separately. There were moments when he knew exactly what the word for something was in French but was unable to translate it into English because it was something that he had never come across before.

I was stunned by his achievement. Whatever happened from this moment on, it would stand him in good stead. It was an enormous advantage for him to have learnt a second language so easily. To be able to do anything well is good for a child's confidence and he was well aware how impressed people were when he flicked between one and the other in front of them. On top of which everyone wanted to learn English, so he could see for himself how much more capable he was in a foreign language than nearly everyone else around him.

He was the right age to pick it all up: it was as simple as that. I could see why the children of diplomats or others who travel with their parents from country to country are able to speak four or five or even more different languages. While he was so receptive it seemed almost a shame not to move on and give him another. But for the moment what we both needed more than anything was stability.

As the weeks passed I soon became accustomed to hearing him talking in French. I quickly took it for granted, as if it was nothing more clever than learning to tie his shoelaces. There were other challenges for this year: he hadn't yet learnt to swim, for a start. And I had learnt to read before the age of five, as had his mother. I wanted him to be able to do the same. We did a few minutes' work every day but there was still some way to go. He was like a sponge. It is a golden age for all children, a moment when they learn so much: to read, to write, to swim, to ride a bike. The hardest task was to put enough in front of him so that he could profit the most from the moment.

We had seen the first year round, experienced all four seasons. We had watched the snow melt away and the blossom appear on the almond and cherry trees. The bare branches and bare ground between the vines had burst into life and colour. We had watched the first fruit appear and ripen, first on the cherry trees then the figs and blackberries and finally the grapes themselves. We had seen so much sunshine, bright and intense in any season, and followed the cycle of life between the vines: cut back hard in the winter, the soil turned over between the rows continually; sprayed, watered and finally harvested by massive machines which towered over workers who drove tractors with trailers to catch the grapes that the monsters spat out.

We watched as the grapes were emptied into pits and the sticks and the leaves churned out by a large screw thread. We saw the juice squeezed and poured into vats to be stored in the cool shade. At our table we drank the wine which was born from the fields we looked out over from our windows.

We saw the leaves turn red and brown around us, the warmth of our trousers and jumpers felt welcome once more. Finally the leaves themselves fell and all was left bare.

Now the almond trees were in blossom once more and, looking at the path that trailed behind us, I could see a little of where we had come from. Alex could stand beside me now without his shoulders rigid with stress and fear. No longer would he leap into my arms at the slightest hint of danger. He was looking out at the world again, instead of shielding himself from it, breathing life back in. I no longer woke up every day to find him beside me in my bed. There were more and more days when he would not bother at all.

As for me? Nothing much had really changed. I felt a little calmer, saw things a little more clearly. But the rage and the frustration and the pain were still the same. The shock and disbelief were hardly any less intense.

The Criminal Injuries Compensation Board were ready to compensate Alex. They wanted to compensate him for the trauma he had suffered and for 'the loss of services' of his mother. We weren't entitled to any compensation for Rachel's life. If she had survived she would have been entitled to compensation for her injuries. But because she was dead her life was worth nothing.

Instead a figure of up to £2,000 was theoretically available for each year until Alex was sixteen. We weren't even offered the maximum. Their offer was an insult to Rachel's memory.

We had appealed. Rachel had provided her child with as much love, as much attention, as much stimulation, as much care, as much devotion as was humanly possible. She was a bright, intelligent woman with her whole future ahead of her. How could it possibly be that her services as a mother were not worth the maximum? The principle was far more important than the sum involved, which was nowhere near a realistic value of the services a mother provides anyway.

But how could you even estimate the cost of the hours and days and weeks and months that had been needed just to get him this far along the road to recovery? If I hadn't found a way to stay with him for so long there was no question in my mind that he wouldn't have been as well as he was now. It wasn't exactly true to say that we had received nothing. We had been sent a cheque for £750. This had been an advance on a final settlement to be awarded 'some time in the future'.

I hadn't known whether to laugh or cry. Whether to tear it up or put it on display. How would we have coped if we had been dependent on that?

Not only had the rest of the settlement not been decided but there was no telling when it would be. On top of all of this I had been told that the money went directly to Alex and could not be touched until he was eighteen.

That there was a system at all was something. I was conscious of that. I had come across a picture of a woman in Rwanda in a French paper one day. She had been bayoneted to death and her tiny child sat crying on her chest. Her body lay within sight of thousands of refugees who were walking by. I knew how much compensation that child was likely to receive. I knew how much public support her surviving family would benefit from.

Even so, the British system was upside down. Families need the money straight away so that they can give the undivided attention that the victim needs from the very first minute. What was the point of a whole load of money at eighteen if by then Alex was more traumatized and more damaged than he otherwise might have been?

But in a way all of that 'stuff' was happening in a distant world. It didn't seem real to me. Most of our news came down a telephone line. When I threw open the doors and windows and looked out over the countryside it was hard to make the connection. I would watch the television news or open a newspaper and see no reference to our lives. Sometimes I asked myself if it had ever even happened. That Rachel was dead, yes, that I knew was true. But had I imagined all the rest in my distress? Being at a distance produced a kind of dual reality. All of that press and police and procedural stuff lived only in a corner of my mind.

We were just beginning to make our mark on another world, just able to anticipate what the seasons would bring us in the months ahead. It was here that the rebuilding was really beginning. Now I was able to tell what shape our lives were likely to take as the year ahead unfolded. But there was a real sense of waiting for the new beginning. And the beginning would be some time after the trial in September. For now the date had been set. What our life would be like after that I wasn't able to imagine. My mind was operating in a flat world in which any thought that sailed past September fell off the edge into an abyss.

There was no telling when the trial would be finished. With so many possible legal arguments I had no reason to believe that it would be over quickly. Unless the defence folded completely under the weight of evidence.

I had been sent official notification that I would be required as a witness. It was something tangible. Something I could hold in my hand which told me that this was actually happening, that the day might arrive when Rachel's killer would be tried and found guilty and sentenced.

'Sentenced.' The word suddenly filled me with dread. What if we got some lunatic judge who passed a ridiculous sentence? Something that meant Rachel's killer would be released while Alex was still growing up. But anybody in his right mind would know that Rachel's killer should never be let out again. That 'life' should mean life.

But I was creating problems before they even existed and there were enough of them already. That could never happen. If the police had the right man and the judge did not put Rachel's killer away for ever, public opinion would ensure that he would never walk the streets again. There were some killers who would never come out again. This one had to join them.

Chapter Twenty-eight

I WAS IN LIMBO. The more the year progressed the more I was aware of what was to come. But the wait was interminable.

The month of September dominated my thoughts. My mind measured everything in terms of how long before or how near to or how long after September such and such might take place. Alex's life now followed an organized pattern. Mine was suspended in time.

Sometimes in my frustration I lost sight of my real achievements. I began to listen more and more to the inner voice which said that a man couldn't just stay at home and do *nothing*. I had to remind myself of what my real job was. Part of the problem was the smoothness with which Alex's life was suddenly going. I was thrown by the fact that I had free time after all the chores had been done. Far from making the most of the opportunity to relax I found myself compelled to do more.

I was managing to keep to my target of a story a month. Living with Alex meant there was no question of running short of inspiration. I worked when Alex was asleep and this took care of most of my evenings. During the daytime I worked on our fourteen-year-old car. This gave me a list of things to do and items to tick off as I went. Just as I had when making our furniture, I found this extremely therapeutic. Once again there were things that I only just understood how to do. Planning the work provided endless hours of mental rehearsal.

On top of this I threw myself back into playing tennis and practised in an effort to expend as much energy as was physically possible. I was only satisfied when my heart was pounding and my lungs were burning. Between all this, dropping Alex off at nine o'clock, picking him up again at twelve, cooking his lunch, cleaning up the kitchen, working on his reading, dropping him at two, picking him up again at five, playing with him, cooking his supper, bathing him, reading him his story, singing his song and doing the other housework and laundry as well, I managed to tire myself out just enough to sleep at night.

My day was marked by making sure that Alex was clean and his clothes were clean and his teeth were brushed and his hair was cut and his nails were cut. I would check the state of the laundry basket and the kitchen table. If the former wasn't overflowing and if the latter was completely clear of dishes, bills and anything else, then I could say that I was keeping up. Anything more was a bonus, anything less and I felt I was going under. It was strange how the mind operated.

The cocoon I had spent so long trying to build around us was ripped into shreds in an instant.

It was all over. All our feelings of safety gone. They had found us. And I knew that somewhere we had been betrayed.

The phone rang one day, and I picked it up and answered in French as usual. But the caller didn't speak French. In English he asked for me formally by name. 'Can I speak to André Hanscombe please?'

Only a handful of people in the UK had our number. This was no one who knew me: not one of the people I knew would ask for me so formally. And this wasn't an official, the voice didn't carry enough confidence. This was a 'journalist'.

I carried on in French and pretended I didn't understand. The speaker knew no French at all. He was soon flustered and hung up. I put down the phone in complete depression, my heart pounding. What was I going to do? Once they had the number it would only be a short time before they had the address. If they didn't have it already. When would they be on the doorstep?

Maybe I had managed to put them off. Maybe I had managed to convince them that they didn't have the right number after all. Or maybe they would come in person to check. It all depended where they were phoning from. If they were phoning from England it was hardly worth their while travelling hundreds of miles on the off-chance that they were on the right lines. If they were somewhere in the area, then that was a different matter. I had the feeling that the connection was an international one, there was a hum on the line.

The problem was that they could turn up at any time. Alex was never on his own but it wouldn't take them long to work out where he was at school. I had never warned the neighbours to look out for reporters. That would have created a drama when all we had wanted was an air of normality. They had targeted his nursery in England. There was no telling that they wouldn't do the same here. I had no idea what some irresponsible lunatic might say within his hearing. The thought was terrifying.

Maybe we should move away as soon as possible. But I didn't want to move, we couldn't hide for ever. And if they had found us once they could do so again. I had to wait. I had to see what their next move was.

I only hoped that they were lightweights. Here the authorities were on our side: privacy laws were strict. They were off their patch, they wouldn't know the rules. And if they didn't even speak the language then at least I had one advantage.

From the moment on I was back on my guard. Paranoia gripped me. But it wasn't paranoia – they *were* after us.

Alex finished his school year completely integrated with his class-mates. He knew all the songs and the poems, and the childhood jargon that went with the playground games. It was hard to tell him from the others in accent or vocabulary or confidence. Now I had to work dou-bly hard to not let my tension affect him. How could they not realize what damage they were doing?

I had learnt that Alex's evidence was no longer going to be used. The appointed barrister had decided his prosecution would concen-trate on the circumstantial evidence and the information which had come to light during the undercover operation.

I had mixed emotions. On the one hand I was relieved that Alex would not be exposed to the ordeal that a personal appearance might involve. He wouldn't have to go through the stress that the whole per-formance, camera links or not, was bound to bring. And he wouldn't have to carry the potential guilt later on if something went wrong or he didn't perform on the day.

On the other hand I now felt completely on the outside of the pro-ceedings. We were no longer to play any positive role in deciding whether this was the monster who had slaughtered Rachel. A convic-tion would still not make things right. But some things were beyond ever being repaired. I wanted Alex to have the satisfaction of knowing he had played a part in helping the jury decide whether this was the man who had slaughtered his mother in front of his eyes; and, if he was guilty, that he should see him get his due punishment. I felt cheated. For him and for me.

But the most important thing was that there should be a conviction. And if the experts considered that the best way to proceed was without Alex's testimony then I had to respect their experience and judgement. I wasn't qualified to have a considered opinion, but I found it difficult to understand why they were not making use of every single scrap of evidence they had at their disposal. I didn't see how it was possible to have too much evidence, too much ammunition.

No longer having an active part to play put me even more in a state of limbo. More than ever there was nothing to do but wait. I spent time going over all the evidence as I knew it and trying to work out how convincing I would find it if I was hearing it for the first time. There was the woman who identified the suspect as being within a hundred and fifty metres of where Rachel's body was found, within ten minutes of the attack. So there was evidence that the suspect had definitely been there, even though he had originally tried to deny it. There was the clothing. This witness's description of the suspect's clothing was exactly the same as that which Alex had given for Rachel's killer.

There were the witnesses who had seen a man answering exactly the same description and wearing the same clothing bending down and washing his hands in the stream where Alex said he had seen his mother's killer looking into the water.

There was the way Alex had reacted to the man with the Alsatian and the strange walk on Hampstead Heath. The suspect had a peculiar walk. The witness who had seen the suspect before Rachel was killed had been even more sure of her identification when she had seen the suspect walking on film.

There were the resemblances to (. . . .), and there was Alex's fear of the life-guard. Both were of a similar facial appearance to the suspect.

But it was the clothing. I didn't even need to consider the evidence gathered during the undercover operation, the similarity of the suspect's violent fantasies to the manner of Rachel's death or even the original psychological profile which so accurately described his lifestyle and habits. The chances of two people of a similar facial appearance, similar hair colour and hair length, wearing similar coloured clothes and both with an unusual walk being so near to Rachel at the same place and time seemed too remote even to be worth considering.

The clothing. The suspect still denied owning the clothing described by the witnesses, but he had already admitted lying once and had had nearly a year until his arrest to get rid of them. Before and after the killing, a man had been identified as wearing these clothes. Alex said that the man who killed his mother wore the same clothes. A witness had said that the suspect wore those clothes. Surely the co-incidences were too great? Alex could have made up any kind of clothing for his description. He didn't know what anyone else had said. I didn't even know what anyone else had said until later. Alex had been too precise. His wasn't a vague description. He had been categorical. White shirt with buttons worn outside his trousers, belt worn over shirt, blue trousers – not jeans, dark shoes. The cash machine receipt that Alex had mentioned, while of no material use, showed how accurate his recall of the day was.

It wasn't a case of sending a man to prison for life on the word of a three-year-old child. It wasn't just the word of a three-year-old child. Alex's evidence seemed to confirm the facts apparently established by adults. And why shouldn't a three-year-old child testify? Now he was not being asked 'Who killed your mummy?' He was being asked 'What colour trousers was the man wearing who killed your mummy?' Or even 'Was he wearing any trousers at all?' In such circumstances his word was as reliable as any adult's.

If I was a member of the jury and had heard just this circumstantial evidence alone, surely the only question I would have left would be: how could this person be anyone other than Rachel's killer?

But the jury would have to hear this person's own evidence and Alex's wouldn't be heard. The police had evidence which was even stronger and even more convincing. But the jury would have to hear this person's own evidence and Alex's. I couldn't see a jury of rational, reasonable human beings, gifted with normal common sense, delivering anything other than a verdict of guilty. It wasn't possible. I was convinced that Rachel's killer was in jail. And he was going to stay there.

★

With every day that passed we were one day nearer to September. The long summer holidays had begun and they really were long. The children broke up three weeks earlier than they did in England. It was a strain to have Alex back with me all day, every day. It took me a while to get into the rhythm again. He had more energy than ever and it took even more to wear him out. I had to pace myself. He simply could not relax or concentrate on anything before he had had the chance to run around and burn off the first burst of energy. Rachel used to tell me she had to get him out of the house before ten o'clock or he would tear the place apart. Nothing had changed; it was never more true.

He was fairly calm in the mornings while he watched his cartoons. But he woke up as early as if it were still school time. I never had the chance of a lie-in. Most of the cartoons were of pretty poor quality. His favourite was a cheap animated Japanese version of *Tom Sawyer*. I could hardly remember the storyline from childhood even if I remembered the characters. Watching as an adult I was surprised to find the adventures so gripping and so undated. Alex was really hooked. He started to wear cut-down dungarees and a floppy hat in imitation of Tom. And I would often find him with a stalk of grass hanging from the corner of his mouth to add to the effect. If we went out early he would insist that I record the programme for him. He laughed at the funny parts and was fascinated by the mischief that Tom and his friends got up to.

He followed the story for weeks. And then came the part when Indian Joe appeared. I couldn't remember what happened but Alex picked up right away that this was a baddy. I never let him watch TV alone, but I was even more careful now, when I knew something sinister was going to happen. Sure enough the moment arrived. From behind a bush in the graveyard one night Tom saw Indian Joe attack his partner in an argument over hidden treasure. He stabbed him to death with a knife.

The viewer was left in no doubt as to what was going on. I hovered on the edge of a chair with the remote control in my hand, half watching the screen, half watching Alex's face. It was a real effort to prevent myself from turning it off, leaping up and throwing my arms around him. But I couldn't protect him from every scary moment that came along. I couldn't wrap him in cotton wool. I managed to limit myself to saying, 'Something scary's going to happen.' It was clear from his expression that he still wanted to watch. But for any child this was potentially the stuff of nightmares.

His eyes widened as the scene continued but he showed no sign of wanting to hide his face or turn away. When the moment had passed he looked at me and shivered, as if to say: 'That was scary!' but carried on watching the rest of the show regardless. It seemed the wrong moment to make an issue out of it. I watched his face and wondered what questions were going to come up in the next few days.

But none came up. I listened out especially carefully over the next few evenings but his sleep was calm. I should have realized. For any other child a scene like that might have been terrifying, but for Alex it was only a pale shadow of what he had actually experienced. He watched over the next few days as the story continued to centre around this violent death. He was more interested in the character of Joe the Indian than any of the others but whatever thoughts he might have had about him he kept to himself.

That he should be so little affected by what he had seen was a tremendous relief. It meant that I no longer had to scrutinize everything he might come into contact with as I had had to in the beginning. It meant that he was developing a more normal resistance to the things that before would have terrified him. Perhaps even more developed than normal as a result of how much we had been through together and had had to work through together. Looking at him now, there was very little sign of the fear that had once dominated his behaviour. It had moved from an obvious to a far more suitable level. A stranger would hardly have noticed his insecurities. Only those who had known him before his mother's death could see that they were still there.

The summer continued. The weeks went past and the interminable wait went on.

There had been more phone calls. Always the same voice, always speaking in English. So far that was the extent of their efforts. In a way their phone calls were a relief. At least I knew they were still struggling to find us. It was a confirmation that they were lightweights. Finding an address from a phone number was child's play.

The waiting was hard. At times I could hardly cope with the most mundane tasks. It was impossible to think of anything else. In my mind I would go over all the events of our last days together. I could remember virtually everything that had happened during that time: the weather, the children's birthday we had been to, the friends we had seen, the bird we had rescued and buried. I spent a lot of time thinking about the mood that Rachel had been in the night before she died. The fact that she wasn't quite the same. People know. I myself had carried a sense of foreboding which went beyond the usual daily neurosis that most of us live with.

Coincidences had run through all of our time together. My imaginary girlfriend called 'Rachel'. The fact that she had chosen Alex's name long before we had ever met. She had decided on Alexander Louis long ago. It wasn't just that she had given him the same initials as me, he would be A.L.H. as well. I found out a long time later that Alexandros, in its original Greek, meant 'protector of Andros' – protector of André. This was the name she had given her unborn son by a yet unknown father. I pondered a long time over that one.

For most of the day before Rachel was killed it had poured with rain. I had sheltered in a newsagent's during one shower. I picked up a book, which was rare for me. I usually flicked through bike or sports magazines as the radio could crackle into life at any moment and it didn't pay to get so absorbed in something that you missed a job. The book was *Black Dogs* by Ian McEwan. I don't know why its cover attracted me more than any other but I picked it up and then found it impossible to put down. I had opened the book at random and had landed on a passage concerning the narrator's relationship with a three-year-old niece.

The description of his niece's behaviour and strength of character made me think immediately of my own son. I had rarely had the time to observe Alex's behaviour in the depth that the narrator had his niece. I read how this tiny child was able to impose its tyrannical will on him and could get him to play exactly how she wanted him to, when she wanted him to. When he was in her presence she dominated everything.

I read how the child's behaviour was degenerating as a result of the lack of attention from her parents. The narrator was clearly expressing guilt about not having stayed in the child's life long enough to give her something solid to lean on. He seemed to be making the observation that even if the child's parents hadn't given her the attention she needed, his presence might have been enough to save his niece from the loneliness and confusion that consumed the rest of her growing up, and what seemed like her adult life as well.

But what really fascinated me were the long descriptions of their play while they had been together. It really hit me how important those moments were in a child's life. These games concerned the whole of a child's relationship with the world. And the world's with it. Those were the moments that decided everything. Like the Jesuit saying: 'Give me a child until he is four and I will give you the man.' In those moments the whole of her life had been in play.

I was fascinated, but at the same time all this was completely irrelevant to me. My small child had the best person possible with him every hour of the day. That was one thing that was sure. I considered my interest in the book to be purely academic. My conviction only had a few hours left to run.

The population of children on the property swelled in the summer: relations come to enjoy the simple pleasures of the countryside. Our neighbour's son and his cousin offered to look after Alex for a little while. Alex was keen, so, begrudgingly, I consented.

Leaving Alex in the care of a responsible adult was traumatic enough for me. Putting his safety in the hands of two twelve-year-old boys, even for a few minutes, was something else. It was only because I knew the boys were absolutely trustworthy that I agreed.

I had to learn to let go. They weren't leaving the estate, and there were other adults around. But reason wasn't enough to stop my hands shaking. As they ran off to play in one of the gardens I wandered away into the shade where I could watch them without being seen.

Once out of the company of adults the two older boys began to swagger in the way that bigger boys always do. Alex's eyes were full of admiration for both of them and clearly he enjoyed the attention they were paying him. I could hear him giggling at their harmless bragging and was just beginning to feel slightly ashamed of myself for acting so furtively when one of the older boys pulled something out of his pocket.

I couldn't make out what it was until the sunlight glinted on the blade. He had unfolded a hunting knife and had begun carelessly waving it around only feet from Alex's head. My heart suddenly felt like it would burst from my chest, the top of my head and the palms of my hands broke out in sweat. My first urge was to rush forward and beat the boy to the ground and the knife from his hand. But I just managed to remind myself that I had played with knives too.

I told myself that I knew this boy well, and that he had always been gentle and well behaved, I told myself that twelve-year-old boys have always played with knives, and always will. I told myself that Alex would have to come to terms with seeing people with knives in their hands going about the most mundane tasks. I told myself that over-protecting him and over-reacting would cause him more problems in his life than he already had. But all I could see was that knife swinging up by his head. It took all my strength to stay where I was.

The older boy tossed the knife in front of him, trying to make the blade stick in the ground. Alex glanced at him. Even from a distance I could tell that Alex had a lot going through his mind. The older boy leant forward and pulled the knife out of the ground before tossing it again. Time stood still. I could hear the birds in the trees and every twig that snapped underfoot. The knife rose in the air and sank into the ground.

I was watching a lesson being learnt. I could see Alex trying to figure out what was going on with this knife. I wondered if he was asking himself if he was safe, but in his conversations with me it was clear that he had never seen himself as a target of violence when his mother had been killed. She had been the victim, not him.

After what seemed like hours the older boy pulled the knife out of the ground, wiped it clean, folded it and put it away in his pocket. My shoulders sagged in relief. The three of them disappeared into the house and I hurried back to ours. A few minutes later they appeared at our front door, all three faces full of carefree smiles.

I thanked the older boys for looking after Alex and they told me to think nothing of it. It was an impossible request.

The second anniversary of Rachel's death arrived. Life had changed beyond all recognition. Alex and I were a universe away from how we had been two years before.

The anniversary was hardly mentioned in the media. This relieved Rachel's parents of the unwanted attention they would otherwise have had to endure. No doubt the calm was due to the approaching trial date.

Alex's birthday was spent with new friends. He was so grown up. He was bursting with life and energy, his face was all smiles. His face had changed even more, the gap between his front teeth more apparent than ever, his mouth even more the shape of his mother's. Even though he was so tanned, I saw Rachel smiling back.

Maybe things get easier. Maybe you just get used to being in pain. But it was the glow in the children's eyes that day which kept me going. There was so much desire for the pleasures that life can bring. I had read somewhere that the ancient Greeks had prescribed the presence of a small child as a remedy for people who are sick. Since the beginning my own small child had emitted so much of that life force the ancient Greeks were so aware of. I had been absorbing it through my skin all along. Who knows what crucial difference this had made in terms of my own survival?

I drove the car into the courtyard at the end of the afternoon. Alex and I unloaded our stuff and I took him inside to give him something to eat. I left him inside and walked out to drop some rubbish in the bin. As I did so a strange car pulled up at the gate. Two young men climbed out and with their eyes on me they walked purposefully forwards.

I knew who they were instantly. I went to cut them off from the house.

'André?'

With rage boiling in my veins I was only just able to control myself. How dare they use my name! They didn't even know me.

'We just want to . . .'

'Get out! Go away!' I shouted, heading towards them.

They turned immediately on their heels and headed back to their car.

'You don't know how much harm you do!' I shouted after them.

'We're sorry . . . !'

The car started and they quickly drove away.

At that very moment Alex appeared on the steps with his food in his hand. He hadn't seen what had happened. His illusions of safety were saved by a fraction of a second.

I had known they would find us. Hadn't they discovered the inscriptions I had written from Alex and myself on the cards placed on Rachel's coffin, cards written only hours before her funeral, when her coffin had been under surveillance from that moment until the cards were burnt at the cremation along with her body? They could discover anything. Nothing was beyond their desecration.

One of the senior detectives had been to see Rachel's parents to prepare them for the trial at the Old Bailey.

He told them something which had previously been kept from us. He said that much of the argument might well turn on the pathologist's evidence, his opinion of exactly how the attack took place and the exact sequence of events. All of which would most likely be challenged by the defence. This much was no surprise, although he was concerned about the possible effect hearing all this read out might have on us.

Recently I had been informed that I did not have to testify. As with Alex, they were trying to save me from any unnecessary ordeal. I had decided that I would not go to hear the evidence itself but only for the summing up. Alex would be back at school and I could not afford to disturb his routine. Also, much of the attention would inevitably be directed at us and it would be hard to keep the press away. We could only expect the worst in that regard. And for him to have me in a state of agitation and anger for weeks on end would hardly be for the best.

But the news that the detective had for us was that Rachel had probably not died exactly as we had been led to believe, and exactly as we had had to come to terms with somewhere in our minds. It was only a question of detail, only a split second's difference, but it was nevertheless very hard for us to accept. He told us that there was hardly any doubt that Rachel would have had enough time to know what was going to happen to her.

To find this out more than two years later was agony for all of us. All of our thoughts were for her. All of the anxieties about what she must have gone through, which we had managed to quieten just a little bit, suddenly burst back out into the forefront of our minds. It would have been better to know at the earliest moment. Now the mental wounds had all been ripped open again.

She had sacrificed herself. In truth I had always suspected this, right from the beginning. Hadn't the thought of this kept me going beyond anything else? She had knowingly given her life so that our child could live. She knew she was going to die. She consciously hadn't struggled in order to save her child from being harmed. Anything I had done since was nothing. Nothing at all. How could I even consider giving up or cutting short a life that she had paid for with her own?

More than ever her killer had to pay. He had to be put away. Someone more evil could not be imagined. I could only think that any jury who heard what we had heard would put this monster away for ever and throw away the key.

A few days after the 'journalists'' appearance I received a letter posted from a nearby town. It was a note of apology scrawled in childish handwriting. In it they said they were sorry for disturbing our privacy and that they would never bother us again. They promised that they would never reveal our whereabouts or our phone number to anyone.

What would have been a fairly honourable gesture was completely undermined by a lack of return address or even the names of those writing. The snivelling cowards had left the note unsigned.

Some time later Rachel's father learnt the names of the two 'journalists' concerned. Despite their 'promise', they had put our address and phone number into free circulation. We were now at the mercy of all and sundry. Our peace was shattered.

The opening of the trial coincided with Alex's return to school. The first week would be taken up with legal argument over the admissibility of evidence. Meanwhile a jury had been sworn in, but were not present at this stage of the proceedings. Rachel's father was in court every day. He phoned every night to keep me informed. He said that the legal terms and jargon were almost impossible for a layman to follow; that the whole thing came down to a battle between the two barristers as to whether the evidence had been legally obtained and admissible. If 'our' barrister did not convince the judge, then there would not be a trial at all! Suddenly we were told by the police to prepare ourselves for the worst.

What did that mean: 'prepare ourselves for the worst'? Hadn't everybody been filled with optimism and confidence right up until now? Nothing was a certainty, but didn't we have the greatest possible chance if obtaining a conviction? It must just be last-minute nerves that were making them react this way.

But, no. It became clear that there was a real chance that the judge could throw out all of the evidence collected during the undercover operation. And because the prosecution's tactics was based so heavily on this, their whole case would be undermined. The realization was a shock. But we had had plenty of those. What were the facts? What were the chances?

Fifty-fifty.

There must be some mistake. How could they have come so far with so much evidence, so much legal advice from the highest-qualified in the land, and after only two days in court admit that they had only a fifty-fifty chance of obtaining a conviction?

Once again we were living on our nerves. Once again the worst that could be imagined was sitting just over our horizon. It couldn't be possible. The judge had spent the whole summer reading through every single piece of evidence that had been collected. If he believed the evidence, surely he knew what the story was. Surely he knew who was guilty? I told myself there was no way that anyone in their right mind could let a man who had slaughtered a defenceless woman and sexually assaulted her in front of her child walk free because of a 'technicality'.

The judge went home to consider his decision. He was due back in court the following day but his decision would not be given until the end of the morning. The waiting was once again excruciating,

I tried to ask myself how I felt. I searched myself for the same feeling of foreboding I had known in the days before Rachel was killed. I couldn't find any. I knew what the judge knew. There was no way that all this was going to stop here. I didn't feel that my life, our lives were going to once more drop over the abyss. Enough was enough. That would surely be stretching the realms of the impossible just too far. There had to be a moment when things turned our way just a little bit.

Rachel's father had prepared a speech in the unlikely event that . . .

I began to wonder if I should get on an aeroplane to be there. But there was nothing I could do. No way I could influence things. But I didn't feel sick. I even managed to sleep that night.

I managed to get Alex ready and take him to school. But the moment I walked back through the door of the empty house the anxiety hit me. I tried to busy myself but I couldn't settle or concentrate on anything. I was compelled to go for a walk in order to calm my nerves. I looked out over the open countryside. So much beauty – and the sickness of man. Nobody with a wife and children of their own could put their head on their pillow at night and know that they had let a killer go free.

My walk had not succeeded in calming my nerves. I still couldn't sit. I went back out three times, willing the time to pass. I was preparing something to eat when the phone finally rang.

A friend had phoned to find out how I was taking the news. The sickness hit my stomach one more time.

Within a matter of minutes the suspect was walking the streets a free man. The judge had considered the evidence as unsafe. He had thrown out the case completely: the verdict was not guilty.